Godzilla FAQ

All That's Left to Know About the King of the Monsters

Brian Solor

APPLAUSE
THEATRE & CINEMA BOOKS
An Imprint of Hal Leonard LLC

Copyright © 2017 by Brian Solomon

All rights reserved. No part of this book may be reproduced in any form, without written permission, except by a newspaper or magazine reviewer who wishes to quote brief passages in connection with a review.

Published in 2017 by Applause Theatre & Cinema books
An Imprint of Hal Leonard LLC
7777 West Bluemound Road
Milwaukee, WI 53213
Trade Book Division Editorial Offices
33 Plymouth St., Montclair, NJ 07042

All images afr from the author's collection unless otherwise noted.
The FAQ series was conceived by Robert Rodriguez and developed with Stuart Shea.
Printed in the United States of America

Book design by Snow Creative

Library of Congress Cataloging-in-Publication Data

Names: Solomon, Brian, 1974– author.
Title: Godzilla FAQ : all that's left to know about the king of the monsters
 / Brian Solomon.
Description: Milwaukee, WI : Applause, an imprint of Hal Leonard LLC, [2017]
 | Includes bibliographical references and index.
Identifiers: LCCN 2016052096 | ISBN 9781495045684 (pbk.)
Subjects: LCSH: Godzilla films—History and criticism. | Godzilla (Fictitious
 character) | Monsters in motion pictures.
Classification: LCC PN1995.9.G63 S65 2017 | DDC 791.43/67—dc23
LC record available at https://lccn.loc.gov/2016052096

www.applausebooks.com

For my wife Jaimee, the Namikawa to my Glenn

Contents

Foreword

Hard as it to imagine now, the first batch of American fans and scholars of all things Godzilla—and the *kaiju eiga* genre generally—pursued their interest with no Internet, no cellphone or instant messaging. There was but extremely limited access to the Americanized versions of these movies; actually owning high-definition, English-subtitled copies of their Japanese counterparts seemed liked something out of *The Jetsons*.

If you wanted to watch, say, *Godzilla vs. the Sea Monster*, you'd have to wait until one of the (ten or fewer) TV channels in your market aired a "Godzilla Week" on the afternoon movie show (with plenty of commercial interruptions and presented "panned-and-scanned," of course). Or maybe if you were more ambitious and could afford it, you hunted down obscenely expensive 16mm prints or maybe bought one of those new, refrigerator-sized contraptions called VCRs so that you could actually *record* movies on videotape and watch them whenever you wanted. Golly.

There was no Skype or iPhone Facetime. If you wanted to reach out and contact another die-hard find on the other side of the country, you could expect to shell out twenty dollars or more (depending on the time of day) for a mere, if exciting, hour-long phone call.

There was no Internet Movie Database, no fan-operated discussion boards with which to exchange information, and, boy howdy, information in those days was sure hard to come by. When a magazine like *Famous Monsters of Filmland* devoted an entire issue to Japanese fantasy films, we studied every square inch of every photo until the magazine fell apart in our hands. I once drove several hundred miles across state lines in search of hard-to-come-by issues of *The Japanese Fantasy Film Journal*.

Gradually, some of us made it to Japan and even got to meet and interview the directors, writers, actors, and special effects artists that created these movies we adored. Many were nonplussed by our keen, sincere interest. Often, they had no previous awareness that their movies had ever been shown outside Japan, much less enjoyed a passionate fan following. Sadly, most of that great Showa-era talent has dwindled to a handful of survivors, but most of them have since become frequent VIP guests of stateside fan conventions. How times have changed.

It seems strange to be writing this foreword so soon after the death of exasperating, irreplaceable Bill Warren, author of *Keep Watching the Skies!*, the seminal genre-study volume so responsible for my entry into *kaiju eiga* scholarship. Bill wrote the foreword for my book nearly twenty-five years ago when he was younger than I am now.

Those of us from the early days, especially pioneers Greg Shoemaker (of *The Japanese Fantasy Film Journal*), Ed Godziszewski (*Japanese Giants*), and the late, talented-but-troubled Guy Tucker (*Age of the Gods*), along with those who followed a bit later, such as my friend and frequent collaborator Steve Ryfle, had varied interests but were all drawn to the same basic quest. We hungered to learn more about these sometimes serious, sometimes goofy, but always (at least in our day) captivating movies. Who were the people behind and in front of the camera? Where do these movies fit in the context of Japanese cinema generally? How did Special Effects Director Eiji Tsuburaya and his team create all those wonderfully vivid special effects?

I daresay Greg or Ed or Steve or myself never could have imagined that, decades later, fans would be banding together for overseas trips to tour Toho Studios or hobnob with actors like Akira Takarada and Haruo Nakajima over drinks at fan conventions in Chicago. Or that, all these years later, I could with my daughter (a budding movie fan) watch a gloriously sharp and colorful Blu-ray of the original Japanese-language (but English-subtitled) version of *Godzilla vs. the Sea Monster* on a 90-inch home theater screen with 5.1 surround sound. Again—golly!

Brian Solomon has meticulously collated all the essentials into a single, highly readable volume, adding another layer of research, personal insight, observation, and perspective to the genre we all love. Enjoy!

Stuart Galbraith IV
Kyoto, Japan

Acknowledgments

As with anything I endeavor, the most important folks to thank first and foremost would be my loving and supportive family. When I insisted on rewatching every single Godzilla movie in order at the beginning of this project, my (more or less) patient and enthusiastic wife Jaimee dutifully sat by me and got through about twice as many of them as a non-aficionado could be expected to survive (she tapped out at *Son of Godzilla*, understandably). But she also supported me in other ways throughout the process, and I probably would have starved to death at my desk without her. My children also provided that extra push, with my son Jack inspiring me further with his shared love of Godzilla (instilled by me, naturally) and his company during several film viewings, as well as my daughter Layla helping me to set the guidelines for productive work habits (she can be a tough boss sometimes).

A couple of years ago, I wrote another "FAQ" book for Hal Leonard Publishing, *Pro Wrestling FAQ*. Having worked in the wrestling industry for years, and enjoying many professional contacts from the experience, that book admittedly came a lot easier than this one. While I've been a lover of Godzilla since my most formative years, for this book I had to work harder and challenge myself further, really doing detailed homework and research in order to turn myself into more than just a superfan, but into as much of an expert as I could within the time allotted. To that end, I am deeply grateful to those genuine experts who consented to be interviewed, and upon whose previous work I built my own humble tome: the infectiously enthusiastic August Ragone, a treasure trove of knowledge; Dr. William Tsutsui, whose insight provided a thoughtful and scholarly perspective; Larry Tuczynski, who was kind enough to offer his thoughts and opinions on the subject of movie music; Peter Brothers, who spoke with me at length about the great Ishiro Honda and his work; Steve Biodrowski, whose strong and carefully considered opinions were invaluable; Stuart Galbraith IV, a giant in the field of Japanese film criticism if ever there was one; and my trusted friend Miguel Rodriguez, who was also gracious enough to offer even more of his time by agreeing to look over portions of the manuscript.

Finally, as usual, I must thank the hardworking staff at Hal Leonard, especially my unflappable editor Marybeth Keating, who was even willing to grant me the extension I desperately needed once I realized that the demands of being a high school teacher meant that the book was going to take me a lot longer to finish than I originally planned.

Introduction
I've *Kaiju* Under My Skin

Up from the depths . . . Thirty stories high . . .
Breathing fire . . . His head in the sky . . .
GODZILLA!

Since 1954, the creature has been one of the cinema's most enduring and popular characters, and with a total of twenty-nine films under his massive belt (not even including two American reboots), he's also the star of the longest-running single-studio franchise in motion picture history. From his home base in Japan, where the legendary Toho Company first put him on the map, Godzilla has gone on to become an international phenomenon—a movie monster unrivaled both in size as well as universal, worldwide appeal.

Godzilla FAQ explores the many facets of the monumental, fire-breathing radioactive lizard that has roared his way into our hearts over a sixty-year reign of terror. Each era of the monster's decades-long legacy is explored here, starting with the groundbreaking original film *Gojira* and moving through the three great "eras": *Showa* (1955–1975), *Heisei* (1984–1995), and *Millennium* (1999–2004). Plus, special attention will be given to both American versions—the notorious 1998 disaster as well as 2014's epic blockbuster that returned the Big G to mainstream relevance for American audiences.

Additionally, fans of the big guy will find detailed looks at the many people responsible for the monster's success, such as director Ishiro Honda, special-effects guru Eiji Tsuburaya, and Akira Ifukube, composer of Godzilla's unmistakable theme music. There is a special rundown of the many members of his supporting monster cast, including Mothra, Rodan, and King Ghidorah; an exploration of Godzilla as the embodiment of Japanese postwar trauma; a special look at how Godzilla met his American match in 1962 in *King Kong*; even a loving retrospective of the short-lived Saturday morning cartoon.

Perhaps no other character in all of international film is as beloved by American audiences as Godzilla. But more than just a movie monster, he has become a pop culture avatar, pervading our consciousness as few fictional creations have. *Godzilla FAQ* dives headlong into the depths of this unstoppable cinematic force of nature.

For me, it all started on those lazy Sunday afternoons close to forty years ago, as I lay on my grandparents' carpet, mesmerized by the glow of those giant monsters doing battle on syndicated television. As a kid, I was easily able to look past the rubber costumes, often clumsily dubbed dialogue, and somewhat puzzling plotlines. To tell you the truth, I still am. I've been in love with Godzilla for as long as I can remember, and in later years, as syndicated TV afternoons gave way to bootleg VHS tapes and convention road trips, my fascination only grew stronger. Today, I'm proud to be passing along the *kaiju* craze to my own son, replacing syndicated TV with Blu-ray and a carpeted floor with hardwood.

Thanks to those formative years, monsters and horror became as much a part of my young life as peanut butter and jelly, and I grew up loving everything from the Universal creature features, to the Ray Harryhausen stop-motion epics, to Italian zombie gorefests and everything in between. But through it all, my fascination with "lowbrow" entertainment has been highlighted by that iconic walking skyscraper with spikes on his back and nuclear fire in his belly. I consider myself a maven of all things creepy, spooky, and fantastical, but there can be no doubt that Godzilla and his *kaiju* compatriots have always held a special place in my heart. And to this day, whenever things in the world get to be a little too much to bear, you'll find me on the couch, transfixed by that same TV glow, as an unmistakable screeching roar fills my living room . . .

A Note About Names

Agreeing on a proper name for each Godzilla film can be a grueling affair. Usually, the original Japanese titles were altered for release in other countries, sometimes with multiple iterations, resulting in films known around the world by many different names over time. For example, as critic Stuart Galbraith IV illustrates in his own book, *Monsters Are Attacking Tokyo!*, the sixth film in Toho's series was originally released in Japan as *Kaiju daisenso*, which translates literally to *The Great Monster War*. However, when the film

The King of the Monsters, in miniature.

Sebastian Dooris/Flickr

was released internationally, it was retitled *Invasion of Astro-Monster*; except in the United States, where it became known as *Monster Zero*. This title was further altered on home video to *Godzilla vs. Monster Zero*. As you can see, this can be quite confusing. For the sake of clarity, I've made every effort to refer to each film primarily using the English-language title most commonly in use in the present day, which is usually the international title (in the given example, that would be *Invasion of Astro-Monster*). In some instances, I also provide the original Japanese title or previous U.S. release title for further clarification.

Furthermore, the monsters themselves often have multiple names. For example, Godzilla himself is known in Japan as Gojira, Mothra is Mosura, and Rodan is Radon. In this book, I have chosen to go with the most "official" English-language versions of the monsters' names, as recognized and endorsed by Toho itself.

In the case of the names of actual human beings, I have elected to use the Western practice of putting the given name before the family name, as opposed to the traditional Japanese practice of doing the reverse (i.e., Ishiro Honda, instead of Honda Ishiro).

Giant Monsters on the Loose

Origins of a Creature Feature Subgenre

n Japan, it is known as the *daikaiju eiga*; the giant monster movie. It is a category of film quite unique to that island nation, combining elements of horror and science fiction, as well as mythology and mysticism. Like *anime* or the historical epics of Akira Kurosawa, it is an entertainment institution immediately identifiable with Japan—one of the country's cultural exports to the world at large, as it were. Featuring nearly impossible-to-destroy and unfathomably huge beasts laying waste to cities and even more popularly, to each other, the Japanese monster film subgenre has fascinated fans around the world—often due to its admirable reliance on practical special effects such as painstakingly molded rubber suits and meticulous miniatures.

It all began in 1954 with the emergence of the one true King of the Monsters, the mighty Godzilla, a monumental radioactive dinosaur with atomic fire breath introduced by the Toho Company in the first of what is now twenty-nine pictures (and counting). The brainchild of producer Tomoyuki "Yuko" Tanaka, director Ishiro Honda, and screenwriters Shigeru Kayama and Takeo Murata, and brought to life by special-effects pioneer Eiji Tsuburaya, the success of the film and of the monster would spawn a decades-long movement in Japanese cinema populated by countless such creatures wreaking havoc in countless ways. Although the height of its popularity occurred decades ago, the subgenre lives on to this day.

And yet, although the Japanese *kaiju* (literally translated as "strange beast") is a unique entity unto itself, as a film category it does derive in part from an earlier tradition of monster-movie-making from across the Pacific Ocean in the United States. For nearly thirty years prior to the original *Godzilla*, Americans had been making movies about giant monsters on the loose. They may have been somewhat different in philosophy and certainly vastly different in technique, but there can be no doubt that the success of these films, both creatively and financially, was a direct inspiration for the Big G and his ilk.

For example, so much on-screen destruction may have never taken place were it not for the efforts of Willis O'Brien, the special-effects genius who helped kick off the giant monster craze in 1925 with the silent epic *The Lost World*, inspired by Sir Arthur Conan Doyle's story of the same name. Still in its early days, the art of filmmaking had finally progressed to the point that significant special-effects films were possible, and O'Brien marveled audiences with his unheard-of technique of stop-motion animation, with which he seemingly brought to life the prehistoric dinosaurs of Doyle's classic tale. For the first time, moviegoers witnessed the concept of giant creatures used as a set piece in a major motion picture, and the spectacle of it could only mean that there would be more to come.

Kong fights a T. rex in one of the first giant monster battles ever created for film.   *Public domain*

The Eighth Wonder of the World

Some eight years later, O'Brien would once again utilize his groundbreaking technique to bring to the world the granddaddy of all giant monster films, RKO Pictures' *King Kong*. Producer/director Merian C. Cooper's classic movie about a fifty-foot-tall gorilla that goes wild in New York City and is famously gunned down by planes at the top of the Empire State Building became a massive success and made the creature an instant cultural icon. This was largely due to O'Brien's startlingly effective stop-motion technique. Constructing metal-frame models and covering them in lifelike skins, O'Brien photographed the models moving in tiny increments, so that when the images were projected one after another, it gave the illusion of movement.

The film was O'Brien's crowning achievement, and worked in large part because the stop-motion technique gave Kong an actual personality, and made audiences both fear and care about him and his unrequited love for Fay Wray's Ann Darrow. The success of the movie set a standard for decades to come, establishing the concept of a film built around the spectacle of a giant monster. Kong was more than just a large beast; he was a character, alongside other movie monster characters of the day like Dracula and Frankenstein. The first true giant monster film turned out to be one of the highest-grossing movies of 1933, and made its way all over the world, wowing filmgoers even as far off as Japan, where Kong would plant the seed of inspiration that led to the *kaiju* craze a generation later.

So transcendent was the Kong craze that it even led to a nearly forgotten 1938 Japanese cash-in knockoff called *King Kong Appears in Edo* (*Edo ni Arawareta Kingu Kongu*). Details of the film are sketchy (even as to whether or not the ape was even giant in size), and it has unfortunately been lost for many decades; nevertheless, it is considered by many to be the very first giant monster movie ever made in Japan. But World War II would put a crimp in the development of the Japanese film industry, and it would be years before the true influence of Kong would be felt in that country.

Master of Stop-Motion Mayhem

Meanwhile, back in the United States, the mantle of Willis O'Brien would be carried on by his even more accomplished protégé, Ray Harryhausen. Idolizing O'Brien as a child, Harryhausen eventually grew up to work alongside the master, and would even supersede him by perfecting the stop-motion technique into something he termed "Dynamation." Harryhausen's great innovation would not only be in streamlining the stop-motion process to create even more expressiveness and movement, but in also compositing the animation with live action in ways that had never been seen before.

"Harryhausen was a man who, basically by himself, spent an insane amount of time creating special effects for his films," says Miguel Rodriguez, film historian and director of the Horrible Imaginings Film Festival. "But Harryhausen also had a lot of time and money to work with, so that's the difference, in comparison [with Japanese *kaiju* films]. Certainly in terms of movements, he could argue that for the special effects of that period his were a little more convincing."

During the 1950s and 1960s, Harryhausen was recognized as a master of special effects. His laborious process required large amounts of time and money, and his tireless dedication resulted in a string of science-fiction and action-adventure epics featuring aliens, creatures of myth and legend, and of course, giant monsters. Because of the level of work he put in to pull off his impressive Dynamation, Harryhausen was known to look askance at what he saw as the cruder "man-in-suit" technique used in later years by Japanese *kaiju* filmmakers; he was often appalled that fans might lump his films together with theirs.

"There was one interview in a magazine called *Castle of Frankenstein*," recalls Steve Biodrowski, editor of *Cinefantastique Online*. "He didn't directly say negative things, what he said was he was surprised the audience couldn't see the difference between what he did and what [the Japanese] did. He was clearly a little bit miffed that no one saw that he was doing something of higher quality. In the U.S. we've always been trained to regard Harry as being the top tier approach, and the Japanese stuff as being the low-rent version, just putting a guy in a suit to knock buildings down."

Nevertheless, ironically, it would be one of Harryhausen's movies that would very directly help to jump-start the *kaiju* movement, namely 1953's *The Beast from 20,000 Fathoms*. Harryhausen would bring to life the ferocious Rhedosaurus, a slumbering dinosaur awakened by nuclear weapons testing in the Arctic Circle. The creature eventually makes its way to New York City, where it terrifies the populace and cuts a swath through the metropolis before finally being defeated by the military in Coney Island. It would be this central concept that would initially get Japanese producer Tomoyuki Tanaka thinking about the creature that would eventually develop into Godzilla. In fact, Tanaka's original working title for his proposed film would be the derivative *The Giant Monster from 20,000 Miles Under the Sea*.

Children of the Atom

Even beyond the works of Harryhausen, American monster movies of the postwar era had another important element that would become essential to the Godzilla formula: nuclear radiation. According to these films, it

Harryhausen's Rhedosaurus rages on the lobby poster for *The Beast from 20,000 Fathoms*.
Rossano aka Bud Care/Flickr

seemed like every other day another nuclear test was causing some creature or another to grow to enormous size and go on a rampage of destruction, whether it be giant ants, giant spiders, even giant praying mantises. You name it, and atomic bomb testing was causing it to mutate into a massive, murderous nightmare. And yet, also distinctive in these types of films was the unrelenting optimism. No matter how bad things got, the American military and scientific elite would always find a way to emerge victorious in the end. And there was no room for moral ambiguity, either. Gone was the touching pathos of King Kong; in the Eisenhower age, the monsters were purely savage and evil, the humans were noble and strong, and that was all there was to it.

"Giant monster movies in the U.S. were either B-pictures (those from Columbia and Universal-International, for instance) or significantly cheaper and more disreputable (e.g., Bert I. Gordon's pictures) from lesser companies," explains Stuart Galbraith IV, author of seminal critical works such as *Monsters Are Attacking Tokyo: The Incredible World of Japanese Fantasy Films*. "Toho's were, up until the end of the 1960s, A-pictures by Japanese standards, targeting a mass market audience. They didn't have the stigma of cheap monster movies made in America."

In developing its own riff on the giant monster formula, Japanese cinema would depart from the American philosophy and head into more morally ambiguous and decidedly darker territory. And this was understandably so, as the Japanese film industry itself had just been shaken to its foundations. Japan did not share America's shiny 1950s optimism, having been humbled in World War II and then subjected to a humiliating and culturally transformative American occupation that lasted from 1945 to 1952. During that time, extensive restrictions were placed on Japanese filmmakers that more or less prevented anything truly subversive or creatively groundbreaking from taking place. But once the occupation ended, so did the years of stagnation, and the Japanese cinema would rebound with the creation of a subgenre that would eventually define it. The seeds planted by the likes of O'Brien and Harryhausen in the minds of a generation of Japanese visionaries would finally start to bear fruit.

More Early Giant Monster Films of Note

Son of Kong (1933)

This quickie sequel to RKO's blockbuster once again enlisted Willis O'Brien to create the great ape's progeny, encountered when the original film's entrepreneur/explorer/filmmaker Carl Denham (Robert Armstrong) returns to Skull Island. A generally silly affair, it's worth noting that O'Brien asked to have his name removed from the credits.

Mighty Joe Young (1949)

O'Brien creates yet another enlarged primate, this time even more lovable and sympathetic than Kong. RKO reunited O'Brien with Merian C. Cooper and even star Robert Armstrong for this one, and it netted the great effects master his first and only Academy Award.

Them! (1954)

Atomic testing in the New Mexico desert leads to the mutation of a colony of ants into gigantic, man-eating monstrosities in what is generally considered the first "giant insect" movie. Genuinely frightening and filled with fine performances from the likes of James Whitmore and Edmund Gwenn, the film kicked off America's 1950s fascination with irradiated terrors.

It Came from Beneath the Sea (1955)

Ray Harryhausen followed up his amazing work on *The Beast from 20,000 Fathoms* with this equally dazzling masterwork featuring a giant octopus that attacks San Francisco. It is especially known for the scene in which the Golden Gate Bridge is destroyed, one of Harryhausen's greatest set pieces.

Tarantula (1955)

With the giant bug craze in full swing stateside, classic monster studio Universal Pictures got into the mix with a tale about—you guessed it—a giant irradiated spider.

20 Million Miles to Earth (1957)

By this point, the original *Godzilla* (re-edited into the Americanized *Godzilla, King of the Monsters*) had already made its way to America, but Harryhausen was still dazzling audiences, this time with the extraterrestrial known as the Ymir, which grows to mammoth size and runs amok in Rome.

The Deadly Mantis (1957)

A prehistoric, two-hundred-foot-long praying mantis is thawed out in a volcanic eruption at the North Pole and unleashes holy hell along the Eastern seaboard before a final confrontation with the military in the Manhattan Tunnel. Once lampooned on an episode of *Mystery Science Theater 3000*, the movie features a young Clint Eastwood in a bit part.

The Giant Claw (1957)

Often referred to as "the American *kaiju* film," this product of veteran schlock-meister Sam Katzman features a giant vulture-like bird from outer space, portrayed rather unconvincingly by a ludicrous puppet (Katzman had wanted to hire Harryhausen but couldn't afford him). Frequently listed amongst the worst movies ever made.

Gorgo (1961)

The wave of giant monster flicks was petering out in the U.S. by the early '60s, and this time the British stepped in to offer up their own sea-creature-on-the-loose story, set, of course, in London. It was first released in the U.S. by M-G-M.

Reptilicus (1961)

A co-production of American International Pictures (AIP) and Denmark's Saga Studios, the film was actually shot twice: once in Danish and then in English using mostly the same cast and with a slightly re-edited story. By this point, giant monster movies had become passé in the West. In the East, however, they were just getting warmed up . . .

English-language poster for the Danish-American co-production, *Reptilicus.*

Public domain

2

Gojira

The Original Classic That Started It All

Toho's *Godzilla* film series is known for its longevity. At sixty-three years and counting, no single-studio film franchise has lasted longer, and only Monogram Pictures' *Bowery Boys* series of the 1940s and '50s can boast more entries (a staggering forty-eight over twelve years). And yet, it had to start somewhere. It certainly wasn't originally envisioned as a series at all. It all began in 1954 with one film; a film that would change the course of Japanese cinema and usher in a whole subgenre of science-fiction movie. Before the franchise, before the giant moths and spiders, before Godzilla Jr. and *kaiju* tag-team matches, there was but one motion picture that completely, and rightly, stood on its own: *Gojira*.

It's a very different type of film from those that followed it, especially the *Godzilla* films of the 1960s and '70s (known as the *Showa* series). Often, those who only know Godzilla as a figure of camp and kitsch are shocked to discover the somber tone, serious message, and outright horror of that original movie. In a class by itself, *Gojira* is a major achievement in Japanese cinema, and from a Western perspective, stands out as one of the finest foreign-language films ever made.

"The original *Gojira* is kind of its own beast, it exists in its own universe," explains Miguel Rodriguez, longtime Godzilla disciple and director of the Horrible Imaginings Film Festival. "It's different than any other that came afterwards and can never be emulated again because it's tied to one specific event and it's so serious."

American Occupation

It was not a film that could have been made in Japan prior to the mid-1950s. Following that nation's surrender to the Allied powers at the end of World War II on September 3, 1945, an American occupation had been put into effect. Ostensibly intended to help the former enemy state rebuild, and

The original Japanese lobby poster for *Gojira*.

Public domain

to engender an alliance from the ashes of the twentieth century's greatest conflict, the occupation also had the effect of forcing Westernization on a country steeped in Eastern tradition, of importing American popular culture, and of stagnating many native industries, including the motion picture industry. Any works of a subversive or controversial nature were out of the question, and certainly films that questioned the status quo, generated genuine horror, and criticized anything American in nature simply couldn't get off the ground.

Just prior to the end of the American occupation in 1952, interest in the concept of giant monsters was piqued with the Japanese rerelease of the 1933 American classic *King Kong*. The reissued film became a huge hit and national sensation, introducing a whole new generation to the idea of a massive behemoth running roughshod through a major metropolitan area. That would be followed the next year with the international release of Warner Bros.' science-fiction smash *The Beast from 20,000 Fathoms*, in which a Ray Harryhausen–created dinosaur terrorizes the eastern seaboard of the U.S. These films would have a strong influence in particular on Tomoyuki Tanaka, a veteran producer working for Toho Co., Ltd., one of Japan's six major film studios of the era.

The Lucky Dragon Disaster

But in addition to media influences, Tanaka would also be affected by something very real; a recent event that had shaken the Japanese people like they hadn't been shaken since the atomic bombings of nine years earlier. On the morning of March 1, 1954, the United States performed a hydrogen bomb test at the Bikini Atoll near the Marshall Islands in the South Pacific. Unfortunately, a Japanese fishing vessel, the *Lucky Dragon No. 5*, got too close to the fifteen-megaton blast, and its entire crew, plus the tons of fish they had caught, were irradiated with toxic nuclear fallout ash. The disaster wasn't reported in the media for another two weeks, by which time the men had already returned, suffering from radiation sickness, and much of their catch had already been sent to market for public consumption. Although most of the fish were successful recalled, the event alarmed the nation, and was a devastating reminder of the true horrors of nuclear weapons.

Tanaka had the *Lucky Dragon No. 5* disaster on his mind as he flew back home from Indonesia that month. A Japanese/Indonesian co-production he had been putting together, *Behind the Glory*, had fallen through, and he needed a new feature film to fill the hole in Toho's schedule and please his boss, executive producer Iwao Mori. The story goes that as he peered into the ocean depths from his plane window, he imagined what unknowable creature could potentially live there, and what would happen if it came to shore and ravaged Japan. Originally calling it *The Beast from 20,000 Miles Under the Sea*, he pitched it to Mori, who hesitantly greenlit the project. The Japanese film industry had never attempted a film like that before—special-effects monster movies seemed to be the domain of the Americans. But Tanaka had leave to try.

Honda and Tsuburaya: Assembling a Creative Team

In order to pull it off, Tanaka would turn to a core group of talented vision-aries and creators. With special effects weighing heavily on his mind, he brought in Eiji Tsuburaya, a respected effects director who had recently emerged from a blacklist during the American occupation due to his participation in creating incredibly lifelike battle sequences (including a re-creation of the Pearl Harbor attack) for Japanese propaganda films during the war. If anyone could pull off the unprecedented work needed, figured Tanaka, Tsuburaya was the man. To take his initial idea and run with it, Tanaka hired prominent fantasy/mystery writer Shigeru Kayama to pen the story, which he did over the course of a mere eleven days. Next on board to work the script into a finished screenplay were screenwriter Takeo Murata and a journeyman Toho director whose name would go on to become nearly synonymous with the film and the franchise, Ishiro Honda. In the early stages, it would ironically be given the name *Project G*, with the "G" standing for "giant."

"Honda not only directed that original film," points out Japanese cinema expert Stuart Galbraith IV, "but also co-wrote the script and was very actively involved in many other facets as well. He helped shape all of the genre's iconography."

The finished script tells the horrifying tale of a hibernating creature irradiated by nuclear testing in the Pacific, who comes ashore and causes far-reaching devastation to Japan. Echoing the *Lucky Dragon* disaster, the script begins with the monster attacking a fishing boat in the open sea, whose burned and traumatized survivors return to the mainland to tell their incredible tale. Following the monster's movements is paleontologist Dr. Yamane, who warns his country of the threat posed by the beast, while also seeking to study it. Meanwhile, Yamane's younger colleague (and fiancé of his daughter Emiko), the mysterious Dr. Serizawa, holds the dreadful secret of the Oxygen Destroyer, a device that just might be destructive enough to end the monster's reign of terror—but at what cost?

"Gorilla-Whale"

With Honda at the helm as director and Tsuburaya in charge of special-effects sequences, the film started to take shape in mid-1954. It would be an equal partnership between the two men, and it was clear from the beginning that unlike American productions of the period in which effects designers worked under the director, Tsuburaya's scenes would be completely under his own supervision. He began to conceptualize what the creature would actually look like. While Tsuburaya's original conception was that of a giant octopus (which would coincidentally be the idea used by Harryhausen for his next film, *It Came from Beneath the Sea*), Tanaka was adamant that he wanted some type of dinosaur-like being.

"As they were figuring out how they were going to do it and everything was falling into place, Mori was probably concerned," says Peter H. Brothers, author of *Atomic Dreams and the Nuclear Nightmare: The Making of Godzilla*. "It was a big gamble because they had never done anything like this in Japan before. The original *King Kong* and *The Beast from 20,000 Fathoms* had played there and done relatively well. But they were just looked at as special-effects pictures, and then when Honda came on board, he said let's do something a little bit more, let's have this reptile represent something that's been terrorizing us Japanese for many years."

Another of Tsuburaya's original ideas was shot down when he suggested the possibility of rendering the monster in stop-motion animation, the way his hero Willis O'Brien had done twenty years earlier for *King Kong* and Harryhausen had done for *The Beast from 20,000 Fathoms*. When Tsuburaya indicated that this process would take approximately seven years, he was informed by Tanaka that he had less than six months. A different approach would need to be taken, and Tsuburaya begrudgingly settled on constructing a rubber suit that would be worn by a human actor—a process that would later become known as "suitmation."

As for what it would actually look like, several designs began to circulate. Comic book illustrator Wasuke Abe was brought in, but his designs—including a rather humanoid model that featured a head shaped like a mushroom cloud to hint at the creature's nuclear origins—were ultimately rejected. Sticking with Tanaka's original conception and inspired by a *Life* magazine pictorial on prehistoric life, production designer Akira Watanabe perfected what would be the monster's ultimate look: an upright cross between a tyrannosaurus and an iguanadon, with stegosaurus-like plates running down its back; a massive tail; and rough, alligator-like skin to simulate the keloid scarring of radioactive burn victims. To fabricate Watanabe's design, Tsuburaya hired former colleague Teizo Toshimitsu, whose team got to work building the monster out of latex and cloth-and-wire frame.

Legend is fuzzy as to how the actual name of the monster came to be. A popular tale that has been often repeated has it that there was a member of the Toho staff (either a PR man or a stagehand, depending on whom you ask) who, due to his immense girth, had been nicknamed "Gojira"—a combination of the Japanese words for "gorilla" and "whale." Numerous attempts over the years to pinpoint the true identity of this mysterious person have proven fruitless, and most (including Honda's widow Kimi) believe that the name of the beast was simply decided upon by the Toho creative team, stemming from Tanaka's earliest notion of a "gorilla-whale"

Godzilla attacks Tokyo for the very first time in this 1954 publicity still.   *Author's collection*

monster. Whatever the origin, the monster would be known as Gojira (later phoneticized to Godzilla for American audiences).

Bringing the Monster to Life

Honda and Tsuburaya's vision called for Gojira to tower over the Tokyo skyline at a staggering height of roughly 50 meters/165 feet (although that number would increase dramatically later in the series). This was larger than any monster in movie history to date, and to accomplish the impressive effect, Tsuburaya would have to construct elaborate miniature sets. Meticulous location scouting was done to be as true to life as possible. Japanese law prohibited the public release of city blueprints, so everything was done by eye. An amusing anecdote from preproduction details how Tsuburaya and Honda were once apprehended by police after being over-heard on the roof of a major department store planning out how the car-nage would unfold, and had to explain that it was only cinematic mayhem they had in mind.

The task of actually putting on the two-hundred-plus-pound Gojira suit was given by Tsuburaya to contract Toho stunt actor Haruo Nakajima, who would go on to become the most celebrated performer in the history of the Japanese suitmation technique, and would play the monster for the next eighteen years. Meanwhile, on the human side of things, Tanaka and Honda assembled a cast of Toho veterans and newcomers: for the role of Dr. Yamane, the legendary Takashi Shimura, a regular in the films of acclaimed director Akira Kurosawa who had just come off starring in *Seven Samurai*; as the brooding Dr. Serizawa, relative unknown Akihiko Hirata, who would become inextricably linked with Japanese science-fiction cinema of the 1950s through the 1970s; as Yamane's daughter Emiko, the young and beautiful Momoko Kochi, who would reprise her role some forty years later in *Godzilla vs. Destoroyah*; and as Emiko's love interest Ogata, the dashing twenty-year-old Akira Takarada, whose presence in the Godzilla franchise is still felt to this day.

Gojira went into production in August 1954 and was completed by October, with Tsuburaya handling the monster effects and destruction, and Honda directing the non-effects scenes that composed the majority of the film. Once filming was under way, the final piece of the puzzle was put into place when prominent classical composer Akira Ifukube was commis-sioned to create the music for the film. Without access to most of the footage being shot, and going mainly on the conceptual material that had been

Momoko Kochi and Akira Takarada as Emiko and Ogata, the young lovers in *Gojira*.

Everett Collection

given to him, Ifukube crafted an orchestral score of thrilling power and inevitable horror, featuring memorable themes that have been associated with Godzilla ever since.

"Ifukube was a composer of military marches, and there's something about that aspect of his score for the original film," says Miguel Rodriguez. "His contribution was two-fold. First of all, it lends a certain gravitas to the monster, because there are some themes that are extremely somber. Some are among the best pieces of movie music ever made. . . . It's not like this crazy action movie kind of score—it's very different."

The Birth of a Genre

On November 3, 1954, Toho released the film upon the unsuspecting Japanese public, and the results were as explosive as the atomic breath the monster used to engulf the fictionalized Tokyo in flames. While many critics of the day deplored what they considered the movie's exploitation of Japan's very real nuclear paranoia and insisted that giant monster movies be left to the Americans, the public overwhelmingly voiced its rapturous approval, and *Gojira* went on to become the highest-grossing Japanese film of the year.

The finished film stands as one of the finest pieces of science-fiction cinema in history, and Honda's realized vision of unstoppable mass destruction pegs *Gojira* as very much a horror film, as well. The monster itself is vividly rendered by Tsuburaya and company and brilliantly shot by cinematographer Masao Tamai using heavy shadows and dramatic lighting for a sense of heightened realism and palpable terror. And yet the human actors shine as well: the seasoned Shimura brings subtlety and gravitas to the film with a striking performance as Dr. Yamane. The movie is also anchored by a poignant love triangle touching on Japan's traditional practice of arranged marriages: Yamane's daughter Emiko (Kochi) has been betrothed to Dr. Serizawa (Hirata), but wants to marry Coast Guard sailor Ogata (Takarada). Serizawa's climactic sacrifice, in which he reluctantly uses his Oxygen Destroyer to kill Gojira, giving up his own life in the process in order to both prevent the weapon from falling into the wrong hands and to allow Emiko and Ogata to be together, is a powerful and touching coda to a monster movie of rare nuance and dramatic force.

Japanese filmgoers were awestruck by the entirely new type of film that Tanaka, Honda, and Tsuburaya had created. Never before had such a film been attempted in Japan, and certainly a movie that so openly courted the country's collective memory of Hiroshima and Nagasaki would never have been permitted during the occupation. Brought to life by the bomb, Gojira rained nuclear fire down upon a helpless Japan, just as American bomber planes had done on August 6 and 9, 1945. One of Honda's main

Dr. Yamane (Shimura) looks on as Ogata (Takarada) and Dr. Serizawa (Hirata) prepare to confront Godzilla in his underwater domain.   *Movie Stills Database*

objectives in making the film was to dramatize the devastating impact of atomic weapons, and his antinuclear message is at the heart of what the film is about. Unlike in later films of the franchise, in which the action, and the monster itself, was treated in a lighthearted and youth-oriented fashion, the original film was unrelentingly grim, putting the loss of human life center stage and generating an atmosphere of pure dread.

"What must the original Japanese audience have felt while watching scenes of such destruction?" asks Steve Biodrowski, editor of *Cinefantastique Online*. "I cannot even imagine. It must've been utterly devastating. It had to bring back so many horrible memories. I imagine it would've been quite an emotional experience."

Gojira was the very first Japanese *kaiju*—a bastardized form of the ancient Chinese term *quai shou* meaning "strange beast" that had come into popular use in Japan in the 1930s with the influx of American monster movies. And not only was the original *Gojira* the first Japanese *kaiju eiga* (monster movie), but it was also the first Japanese special-effects film—a subgenre known as *tokusatsu* that was drastically unlike the subtle dramas, historical epics, and war pictures that the Japanese cinema had been known for up to that time. The success of the film led to an explosion of *kaiju* cinema that continued for decades, and kicked off the greatest international film franchise of all time.

3

King of the Monsters

Godzilla's First Introduction to American Audiences

T he original *Gojira* had been a smash success in its native Japan—the most lucrative film of 1954, in fact. But success in Japan and success worldwide were two very different things. Specifically, mainstream success in the United States was a Holy Grail of sorts—the ultimate goal that had yet to be achieved by any Japanese-made film, and in fact by very few non-American films in general at that time. But thanks to some enterprising producers, some liberal and creatively questionable editing, and the addition of a friendly Caucasian face, that was about to change. When *Gojira* became *Godzilla*, it began a relationship between American audiences and Japanese movies that would truly turn the monster into a household name.

An original 1956 lobby card from the American release of *Godzilla, King of the Monsters*. *Tom/Flickr*

The 1950s was a time when American distributors were beginning to take chances on prominent foreign-language films, including the works of Italian director Federico Fellini and even Toho-produced films from director Akira Kurosawa such as the highly influential *Rashomon*. Art houses were buzzing with films from across the seas, and their unique perspectives and values were even starting to have an effect on the way American movies were made. The time was ripe for a truly crossover blockbuster hit to make an impact in the United States, and that hit would be the film that became known as *Godzilla, King of the Monsters*.

It was through success in the States, and also throughout the world, that the franchise was assured longevity as part of American popular culture, and achieved a level of prominence it never would have achieved had it remained confined to native shores as so many other successful Japanese films and franchises have since. But in order for that to happen, it was judged that some changes would have to be made—this was, after all, a film produced by a nation that America had very recently been at war with, which portrayed that nation in a positive light, while at the same time drawing attention to the atomic nightmare it had endured at American hands. It was touchy material for the time, and for this reason the film that American audiences eventually saw in 1956 would be significantly altered from the original vision of director Ishiro Honda.

From Gojira to Godzilla

Contrary to popular belief, the original, unedited version of *Gojira* did make its way to American shores shortly after its initial Japanese release in 1954. However, the release was extremely limited, confined to small Japanese American enclaves in cities like New York and San Francisco, where Toho deemed it would have an appeal. It was in a small theater in the Chinatown section of Los Angeles in 1955 that American movie producer Edmund Goldman discovered the picture and immediately recognized its potential appeal to a much wider domestic audience.

Goldman purchased the international distribution rights from Toho for $25,000, then quickly sold them to Jewell Enterprises. The small studio set out to develop and prepare the film for American distribution, with significant financial backing from businessmen Terry Turner and that master of ballyhoo Joseph E. Levine, whose Embassy Pictures would go on to produce and/or distribute such major films as the 1962 adaptation of Eugene O'Neill's *Long Day's Journey into Night*, the war epic *Zulu* (1964), director Mike

Nichols's groundbreaking film *The Graduate* (1967), Mel Brooks's directorial debut *The Producers* (1968), the Katharine Hepburn/Peter O'Toole historical drama *The Lion in Winter* (1968), and the early Anthony Hopkins vehicle *Magic* (1978).

Levine and his Jewell associates determined that before giving the film a wide theatrical release, some doctoring would need to be done. First would be the name itself. Although many have assumed that it was the American producers who changed the name of the movie (and the creature), the change was actually made by Toho's own marketing department, which felt it wise to use "Godzilla," a word that sounded phonetically in English closer to how "Gojira" is pronounced in Japanese ("Goh-dzhi-la"). But that was just the beginning, and the most superficial of changes compared to what was to come.

The idea was to make the movie "palatable" to 1950s American audiences, so elements that accentuated its "Japanese-ness" would have to go. Freelance TV writer Al C. Ward was brought on board to rework the story. The tragic arranged marriage of main characters Emiko and Serizawa, an alien concept to Americans, was downplayed; further neutering the romantic subplot, Ward toned down hints of Emiko's unfaithfulness to Serizawa with her true love Ogata, to avoid clashing with conservative 1950s American family values. But most importantly, the film's antinuclear

The American re-edit of *Godzilla, King of the Monsters* actually received a Japanese release in 1957.

Public domain

message—particularly the manner in which it subtly laid blame at the feet of the nation that had once attacked Japan with nuclear weapons—had to be reined in. As crucial to the film as it was, it couldn't be completely eliminated, but several key moments—including a debate in the Japanese senate over the Hiroshima and Nagasaki bombings and a heartrending scene during Gojira's devastation of Tokyo in which a distraught mother tells her children that they will soon join their father (presumably killed in World War II) in heaven—were liberally truncated. In the end, more than fifteen minutes of footage was removed from Honda's original film.

Enter Raymond Burr

Yet more revision was to come. Easing the tension raised by the nuclear themes, producers felt that American (read: non-Asian) audiences would feel more comfortable and less threatened with a Caucasian character as the story's lead. Needless to say, this would require significant rewriting and editing, as well as entirely new scenes to be shot and cut into the film. Independent director/editor Terry O. Morse was brought in to direct new footage. The character of intrepid newspaper reporter Steve Martin (no relation to the famous comedian, who was only ten years old at the time) was created, and cast in the role was a somewhat obscure Canadian-born actor named Raymond Burr, best known at the time for a brief role as the heavy in Alfred Hitchcock's *Rear Window* (1954), who would later go on to great renown in starring roles on the long-running TV series *Perry Mason* and *Ironside*.

"There's been a lot of controversy about that," says Peter H. Brothers, who chronicled the film's Americanization closely in his book *Atomic Dreams and the Nuclear Nightmare: The Making of* Godzilla. "I think there were two reasons. One was to make it a more linear, straightforward, run-of-the-mill monster movie, without all the social subtext. But there are also a lot of references to the atomic bombs, to the contaminated fish, to the Lucky Dragon incident, a lot taken out for political reasons. The war was over, it had been about ten years; no one really want to be reminded about that stuff, particular the A-bomb."

The altered film, eventually titled *Godzilla, King of the Monsters*, is structurally quite different from the original. Gone is the opening scene of the fishing boat attack, meant to evoke the real-life *Lucky Dragon No. 5* disaster; instead, the movie opens *in media res*, documenting the devastated Tokyo immediately following Godzilla's attack, and then jumping back in time

Burr was a mere year away from superstardom as TV's Perry Mason.   *Everett Collection*

to demonstrate how it all happened. The chief witness is Burr's Martin, a journalist on a stopover in Japan who had been following the events leading up to and including the emergence of the monster—it is through his perspective that we experience the events of the story, and a somewhat clumsy connection between himself and the original Japanese characters is concocted to keep him relevant to the action. Morse went so far as to shoot scenes featuring Burr interacting with stand-ins, often shot from behind to strengthen the illusion that Burr is interacting with the original cast. All in all, Burr's screen-time is not very long, and some accounts indicate that his scenes may have been shot in as little as twenty-four hours. Nevertheless, the re-edited film as put together by Ward and Morse places Steve Martin at the center of the action, commenting on everything he sees with a sense of Western authority while actually influencing the plot very little.

Godzilla Takes America

Once Burr's scenes were finished and had been edited into the reworked film, *Godzilla, King of the Monsters* was ready for mass consumption, and the movie was given a wide release as a full-fledged A-picture on April 27, 1956, distributed by Levine's Embassy Pictures and Jewell Enterprise co-owner Richard Kay's Transworld Releasing Corp. Just as they'd hoped, an American audience primed for giant monster action during the height of Hollywood's post-World War II science-fiction boom ate it up and made *Godzilla* an instant hit. Critics weren't kind, but just as in Japan, that mattered little. American audiences embraced what they saw as the brand-new giant monster (little did they know that back in Japan he had already appeared in a sequel, Toho's hastily produced *Godzilla Raids Again*, which wouldn't reach America until 1959).

"The Americanized version played around the world to great success, and was instrumental in promulgating the series," says Peter H. Brothers. "Eventually, companies like American International would be co-producing some of these films with Toho. A lot of people think Godzilla was a Japanese export; I see him more as an American import. Because the inspiration for Godzilla was America, and he really is a Japanese/American creation."

And yet, what American audiences also didn't know, and really wouldn't be widely aware of for decades thereafter, was that the movie they saw wasn't the movie as it had originally been made. With Ishiro Honda's critique of the dangers of nuclear weapons muted, *Godzilla, King of the Monsters* is indeed more of a conventional giant-monster-on-the-loose picture, less likely to make its viewers feel guilt than to provide creature feature thrills and chills. Burr's reporter is a straightforward protagonist more familiar to fans of American monster movies than the sober, nuanced, hand-wringing protagonists of the Japanese *Gojira*. Its conclusion is also much more open-and-shut, as opposed to the more ambiguous Japanese finale, in which Yamane warns that more such creatures could arise if we don't learn our lesson.

"Back in the '50s, it was maybe necessary in order to get a film into a theater where a US audience would see it," speculates Steve Biodrowski, editor of *Cinefantastique Online*. "Even Ishiro Honda said as far as he was concerned it was OK for the rest of the world to see the Americanized version. Putting Raymond Burr in there gave Americans someone to relate to. What they did in that film was fairly respectful. Most of it was to make it understandable to US audiences. I still think the Japanese cut is much better, but all things being equal, that was the way to get American audiences to pay for tickets."

Nevertheless, in later years, Honda himself would claim to have never even seen the American re-edit of his film. And yet the movie does have its defenders to this day; despite the questionable reasoning behind the revision, *Godzilla, King of the Monsters* is not without power and the ability to horrify as well as entertain. Burr puts in a solid performance, highlighted by his grim firsthand narration of what he believes to be his final moments as he watches Godzilla trample through the heart of the city. The flashback framing of the narrative, while lacking the immediacy of the original, turns out to be an intriguing choice that draws the viewer in.

Whatever its merits and faults, *Godzilla, King of the Monsters* would directly kick off the American love affair with *kaiju* cinema, and also spread the gospel of Godzilla all over the world (the American version would even be released in Japan to great success in 1957). Generations of film fans would grow up knowing only this version, as it continued to be popular in late-night showings, drive-ins, and TV over the years. Only the most hardcore of Western *kaiju* fans would even be aware of the original *Gojira* until 2004, when Rialto Pictures commissioned a digital restoration of the film and finally gave it a proper American theatrical release to commemorate its fiftieth anniversary, including a DVD release that would allow fans to discover what they had missing all these years.

Today, the original *Gojira* has at last earned a place in America as a recognized classic of world cinema, as fans have discovered just how superior it is to the version they'd known before. And although the memory of Raymond Burr and the American re-edit is still cherished, particularly by those of the generations that grew up with it, with each passing year it becomes more a curiosity of the Cold War era.

Kaiju Italiano: The Forgotten Story of "Cozzilla"

Whether praised or avoided, the American version of **Gojira** is widely known to most fans around the world. However, not nearly as known is another alternate edit produced for release outside Japan some twenty years later. An Italian version, it was a bizarre project undertaken by an enterprising producer looking to capitalize on the *kaiju* craze long after it had run its course in other corners of the globe. The result is a rarity that continues to be sought after by Godzilla completists the world over.

In 1977, Luigi Cozzi, a young Italian writer-director of science-fiction and horror films and a protégé of Italian horror maven Dario Argento, got the idea to bring the original Japanese *Gojira* to Italy for the very first time. However, when he failed to obtain the rights from Toho, he instead wound up with the American version starring Raymond Burr. Since this cut had already been seen in Italy and Cozzi had his heart set on giving Italian audiences something they hadn't seen before, he took the liberty of creating his own cut—without Toho's explicit blessing.

Because Italian distributors refused to exhibit a black-and-white film by that point, Cozzi's first move was to colorize the picture using an experimental technique called Spectrorama 70, making the film one of the first thus altered. But that was only the beginning. Cozzi liberally re-edited the already re-edited movie, removing certain scenes and adding so much stock footage of destruction that the film's running time was padded by an additional twenty-five minutes. Akira Ifukube's superb original musical score was jettisoned in favor of a score re-edited by film composers Fabio Frizzi, Vince Tempera, and Franco Bixio, known for their soundtracks for the films of Italian gore-master Lucio Fulci. In a choice reminiscent of 1950s schlock impresario William Castle, Cozzi even augmented the soundtrack with a special in-theater effect that shook viewers' seats each time Godzilla took a thunderous step.

Infamous today as "*Cozzilla*," Luigi Cozzi's *Godzilla* has only been officially released in Italy, aside from brief exhibitions in Turkey and Japan. Reportedly, Toho, none too pleased with Cozzi's tampering, has decreed that this version of the film may only be legally distributed in Italy. That hasn't stopped bootleg versions of the coveted *Cozzilla* leaking out over the years, whether on VHS or on YouTube. Unfortunately, most original prints of the film have been lost, making it perhaps the rarest of all Godzilla movies.

4

Golden Age

The Early Showa Era

F ans of Godzilla films—and of *kaiju* and *tokusatsu* films in general—
usually recognize three distinct eras in the history of their beloved
franchise: *Showa, Heisei,* and Millennium (not to mention a brand-
new fourth era only now beginning). Of these three eras, the one that is
often the most revered, particularly amongst older fans who were around
for it, is the original one. From an American pop cultural perspective, it
is even very often the only era of which casual fans are aware, even if they
don't necessarily know what it's called.

The origin of the term comes from the name of the reigning Emperor
of Japan at the time, Hirohito, who was known as the "*Showa* Emperor" due
to his use of the term—roughly translated as "enlightened harmony"—
during his 1925 coronation speech. As is the custom in Japan, history is
divided into these Imperial reigns, and since Hirohito reigned until 1989,
it was easy to categorize the Godzilla films made during that period as
"*Showa*" films.

Thanks to the success of the groundbreaking original *Gojira* in 1954,
Toho decided to stick with the winning formula, and immediately began
producing a string of *tokusatsu* movies. From the beginning, chief among
them was Godzilla himself, the creature that had started it all. From 1954
through 1975, a string of Godzilla films was released that include some of
the most cherished entries in the long-running series. It was this era that
introduced fans to most of the standard tropes of *kaiju* cinema, as well as a
colorful cast of giant monsters.

Characterized by a sense of fun, adventure, and inventiveness sometimes
lacking in the other eras, it also helps that the *Showa* era was first—making
it difficult to top in the minds of many, since it set the original standard.
And yet the *Showa* era itself lasted so long that it is sometimes divided into
two distinct subsections, owing in part to the dramatic shift in tone that
was occurring, not to mention the change in key personnel as well as the

changing fortunes of the Japanese film industry going from the 1960s to the 1970s. Often considered the finest period of Godzilla pictures—not to mention the heyday of the Japanese movie industry in general—the time between 1955 and 1968 gave us some truly classic *kaiju* cinema, and transformed Godzilla from the titular monster in a one-off disaster movie into a bona fide international movie star.

"The original ones started off serious, were meant to be warning films, real science fiction films," says Steve Biodrowski of *Cinefantastique Online*. "And they gradually descended into being just entertainment films. But always there was an attempt to do something that would be entertaining to the entire audience."

Godzilla Raids Again

Japanese Title: *Gojira no gyakushû*
Literal Translation: *Godzilla's Counterattack*
Also Known As: *Gigantis: The Fire Monster* (U.S. title)
Release Date: April 24, 1955

As is often the case, the massive success of the original *Gojira* led to a sequel being immediately fast-tracked. Toho wanted to capitalize right away on its surprise smash, and struck while the iron was hot by kicking off production on a new Godzilla movie mere weeks after the first one had opened. The result was a movie that tended to show the strain of its rushed nature—a far cry from its predecessor, yet nevertheless the movie that helped set the *Showa* era in motion.

A largely new cast and crew was assembled for the hastily produced sequel, with Ishiro Honda being replaced as director by Motoyoshi Oda, a contemporary of both Honda and Akira Kurosawa at Toho, for whom the picture would be the only *daikaiju* film he would ever helm. Taking the place of composer Akira Ifukube was Masaru Sato, who would eventually become the second most prolific contributor of Godzilla film scores. Takeo Murata, co-writer of the original *Gojira* script, was brought back and, with the assistance of new young screenwriter Shigeaki Hidaka, penned the story of a second Gojira-like mutated dinosaur that emerges from the Pacific, much to the dismay of Takashi Shimura's Dr. Yamane, the only returning character from the original film.

This time out, however, the monster would not be alone. In what would be the very first time two *kaiju* did battle against one another, in *Godzilla Raids Again*, the big guy is challenged by a second giant mutated dinosaur, an ankylosaurus named Anguirus that would go on to become his longest-running ally in later films of the series. The site of their destruction would not be Tokyo in this installment, but the port city of Osaka. At the time, the concept of dueling giant monsters was quite the novelty, and was without a doubt the most interesting thing about the movie.

Eiji Tsuburaya returned to mastermind the special effects, lending a unique flair to the scenes in which the creatures do battle. Typically, Tsuburaya's strategy was to record the monsters' movement at an extra fast speed, so that when the film was run at normal speed, they would appear to move slower, lending them the illusion of great size. However, it appears that someone in Tsuburaya's unit accidentally recorded the Godzilla/Anguirus

When Godzilla and Anguirus clash, Osaka Castle doesn't stand a chance.   *Author's collection*

battles not at extra-fast speed but rather at extra-slow speed, resulting in surreally quick-moving monsters. Legend has it that despite the mistake, Tsuburaya liked the bizarre results so much that he left them in the picture (or perhaps he just bowed to the reality of a tight schedule and even tighter budget).

Unfortunately, what didn't move along very quickly was the plot; revolving around a team of fishing spotter pilots who help defend their waterfront community from Godzilla's onslaught, the story line is rather lackluster compared to that of the original, with characters who simply do not spark interest in the way that Yamane, Emiko, and Serizawa did. Nevertheless, the sequel does introduce Godzilla fans to Hiroshi Koizumi, the actor who would go on to appear in five more Godzilla films, including *Godzilla: Tokyo S.O.S.* some forty-seven years later.

Just as *Gojira* had a tortuous road to U.S. distribution in 1956, so too was the distribution of *Godzilla Raids Again* fraught with tampering and misguided editing. The first American company to purchase the rights from Toho, AB-PT Pictures (co-owned by Richard Kay, one of the distributors of *Gojira*), had no intention of actually releasing the film; rather, they intended to use only the monster sequences, then add new scenes with Caucasian actors, set the whole thing in San Francisco, and call it *The Volcano Monsters*. Toho went so far as to ship over new Godzilla and Anguirus costumes in case AB-PT needed them, but the company went belly-up before the project came to fruition.

Instead, the venerable Warner Bros. wound up snatching up the rights in 1959. American producers were still skeptical that their audiences would accept an unadulterated Japanese product, and so the film was re-edited, with a voice-over narration added. Sato's score was replaced with stock music from previous films. And finally, in a cynical move to dupe moviegoers, Warner Bros. changed Godzilla's name to Gigantis, even replacing his trademark roar in an effort to make it seem that the movie featured a brand-new monster. The resulting film, *Gigantis: The Fire Monster*, is considered vastly inferior to its original Japanese version, which didn't see the light of day in the States for decades.

Godzilla Raids Again performed quite well at the box office in Japan; nevertheless, Toho decided to put Godzilla in mothballs for a little while, focusing instead on developing new *kaiju* and *tokusatsu* properties like *Rodan* (1956), *The Mysterians* (1957), *The H-Man* (1958), *Battle in Outer Space* (1959), and *Mothra* (1961). It would be seven years before the Big G would once again rear his scaly head, and the *Showa* era would continue in earnest.

King Kong vs. Godzilla

Japanese Title: *Kingu Kongu tai Gojira*
Release Date: August 11, 1962

The highest-grossing Japanese Godzilla film of them all, and arguably the most popular worldwide, King Kong vs. Godzilla *gets an entire chapter all to its mighty self. Please see Chapter 9 for more information!*

Mothra vs. Godzilla

Japanese Title: *Mosura tai Gojira*
Also Known As: *Godzilla vs. The Thing* (U.S. title)
Release Date: April 29, 1964

Often hailed as one of the finest, if not the very finest of all the *Showa* Godzilla sequels, *Mothra vs. Godzilla* represents Toho firing on all cylinders, at the very height of its powers both commercially and creatively. The Japanese film industry was still booming, and the towering success of *King Kong vs. Godzilla* ensured that audiences would not have to wait another seven years before the giant reptile showed up once again. In fact, beginning with *Mothra vs. Godzilla,* Toho would not cease regular production on Godzilla movies for the rest of the decade. The great "*kaiju* boom" of the *Showa* era was now in full effect.

Composer and screenwriter Shinichi Sekizawa, who was quickly becoming Toho's go-to writer for *tokusatsu* films after penning scripts for *Giant Monster Varan* (1958), *Battle in Outer Space* (1959), *Mothra* (1961), and *King Kong vs. Godzilla* (1962) was brought to the Godzilla series for the second time to create yet another crossover; except this time, the crossover would be between two established and popular Toho properties. The giant, mystical insect/goddess Mothra, joined by her tiny twin guardians the *shobijin,* was the second-best-known Japanese *kaiju* at the time after making her first appearance in the stand-alone picture Sekizawa wrote three years prior, and it was only natural that he would bring her back to take on Godzilla.

With Ishiro Honda back at the helm, the director's penchant for social consciousness is once again at the fore, this time with a decidedly anticorporate message. When Mothra's giant egg appears off the Japanese coast, it is "claimed" by ruthless profiteers Kumayama and Torahata of "Happy Enterprises" (played with relish by Yoshifumi Tajima and series regular Kenji Sahara), who seek to exploit it as a tourist attraction. When Godzilla also shows up, the dollar signs in their eyes initially grow larger, until they realize they cannot control the monster. With Japan experiencing an explosion of big business growth at the time that clashed with the country's pre-World War II traditions, the story line resonated greatly with audiences that were troubled by some of the moral issues it raised.

But a great Godzilla movie also has to have great action, and that was in no short supply thanks to innovative work from Eiji Tsuburaya, who by this point had formed his own separate special-effects company, Tsuburaya Productions. The "Old Man" and his team, including art director Akira Watanabe, assistant director Teruyoshi Nakano, and suit designer Teizo Toshimitsu, crafted some of the finest *kaiju* battles ever put to celluloid. The Godzilla suit itself, worn for the fourth time by Haruo Nakajima, is among the most memorable and popular with fans. Two new Mothra larvae, realized through mechanical fabrication and operated by remote control, join in on the action along with the original wire-operated ten-foot-long Mothra marionette. Tsuburaya and cinematographer Hajime Koizumi used strobe effects and a form of stop-motion photography to ensure that the fight scenes between the titular creatures would be truly unique.

"Imagine being Eiji," ponders Godzilla expert Miguel Rodriguez. "You have Godzilla and now you have this big moth, and you make them fight: How in the world is that going to happen? They're so completely different. And he does a lot of interesting things, like Mothra grabbing the back of his head, and pulling him by the tail. And then Godzilla has to fight the Mothra larvae, for crying out loud! So I have to take my hat off to *Mothra vs. Godzilla*, one of my favorite movies of all time, just pure brilliance."

In addition to Tajima and Sahara, *Mothra vs. Godzilla* also brought back Akira Takarada, who had starred in the original *Gojira*, to play protagonist Ichiro Sakai, the reporter joined by photographer Junko Nakanishi (Yuriko Hoshi), who opposes the interests of Happy Enterprises and, with the help of the *shobijin* fairies, brokers the peace with Mothra to ensure that the benevolent monster will help defend Japan from Godzilla's destruction. In the roles of the fairies were Emi and Yumi Ito, beloved in Japan at the time as the pop-singing sensation known as the Peanuts. Not only did the Ito twins reprise their iconic "Mothra Theme" from the original *Mothra* film, but they were also given a second, gorgeously melodic tune, "Sacred Springs," composed for them by Godzilla music-master Akira Ifukube, who had also returned to the series.

Godzilla was now a hot property over in the United States, and so there would be no delay in getting the film American distribution. The movie was picked up by American International Pictures (AIP), making it the first of three Godzilla films to be distributed in the States by the production house that had already made a name for itself as one of the premier purveyors of low-budget terror and science fiction, introducing American audiences to the movies of British horror studio Hammer Films, American producer Roger Corman, and Italian director Mario Bava, not to mention Toho's own submarine vs. *kaiju* picture *Atragon* (1963).

With Godzilla a well-established American success by this point, *Mothra vs. Godzilla* would be the first of the series released in the U.S. with almost no editorial tampering (one extra scene was filmed for American audiences only). Nevertheless, when the movie came out in the U.S. in August 1964, the title would be changed to *Godzilla vs. The Thing*, in what appears to be a lame attempt to tie into Howard Hawks's legendary 1951 alien monster movie, *The Thing from Another World*. But if AIP was worried American audiences wouldn't buy Godzilla fighting a giant moth, they were wrong; the movie became one of the most successful of the entire series.

Ghidorah, the Three-Headed Monster

Japanese Title: *San daikaijû: Chikyû saidai no kessen*
Literal Translation: *Three Giant Monsters: Earth's Greatest Battle*
Release Date: December 20, 1964

By this point, the Godzilla machine was moving full speed ahead. Toho had officially put the series into continuous production, and in fact, 1964 would be the first and only year in which not one but two Godzilla films were made. This time, it would be a *kaiju* extravaganza unlike anything before it, and a picture that would introduce the world to the monster's greatest foe. It would also begin the shift of the character of Godzilla from destructive force of nature to benevolent protector of the Earth.

Ghidorah, the Three-Headed Monster is also the first film in the franchise to introduce pronounced elements of science fiction, which would remain prevalent throughout much of the remainder of the *Showa* era. In Sekizawa's script, the titular creature, a golden, scaly, dragon-like monstrosity that fires bolts of lightning from each of its three reptilian heads, arrives via meteor from outer space. We learn from an ancient Venusian prophecy spouted by the captivating Princess Selina of the fictional kingdom of Selgina (inexplicably possessed by a Venusian intelligence of some kind) that Ghidorah destroyed the civilization of Venus many centuries ago, and now threatens to do the same on Earth. As if that's not bad enough, the princess also correctly predicts the return of both Godzilla and even the giant pteranadon Rodan, who hadn't been seen since seemingly meeting his fate in the volcanic Mt. Aso at the conclusion of the 1956 film of the same name.

In order to drive Ghidorah from the Earth and ensure that he doesn't do to Earth what he did to Venus, the people of Earth must enlist the aid of none other than Mothra, a new version grown from one of the larvae of the previous film, to "persuade" the seemingly uncontrollable Godzilla and Rodan to fight the three-headed menace. In a very odd scene that was a sign of some of the wackiness to come in the series, the very anthropomorphized monsters engage in a "conversation" in their own tongue, which results in Godzilla and Rodan reluctantly joining forces to defeat Ghidorah.

For the first time ever, Godzilla was working not to wipe out human civilization, but to save it. And even though the monster was still presented in a dangerous, unpredictable light, this plot twist represents the beginning of a character evolution that occurred over the course of the 1960s. Responding to Godzilla's increasing popularity among children, many of whom were far too young to even remember the nuclear annihilation for which he was originally a cipher, Toho wanted to make the monster less evil and more of a figure that could be cheered. And although this development reportedly did not sit well with director Ishiro Honda, who also disapproved of the "humanization" of the monster, this trend would only get stronger in the films to come.

With the James Bond phenomenon in full swing, it's clear that Sekizawa was looking to add an atmosphere of intrigue and espionage to the film, which features assassins, detectives, and high-octane chase and shootout scenes mixed in with the giant monster action. And although the plot may not be entirely cohesive, it's a valiant effort that results in a unique kind of *kaiju* movie. Also unique is the joining of four different *kaiju* in a single film, something that had never been tried before. Appearing for the first time, Ghidorah would become one of the most regular foes in the entire series, appearing to antagonize the Big G repeatedly in all three eras of the franchise.

The film was brought to the United States nine months later by the Walter Reade Organization, a Northeast-based distributor specializing in foreign pictures. The company had experienced little success with arthouse fare, and so turned to more populist entertainment like Godzilla (they would have their greatest hit three years later with a domestic release, George Romero's zombie opus *Night of the Living Dead*). Although the

American version was largely untampered-with, unfortunately much of Akira Ifukube's excellent score (featuring his memorable new Ghidorah theme, adapted from the theme to 1958's *Giant Monster Varan*) was excised in favor of less "Oriental-sounding" stock music from American monster flicks.

A certain juvenilization was certainly coming into play with *Ghidorah, the Three-Headed Monster*, as the serious tone of earlier films continued to be lightened up. Consequently, the appeal of the series started to skew even younger, with effects director Eiji Tsuburaya leading the charge. The film is a major turning point in the series, with the emphasis put more on fun monster action and less on sober social commentary.

Invasion of Astro-Monster

Japanese Title: *Kaiju daisenso*
Literal Translation: *War of the Monsters*
Also Known As: *Monster Zero* (U.S. theatrical title)
Godzilla vs. Monster Zero (U.S. home video title)
Release Date: December 19, 1965

Although there were certainly greater Godzilla films made, there were perhaps none that more typified all that the *Showa* era was about quite like *Invasion of Astro Monster*, a rollicking romp of a picture that combines the *kaiju* concept for the first time with the space opera aesthetic Toho had been exploring in films like *The Mysterians* (1957) and *Battle in Outer Space* (1959). In a sign of the continuing success and growing prominence of Godzilla in the United States, the film would actually be co-produced by United Productions of America (UPA), the animation-studio-turned-production-house headed by B-movie mogul Henry G. Saperstein. Bursting with imaginative special effects and colorful performances, it is pure fun from beginning to end.

The first in a long line of alien invaders bent on taking over Earth in Godzilla movies, the sinister and duplicitous Xiliens of the newly discovered Planet X promise the world a cure for cancer if only Earth will lend them the services of Godzilla and Rodan to defeat the mysterious Monster Zero that allegedly has been terrorizing them. Of course, the Xiliens' real agenda involves brainwashing the two Earth *kaiju* to join forces with Monster Zero (who turns out to be none other than King Ghidorah) in wiping out human civilization so that they may harvest all of the planet's water supply.

In order to pull off this outlandish story line, Tsuburaya and his team develop some of their finest special effects to date, including gorgeous matte paintings of Planet X and its environs, meticulously detailed spaceship and city models, and stunningly convincing composite shots. Above all, the film is engaging to look at, and light in tone. This lightness would be accentuated by Tsuburaya in his direction of the monster scenes; motivated more and more to appeal to children, Tsuburaya continued to infuse whimsy amidst the action.

This whimsy is typified by the infamous "shie" victory dance performed by Godzilla at the conclusion of his first battle with King Ghidorah. Also commonly known among American fans as the "highland fling," this leaping maneuver was very popular at the time in Japan as a trademark of the humorous manga comic book *Osomatsu-kun*. Tsuburaya believed young fans of Godzilla would eat it up, but was opposed by many, like director Honda and suit actor Haruo Nakajima, who felt the dance move was a "bridge too far" as far as Godzilla's descent into silliness was concerned. But Tsuburaya won out, and the moment remains one of the series' most polarizing.

The lively cast is highlighted by the terrific chemistry of series veteran Akira Takarada as Astronaut Fuji and American actor Nick Adams as Astronaut Glenn, the two space explorers who first encounter the Xiliens on Planet X. Nominated for an Oscar for his role in *Twilight of Honor* two years earlier, Adams was an intense method-style thespian in the stripe of Jack Palance, Marlon Brando, and James Dean (a very close friend) who had first appeared for Toho earlier in 1965 in *Frankenstein Conquers the World*, another Saperstein co-production. Confident that American actors would add to his films' appeal, Saperstein was responsible for the casting of Adams, whose Hollywood career had begun to stagnate (he also had Russ Tamblyn of *West Side Story* fame cast in Toho's *War of the Gargantuas* the following year). Whether Adams helped the films' American appeal or not, his performance is a joy to behold, his Actors Studio posturing, brooding angst, and confident American swagger contrasting surreally with the traditional acting of his Japanese co-stars in a manner that somehow works.

Joining Takarada and Adams is the lovely Kumi Mizuno as Miss Namikawa, Glenn's love interest and undercover Xilien. Rumored to be Adams's love interest in real life as well, Mizuno also demonstrates a natural charisma that would lead to several more appearances in the series. As the evil Controller of Planet X and leader of the alien invasion, accomplished character actor Yoshio Tsuchiya acquits himself with great flair, even improvising snippets of alien language (unfortunately deleted from the American version).

Despite Saperstein's involvement, the film (along with *War of the Gargantuas*) would remain unreleased in the United States for almost five years due to UPA's failure to find a willing distributor. Finally, in 1970, Saperstein hooked up with Maron Films, which put out both of his Toho co-productions as a double feature.

If there is any major negative to *Invasion of Astro-Monster*, it is the start of a major trend in the *Showa* series, with the heavy use of stock footage from previous Toho pictures. It had been done before, but never to the extent that it was this time, and the practice would only get worse in future years as Toho's budgets grew smaller. Nevertheless, the film remains a series favorite, and the *Showa* era would never again equal its financial success—or, some would argue, its creative energy.

"People were getting tired of the fantasy films, so it was a commercial decision to make them more juvenile," says Peter Brothers, author of *The Making of Godzilla*. "Mr. Honda, who was a very accommodating person and a real company guy, said OK I'll go ahead and do it for a little while, but after that it was pretty much it for him. He really didn't want to be involved."

Godzilla vs. the Sea Monster

Japanese Title: *Gojira, Ebirâ, Mosura: Nankai no daiketto*
Literal Translation: *Godzilla, Ebirah, Mothra: Big Duel in the South Seas*
Also Known As: *Ebirah, Horror of the Deep* (international title)
Release Date: December 17, 1966

At the end of the mid-1960s, there was major change in the air, both for Toho Company and for the entire business. The so-called golden age of Japanese filmmaking was coming to an end. Moviegoing audiences were dwindling dramatically, as the newer medium of television, which had first exploded in Japan nearly a decade later than it did in the United States, took its toll. The youth audience was being captivated by TV shows like *Ultraman*, ironically a creation of Tsuburaya Productions. Perhaps in response, Toho decided to shake things up with its next Godzilla installment, with a largely new creative team.

The result, *Godzilla vs. the Sea Monster*, is often seen as the start of a downturn in the series. Whereas previous Godzilla pictures had been A-releases with state-of-the-art special effects for their time, now Godzilla films would begin to be treated as B-pictures with decidedly smaller budgets. Honda was given a break from the series, and in his place Jun Fukuda, a director of comedies and mysteries, was brought in. With more of a "popcorn flick" sensibility, Fukuda was certainly more in line with the lighthearted direction of the series than the more serious and socially conscious Honda, and *Sea Monster* would be the first of an eventual five Godzilla movies Fukuda would helm, second only to Honda himself in the history of the franchise.

In keeping with the lighter tone, Fukuda declined to bring back Ifukube as the composer, rejecting his intense and morose themes for the jazzier work of Masaru Sato, previous contributor to *Godzilla Raids Again*. Consumed more than ever with the work of his own production company, Eiji Tsuburaya took less of a direct role in special effects beginning with this picture, turning over the reins largely to his assistant Sadamasa Arikawa (while still maintaining effects director credit).

The first of what would become known as Godzilla's "island pictures," *Godzilla vs. the Sea Monster* makes the most of its tighter budget by relocating the action from the big cities of mainland Japan to the exotic South Seas, resulting in simpler set design and less in the way of complicated model-making. This time out, Godzilla encounters a new foe, the monstrously huge shrimp known as Ebirah (often erroneously described as a lobster). Ebirah has been making life difficult for the Red Bamboo, a terrorist organization that has been enslaving the natives of Mothra's Infant Island in the manufacture of heavy water for the production of nuclear weapons. Headed by the diabolical Capt. Ryuui, played by Akihiko Hirata (Dr. Serizawa in the original *Gojira*), the Red Bamboo's plot is foiled by shipwrecked fugitive Yoshimura (Akira Takarada), as well as a rampaging Big G, who destroys their base during his battle with Ebirah.

Interestingly, the film seems to have begun life as a vehicle not for Godzilla but for another equally famous giant monster: King Kong. Toho was interested in bringing back the Eighth Wonder of the World, whom they had used four years earlier in *King Kong vs. Godzilla*. However, unlike in 1962, this time they were unable to successfully negotiate the rights from RKO, the American movie studio that owned the giant ape, and so Shinichi Sekizawa's script had to be retooled to feature a monster that Toho already owned the rights to. Still, the original concept can still be glimpsed in certain vestigial elements of *Godzilla vs. the Sea Monster*, including Godzilla's ability to absorb energy from electricity (which had been established as a property of King Kong in *King Kong vs. Godzilla*), as well as Godzilla's affinity for the beautiful island girl Dayo (Kumi Mizuno), reminiscent of Kong's infatuation with Ann Darrow. Nevertheless, Toho would finally succeed in relicensing Kong the following year for Ishiro Honda's *King Kong Escapes*.

Perhaps Toho's instincts in wanting to switch out Godzilla were sound, as with *Godzilla vs. the Sea Monster*, the series begins to flag a bit in popularity. Ticket sales were flattening out from the franchise's early 1960s heyday. A by-product of the sagging Japanese film industry, it also became reflected in Godzilla's demotion to B-movie status. Though an entertaining film with a fresh creative team, it's a noticeable drop from the Honda gems that preceded it. The movie's comparative lack of ambition was even reflected in its U.S. distribution, as *Godzilla vs. the Sea Monster* was released by the Walter Reade Organization directly to television in America, bypassing theaters entirely.

Son of Godzilla

Japanese Title: *Kaijûtô no kessen: Gojira no musuko*
Literal Translation: *Monster Island's Decisive Battle: Godzilla's Son*
Release Date: December 16, 1967

If there was any doubt that Toho had begun to target the Godzilla franchise squarely at the juvenile market, all doubt was put to rest once the second Jun Fukuda entry in the series was released. Whereas audiences for the original *Gojira* were largely adults, the films of the early 1960s had begun to attract an audience that seemingly kept getting younger and younger. And so it only made sense to introduce a character crafted entirely with little kids in mind: none other than Godzilla's progeny, the irrepressible and somewhat infamous Minya.

From the beginning of the film, with its whimsical Minya musical theme courtesy of Masaru Sato (sounding suspiciously similar to Henry Mancini's 1962 smash hit "Baby Elephant Walk"), it's clear we are far, far away from the stark world that had been scored by Akira Ifukube. The second of the "island films," it introduces a setting that would become quite familiar in later entries: the as-yet-unnamed Monster Island, home to a rotating bevy of *kaiju*. This time around, those *kaiju* include the giant irradiated mantises known as Kamacuras (or Gimantis in the dubbed American version) and a massive web-spinning spider named Kumonga (or Spiga in English).

The mantises in particular are by-products of radiation caused by scientists using the island as a base for weather-control experiments. When the mantises uncover a gigantic egg that turns out to contain a baby version of

The 1988 American VHS box cover of *Son of Godzilla*.   *Author's collection*

Godzilla, it isn't long until the Big G himself shows up to tend to the young-ster, ruining the scientists' plans in the process. As to the source of the infant creature, it's never made quite clear: How did he come to be? Assuming Godzilla is the father (an assumption never definitively proven), who is the mother? In the end, it doesn't matter.

The result is a decidedly strange creation of Tsuburaya protégé Sadamasa Arikawa and designer Akira Watanabe. The suit itself, occu-pied by Japanese midget wrestler Little Man Machan, is cartoonish and grotesque, and the sounds he makes, produced by sound effects designer Minoru Kaneyama, are more unsettling than cute. The film is remembered by fans for its scenes of Godzilla instructing Minya in the finer points of monstering, including the proper production of atomic breath (Minya is notoriously capable only of smoke rings at first). In order to more convinc-ingly pull off the difference in size, in addition to the casting of Little Man Machan as Minya, many of Godzilla's scenes feature not Haruo Nakajima in the suit (considered by most to be the worst-looking suit of the entire Godzilla series), but the much taller Seiji Onaka.

In spite of the lackluster Godzilla suit design, *Son of Godzilla* does contain impressive monster fight choreography, including some fine wirework with both the Kamacuras and Kumonga marionettes. The trend of stock footage is more pronounced than ever, with segments of *Godzilla vs. the Sea Monster*, including the battle with Ebirah, lifted wholesale. An enjoyable family film despite its flaws, its lighthearted sense of fun is tough not to like, and the closing scene, in which Godzilla shelters Minya during a snowfall, is genuinely endearing.

The audiences were shrinking and the budgets were getting smaller, and Toho's introduction of a baby Godzilla helped make the transition of the franchise into children's entertainment pretty complete. Just as it had done with *Sea Monster*, the Walter Reade Organization brought *Son of Godzilla* to America via direct-to-TV distribution in 1969.

Destroy All Monsters

Japanese Title: *Kaiju sôshingeki*
Literal Translation: *Monster Invasion*
Release Date: August 1, 1968

At the time, it was supposed to be the end of the Godzilla series. Seeing the writing on the wall as far as dwindling returns, Toho wanted to send

© TOHO CO., Ltd. 1968

カラー作品〉　怪獣総進撃　　キラアク星人の切り札、宇宙の超怪獣キングギドラが襲ってきた。
迎え撃つはゴジラ、ラドン、モスラ、ミニラなど10匹の地球怪獣。富
士山麓は一大決戦場と化した。　　　[映倫]

Godzilla and the whole Monster Island crew take it to King Ghidorah in this publicity shot.

Movie Stills Database

Godzilla off with a bang, and to do so they reassembled some of the key players who had made the Big G great in the first place, in what was theoretically one last big hurrah monster blowout. And even though it turned out not to be the end, *Destroy All Monsters* is often considered the last great Godzilla film of the *Showa* period, and certainly an end of an era.

Kicking off with a stirring new composition from returning composer Akira Ifukube, *Destroy All Monsters* is something of a return to form. Ishiro Honda is back in the director's chair, and just as with the original *Gojira*, served as co-writer of the script. Set in the then-futuristic year of 1999, the film brings together a veritable who's who of Toho monsters—not just the usual suspects of Godzilla, Mothra, and Rodan, but also lesser-seen *kaiju* such as Baragon, Varan, Gorosaurus, and Manda. An alien race known as the Kilaaks attempt to annihilate humanity by taking control of all the monsters, who have been corralled on Monster Island to keep them away from civilization, and unleashing them on cities all over the globe. When the United Nations Science Committee (UNSC) wrests control of the monsters away from the Kilaaks, the aliens unleash the mighty King Ghidorah for one final *kaiju* battle royal at the base of Mt. Fuji.

A favorite amongst *tokusatsu* fans, *Destroy All Monsters* brings the series back to its glory days with a more serious tone, inventive set design by Takeo Kita, and superb miniatures by Tsuburaya's team, headed once again by Arikawa. Despite the return of Minya and the presence of the usual stock footage, the film fairly crackles with energy and is a satisfying coda for Godzilla fans, even if it did not turn out to be one. With an impressive lineup of Toho creations the likes of which had never been assembled in one movie, it was the last gasp of the golden age of Godzilla.

As it had done with *Mothra vs. Godzilla*, B-movie mavens American International Pictures (AIP) brought *Destroy All Monsters* to the United States in the summer of 1969. Unfortunately, as much of a creative success as the film was, it was unable to reverse the box-office trend of the series both domestically and abroad, with another lukewarm performance. For a variety of reasons, the *Showa* era of Godzilla would continue in the years ahead, but the franchise was soon to become a shadow of what it once was.

"There's a certain innocence to the way those films are made," reflects Miguel Rodriguez on the glory of the *Showa* era. "They're very tied to the culture of the '60s. There's something about the '60s and early '70s that can never be recaptured again, that very otherworldly strangeness that they not only had, but embraced."

5

Father of Godzilla

The Vision of Tomoyuki Tanaka

His films have been seen all over the world more than any other producer in the history of Japanese cinema. Many of these films are responsible for sparking the imagination of millions and opening their minds to the possibilities of science-fiction and fantasy filmmaking. There are several men who can lay claim to playing an important role in the creation of Godzilla, but there is no single person more responsible for not only the conception but also the proliferation and endurance of the King of the Monsters as a cultural icon than Tomoyuki "Yuko" Tanaka.

And yet, of the more than 220 pictures he produced as one of the shining lights of the Toho Company firmament, only about a quarter were what would be considered "genre" films, and his body of work contains period pieces, wartime dramas, comedies, and much more. In fact, one of Tanaka's frequent collaborators was celebrated director Akira Kurosawa, with whom he produced six films. And yet it is inevitable that his lasting legacy is the creation of the *tokusatsu* and *daikaju eiga* subgenres—which he helped to define and popularize over an incredibly fruitful and innovative forty-year period.

A Movie-Loving Childhood

He was born on April 26, 1910, in Japan's Yamanashi Prefecture, near the city of Osaka. His love of cinema came very early during his childhood, which happened to coincide with the golden age of silent movies. That meant not just the films of his native Japan, but also the influx of American movies that would continue to influence and awe him throughout his formative years and beyond. As a boy, he was said to walk many miles to the nearest movie theater, just to be able to catch the latest pictures. Naturally, his attention was especially captured by tales of adventure, and in particular he would recall the 1924 epic of American expansion in the Old West, *The Covered Wagon* starring J. Warren Kerrigan, Lois Wilson, and Alan Hale, as his very favorite. From that early age, he knew he wanted to do something in the movies, he just didn't know what.

However, Tanaka's family was quite affluent, and had greater ambitions for their son than simply following his movie passion, which they viewed as a pursuit that was beneath him. Following the wishes of his family (who had once even gone so far as to disown him over his preoccupation with the movies), Tanaka enrolled in the newly established Kansai University in nearby Osaka Prefecture, majoring in economics. Nevertheless, the lure of performing arts was just too strong, and in the end Tanaka strayed permanently from his parents' wishes. In fact, it was while at university that Tanaka would meet up with a group of stage actors that sparked an interest in theatrical performance.

While still in school, Tanaka became part of a new movement in Japan, away from the traditional forms of theater such as *kabuki* and favoring a modern, Westernized style of performance. Known as *shingeki*, it also gave him enough experience to learn that he only possessed middling skill as an actor, and if he wanted to be involved with the stage or screen, it would have to be in another capacity. Since he had such a fascination with what went on behind the scenes in producing entertainment, the young Tanaka next gravitated to directing and producing, which is where his ultimate destiny would lie.

Enter Toho

At first, live theater would be where Tanaka gained his experience, producing plays throughout his twenties. But by 1940, he achieved his first break in the industry that originally caught his attention, when he was hired by Tokyo movie studio Taisho Film Company; the studio would be acquired the following year by Toho, and it would be there that Tanaka would spend the vast majority of the remainder of his career, making not only his own greatest mark on the cinema industry in the process, but also just about the greatest mark that any Japanese producer could have ever dreamt to have made anywhere.

Tanaka began his tenure with Toho in the literature department, researching and developing new material to be turned into motion pictures. But before long, he attracted the attention of the head of the studio,

Iwao Mori, who recognized the young man's talent and potential and promoted him to producer. With the Japanese movie industry under a watchful Imperial eye during World War II, the first project that crossed Tanaka's desk to produce was the wartime propaganda film *Until the Day of Victory* (*Shôri no hi made*), released seven months prior to Japan's surrender to the Allied Powers (of which only a fifteen-minute fragment still survives).

After the war, Tanaka's prospects at Toho only improved during the American occupation. He produced one of the earliest films of a maverick young director who would go on to become perhaps the most celebrated in the history of Japanese cinema, Akira Kurosawa. On *Those Who Make Tomorrow*, Kurosawa was one of three directors brought together by Tanaka for the project, and the now-rare film (which has never been exhibited publicly since its original 1946 release) began a lifelong producer-director partnership between the two that would also include such Kurosawa classics as the samurai epics *Yojimbo* (1961), *Sanjuro* (1962), and *Kagemusha* (1980) (on which he shared executive producer credit with the likes of Francis Ford Coppola and George Lucas), as well as the thriller *High and Low* (*Tengoku to jigoku*) (1963) and the period medical drama *Red Beard* (*Akahige*) (1965).

During his early Toho years working with Kurosawa, Tanaka also met and fell in love with one of the director's young ingenues, Chieko Nakakita, best known for her turn in Kurosawa's *Drunken Angel* (*Yoidore tenshi*) (1948). Tanaka married the actress, who remained by his side for the rest of his life. While raising their three sons, she also continued to pursue her own career, remaining a Toho studio contract player all the way through the demise of the studio system at the end of the 1960s (one of her last roles being a bit part in Tanaka's *Godzilla vs. the Sea Monster* in 1966).

Just as Imperial rule had been tumultuous for the Japanese film industry, so did the occupation period come with its own challenges. In 1948, Tanaka (and many others) walked away from Toho when the studio unceremoniously dumped roughly twelve hundred workers suspected of communist tendencies (a sign of controversies to come in the American film industry, as well). This, in addition to ongoing union disputes, led Tanaka to spend the next four years producing films independently as part of the renegade Society of Film Artists (co-chaired by his friend and fellow Toho walkout Kurosawa). Once the occupation ended in 1952, Iwao Mori was finally able to convince his former protégé to return to the Toho fold, where he'd remain for the rest of his career.

Making a Monster

If Tanaka was looking to impress his superiors upon his return to the studio, he couldn't have planned it any better than what occurred in 1954, when he kicked off what would be not only Toho's longest-running franchise and a cash cow that continues to reap dividends for the company, but also the invention of an entirely new type of Japanese film in the process. The original *Gojira*, the brainchild of Tanaka that was further developed by screenwriters Shigeru Kayama and Takeo Murata, as well as screenwriter-director Ishiro Honda, took the Japanese moviegoing public by storm and helped make Tanaka into one of Toho's most successful and influential producers. He would remain the executive producer of what would become the Godzilla film series all the way through 1995, encompassing the entirety of both the *Showa* and *Heisei* eras of the franchise.

"He made some very shrewd decisions with that first film," explains Peter Brothers, author of *The Making of Godzilla*. "Omori deserves credit too,

By securing the services of the respected Takashi Shimura, Tanaka helped ensure *Gojira* would be a major success.   *Movie Stills Database*

because he was the executive producer who greenlit the project. He believed in Tanaka when Tanaka got all these very skilled people to work on it. Tanaka sometimes doesn't get enough recognition for that."

Lobby poster for *Rodan*, Tanaka's second major *tokusatsu* success for Toho.

Public domain

Thanks to his tremendous smash hit with *Gojira*, Tanaka came to be known as Toho's producer of special-effects extravaganzas, known in Japan as *tokusatsu*. Prior to Tanaka's innovations, special-effects films had been seen as the exclusive domain of Hollywood, but by nurturing the newly born subgenre with the recruiting of effects genius Eiji Tsuburaya, Tanaka changed the course of Japanese cinema. Amongst his specialties would be the giant monster movies, or *daikaiju eiga*, that followed in the wake of *Gojira*, and included the likes of *Giant Monster Varan* (1958), *Mothra* (1961), *Atragon* (1963), *Dogora* (1964), *Frankenstein Conquers the World* (1965), *War of the Gargantuas* (1966), *King Kong Escapes* (1967), and *Yog: Monster from Space* (1970). One of them, *Rodan* (1956), even sprang from an original idea that came to Tanaka in a dream, later developed into a screenplay by novelist Takashi Kuronuma.

During the 1950s through the 1970s, although he continued to handle many other projects (including his ongoing prestigious work with Kurosawa), nearly all of Toho's science-fiction output was produced under Tanaka's watch, also including other non-*kaiju* fare as *The Mysterians* (1957), *The H-Man* (1958), *Battle in Outer Space* (1959), *The Human Vapor* (1960), *Gorath* (1962), *Matango* (1963), *Latitude Zero* (1969), and *The War in Space* (1977). The majority of Tanaka's *tokusatsu* output during this period was a product of another very fruitful producer/director relationship Tanaka cultivated with Ishiro Honda, including eight of the fifteen Godzilla films of the *Showa* era.

Tanaka was very involved in the development of the movies he produced, especially when it came to what was now his bread and butter, *tokusatsu*. He had a say in story ideas, and was strongly involved in marketing efforts both domestically and perhaps even more importantly, internationally. Tanaka's goal was to make Godzilla and his other science-fiction efforts into hits not just in Japan but the world over, especially the United States, the country that had produced many of the movies that made him fall in love with the business as a child. He negotiated partnerships with producer/distributors like Henry G. Saperstein of United Productions of America. He shepherded the development of the *kaiju* subgenre, especially his beloved Godzilla.

In fact, it was under Tanaka's reign that Godzilla transformed from a terrifying monster into the adored savior of the Earth and hero to children over the course of the 1960s and '70s. This was a very conscious decision on the part of Tanaka and the rest of the Toho brass, who were looking to cater to the youth market that was more and more a part of the audience as the landscape of the Japanese film industry changed. It was a move made in

The Peanuts pose for this publicity shot from *Mothra*, Tanaka's first major hit of the 1960s.
Movie Stills Database

response to the monster's already existing popularity among children, but one that the producer later came to regret, as he felt it diluted the character, and may have even contributed to his (temporary) demise in the mid-1970s.

"Credit goes entirely to Tanaka for Godzilla's longevity," says Stuart Galbraith IV, who has written of the producer's career in such books as *Japanese Science Fiction, Fantasy and Horror Films*. "The argument could be made that the series suffered in some respects because of the market Tanaka catered to at various points. On the other hand, there is absolutely no way Godzilla would have lasted and continued for as long as it has without his guidance."

A Return to Prominence

By the time the Godzilla series was put in mothballs in 1975, Tanaka was more powerful than ever, having been promoted to president of the studio's main production unit, Toho Films. But the Japanese *tokusatsu* subgenre as a whole seemed to have run its course as a result of dwindling audiences and hard economic times for the industry, and Tanaka focused on his work with Kurosawa, as well as other projects such as *Deathquake* (*Jishin retto*), a 1980 knockoff of the American disaster film *Earthquake*, as well as World War II period pictures like *Zero Pilot* (*Ozora no samurai*) (1976) and *The Imperial Navy* (*Rengo kantai*) (1981) that hearkened back to Tanaka's earliest work at Toho. But business had slowed since his heyday in the 1960s—*The Imperial Navy* would be the only film Tanaka produced in 1981, as opposed to his busiest year, 1961, in which he produced a grand total of thirteen films, including Kurosawa's *Yojimbo* and Honda's *Mothra*.

It was no secret that Tanaka had been interested in eventually bringing back his greatest creation, and in fact he had been involved for several years in the early 1980s in attempting to come up with a suitable concept. He had even been getting back into the *tokusatsu* market for the first time in years, bringing the science-fiction epic *Bye, Bye Jupiter*, based on the popular novel by Sakyo Komatsu, to the big screen in March 1984. Following that project, Tanaka himself put together a story idea he called "The Resurrection of Godzilla." It was the only time he ever actually worked up a script treatment himself, and it would soon be developed by screenwriter Hideichi Nagahara (who had written *The War in Space* for Tanaka in 1977) into the full script for the movie originally known in Japan simply as *Gojira*, and later altered to *Godzilla 1985* for American release.

The new film helped to kick off a complete resurgence in the Godzilla franchise, soon to be known as the *Heisei* era. Although well into his seventies and seemingly near retirement, the resurgence of Godzilla also meant a resurgence for Tanaka. By the end of the 1980s, he was promoted once again to chairman of Toho Films, as well as overseeing the production of the second *Heisei* Godzilla film, *Godzilla vs. Biollante*. A rejected script for the new Godzilla film, in which Godzilla was to fight a supercomputer (reminiscent of the plot of *Superman III* some six years earlier, in which the Man of Steel did the very same thing), was transitioned by Tanaka into the *Terminator*-influenced *Gunhed*, a project in which Toho Company partnered with the entertainment division of toymaker Bandai, as well as Sunrise, producers of the popular *Mobile Suit Gundam* franchise.

Tanaka continued executive producing Godzilla films well into the 1990s, along the way correcting what he saw as his *Showa*-era mistake by returning the monster to his original, destructive roots. He even produced his final non-Godzilla *kaiju* film in 1994, the historical fantasy *Orochi the*

Eight-Headed Dragon (*Yamato Takeru*). In 1995, Tanaka oversaw what was supposed to be the final Toho Godzilla picture, *Godzilla vs. Destoroyah*, in which the monster meets his death. At the age of eighty-five, he chose that appropriate time to finally step down as chairman of Toho Films and go into semi-retirement, continuing on as an advisor to Toho Company. He assisted in conceptualizing the first two movies in Toho's *Rebirth of Mothra* trilogy, an attempt to return to the spotlight another classic company property.

But Tanaka would not live to see the release of the second of those films. As his great creation had done in fictionalized form two years earlier, Tomoyuki Tanaka passed away on April 2, 1997, less than four weeks shy of his eighty-seventh birthday. The *Heisei* Godzilla films had been largely financial successes for Toho, and proved a satisfactory conclusion to the career as well as the life of the celebrated producer who helped give *kaiju* and *tokusatsu* to the world. As a testament to his crucial importance to the legacy of Godzilla, when TriStar Pictures produced their American version in 1998, the film was dedicated to the memory of Tomoyuki Tanaka, the man who, more than any other, can rightly be called "The Father of Godzilla."

Keeper of the (Atomic) Flame

After the death of Tomoyuki Tanaka, it seemed that Godzilla had been handed over to the Americans for safekeeping forever, with a whole new franchise planned from TriStar Pictures. However, when the first American film turned out to be an unmitigated disaster, all of a sudden the future of the Big G seemed to really be up in the air. Toho decided to take their character back, but for the first time since Godzilla's creation, there was no Tanaka to shepherd it along. It would fall to his successor as executive producer of the Godzilla series to see to it that the great beast did not go gentle into that good night.

Born February 27, 1952, Shogo Tomiyama was a young producer making a name for himself within the Toho ranks in the 1980s. At the age of thirty-two, he worked alongside Tanaka for the first time as an associate producer on the period film *Ohan*. The following year, he got his first full producer credit for *Lost Chapter of Snow: Passion* (*Yuki no dansho—jonetsu*). By 1989, he had been promoted to an executive producer, just at the time that the *Heisei* series of Godzilla films was taking off under the watchful eye of elder statesman Tanaka.

With Tanaka pushing eighty and unable to handle the day-to-day responsibilities as he once did, Tomiyama entered into a producer's role on the Godzilla series for the first time with *Godzilla vs. Biollante* (1989). He continued on as

Tanaka's second-in-command, spearheading production on the next five films of the *Heisei* series as well. Before long, he found himself taking on the mantle once worn by Tanaka himself as Toho's resident producer of *kaiju* and *tokusatsu* cinema. In addition to Godzilla, he would produce *Reiko, the Psyche Resurrected* (1991), *Orochi the Eight-Headed Dragon* (1994), and the *Rebirth of Mothra* trilogy that ran from 1996 to 1998.

Following Tanaka's passing in 1997, Tomiyama's star rose even higher within Toho. Once it became clear that the company would be taking back the reins of Godzilla from TriStar following the failure of the American *Godzilla* (1998), it only made sense that Tomiyama would take Tanaka's place as executive producer of the series. Under Tomiyama's control, Godzilla would once again return to Japan in what would come to be known as the Millennium series, the third great era of the Godzilla franchise.

The new series struggled from the beginning, never really achieving the financial success in Japan that Godzilla had in the past, and yet Tomiyama worked hard to keep it going, recruiting innovative directors and executive producing a total of six new Godzilla pictures from 1999 through 2004. By the time of his last entry, *Godzilla: Final Wars*, Tomiyama had been promoted to president of Toho Company, only the fourth person to hold that position. It was a fitting reward for the man who had kept Godzilla alive into the twenty-first century.

Nevertheless, Tomiyama rightly recognized that Godzilla seemed to have worn out his welcome with Japanese audiences, and would need to go away for a while. He declared that the monster would be going into cinematic hibernation for at least a decade, and Toho followed his edict, not even contemplating bringing back the creature until the smashing worldwide success of the second American Godzilla reboot in 2014. However, by that time Tomiyama had stepped down as Toho president, being replaced in 2010 by Yoshinari Shimatani.

Though no longer part of the Toho organization, Tomiyama continues to be involved in the business of producing movies in Japan. In 2015, in time for the sixtieth anniversary of the King of the Monsters, he authored the book *Managing Godzilla*, in which he discussed his experiences carrying on the legacy of the great Tomoyuki Tanaka.

6

Godzilla's Soul

The Philosophy of Ishiro Honda

Monsters are born too tall, too strong, too heavy," Ishiro Honda once said. "That is their tragedy." Such a sentiment sums up perfectly the director's very thoughtful, even melancholy attitude toward the creatures he helped bring to life on the silver screen. More than any other director, Honda is inextricably linked to the Godzilla franchise, and to Japanese *tokusatsu* cinema in general. A skilled craftsman who helmed a total of forty-four films during his career, he is also responsible for eight of the *Showa*-era Godzilla films, including the groundbreaking 1954 original, which he had a direct hand in writing as well as directing.

His work is marked by a social sensitivity and carefully nurtured worldview that was frankly not normally seen in the monster movies being made across the Pacific in Hollywood at the same time. Using his films as a platform to advocate for universal peace and nuclear disarmament, he helped ensure that Godzilla would not simply be another simplistic creature feature, but rather a lasting commentary and a character that has resonated with generations. From the beginning, he saw Godzilla as a metaphor for the atomic bomb, and knowing firsthand what that horror was like, he was able to transform it into a unique, impactful cinematic experience. Even if the series eventually moved in a direction that didn't quite suit him, his fingerprints can still be seen on everything that came after.

"There was a feeling of integrity and passion that went into his work, unlike a lot of people who make these films to capitalize on the genre," explains Peter H. Brothers, author of the first English-language book on the director, *Mushroom Clouds and Mushroom Men*. "Mr. Honda and his team were really concerned about how well they could make these pictures. He cared very strongly about the message."

An Early Love of Film as Art

He was born May 7, 1911, in Yamagata Prefecture in the town of Asahi (present-day Tsuruoka), the son of a Buddhist priest. His father's devout Buddhism would actually lead to the young Honda's love of the movies, as he would avidly attend the nearby cinema as a child by himself, and then hurry home to describe and act out what he'd seen to his father, who never went to the movies himself. He grew to love the act of telling the stories, a sure hint of his future aptitude as a director. In particular, he was fascinated by the Japanese practice in those days of silent films having live narrators, known as *benshi*, in the theater to provide verbal accompaniment to the movie. His interest in storytelling further piqued, Honda became determined to enter the movie business from an early age.

Immediately after graduating high school, Honda enrolled in Nihon University's recently established College of Art (*Nichigei*) in Tokyo's Nerima ward, which featured one of the world's first programs in film studies and technique. It's known today as a leading producer of future theater and film luminaries, and Honda was among the earliest graduating classes. Just prior to his graduation, he began an apprenticeship in 1932 with the newly established Photo Chemical Laboratory (PCL), a company at the cutting edge of developing sound technology for motion pictures (which had already become standard in the United States a few years earlier).

While apprenticing at PCL, Honda came under the supervision of Iwao Mori, the future Toho president who would one day greenlight his greatest film, *Gojira*. Mori recognized Honda's burgeoning talent right away, and he was hired full-time by PCL as a cameraman in the summer of 1933, before he had even completed his degree. He was working in the production department when, two years later, the company was acquired by the Toho Company, an outfit quickly ascending to the status of one of Japan's leading producers of motion pictures. By that point, Honda had attained the position of assistant director, beginning with his work in 1934 on a film called *Life Study* (*Tadano bonji: Jinsei benkyo*).

The Real-Life Horrors of War

Honda would continue to work as an assistant director for Toho Company for the next fifteen years, but along the way, world events would provide a temporary obstacle to the growth of his career. The Empire of Japan had expansion on its agenda, having already conquered the region of Manchuria in 1931 and with an invasion of mainland China in the works. Honda was drafted into the Japanese army in 1936, and would serve three tours of duty over the course of the next eight years in both Manchuria and China. A gentle, peace-loving person, Honda was troubled by the conflict: first the Chinese invasion in 1938, followed by the full-scale outbreak of the Second World War in 1939. The terrors of war would remain with him always, and informed his work in later years.

Despite the escalating aggressions and Honda's overseas wartime activities, he continued to work at Toho whenever he was back home. As an assistant director, he worked regularly under Kajiro Yamamoto on a series of films that included *Enoken's Ten Millions* (1936), *A Husband's Chastity: Fall Once Again* (1937), *The Beautiful Hawk* (1937), *Tojuro's Love* (1938), and *Uma* (1941). In 1937, his path crossed for the first time with another budding young Toho directorial talent, Akira Kurosawa. *Uma* would be one of the first projects the two men would work on together, forging a lifelong bond that saw them continue to consult on each other's projects for the remainder of their respective careers. Also in 1937, Honda met and married another fellow Toho Company employee, a young script girl named Kimi who would become a lifelong companion as well.

During the war, Honda also became acquainted with the work of a special-effects supervisor whose status within Toho was on the rise: Eiji Tsuburaya, the very man with whom he would one day collaborate on a plethora of *kaiju* and *tokusatsu* films. With World War II still raging, at the time Tsuburaya's expertise was in the precise re-creation of realistic battle sequences. In 1943, Honda and Tsuburaya would work together for the first time on one of Yamamoto's war epics, *Kato's Flying Falcon Forces*.

But even though he was working to simulate war in the studio, abroad, Honda was still engaged in the very real war. In early 1945, he was captured by the Chinese and held as a prisoner of war until the Japanese surrender in August resulted in his release. The surrender itself had been the result of the devastating nuclear bombardment of Hiroshima and Nagasaki, which Honda and his fellow prisoners had only heard rumors about during their captivity. Rumors turned to harsh reality when those released prisoners passed near the crumbled ruins of Hiroshima on their return home. In several interviews given in later years, Honda would speak with great gravity of the impact viewing that wreckage had on him. He had witnessed the aftermath of the bomb firsthand; the impression never left him, and would inform much of his later work, most notably, *Gojira*.

A Return to the Director's Chair

Following the war, the American occupation of Japan put significant stress on the Japanese film industry, and Toho Company was embroiled in a series of labor disputes that led many, including Honda, to seek work elsewhere for a time. Nevertheless, Honda's exile from Toho was not as long as most, and he was back to his assistant directorial duties at the studio in 1949, collaborating on one of his dear friend Kurosawa's films, *Stray Dog* (*Nora inu*). Kurosawa had already broken out as a maverick star director for Toho during the war, and would go on to become arguably the most celebrated director in his nation's history.

There can be no doubt that the career paths of Kurosawa and Honda progressed along different trajectories from that point on, with the former attaining respected auteur status while the latter was more of a reliable studio journeyman not necessarily known for producing great works of art. Nevertheless, Honda himself finally ascended to the director's chair in 1949, with the documentary short *The Story of a Co-op*. Two years later, he followed up with his feature film debut, *The Blue Pearl* (*Aoi shinju*), a groundbreaking film about female pearl divers, which he wrote as well as directed. And although Honda was not destined to have a career with the prestige of Kurosawa, with whom he remained very close, he was nevertheless on the verge of a directorial career that would one day be celebrated for other reasons.

Honda began to establish himself as a director for Toho in the early 1950s. He directed acclaimed actors Toshiro Mifune (Kurosawa's favorite) and Takashi Shimura (who would later star in *Gojira*) in *The Man Who Came to Port* (*Minato e kita otoko*) (1952), and achieved particular notoriety with the World War II drama *Eagle of the Pacific* (*Taiheiyo no washi*) (1953), in which he utilized the expertise of none other than Eiji Tsuburaya to create his usual show-stealing battle simulations. Honda's body of work was taking shape, and included romances and "slice-of-life" pictures. However, there was a project on the horizon that would define the rest of his career, while also changing the course of it permanently.

Project G

In June 1954, Honda was brought on for a pet project being developed by Toho producer Tomoyuki Tanaka. Known at the time only as "Project G," it was the story of a giant irradiated monster called Gojira that terrorizes mainland Japan. The basic structure had already been developed by novelist Shigeru Kayama, but Honda and screenwriter Takeo Murata were brought in to turn the story into a full script; Honda himself was officially named director. Together with Murata, Honda refined the story into something quite a bit more sophisticated, intelligent, and nuanced than virtually any monster film that had ever been made. It was Honda, for example, who worked out the love triangle involving main characters Dr. Serizawa, Emiko, and Ogata.

Most importantly, it was Honda who was immediately struck by the notion of the monster as a physical representation of the atomic bomb. The kernel of that idea had been there from the beginning, but through Honda it became a centerpiece of the work, not just in the script, but in the way he would direct the overall film, working hand-in-hand with Tsuburaya, who was brought in to direct the special-effects sequences. Having seen the effects of the bomb, Honda wanted to represent it in his film, and

Honda's sensitive approach to his actors' scenes helped make sure *Gojira* would be about a lot more than a giant monster.   *Movie Stills Database*

lent a somber tone to the proceedings with an almost documentary-style approach.

No Japanese director had ever attempted a film of this kind; the finished product, *Gojira*, was unlike any giant monster film that had preceded it anywhere in the world, and became an instant hit. Honda's personal anti-nuclear stance lent the film much of its raw power, and most would agree it was his greatest work. At the time, the director's optimistic dream was that the success of the movie could somehow lead to an end to nuclear weapon proliferation. This did not occur, needless to say, but what did proliferate in the wake of *Gojira* was a vast wave of *kaiju* and *tokusatsu* cinema in Japan, and very quickly, Honda became more closely linked to the genre than any other director.

The Kaiju Director

It didn't happen immediately. Honda didn't even return to direct the initial *Gojira* sequel, *Godzilla Raids Again* (*Gojira no gyakushu*), later that year. For a few years, he continued to make the typical melodramas and comedies he had done in the past. He got his second *kaiju* assignment in 1956 with *Rodan*, a film for which he consulted a bit behind the scenes with his old friend Akira Kurosawa. The following year, he directed *The Mysterians* (*Chikyu boeigun*), an alien invasion film often considered one of the predecessors of modern space opera. The so-called *kaiju* boom was taking hold of Japan, and the tide of *tokusatsu* projects in development was about to consume Honda completely.

By 1958, the year he helmed *The H-Man* (*Bijo to ekitai ningen*), *Giant Monster Varan*, and *Half Human* (*Jujin Yukiotoko*), Honda's slate was almost totally taken over by science-fiction films, and it would remain so for pretty much the rest of his career. Although he may have been concerned by the pigeonholing that was taking place, Honda was a company man through and through, and took on the projects assigned to him by Toho with enthusiasm and genuine heart. Those close to him indicated that he did wish to be able to direct other kinds of films, but also that he truly enjoyed the work he did on *tokusatsu* movies.

Taking what some might consider immature subject matter, Honda added layers that other directors would likely not have, infusing earnest social messages that expressed his own positive outlook and hope for the future. In films like *Battle in Outer Space* (*Uchu daisenso*) (1959), he portrays a world that puts aside its differences to combat a common threat; in *Mothra* (1961), he condemns the marginalization of native peoples. Much like Gene Roddenberry would do with his *Star Trek* TV series of the 1960s, Honda used science fiction to highlight social ills and paint an optimistic view of a world that had the moral rectitude to overcome them.

Although Honda sometimes felt pigeonholed directing *kaiju eiga* like *Rodan*, he dutifully fulfilled his obligations to the studio.   *Public domain*

Godzilla Reunion

After a seven-year hiatus, Toho at last brought back Godzilla for 1962's *King Kong vs. Godzilla*, and Honda was given the opportunity to return to the franchise that he helped to begin. A testament to the director's versatility, the sequel had a decidedly comedic tone, a far cry from the chilling nightmare of the 1954 original. Following the unprecedented success of that film, Honda remained with the series, directing three more Godzilla films in 1964 and 1965: *Mothra vs. Godzilla*, *Ghidorah, the Three-Headed Monster* (*San daikaiju: Chikyu saidai no kessen*), and *Invasion of Astro-Monster* (*Kaiju daisenso*). Once again, the spectrum of tones demonstrates Honda's consummate skill, going from a sophisticated fantasy that takes aim at corporate greed, to a tale of espionage and sci-fi mystery, to an all-out space adventure.

"He was the one who put the most sincere efforts into giving his creations subtext," says *kaiju* aficionado and film festival maven Miguel Rodriguez. "His subtext has not only been the most sincere, it has also been probably the most profound. He thought about what these creatures meant, more than any other directors have."

Nevertheless, there can be no doubt that the studio's attitude toward Godzilla was changing vastly from what Honda's original intentions had been. The films were getting goofier, and the monster was getting more and more likeable; no longer the atomic terror he had been invented to be, he was becoming a lighthearted figure of children's entertainment. Honda was opposed to such scenes as the "monster summit" in *Ghidorah* in which Mothra tries to "convince" Godzilla and Rodan to help her, as well as Godzilla's infamous "chie" victory dance in *Invasion of Astro-Monster*. For this reason, as well as Toho's desire to try a fresh director on the series (namely Jun Fukuda), Honda was taken off the series. This did not stop his *kaiju* output, however, as he was immediately put to work on films like *War of the Gargantuas* (*Furankenshutain no kaiju: Sanda tai Gaira*) (1966) and *King Kong Escapes* (*Kingu Kongu no gyakushu*) (1967).

"People were just getting tired of the fantasy films, so it was a commercial decision to make them more juvenile," says Peter H. Brothers. "Mr. Honda, who was a very accommodating person and a real company guy, said OK I'll go ahead and do it for a little while, but after *Ghidorah* that was pretty much it for him. He really didn't want to be involved. But typical of his loyalty to the company that had given him his start and kept him on the ledgers when he was away on three separate war tours, he stayed on and just did films for them. I'm sure it was very frustrating, [but] he went and made them the best way he knew how."

Of course, the Godzilla series was far from over, even if it may have been running out of steam. As Toho looked to inject life back into the Big G in the late 1960s, Honda was brought in to make two more films: the ambitious *Destroy All Monsters* (*Kaiju soshingeki*) (1968), originally designed to be a swan song for the series, and the often-maligned *All Monsters Attack* (*Gojira-Minira-Gabara: Oru kaiju daishingeki*) (1969), a bizarre, juvenile fantasy that Honda still managed to invest with pathos and thematic depth as a poignant coming-of-age story. But it was clear that much of the magic was gone. Audiences weren't responding like they used to, and the series had undeniably devolved.

"I think he was disappointed, he was somewhat regretful, but he had a very great career," says Brothers. "I don't think his career was for nothing. But every interview he did, they always mentioned his Godzilla films and he was proud of that, but he was always like, 'You know, I did other films, too.' I think he got a little fed up with that."

Walking Away from Toho

Honda directed one more film for Toho, *Yog: Monster from Space* (*Gezora, Ganime, Kameba: Kessen! Nankai no daikaiju*), in 1970, and then walked away from feature film directing permanently. There were a few factors, including disappointment over the lack of variety in his assignments, and political problems with the studio brass over a perceived lack of respect given to his esteemed colleague Eiji Tsuburaya during the special-effects master's final, dying days. Honda instead opted for the world of television, which by the 1970s had supplanted cinema as Japan's foremost medium for popular entertainment, anyway.

He directed episodes for such Tsuburaya Productions TV series as *The Return of Ultraman* and *Mirror Man*, as well as the Toho-produced series *Rainbow Man*. In 1975, as Godzilla was finally being put out to pasture (for a decade, anyway), Honda was coaxed back one last time to direct the fifteenth film in the series, *Terror of Mechagodzilla* (*Mekagojira no gyakushu*). Reunited with composer Akira Ifukube as well as star Akihiko Hirata, Honda was once again able to infuse gravitas and depth into a franchise that had by that point reached even more ridiculous levels of silliness, producing a dark film that was a fitting swan song to the *Showa* era.

"If you just look at the difference between Fukuda's *Godzilla vs. Mechagodzilla* and Honda's *Terror of Mechagodzilla*, which is a direct sequel, and the tonal differences between those films, it's pretty profound," Miguel Rodriguez points out.

A Friendly Collaboration

Now age sixty-four, Honda attempted to retire from the industry, feeling he had accomplished all he wanted to (or would be allowed to) as a director. He continued to remain close to Akira Kurosawa, who by that point had become Japan's most respected auteur worldwide. In fact, with his own directorial career behind him, Honda opted to assist his friend in future projects, taking great pleasure in the chance to contribute to films he had chosen to work on himself. He worked behind the scenes as an assistant director and production coordinator on Kurosawa's masterpieces *Kagemusha* (1980) and *Ran* (1985). It was quite telling that in 1984, when he was approached by producer Tomoyuki Tanaka to direct Godzilla's big comeback film, he turned the project down flat, reportedly due to creative differences with the micromanaging Tanaka and a desire to remain free of Toho's control.

"He appreciated the offer, but at the same time appreciated the irony, of being asked to do this thing when they wouldn't let him do what he wanted with all these other things," says Brothers. "It also might not have been a totally genuine offer; it might've been just to make Tanaka look good, or maybe for commercial appeal . . . I think he felt, 'This is all you think I'm good for, another Godzilla movie? Let me do something else!'"

Honda instead continued working with Kurosawa. He even had the opportunity to direct sequences within Kurosawa's films, including *Dreams* (*Yume*) (1990) and *Rhapsody in August* (*Hachi-gatsu no kyoshikyoku*) (1991). In his seventies and eighties, he even took on a few acting roles here and there, playing grandfatherly figures in front of the camera. He was an uncredited writer and editor on Kurosawa's *Madadayo* (1993), but would not be able to enjoy the finished product. During postproduction of the film, the eighty-one-year-old Honda suffered a heart attack and died of respiratory failure the evening of February 28, 1993.

A respected craftsman, Ishiro Honda may never have achieved the auteur status enjoyed by his lifelong comrade Akira Kurosawa, but it can never be said that he didn't leave an indelible mark on the history of his nation's cinema, namely, helping to realize its greatest screen character and most popular movie export. His gentle principles came to define the

Godzilla series, and continue to do so to this day, just as they have inspired fans and filmmakers alike as to the possibilities of genre filmmaking. It is quite appropriate that, when visionary director Guillermo del Toro released his own contemporary *kaiju* opus *Pacific Rim* in 2013, he dedicated the film to two individuals: American special-effects pioneer Ray Harryhausen and Ishiro Honda.

Lights, Camera, Kaiju!

As prolific as he was, Ishiro Honda was far from the only director to tackle the Big G. Here are a few of the notable helmers who have also left their prodigious mark on Godzilla's legacy . . .

Jun Fukuda

- *Godzilla vs. the Sea Monster* (1966)
- *Son of Godzilla* (1967)
- *Godzilla vs. Gigan* (1972)
- *Godzilla vs. Megalon* (1973)
- *Godzilla vs. Mechagodzilla* (1974)

After Honda himself, Fukuda is the director most associated with the Godzilla series, and rightfully so. Between 1966 and 1974, he directed five of the fifteen *Showa*-era Godzilla films, bringing a very different sensibility to the material that made him an interesting counterpart to Honda. Whereas Honda was sober and introspective, Fukuda tended to take the material less seriously, with more of a pop art/comic book approach. He had fun with Godzilla; after all, it was under Fukuda's watch that the monster would have a child, speak, and engage in outrageous battles that often resembled professional wrestling matches.

Born in the Chinese region of Manchuria on February 17, 1923, Fukuda was just a small child when the Japanese invaded and conquered the region, and it wasn't until the age of sixteen that he migrated on his own to his family's nation of origin, Japan, at the very beginning of World War II. He joined Toho in 1949 and began working as an assistant director two years later. His first gig as assistant director, in fact, was on an Ishiro Honda picture, *The Man Who Came to Port* (*Minato e kita otoko*).

By the end of the decade, he had become a director himself, starting with *Dangerous Playing with Fire* (*Osorubeki hiasobi*) (1959), the first of several *seishun eiga*, or "youth films" that he would make throughout his career. Also among these youth films were several entries in the popular "Young Guy" teenybopper series, including *Japan's Number One Young Guy* (1962), *Young Guy in Hawaii* (1963), *Young Guy Graduates* (1969), and *Young Guy in New Zealand* (1969). In addition to his lighthearted comedies, Fukuda also became known as a director of gritty mysteries such as the tense thriller *The Merciless Trap* (*Nasake muyo no wana*) (1961) and the crime drama *Ankokugai gekitotsu sakusen* (1965).

It was right after his 1965 James Bond send-up, *Ironfinger* (*Hyappatsu hyaku-chu*), that Fukuda was approached about replacing Honda as director on the Godzilla series. He'd be responsible for kicking off the Godzilla "island" films with back-to-back entries *Godzilla vs. the Sea Monster* (1966) and *Son of Godzilla* (1967), two movies that took the monster in a decidedly more whimsical direction, which was exactly what Toho wanted. And although Honda would be brought back to the series after that, Fukuda would eventually return to the fold in the 1970s, during a time when Honda had completely walked away from directing feature films.

"He was a much more dynamic filmmaker [than Honda], visually certainly," offers Stuart Galbraith IV. "His two 1960s entries are, for my money, the best-directed entries, other than perhaps the original . . . Those are maybe the only two films in which one could remove Godzilla and you'd still have a pretty wonderful movie. Both are directed with a lot of energy, have strong characters, great scores very different from Ifukube's, involving story lines, effects that are technically great for the most part but which also expand upon Tsuburaya's original work in interesting ways."

In Honda's absence, Fukuda began to assume his place as Toho's resident *tokusatsu* director. Between 1972 and 1974, he helmed *Godzilla vs. Gigan*, *Godzilla vs. Megalon*, and *Godzilla vs. Mechagodzilla*. At a time when Toho was hurting financially and the Godzilla movies weren't doing anywhere near the business they used to, Fukuda made do with shoestring budgets and often inane scripts to create entertaining, unapologetic *kaiju* flicks that are a lot of fun despite, or perhaps because of, their B-movie status.

Near the end of his career in 1973, Fukuda and Honda would actually work together on a TV project, sharing directing duties on the sci-fi adventure series *Zone Fighter* (*Ryusei ningen zon*), Toho's answer to Tsuburaya Productions' wildly successful *Ultraman*. Fukuda directed his final feature film, Toho's lackluster *Star*

Wars cash-in *The War in Space* (*Wakusei daisenso*), in 1977, and subsequently retired from filmmaking at the age of fifty-four. He did not think highly of his *kaiju* work, since he apparently did not share Honda's deep affinity for the material and its social implications, and rather resented the pigeonholing that occurred late in his career. He died on December 3, 2000, in Tokyo at the age of seventy-seven.

Kazuki Omori

- *Godzilla vs. Biollante* (1989)
- *Godzilla vs. King Ghidorah* (1991)
- *Godzilla & Mothra: The Battle for Earth* (1992) (writer)
- *Godzilla vs. Destoroyah* (1995) (writer)

Not since the days of Ishiro Honda had a director invested as much of his heart and soul into Godzilla as Kazuki Omori, who was brought on board by Toho in 1989 when the company was looking to resume full-time production of what is now known as the *Heisei* era of the franchise. With the mandate to maintain the monster's more menacing roots and remain faithful to the spirit of the 1954 original, Omori was the man who helped guide much of Godzilla's return to the public consciousness and to the cinematic landscape during the final years of the twentieth century.

Born in Osaka on March 3, 1952, Omori was but a very small child when the original *Gojira* emanated from theatrical projectors for the first time, and grew up during the heyday of the *Showa* era and the work of Honda and Fukuda. But initially, film was not to be his main calling, as he attended medical school in the 1970s, obtaining a license to practice medicine that he would never use. While still a student, the film bug bit him, and he began directing his own independent movies as early as age seventeen. He continued to make films during his medical school years, and began to attract the attention of major studios.

Omori was becoming not only a skilled director, but a skilled writer as well, and when his script for *Orange Road Express* won an award in 1977, he received an offer from venerable Japanese film company Shochiku to produce the picture, marking his professional debut at the age of twenty-fix. Over the next decade, he received critical acclaim for several of his films, most notably *Disciples of Hippocrates* (1981) and *Koisuru onnatachi* (1986), for which he was nominated for a Japanese Academy Award.

Omori was known primarily for these films when he was hired by Toho in 1989 to make *Godzilla vs. Biollante*, the first Godzilla movie since the franchise had

The dynamic Japanese poster for *Godzilla vs. Biollante*, Omori's first entry in the series. *Everett Collection*

been restarted four years earlier. It was quite a coup for Toho to acquire Omori's services, and the director did not disappoint, delivering a picture that, although not a stellar success at the box office, is today considered one of the finest entries in the entire series.

He would remain on board with Toho for much of the remainder of the *Heisei* series, next helming the more financially successful *Biollante* follow-up, *Godzilla vs. King Ghidorah* (1991). Although that would be his final stint on the series as director, Toho appreciated Omori's take on the material so much that he continued to contribute scripts for future installments. The first of these was for *Godzilla & Mothra: Battle for Earth* (1992), and three years later, it would be Omori that Toho tapped to script the ultimate demise of their beloved *kaiju* for the smash hit *Godzilla vs. Destoroyah*, Toho's final Godzilla picture before handing the reins over for TriStar Pictures' American reboot.

Unlike the studio-bound directors of an earlier generation, Omori had much more creative control over his career, even founding the Director's Company, a group dedicated to providing an outlet for young directors to work completely outside the studio system during the 1980s. In more recent years, his directorial output has slowed somewhat as he has taken on teaching positions, first at Osaka Electro-Communication University in 2000, and then Osaka University in 2005. His most recent film, *Vietnam no kaze ni fukarete*, was released in September 2015.

Takeo Okawara

- *Godzilla & Mothra: The Battle for Earth* (1992)
- *Godzilla vs. Mechagodzilla* (1993)
- *Godzilla vs. Destoroyah* (1995)
- *Godzilla 2000* (1999)

With a body of work that bridges the *Heisei* and Millennium eras of Godzilla, Takeo Okawara may not have been as prolific a filmmaker as his predecessors on the franchise, but he is responsible for some of the series' fan favorites, and was trusted enough for Toho to turn to when looking to resurrect their cash cow following the disastrous 1998 American effort.

Born December 20, 1949, in Tokyo, Okawara signed on with Toho right out of film school in 1972 and was put to work as an assistant director. Although this was during the last years of the *Showa* era, Okawara never worked on Godzilla films during this period, instead cutting his teeth on the disaster epic *Tidal Wave*

(*Nippon chinbotsu*) (1973), starring Canadian-born actor Lorne Greene, as well as *The Last Days of Planet Earth* (*Nosutoradamusu no daiyogen*) (1974), Toho's attempt to cash in on the burgeoning Nostradamus craze. Okawara also worked with Akira Kurosawa on one of the great director's samurai films, *Kagemusha* (1980), on which he shared assistant director credit with the semi-retired Ishiro Honda.

Okawara finally crossed paths with the Big G in 1984, when he worked as chief assistant director on *Godzilla 1985*, Toho's full-fledged reboot of the franchise that kicked off the *Heisei* era. His next project would mark his directorial debut, *Super Girl Reiko* (*Cho shojo Reiko*) (1991), for which he also wrote the script and won the prestigious Kido Screenplay Award in the process. This would lead directly to his role as a full-scale director on the Godzilla franchise. Two more films had been made since Okawara's assistant director stint on the series, but now Okawara was pegged to take the director's seat for *Godzilla & Mothra: The Battle for Earth*, the fourth film in the *Heisei* series.

Toho kept Okawara on tap for two of the last three *Heisei* pictures, *Godzilla vs. Mechagodzilla II* (1993) and the final chapter, *Godzilla vs. Destoroyah* (1995), perhaps his finest hour on the franchise. A company man in the truest sense of the term, Okawara was a dependable craftsman in the Honda mold, even if he lacked that director's more noble ambitions, preferring to view the material as mere popcorn entertainment, more like his other predecessor Jun Fukuda did. He delivered product that was satisfactory to the studio while also pleasing the public, which is no mean feat in the grand scheme of things. He also developed an ongoing working relationship with Koichi Kawakita, the new special-effects director on the Godzilla series, which echoed the relationship of Ishiro Honda and Eiji Tsuburaya in years gone by.

Ironically, the film for which Okawara may be best known by mainstream Japanese audiences was the one immediately following his big Godzilla run, namely *Yukai* (1997), a popular thriller that was nominated for the Japanese Academy Award for Best Film, and for which he himself received a nomination for Best Director.

That success, combined with his proven track record, made Okawara the director of choice when Toho once again rebooted the Godzilla series in 1999. Reeling from the critical (and to a lesser extent, box-office) disaster that was TriStar's *Godzilla* (1998), Toho wanted someone they could trust to help restore the monster to his former glory. And although it is a flawed film, *Godzilla 2000* did begin the third phase of Godzilla's on-screen career, the Millennium series. It would also be Okawara's final film to date.

Masaaki Tezuka

- *Godzilla vs. Megaguirus* (2000)
- *Godzilla Against Mechagodzilla* (2002)
- *Godzilla: Tokyo S.O.S.* (2003)

The most dominant director of the Millennium series, with three of the six films to his credit, Masaaki Tezuka was the one director Toho kept coming back to, despite their original vision for the Millennium series as being an ever-changing showcase for new creative talent. The days of a single director charting the course of the franchise seemed to be in the past, and yet the work of Tezuka has been the closest the series has gotten to it in the twenty-first century.

Born January 24, 1955, north of Tokyo in the city of Tochigi, Tezuka came into the world not long after Godzilla himself. He attended Nihon University's College of Art, where Ishiro Honda had learned his trade some fifty years earlier, and by 1979 he had followed Honda's course to Toho. There he would spend the next twenty years as an assistant director, starting with the torrid romance *White Love* (*Howaito rabu*).

For a time during his early career, he formed an ongoing partnership with legendary cult director Kon Ichikawa, collaborating with him on such films as *Koto: The Ancient City* (1980); *The Burmese Harp* (*Biruma no tategoto*) (1985); the fantasy *Princess from the Moon* (*Taketori monogatari*) (1987), based on a beloved Japanese fairy tale; the samurai piece *47 Ronin*; and *The 8-Tomb Village* (*Yatsuhaka-mura*) (1996). In the midst of his Ichikawa partnership, however, Tezuka would also get a taste of what the future held, serving as assistant director under Takeo Okawara on *Godzilla vs. Mechagodzilla II* (1993).

Tezuka worked with Okawara again on the acclaimed hit *Yukai*, before continuing his *kaiju* education as assistant director on the last two films of the *Rebirth of Mothra* trilogy in the late 1990s. That experience would prepare him to finally take the reins as a full-fledged director in 2000 at the age of forty-five. The project was *Godzilla vs. Megaguirus*, the second film of the Millennium series.

Although Tezuka tried to put his own spin on the series with elements of horror and '70s-style *kaiju* action, unfortunately the film was the poorest box-office attraction the franchise had seen in years. The next film in the series, *Godzilla, Mothra and King Ghidorah: Giant Monsters All-Out Attack* (2001), would be handed over to a new director, but Tezuka had so enjoyed working with Godzilla that he signed on to the project as an assistant special-effects director.

But that wouldn't be the end of Tezuka's directorial career. Up to this point, each new Millennium series entry had been helmed by a different director, but

Toho decided to give Tezuka another try, and he experienced much greater success with *Godzilla Against Mechagodzilla* (2002). With its military-themed plot, the film was a hit with audiences, and when Tezuka pitched his own concept for a direct sequel, Toho brought him back to write and direct *Godzilla: Tokyo S.O.S.* (2003).

Tezuka's work as a director did not extend much beyond the Godzilla Millennium films. After a few lackluster action and sci-fi projects, including *Go! Godman*, a one-shot TV special reviving a popular 1970s Toho TV show of the same name and featuring the return of the *kaiju* Gaira of *War of the Gargantuas* fame, Tezuka would hang up his director's mantle in 2008. Having established himself as a special-effects director following his work on *Giant Monsters All-Out Attack*, he continued his career in that capacity.

7

Creating a Monster

The Special Effects of Eiji Tsuburaya

To this day, he is regarded with great warmth and fondness as the "Father of *Tokusatsu*." He was perhaps the most integral member of what came to be known as Toho's "Golden Trio" of creators most responsible for the smashing success of *kaiju* cinema, and Godzilla in particular. To those who worked with and respected him, he was "the Old Man." And although his work came to be unfairly criticized by the uninformed in later years, he was at the very cutting edge of special-effects technology in his time, and one of a handful of individuals who were the stewards of the evolution of science-fiction cinema in the twentieth century.

In his native Japan, the name of Eiji Tsuburaya came to connote something to movie fans similar to what names like Spielberg and Disney conjure up in the minds of American moviegoers. Before him, there really was no Japanese special-effects industry to speak of, but during his peak years he set a standard that continues to influence the way genre films are made in Japan. It was Tsuburaya who pioneered what came to be known as "suitmation," who innovated the use of intricate and meticulous miniatures, who spearheaded the distinctive look and feel of Japanese fantasy cinema. It is remotely conceivable that Godzilla could have somehow succeeded without the vision of producer Tomoyuki Tanaka, the music of Akira Ifukube, or even the direction of Ishiro Honda; however, it is beyond reasonable conception that it could have happened without the genius of Eiji Tsuburaya.

Inspired by the great Willis O'Brien and his landmark achievement on *King Kong* (1933), Tsuburaya used determination and rare creative gifts to become the greatest maker of movie magic his nation has ever known. In addition to his work with Toho, he founded his own company, Tsuburaya Productions, which is responsible for, among many other things, *Ultraman*, the single most prolific science-fiction TV franchise in history. And he approached it all with a sense of unparalleled wonder, and the firm conviction that his most important audience was young people, whose imaginations he hoped to inspire in the same way that his own had been.

"He was a genius," says Dr. William Tsutsui, author of the cultural study *Godzilla on My Mind: Fifty Years of the King of Monsters*. "One of the great special effects talents. He had no budget and no technology, he essentially had to invent what he did. I'm a big fan of suitmation, I love the person in the suit. Having that human connection with the monster on some level, to recognize there are human beings inside that costume really makes Godzilla special, especially if you're a kid. It's the relatability of the humaneness of Godzilla, as opposed to the sterileness of CGI."

From Flying to Filming

He was born Eiichi Tsuburaya on July 7, 1901, in Sugasawa City, Fukushima Prefecture. Although surrounded by a large extended family, he essentially lost both parents at an early age, his mother dying when he was only three years old, and his father relocating to China shortly thereafter for business reasons. The boy would be raised by his grandmother Natsu and Uncle Ichiro, who was only a few years older than he was.

The young Eiichi's first love was not motion pictures; the movie industry in Japan barely existed in the first decade of the twentieth century. What was very popular in those early years was a new technology of a different kind: aviation. At a time when Japan was swept up in an aviation craze and brave early pilots were heroes to a generation of little boys, Eiichi longed to fly his own plane. He began putting model planes together at the age of nine, and it was his curiosity and interest in assembling intricate structures that eventually led him to the movies—but from the beginning, it was the technical aspect that interested him. By the age of ten, he was alleged to have gotten his hands on a film projector, which he disassembled and then taught himself to reassemble.

After high school, he convinced his family to allow him to attend aviation school, studying under nationally famous pilot Seitaro Tamai. However, tragedy struck in 1917 when Tamai was killed in a freak crash that occurred while taking photographers on a flight over Tokyo. The Nippon Flying School was shut down in the wake of Tamai's death, and the teenaged Tsuburaya's piloting ambitions would unfortunately have to be shelved. Instead, he entered trade school and put his thirst for tinkering to work in research and development for a prominent toy manufacturer.

It was while working in the toy industry that Tsuburaya finally found his way to the film industry, when at a company party in 1919 he encountered director Yoshiro Edamasa, who offered him a job as a cameraman for the Nihon Cinematograph Company, the studio that would eventually evolve into Nikkatsu, one of Japan's major motion picture outfits. The eighteen-year-old Tsuburaya didn't yet fully understand how to operate a motion picture camera, but his formidable technical prowess allowed him to overcome that hurdle with relative ease, and before long he was an assistant cinematographer on *Hunchback of Enmeiin* (*Enmeiin no semushiotoko*) (1920), his motion picture debut.

Early Innovator

The film industry in Japan was, like in the United States, experiencing its first golden age at the time, and the young Tsuburaya was getting in on the ground floor. While gaining valuable experience in the early 1920s, he was also approached by the Japanese government for the first time and began doing propaganda work for the military, a specter that would grow in later years and come back to haunt him just at the peak of his career. But the reason for the military's interest in Tsuburaya's talents was his growing knack for innovation, and willingness to learn any and all new techniques— qualities that served him well as he lent his skills to a series of different studios over the course of the late 1920s and early 1930s, most notably Shochiku Kyoto Studios.

While at Shochiku, Tsuburaya began experimenting with a variety of new filming techniques, and was in fact the first in the Japanese industry to use a camera crane, introduced a decade earlier in the U.S. by D. W. Griffith on *Birth of a Nation*. It was a thrilling time to work in the industry, with the transition to sound just around the corner, opening up even newer possibilities. Although still working primarily as a cameraman, in 1930 Tsuburaya produced the earliest special effects of his career, creating superimposed imagery for the film *Chohichiro Matsudaira*. It would be an epiphany of sorts, and a sign of things to come as far as where his career path was headed.

In the early 1930s, life-altering experiences would occur in Tsuburaya's life on both a personal and a professional level. On February 27, 1930, the twenty-nine-year-old Tsuburaya married nineteen-year-old Masano Araki, the daughter of a prominent businessman, who had first become smitten with Tsuburaya during a tour of Shochiku Studios, when she witnessed the young man suffer a disastrous fall from his crane and began visiting him in

Seeing *King Kong* for the first time in 1933 changed Tsuburaya's life forever.   *Public domain*

the hospital. The first two of the couple's three sons, Hajime and Noboru, would follow soon after in 1931 and 1935 (the third and youngest, Akira, came along a decade later in 1944). Additionally, Tsuburaya's marriage to the Roman Catholic Araki led to his conversion from his original Buddhist faith; he would remain devout in his new religion for the remainder of his life.

The other major occurrence was the inspiration that would truly open his mind to the potential of motion picture effects. After transitioning from Shochiku back to Nikkatsu in the early 1930s, Tsuburaya first saw the groundbreaking giant monster movie *King Kong* when it came to Japan in 1933. Much like his future collaborator, director Ishiro Honda, he was immediately enthralled by the film, but in a different way. Whereas Honda decided he wanted to make films like *King Kong*, Tsuburaya wanted to create Kong himself; the work of stop-motion pioneer Willis O'Brien awakened him to the possibilities of what movie magic was capable of producing, and Tsuburaya began looking into the logistics of bringing genuine special-effects techniques to Japanese film. Up until that point, there had been no real Japanese special-effects industry to speak of. Tsuburaya was about to change that.

By the end of 1933, after expounding to his Nikkatsu superiors on what special effects could do for the movies, Tsuburaya was commissioned to begin researching and executing these techniques. But his ambition proved to be too lofty for his bosses to understand, and he quit the company the following year when the studio began complaining that he was spending too much money. He was quickly brought on at J.O. Studios (formerly "J.O. Talkies") as deputy chief of staff for research and development, then chief cinematographer. His new bosses were excited by his interest in such screen process techniques as rear projection, and also helped him construct his first iron camera crane (previous models had been wooden).

The Specter of War

Meanwhile, the Japanese government would come calling again as they were looking for talented filmmakers to put together propagandist films to support their growing militaristic ambitions. As Japan was poised to invade China and eventually start the Second World War, Tsuburaya was enlisted to work as director and cinematographer on such films as the documentary *Three-Thousand Miles Across the Equator* (*Kotei sanmanri sekido-o koete*) (1935), designed to show the might of the Imperial Navy.

Back home, he would begin incorporating elaborate effects into his pictures. On J.O. Studios' highly successful *Princess Kaguya* (1935), a retelling of an ancient Japanese fairy tale, he would employ detailed miniatures for the first time. The initial time Tsuburaya would officially work as a special-effects director was not at Toho, but for his old employers at Nikkatsu. The film was a Japanese/German co-production entitled *The New Earth* (*Atarashiki tsuchi*) (1937), a samurai-era period picture that included Tsuburaya's first full-scale rear-screen process.

However, Tsuburaya found himself a part of a grand new motion picture company the following year, when several smaller companies, J.O. Studios among them, were merged into the giant conglomerate that became known as the Toho Motion Picture Company, Ltd. A thoroughly modern company with forward-thinking brass eager to take Japanese filmmaking beyond what it had been, Toho embraced the innovative and enthusiastic Tsuburaya, naming him head of what they called the Special Arts Department, an independent division dedicated to special effects. His first Toho film was *Major Nango* (*Aa, Nango shosa*) (1938).

With the onset of World War II, much of the motion picture industry was compelled to aid in the war effort, and Toho was no different. Tsuburaya was brought on to the Imperial Army Air Corps Training Academy and commissioned to make flight training films, fulfilling a lifelong dream in the process by earning a master's certification in acrobatic flying. Also, as part of his duties at Toho he was put to work creating painstakingly elaborate battle simulation special effects for a number of pro-military Japanese propaganda films. Most notable among these was *The War at Sea from Hawaii to Malaya* (1942), made on the heels of the attack on Pearl Harbor. It became the highest-grossing Japanese movie of the year, and included an incredible re-creation of the Pearl Harbor bombardment that was considered so realistic it was later mistaken for actual footage and would even turn up in documentaries made after the war.

Though the product of government coercion, Tsuburaya's propaganda films brought him great attention and respect as a special-effects director. However, things would turn bad for him just as they turned bad for all of Japan in 1945. Following a massive napalming of Tokyo by Allied forces in March that Tsuburaya and his family narrowly survived, the nuclear assaults on Hiroshima and Nagasaki in August led to the Japanese surrender, and subsequent American occupation. Suddenly, Tsuburaya's connection to Japan's propaganda efforts made him the target of suspicion by occupation forces, which wrongly believed that his detailed simulation of Pearl

Harbor could only be the result of wartime espionage. Tsuburaya was let go from Toho in 1948, and would remain in exile from the company for the remainder of the occupation.

The Birth of Tokusatsu

Tsuburaya did not return to Toho until 1953, when he was quietly brought back by studio head Iwao Mori, who reinstated him as head of the Special Arts Department (later known as the Visual Effects Department). Almost as a counterbalance to the 1940s propaganda work he had done, Tsuburaya's first major project was *Eagles of the Pacific* (*Taiheiyo-no Washii*) (1953), a film designed to chronicle the real-life toll of losing the war and to pay tribute to those who had lost their lives. It was on this movie that Tsuburaya worked for the first time with Akira Watanabe, the production designer who would play such an important role in the work that was soon to come.

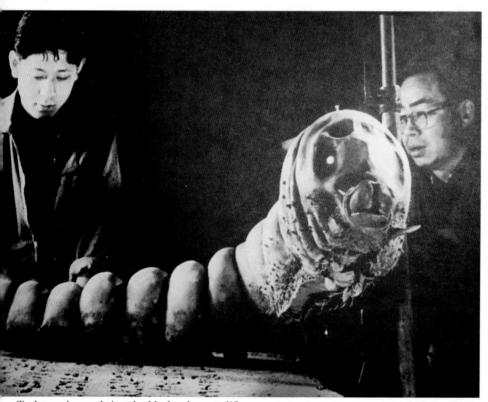

Tsuburaya's crew bring the Mothra larva to life.   *Author's collection*

Tsuburaya was fifty-three years old when he first embarked on the phase of his career for which he would become best known. Already a well-established and respected special-effects designer, he was immediately tapped by Toho head honcho Iwao Mori to join forces with producer Tomoyuki Tanaka on what up to that point was known only as "Project G"—the ambitious giant monster movie *Gojira*. Together with director Ishiro Honda, they formed what Toho's PR department labeled "the Golden Trio." But of all three men, perhaps Tsuburaya was the one under the most pressure. After all, he had to deliver the monster. Given his reputation at the time, Mori and Tanaka had complete faith that he could do just that.

In some ways, it was the dream job he had always hoped for. Finally, the full potential of what had been awoken inside him after first seeing *King Kong* twenty years earlier could come to fruition. Tsuburaya had always wanted to do a monster movie just like his hero Willis O'Brien. However, compromises would have to be made, and it's a testament to Tsuburaya's ingenuity that he still pulled it off. When he informed Toho that he'd need about seven years to create a fully realized stop-motion dinosaur in the style of Kong, Tsuburaya was told that he had less than six months. Naturally, this required a shifting of gears. Although disappointed, Tsuburaya opted instead to create the monster using an elaborate rubber suit that could be worn by an actor, to be built by his art director Akira Watanabe. This, combined with the meticulous miniature construction and photography techniques he had mastered years earlier, would generate the illusion of a massive reptilian beast on the loose in Japan.

As would be the style on all Toho's special-effects pictures, Tsuburaya had total responsibility for all special-effects sequences (Honda directed everything else). This made him more than just a special-effects director—his vision would be largely relied upon to make the movie a success. Tsuburaya supervised the re-creation of downtown Tokyo using firsthand surveys of the city, as well as the construction of the suit itself, a latex rubber and metal wire contraption to be worn by stunt performer Haruo Nakajima. For the start of special-effects photography in August 1954, Tsuburaya divided his team into three units: location photography, miniature photography, and optical photography/animation (the unit responsible for creating Godzilla's glowing atomic breath). It took Tsuburaya and company a total of sixty-two days—more than 50 percent longer than Honda's crew—to complete their end of the job.

The results were unlike anything seen in Japanese cinema up to that point: Tsuburaya had produced the first *kaiju* film, in the process inventing an entirely new genre of special-effects films in Japan, known as *tokusatsu*. Pretty soon, Toho was eager to re-create the success of *Gojira*, and a plethora of *tokusatsu* movies were put into production in the immediately subsequent years. The common denominator to all of them was Eiji Tsuburaya, the man who was literally defining the very look of Japanese science-fiction film. His processes, including the later-dubbed "suitmation," as well as high-speed photography designed to make the monsters appear unthinkably huge, and his startling attention to detail in all miniature work, became hallmarks of *tokusatsu*, not just during Tsuburaya's own lifetime but also beyond, and are still largely carried on (with some modern CGI augmentation) by filmmakers who are respectful of the tradition he began.

A Special-Effects Philosophy

Excited at the opportunity to use his talents to create monsters and other fantastical effects, Tsuburaya continued to hone his distinctive style on such films as *Rodan* (1958), *Giant Monster Varan* (1958), *The H-Man* (1959), *The Mysterians* (1957), and *Battle in Outer Space* (1959), as well as the *Gojira* sequel, *Godzilla Raids Again* (1955). Whether called upon to depict flying saucers, giant winged terrors, or bizarre and frightening mutants, Tsuburaya approached each project with relish and a desire to break new ground, inventing as he went along. A firm believer in the value of fantasy, he was not so much concerned with entirely "believable" realism, but rather with creating a unique, otherworldly look in which both his imagination and the imagination of the viewers could run free. For this reason, Western fans in Europe and America, unused to his personal aesthetic, would often unfairly judge his effects work as hokey or cheesy. These cynical critics miss the point: 100 percent photo-reality was never Tsuburaya's goal. He tackled the outlandish tasks put in front of him with the intention of transporting viewers to a surreal place that was clearly not their own—a cinematic domain in which color and creativity were the goals.

In fact, what's often lost on those looking back is the fact that during Tsuburaya's *tokusatsu* heyday of the 1950s and 1960s, Toho's visual effects department was producing work that was cutting edge for the industry at the time, rivaling and in some cases surpassing what was being done in American science-fiction cinema. Tsuburaya was setting the standard, and his work was decidedly state of the art in its day, not the second-rate schlock it is sometimes termed by the uninformed.

"There's no overstating just how charming the movies are with regards to Eiji Tsuburaya's special effects and the special effects he pioneered that others were able to run with," says Miguel Rodriguez. "It's a different world that you look at as you watch these films, and there's a beautiful artifice to everything that is very charming. You can't help but be a little bewitched by it."

Tsuburaya's profile was higher than ever, and Toho acknowledged that his work was a major element of why the new string of *kaiju* and *tokusatsu* films had become such a sensation. He even designed the distinctive Toho Company logo that would appear at the beginning of the studio's films for years to come. With greater power at the studio, and a staff that now included some two hundred employees, he was given more leeway to innovate. In 1959, he designed the "Toho Versatile Process," a complete update of the company's optical printer that optimized the creation of widescreen color films. The following year, Toho approved the construction on their lot of what came to be known as "The Big Pool." Containing nearly three hundred thousand cubic feet of water, the pool was utilized on everything from naval battle re-creations for Tsuburaya's return to the war film genre, *Tempest Over the Pacific: The Air Battles of Hawaii and Midway* (1960), to the next wave of *kaiju* films that was to come, including perhaps Tsuburaya's most ambitious monster movie to date, *Mothra* (1961).

The 1960s also saw the return of Godzilla to full-time action, and Tsuburaya was front and center to realize the monster's full-color exploits. In 1962, he fulfilled a lifelong dream by creating his own version of the Eighth Wonder of the World for *King Kong vs. Godzilla*. He united the Big G with his other great creation in *Mothra vs. Godzilla* (1964), designed his most elaborate *kaiju* to date for *Ghidorah, the Three-Headed Monster* (1964), and supervised the construction of jaw-dropping matte painting and spaceship miniature effects for *Invasion of Astro-Monster* (1965).

With the new decade came a new approach to *kaiju*, a lighter approach that was largely due to Tsuburaya's growing influence. Although earlier films like the original *Gojira* had been quite dark and geared for adults, Tsuburaya was a strong proponent of the wonder of fantasy cinema, and its ability to connect with children. Perhaps recalling his own childhood of idolizing early pilots and discovering the power of silent movies, he sought to appeal to youngsters, downplaying intense violence and playing up the whimsical whenever possible (it was Tsuburaya, for example, who pushed for Godzilla's exuberant victory dance to be included in *Invasion of*

The "Old Man" always took his work seriously, even while directing Mushroom People in *Matango*.
Movie Stills Database

Astro-Monster). Keenly aware that children were becoming a large part of the *tokusatsu* audience, Tsuburaya felt a responsibility toward them, wanting his special effects to nurture their imaginations rather than give them nightmares.

"There's no getting over how much Tsuburaya had fun when creating his miniature cityscapes and monsters," says Miguel Rodriguez. "That enjoyment comes through the screen. He's even been quoted talking about what an enjoyable time it was, and how much he loved it . . . It's not really trying to fool you into thinking this is real, per se. It's incumbent on the viewer to use their imagination a little bit, and I think that's part of the charm. When the audience can participate in that way, where their imagination is being called upon to bring these characters to life, then it makes the characters seem a little more real."

A Company of His Own

Tsuburaya would have an even greater opportunity to translate his personal vision directly to the screen beginning in 1963, when he started his own special-effects studio, Tsuburaya Productions. Although a separate and distinct entity from Toho Company, Tsuburaya Productions and Toho worked hand-in-hand, fostering a relationship built on Tsuburaya's lofty status at Toho. Tsuburaya Productions took on all the special effects for Toho films going forward, as well as their own in-house projects, which were mainly for the new medium of television that was quickly supplanting the movies as Japan's most popular entertainment source.

Tsuburaya continued working with Toho, but with so much now on his plate with his very own company, "the Old Man" was becoming less directly involved with day-to-day operations, taking on more of a supervisory role. Starting with *Godzilla vs. the Sea Monster* (1966), Tsuburaya's right-hand man Sadamasa Arikawa took on the role of special-effects director previously filled by Tsuburaya himself, although Tsuburaya continued to receive full credit, and indeed remained creatively involved at all times. Now and then, such as with the 1965 Toho-Warner Bros. joint production *None but the Brave*, Tsuburaya would return to more of a hands-on position as special-effects director, in this case working alongside the film's director and star, Frank Sinatra.

But Tsuburaya Productions was keeping him more than busy, thanks to a new franchise that was capturing the imagination of the Japanese public. Inspired by Rod Serling's *Twilight Zone*, in 1966 Tsuburaya spearheaded the creation of *Ultra Q*, a fantasy anthology series that has come to be regarded as some of the finest television ever produced in Japan.

But TV executives wanted more giant monsters and the type of work Tsuburaya had been creating for Toho, and so the black-and-white *Ultra Q* gave way to the full-color *Ultraman*, a science-fiction superhero series that became a monumental hit with the youngsters of Japan—so much so that it would spawn a lengthy franchise that continues to this day and includes countless spin-offs, continuations, motion picture adaptations, and other ancillary incarnations, starting with the first *Ultraman* spin-off, *Ultra Seven*, unleashed by Tsuburaya in 1967. In fact, *Ultraman* is listed in the *Guinness Book of World Records* as the longest continuously running franchise in television history.

Tsuburaya Productions became one of the most successful Japanese TV studios during the late 1960s. Other major hits for the company included *Booska the Friendly Beast* (*Kaiju Booska*), Tsuburaya's first overtly juvenile *kaiju* creation, as well as the spy action series *Mighty Jack*, which he considered his masterpiece. But none could compare to the overwhelming success of *Ultraman*, with its weekly battles between invading monsters and the titular alien superhero. Children thrilled to the adventures of pilot and scientist Shin Hayata, a member of the Science Special Search Party who had merged with Ultraman and could call the hero forth whenever danger appeared. The format of the series would inspire numerous series from other companies over the years, including the likes of *Kamen Rider* and *Super Sentai* (known in the U.S. as *Power Rangers*), and can rightly be said to have founded an entire genre.

By the end of the 1960s, age and illness were beginning to take a toll. Pushing seventy, diagnosed with angina and suffering from diabetes, Tsuburaya had been under doctor's orders to take it easy, but continued to push himself, burning the candle at both ends with TV and movie projects. He took on the production of a special film to be shown at Expo '70, the first World's Fair ever held in Japan. But his weakened health forced him to stay home and rest. Unable to contribute, out of respect he still continued to receive special-effects director credits on Toho productions such as *All Monsters Attack* (*Gojira-Minira-Gabara: Ōru Kaijū Daishingeki*) (1969), the final Godzilla film produced under his watch. On January 25, 1970, while vacationing with his extended family in Shizuoka Prefecture, Eiji Tsuburaya died in his sleep of a heart attack at age sixty-eight.

Amongst the pantheon of twentieth-century motion picture fantasists, the light of Eiji Tsuburaya shines brightly alongside the likes of Georges Méliès, Walt Disney, George Pal, Ray Harryhausen, George Lucas, and his great inspiration, Willis O'Brien. The Father of *Tokusatsu*, his singular ambition and relentless work ethic gave birth to an aesthetic that was completely ingenious, robustly influential, and most importantly, the result of an individual vision. Without Tsuburaya, there could not have been a golden age of *daikaiju eiga*, and there would not have been a Godzilla as we know the creature today. For this reason, "the Old Man" remains an inspiration and a comfort to all who seek escape through the exciting medium of the cinema of the imagination.

Carrying the Torch of Tokusatsu

It was Tsuburaya who created the template, setting a standard for special effects that continues to be adhered to today in Japan, where practical effects have never been supplanted by CGI as they have in the United States. Understandably, when the master passed away in 1970, it left a hole that was difficult to fill. And yet these disciples did their best to pick up where Tsuburaya left off, and ensure that Godzilla would continue to rampage to his heart's content.

Sadamasa Arikawa

Sometimes credited as Teisho Arikawa, the man who cut his teeth as the special-effects cameraman working directly under Tsuburaya would also be the one to immediately take over when his boss suddenly found himself swamped with work thanks to the launch of Tsuburaya Productions. Although he never received the credit he deserved at the time, as Tsuburaya still retained "Special Effects Director" credit, from 1966 to 1970, Arikawa was the man in charge of bringing Godzilla and many other *kaiju* to life.

Born in Tokyo in 1925, Arikawa first came to work for Toho Company in 1953 at the age of twenty-eight. From the beginning of his career, he was under Tsuburaya's tutelage, debuting as head special-effects cinematographer on *Operation Kamikaze* (*Taiheiyo no washi*), an Admiral Isoroku Yamamoto biopic directed by Tsuburaya's longtime collaborator Ishiro Honda.

Arikawa was behind the camera during Tsuburaya's brilliant special-effects sequences for the original *Gojira*, the first of many *tokusatsu* films on which he would work alongside the master. His cinematography can be seen on subsequent Godzilla sequels, including *Godzilla Raids Again*, *King Kong vs. Godzilla*, *Mothra vs. Godzilla*, *Ghidorah, the Three-Headed Monster*, and *Invasion of Astro-Monster*, as well as filming Tsuburaya's work on such non-Godzilla *tokusatsu* movies as *Rodan*, *The Mysterians*, *The H-Man*, *Giant Monster Varan*, *Battle in Outer Space*, *The Human Vapor* (1960), *Mothra*, *Gorath* (1962), *Matango* (1963), *Atragon* (1963), *Dogora* (1964), and *Frankenstein Conquers the World* (1965).

By the mid-1960s, Arikawa had gained valuable experience, and was being given more and more responsibilities. In 1965, Tsuburaya named him special-effects director on Tsuburaya Productions' first major effort, the anthology series *Ultra Q*. This was followed by similar duties on the even more successful follow-up smash-hit superhero series *Ultraman*, which demonstrated more than ever that Arikawa was up to the task of orchestrating *kaiju* action sequences on his own. For this reason, when Tsuburaya began to relinquish direct control of day-to-day operations on Toho's *tokusatsu* projects, it was Arikawa who stepped in to take over, beginning with *Godzilla vs. the Sea Monster*, alongside director Jun Fukuda.

Some of Arikawa's finest work can be seen in his subsequent film, *Son of Godzilla* (1967), in which he orchestrated complex battle scenes involving the eight-legged Kumonga spider, which fired "webbing" in the form of rubber glue and had to be operated by as many as twenty assistants, as well as the giant Kamacuras praying mantis marionettes. He also pulled off more composite shots involving human characters and *kaiju* than had ever been seen before. This was followed by the *kaiju* battle royal extravaganza *Destroy All Monsters* (1968), as well as other *tokusatsu* films like *King Kong Escapes* (1967) and *Latitude Zero* (1969). His final film for Toho would be *Yog: Monster from Space* (1970), completed following the death of his mentor Tsuburaya.

In the wake of Tsuburaya's passing, and a complete restructuring of the studio, Arikawa departed Toho and took on sporadic projects over the course of the 1970s. These included *Goliathan* (1977), a cult classic King Kong spin-off designed to capitalize on the success of the 1976 *Kong* remake that was a co-production of Japan's Shochiku Films and the famous Shaw Brothers of Hong Kong, known for their copious kung-fu flicks. He also did some television, and even got to direct for the first and only time, helming *Phoenix*, an American/Taiwanese sci-fi/fantasy film that was shot in 1978 and finally found a distributor in 1983.

Arikawa left the business after the 1970s, and would later gain renewed popularity thanks to the rise of Godzilla fandom and the spread of conventions, where fans could properly thank him for taking up Tsuburaya's reins at such a crucial point in Godzilla's history. He died of lung cancer in 2005 at the age of eighty.

Teruyoshi Nakano

After the death of Eiji Tsuburaya in 1970, it was not Sadamasa Arikawa but Teruyoshi Nakano, another of "the Old Man's" chief assistants, who was chosen by Toho as his official successor. From 1971 to 1987, he served as the head of Toho's visual effects department, supervising not only the late *Showa*-era Godzilla films, but even the first film of the later *Heisei* series. Though not as revered as the pioneering Tsuburaya, and sometimes criticized for the deterioration in the quality of *tokusatsu* during the 1970s, he made the most of tough times for the studio and kept Godzilla stomping along on a shoestring budget.

Born in 1935 in the Manchurian region of what was then the Empire of Japan, Nakano entered the motion picture business at the age of twenty-one, working as an assistant director to none other than Ishiro Honda on *Yakan chugaku* (1956), one of the director's rare non-Toho projects of the 1950s. It would be three years later that Nakano made his way to Toho, and to the special-effects unit run by Eiji Tsuburaya. His first Toho project under Tsuburaya was the war picture *Submarine I-57 Will Not Surrender* (1959).

By that point, the "*kaiju* boom" was already in full swing, and Nakano was right there alongside Tsuburaya for the classic *tokusatsu* films of the golden age of Japanese filmmaking during the early 1960s. Although the first two Godzilla films of the 1950s had been just a bit before his time, he gained hands-on experience with the greatest *kaiju* of them all for the lucrative string of sequels made during the 1960s. This experience served him well when, in 1969, with Tsuburaya too ill to supervise and his protégé Arikawa off on other projects, he stepped in as the unofficial director of special effects on *All Monsters Attack* (aka *Godzilla's Revenge*), working directly with Ishiro Honda to hastily cobble together some passable effects sequences (combined with liberal use of stock footage from previous films).

They were not ideal circumstances with which to prove oneself, but nevertheless by 1971, what had been unofficial became official when Nakano was promoted to Tsuburaya's old position. Over the next four years, he supervised the final five films of Godzilla's *Showa* era: *Godzilla vs. Hedorah* (1971), *Godzilla vs. Gigan* (1972), *Godzilla vs. Megalon* (1973), *Godzilla vs. Mechagodzilla* (1974), and *Terror of Mechagodzilla* (1975), crafting a whole new generation of *kaiju* villains for Godzilla to tangle with.

Unfortunately, by this point the Japanese film industry was in shambles, with the studio system wiped out and an oil crisis crippling the national economy. This lack of funding is on full display in the markedly shabbier special effects of the 1970s Godzilla films, including creature designs that simply weren't up to the standards Tsuburaya had set a decade earlier. Nevertheless, Godzilla fans still find much to love in Nakano's work from this period, including the often horrifying attacks of the bizarre "Smog Monster" Hedorah and the design of Mechagodzilla, as well as the animations created to produce the robot monster's laser assaults.

Despite Godzilla being shelved, Nakano continued to work for Toho through the late 1970s and early 1980s. In 1984, when producer Tomoyuki Tanaka decided to finally dust off the Big G, Nakano was tapped to come back, with a bigger budget this time, and return the monster to his former glory. And while *Godzilla 1985* would be Nakano's final Godzilla film, it also finally granted him the platform to show more of what he was capable of with proper funding.

Nakano continued on with Toho for three more years. In 1985, he and his team were brought to North Korea for a controversial project called *Pulgasari*. The product of North Korea's oppressive dictatorship government, whose heir apparent Kim Jong-Il was a rabid fan of Godzilla and other *kaiju* movies, *Pulgasari* was designed to be North Korea's own *kaiju* film, directed by Shin Sang-ok, a celebrated South Korean director who had been kidnapped by Jong-Il seven years earlier for the express purpose of making pro-government propaganda pictures. Following this bizarre project, Nakano ended his tenure as Toho's special-effects director with Kon Ichikawa's *Princess from the Moon* (1987).

Much like Arikawa, Nakano has enjoyed great popularity on the convention circuit in recent years, and was even the guest of honor at the 2004 edition of G-Fest, America's premier annual Godzilla convention.

Koichi Kawakita

The work of Kawakita has defined the Godzilla series like that of no other special-effects director but Eiji Tsuburaya himself. Like the master, Kawakita left an indelible mark on the development of the Big G, establishing his own unique look and feel over the course of the last six films of the *Heisei* era made from 1989 to 1995. To this day, there are many who feel that the "default Godzilla" most latter-day fans envision when they think of the Big G is the version created by Kawakita during his enormously successful run as Toho's director of special effects.

Born December 5, 1942, in Tokyo, Kawakita first joined Toho after dropping out of college at the tender age of nineteen, learning his craft as part of Tsuburaya's extensive special-effects team. His first major project was one of "the Old Man's" finest pieces of work, *Gorath*, on which he served in an uncredited role as an assistant optical technician. Decades before he would take over the *Heisei* series, he first crossed paths with Godzilla in 1962, when he worked as an assistant cameraman on Tsuburaya's special-effects shoots for *King Kong vs. Godzilla*, the monster's first color feature.

Among Kawakita's memorable creations were Space Godzilla and MOGUERA, seen in *Godzilla vs. Space Godzilla*.
Everett Collection

Following the death of Tsuburaya, the special-effects division of Toho was restructured along with much of the entire company. His time with Tsuburaya left a lasting impression, however, and he found significant work with Tsuburaya Productions as the special-effects supervisor for *The Return of Ultraman* (1971), the third series in the enormously successful Ultraman franchise and the first to be mounted since Tsuburaya's passing. The following year, he would return to the franchise for the fourth series, *Ultraman Ace* (1972), a show that would mark his first time as a full-scale special-effects director.

Kawakita returned to Toho shortly thereafter, this time with much more experience under his belt. As a result, his first project back was the Toho TV series *Zone Fighter* (*Ryusei Ningen Zon*) (1973), an obvious *Ultraman* copycat. He continued to work for Tsuburaya Productions as well, following up his previous *Ultraman* work with duties on the next series, *Ultraman Leo* (1974). It was also at this time that Kawakita became the first assistant to the new director of special effects at Toho, Teruyoshi Nakano. While working with Nakano, Kawakita would return to the world of Godzilla just in time to work as assistant special-effects director on the second-to-last of the *Showa*-era films, *Godzilla vs. Mechagodzilla* (1974).

During Nakano's regime, Toho began assigning more responsibility to Kawakita. In 1976, he was given the opportunity to serve for the first time as chief special-effects director on a feature film, *Zone Fighter* (*Ozora no samurai*). He did the same on *Bye, Bye Jupiter* (1984), one of Toho's first forays back into the realm of science fiction since the heyday of *tokusatsu* years earlier. His impressive body of work made him Toho's choice to succeed Nakano as head of the company's visual effects department in the 1980s.

The Godzilla franchise had already been rebooted in 1984, but it took five full years for another film to be made, and at that point, Kawakita was handed the special-effects reins. Beginning with the extraordinary *Godzilla vs. Biollante* (1989), he set to work creating his very own unique version of the Big G, paying homage to what Tsuburaya, Nakano, and others had done in the past, but at the same time making the monster (and his many allies and foes) completely his own. He reimagined classic *Showa* monsters King Ghidorah, Mothra, and Mechagodzilla for *Godzilla vs. King Ghidorah* (1991), *Godzilla & Mothra: Battle for Earth* (1992), and *Godzilla vs. Mechagodzilla II* (1993), respectively (the latter not to be confused with the film of the exact same name that he had worked on twenty years earlier). And he created all-new *kaiju* as well, including Space Godzilla in *Godzilla vs. Space Godzilla* (1994), as well as Destoroyah, the monster that would best the *Heisei* Godzilla for good in *Godzilla vs. Destoroyah* (1995). In keeping with the grittier, more realistic approach to the *Heisei* films, Kawakita brought a more grounded philosophy to his effects, eschewing the more fanciful aspects of Tsuburaya's aesthetic for an often darker and more serious style.

Following the end of the *Heisei* series, Kawakita directed special effects on the first two films of the *Rebirth of Mothra* series of the late 1990s. He finished out his time with Toho in 2003 on the TV series *Super Star God Gransazar* (*Choseijin Guranseiza*), a hit for the studio that achieved international distribution. After stepping down from Toho, just as Tsuburaya had done, he started his own effects company, Dream Planet Japan. He continued to make convention appearances and took part in public Godzilla exhibitions right up until his unexpected death from liver failure on December 5, 2014, at the age of seventy-two.

Just as Tsuburaya had done in the 1950s and '60s, Kawakita defined the look of Godzilla, and of Toho *tokusatsu* in general, for the late 1980s and '90s. His contribution was an important one, bringing something new and fresh to a creation that by that point was more than thirty-five years old. And just as *Showa* Godzilla will always be associated with Tsuburaya, so will *Heisei* Godzilla forever be associated with Kawakita.

8

Man in Suit

The Work of Haruo Nakajima

lthough special-effects maven Eiji Tsuburaya had first envisioned Godzilla as a stop-motion creation, the limited schedule and budget of the original *Gojira* meant that he'd have to realize the creature using a technique later termed "suitmation"—using a monster suit that could be worn by an actor on a miniature set designed to make him look gigantic. In order to make his revised vision work, Tsuburaya needed the right actor for the job; a physical performer with the humility to allow himself to be completely obscured from the camera, willing to work inside a stifling and ponderously heavy rubber suit.

That actor turned out to be Haruo Nakajima, a young stunt performer under contract to Toho who not only played Godzilla to great effect in the original film, but when the franchise took off in popularity, went on to don the costume for a total of twelve different films in the series, far more than any other performer ever has. For the majority of the *Showa* era, during what most consider to be Godzilla's heyday, Nakajima was the literal embodiment of the irradiated dinosaur, bringing him to life through his unique approach to the character, giving him a personality and a presence that are unmatched in the history of *kaiju eiga*, suffering for his art along the way.

An Actor of a Different Kind

Nakajima was born on New Year's Day 1929, in the waterfront city of Sekata, in Japan's Yamagata Prefecture. As a small child, he began to work gathering seaweed from the ocean when not in school. At only fourteen years of age, with World War II raging, he joined the Imperial Navy as a pilot trainee. In his later teenage years, he helped out at his family's meat store, and also drove a truck for the American occupation forces after the war.

But none of those jobs really held his attention, and by the age of twenty, he had enrolled in Tokyo's International Film Acting School, with a dream of making it to the silver screen. While still studying there, he landed his first bit part, in an Akira Kurosawa picture from Toho entitled *Stray Dog* (*Nora inu*) (1949); but the part unfortunately remained on the cutting-room floor. It wouldn't be until the following year, when one of his teachers helped him secure a formal contract with Toho, that he started to make his earliest appearances on film, starting with *Sword for Hire* (*Sengoku burai*) in 1952. He was called upon to do stunt work in that film, revealing a talent that would serve him throughout his career.

Director Ishiro Honda first used Nakajima in 1953 in his prestigious war film *Eagles of the Pacific* (*Taheiyo no washi*), in which he played a fighter pilot. That same year, Nakajima would finally make it into the final cut of a Kurosawa film, and no less than what was arguably the director's finest effort, *Seven Samurai*. But it would be Honda's next project, mysteriously titled "Project G," that would alter Nakajima's career forever.

The Role of a Lifetime

When he was assigned the script by the head of the acting department, Nakajima was intrigued, and wanted to know about the role he would be playing. But the project was such a secret that no one but special-effects director Eiji Tsuburaya knew enough to help him understand. Tsuburaya explained that Nakajima would be wearing a massive rubber costume to play the giant monster Gojira (Godzilla), and showed him images from the illustrated storyboards of what the creature might look like. The suit had not yet been finalized, but to prepare the young actor for the part, Tsuburaya showed him *King Kong*, another film about a giant beast on the loose in a major city.

But Kong existed on a much smaller scale than what was envisioned for Godzilla, and that monster had been achieved through stop-motion. In order to play Godzilla, Nakajima would have to enter uncharted waters, creating something that had never been seen in Japanese cinema up to that time. To add to his preparations, he started making frequent visits to Tokyo's Ueno Zoo, observing the motions of bears, elephants, and other enormous animals to give him ideas for the movement of the fictional behemoth he'd be portraying.

No amount of preparation, however, could have equipped him for what awaited him that first day on Stage 3 of the Toho studio lot. In trying on the

Nakajima takes a much-needed break during filming of *Godzilla Raids Again*.   *Public domain*

first prototype of the Godzilla suit, Nakajima discovered just how difficult it was going to be to pull off a worthwhile performance. That initial version was constructed of a hard, stiff rubber, making it not only extremely heavy (approximately 220 pounds), but also next to impossible to move around in. Once a new, more practical suit was made, one that also better fit Nakajima's specifications, things got a bit easier, with "easy" being a relative term. Still weighing close to 150 pounds, it remained difficult to maneuver, not to mention the heat inside the costume was almost beyond human endurance levels. Nakajima knew it would be a supreme challenge, but his unflagging enthusiasm compelled him on.

Filming was a grueling process for Nakajima, only heightened by the need for him to move at accelerated speed due to the fact that the film would be slowed down later in order to give the illusion of great size. When the actor slipped a thermometer inside the suit out of curiosity, it came out showing 60 degrees Celsius (140 degrees Fahrenheit). There were times he had to be removed from the suit for fear that he might pass out. Buried inside layers of rubber and cloth, not to mention the large wooden sandals inside the costume's enormous feet, Nakajima would build up so much perspiration that he would need to wring it out of his clothing periodically. By the end of a shoot, nearly a cup of sweat had dripped from his body into the bottom of the suit.

Although he had help from a second actor, Katsumi Tezuka, who is believed to have filled in for him during the shoot from time to time (and who went on to an impressive suit-acting career of his own), Nakajima worked hard to establish the Godzilla role as his own. As difficult as it was to perform or emote on any level within the suit that required so much concentration just to maneuver, Nakajima did his best to convey a sense of the monster's size and even personality through his movements. And part of the film's success once it was released in the fall of 1954 can be attributed to his impressive portrayal of the title character. Nakajima witnessed firsthand the impact his performance had on audiences: The actor later would describe attending a premiere and being brought to tears by the riveted response of theatergoers, particularly children, when he appeared on-screen in costume.

Toho's Favorite Suit Performer

The success of *Gojira* helped kick off Nakajima's reign as the master of *kaiju* suit acting, the most often-used performer in the history of the genre, and the man who set the standard for all who came after. For nearly two decades, Nakajima found himself inside a rubber suit on an almost regular basis. He reprised his Godzilla role for the 1955 sequel, *Godzilla Raids Again*, and took on the challenge of the flying monster Rodan in the 1956 film of the same name. He played the giant robot Moguera in the 1957 sci-fi epic *The Mysterians*, as well as the title beast in the one-off *kaiju* feature *Giant Monster Varan* (1958). He was even inside the partially motorized larva costume for *Mothra* (1961). Once the Godzilla franchise was kicked into high gear in 1962 with *King Kong vs. Godzilla* (1962), it was only natural that Nakajima was pegged to once again play the famous dinosaur.

It was a role he would dominate for the remainder of the 1960s, and even into the 1970s. Nakajima became so trusted as Toho's *kaiju* performer deluxe that he was given carte blanche to choreograph his own fight sequences, meaning that he was able to contribute significantly to what made so many of those classic *Showa* Godzilla movies work, staging the many battles between the King of the Monsters and his numerous foes. He brought a visceral sense of being to the creature, rooted in animal movement, although increasingly becoming anthropomorphized as the series progressed. It was not uncommon in later Godzilla pictures like *Invasion of Astro-Monster* (1965), *All Monsters Attack* (1969), and *Godzilla vs. Hedorah* (1971) for Nakajima to strike martial arts poses, engage in victory dances, and even incorporate professional wrestling maneuvers (due in large part to the enormous popularity of pro wrestling in Japan during the 1960s and '70s).

During this era, only one Godzilla film, *Son of Godzilla* (1967), relied on other actors to play the monster: Stunt performers Yu Sekida and Seiji Onaka were used due to their great height, which would help establish the size difference between Godzilla and his son Minya, played by midget wrestler Little Man Machan. Nakajima was only used for the water scenes; partly because he didn't need to stand next to Machan, and also because he had become so adept at maneuvering the costume around Toho's "Big Pool" aquatic set.

Nakajima continued taking on other *kaiju* roles during this period, including the title parts in *Matango* (1963), the monster Baragon in *Frankenstein Conquers the World* (1965), and the part of Gaira, one of the twin giants in *War of the Gargantuas* (1966). That latter role was one of Nakajima's most physical, allowing for more agile mobility and also displaying the actor's eyes, giving more of an opportunity to portray emotion. He even got a chance to portray the Eighth Wonder of the World for the only time in his career, in *King Kong Escapes* (1967). A trusted member of Eiji Tsuburaya's team, he took on roles for several of Tsuburaya Productions' TV series, including *Ultra Q* (in which he donned an old refitted Godzilla suit to play the monster Gomess), as well as *Ultraman* and *Ultra Seven*, on which he played a variety of evil *kaiju* adversaries.

Stepping Out of Costume

Following Tsuburaya's death in 1970, Nakajima's once unbounded enthusiasm for his work began to dissipate. A decade and a half of lumbering around under intense heat and weight, of being burned by explosives and even nearly drowning inside the costume, had taken a toll. Also, Toho Company was experiencing some serious upheaval and a major restructuring that saw them release all of the actors they had signed to long-term contracts, of which Nakajima was one. His final turn as Godzilla would be in 1972's *Godzilla vs. Gigan*. His last role would be without a costume, playing a chauffeur in Toho's disaster epic *Tidal Wave* (*Nihon Chinbotsu*) (1973). Afterwards, Toho unceremoniously relegated him to working in the bowling alley located on the studio lot. Although seemingly a shocking demotion for the man who once was Godzilla, Nakajima has maintained that he no longer had any desire to perform, believing that at the age of forty-four, he was no longer young and spry enough to get the job done.

There was a certain anonymity derived from playing roles in full costumes for so long, and for many years only the most ardent of *tokusatsu* fans were even aware of who Haruo Nakajima was. That began to change in the 1990s due in part to the rise of the Internet and strengthening of film fan culture on a worldwide basis. Nakajima had put his own distinct mark on the portrayal of Godzilla that was missing from what later actors brought to the role, and more and more fans began to recognize the importance of his contributions. He began making convention appearances starting in 1996 with Chicago's famous G-Con (later known as G-Fest, the world's premier annual Godzilla-themed fan event). Subsequent appearances in New York, Los Angeles, and other locations only helped to further cement his position as one of the legends of *kaiju eiga*. In 2010, at age eighty-one, he published his autobiography, *Monster Life: Haruo Nakajima, The Original Godzilla Actor.*

Universally acknowledged as the most celebrated suit actor of all time, Haruo Nakajima took what could have been a completely thankless responsibility and turned it into a truly enviable legacy. For years, the "suitmation" technique was shrouded in mystery, and much of the tremendous efforts of Nakajima (and his fellow suit performers) went unheralded outside of the industry, due to the desire for trade secrecy. But today that secret is an open one, and fans are able and willing to show respect and admiration for the unique and groundbreaking work of a man who was, first and foremost, an actor. Many great and talented individuals combined their abilities to help make Godzilla a success. But throughout his career, Nakajima did not simply contribute to Godzilla; rather, he *was* Godzilla.

Being Godzilla

It was Haruo Nakajima who originated the role of Godzilla in 1954, and he proudly reprised it over the course of eighteen years and eleven additional Godzilla movies. And although no one has ever donned the suit more times than he did, there were others who took on the rubber mantle once the time came for Nakajima to step down as the king of Toho *kaiju*. Following Nakajima's final turn in *Godzilla vs. Gigan*, a series of stalwart stuntmen took on the part for the remaining three films of the *Showa* era: Shinji Takagi for *Godzilla vs. Megalon* (1973) (minus some stock footage of Nakajima from previous installments), Isao Zushi in *Godzilla vs. Mechagodzilla* (1974), and Toru Kawai in *Terror of Mechagodzilla* (1975). (As a side note, Kawai had previously played Godzilla in an appearance on Toho's *Zone Fighter* TV series, and can also lay claim to being the only man to portray both Godzilla and Gamera, having briefly played the monstrous turtle in *Gamera: Super Monster* [*Uchu Kaiju Gamera*] [1980], the last of the *Showa*-era Gamera pictures.)

But none of those performers were ever invited back, and no one else in the *Showa* era was ever able to make the Godzilla part their own in the way that Nakajima did, instead merely attempting to fill his spot for a moment in time. It wasn't until the later eras of the Godzilla franchise that other actors were able to truly once again inhabit the role, and add to the legacy of the famous creature the way his original interpreter had done for so many years.

Nakajima greets fans at Weekend of Horrors in Oberhausen, Germany, 2013.

Michael Koschinski/Wikimedia

Kenpachiro Satsuma

- *Godzilla 1985* (1984)
- *Godzilla vs. Biollante* (1989)
- *Godzilla vs. King Ghidorah* (1991)
- *Godzilla & Mothra: Battle for Earth* (1992)
- *Godzilla vs. Mechagodzilla II* (1993)
- *Godzilla vs. Space Godzilla* (1994)
- *Godzilla vs. Destoroyah* (1995)

An even more physical actor than Nakajima, Ken Satsuma took over the reins of the Big G for the second great iteration of the franchise, known as the *Heisei* era. With a background in martial arts, Satsuma was known for bringing great preparation to the role, often taking a long time just to warm up his body and get into the right frame of mind to don the suit. This was reflected in the intense manner in which he portrayed the monster, a manner that was more in keeping with the serious tone of the *Heisei* series in general.

Satsuma was no stranger to *kaiju* work, or even to the Godzilla franchise itself, by the time he first took on the role in 1984. In fact, he had first come to Toho in 1971 at the age of twenty-three, during the final years of the *Showa* era. His first appearance in a Godzilla film came in Yoshimitsu Banno's *Godzilla vs. Hedorah*, in which he played the latter creature in the title, the notorious Smog Monster who battles a very heroic Godzilla in his attempt to "save the Earth." The Hedorah costume was something of a baptism of fire, being even heavier and more difficult to maneuver than the Godzilla suit itself. In fact, when Satsuma suffered the misfortune of appendicitis while in costume, he had to be rushed to the hospital in the suit, which was so difficult to get off that doctors had to cut through it to perform emergency surgery.

In addition to Hedorah, Satsuma also took on the role of the cyborg/avian/lizard *kaiju* Gigan, one of Godzilla's greatest foes of the 1970s, and a role he played in both *Godzilla vs. Gigan* (opposite Nakajima as Godzilla) and again in *Godzilla vs. Megalon*. After the end of the *Showa* series, Satsuma parted ways with Toho until, eleven years later, when the company was rebooting its Godzilla series, they turned to Satsuma, a proven suit actor from previous Godzilla films, to step up and take the lead *kaiju* role at last. Satsuma was only too happy to accept, having grown up during the *kaiju* boom of the 1950s and '60s, and longing for the opportunity to play the King of the Monsters.

This time, Toho was looking for an actor to play more of a long-term role, as Nakajima had done during the *Showa* era. When the *Heisei* series took off in the late 1980s, it soon became apparent that Satsuma would have steady work as Godzilla. And much like Nakajima, Satsuma was given free rein to choreograph fight scenes—which, given his training, was something at which he was quite adept. This was a different Godzilla for a different time; gone were the goofy dances, wrestling moves, and other anthropomorphic trappings that Eiji Tsuburaya had encouraged Nakajima to play up. Satsuma's Godzilla was a more majestic throwback to the original *Gojira*, emphasizing massive size and slower, steadier movement. It may not have been as much fun, but it was certainly more terrifying than what had been seen before. Also unlike in the past, the suits were now being made using rubber injection molds; nevertheless, although their construction may have been streamlined, wearing them was no less arduous, and Satsuma often fell prey to passing out from lack of oxygen or extreme heat.

After playing Godzilla in seven consecutive films, Satsuma's time in the suit came to an end when the *Heisei* era itself did, in 1995 with *Godzilla vs. Destoroyah*, in which the actor pulled off the rare task of Godzilla's death scene. With the monster behind him, Satsuma nevertheless continued on for a time doing *kaiju* work, including *Orochi, the Eight-Headed Dragon* (*Yamato Takeru*) (1994), one of the last films produced by Toho legend Tomoyuki Tanaka, as well as in the bizarre independent *kaiju* flicks of cult director/producer Teruo Ishii, including the 1999 remake of the occult thriller *Jigoku* and Satsuma's last film to date, the dark fantasy *Blind Beast vs. Killer Dwarf* (*Moju tai Issunboshi*) (2001).

By his mid-'50s, Satsuma's athletic method of performance was becoming more difficult, and the actor phased out the suit-acting portion of his career. He remains active as a trainer and physical culturist, and is also involved in charity work to provide relief from starvation and environmental calamity in North Korea—a passion that stems from his time working on the infamous Kim Jong-Il–financed North Korean *kaiju* film *Pulgasari* back in 1985. His time as Godzilla remains special to him, as was evidenced by his very publicly walking out of a screening of the American remake of *Godzilla* in 1998, echoing the feelings of many fans by declaring, "It's not Godzilla; it doesn't have the spirit."

Tsutomu Kitagawa

- *Godzilla 2000* (1999)
- *Godzilla vs. Megaguirus* (2000)
- *Godzilla Against Mechagodzilla* (2002)
- *Godzilla: Tokyo SOS* (2003)
- *Godzilla: Final Wars* (2004)

With Satsuma in semi-retirement, a new actor was brought into the fold for the third phase of the Godzilla franchise, the Millennium series, beginning in 1999 with *Godzilla 2000*. For the twenty-first century's take on Godzilla, Toho went for a completely different performance style, to go with a completely redesigned Godzilla suit. To fill that suit, the company turned to an actor who was new to the studio, but had extensive experience as part of what is perhaps Japan's second-most internationally known entertainment property, the *Super Sentai* TV series produced by rival studio Toei Company, known in the United States as *Power Rangers*.

Tsutomu "Tom" Kitagawa's earliest stunt acting work came at the age of twenty-one on the *Super Sentai* franchise, starting in 1979 with the third *Sentai* series, *Battle Fever J*. He became a series regular, appearing in seven of the next eight seasons of the series over the course of the 1980s. Clad from head to toe in the trademark suit and mask, he alternately played the "blue" and "black" members of the multicolored *Sentai* team, known in the American version as the Blue Ranger and the Black Ranger. A stunt performer first and foremost, Kitagawa only played the part during the masked battle sequences. He returned to the franchise for two more seasons during the mid-1990s.

Kitagawa was already forty years old when he first signed on with Toho— nearly the age that Nakajima was when he *retired* from suit acting. His first *kaiju* role would turn out to be Godzilla's greatest nemesis, King Ghidorah, which he played in 1998 in the third film of the *Rebirth of Mothra* trilogy. After the creative flop that was the American *Godzilla*, Toho reclaimed their beloved monster and relaunched the franchise on Japanese soil. Having proven himself as the three-headed dragon, Kitagawa was tapped to play the Big G himself.

With the exception of 2001's *Godzilla, Mothra and King Ghidorah: Giant Monsters All-Out Attack*, in which the creature was played by Mizuho Yoshida, Kitagawa remained Godzilla for the entire Millennium series. The suit had been totally revamped once again, and an entirely new approach was taken to the performance of the role. Inspired by the more naturalistic style of the CGI creations of *Jurassic Park*, this new Godzilla was more dinosaur-like, with a more horizontal stance that was very different from the traditionally upright position seen in Godzilla films up to that point. As a result, Kitagawa was more hunched over in his performance, making for the least humanoid Godzilla of them all. In some ways, this made his work some of the most challenging suit acting seen in the entire series.

During his run as Godzilla, Kitagawa also embarked on a second career as a motion-capture performer for videogames, including games in the *Dead or Alive* and *Dynasty Warriors* series. His last turn as Godzilla was in 2004's *Godzilla: Final Wars*, the film that would shut the door on Toho's franchise for the next dozen years. At age forty-six, he retired from suit acting, focusing on motion-capture work. In 2014, he made a cameo appearance out of costume in the thirty-eighth series of the ongoing *Super Sentai* franchise, in honor of his previous contributions.

9

When Godzilla Met Kong

How the Ultimate Monster Showdown Came to Be

Throughout the course of cinematic history, there have been several memorable clashes between characters from different film franchises. *Frankenstein Meets the Wolf Man. Alien vs. Predator. Freddy vs. Jason.* More recently, audiences watched the Dark Knight and the Man of Steel duke it out in *Batman v Superman: Dawn of Justice.* But no inter-franchise mash-up ever captured the imagination of millions quite like the time that the Eighth Wonder of the World and the King of the Monsters himself finally met and battled it out to the end. In what turned out to be the most popular *kaiju* picture of all time, this dream match of epic proportions unfolded as a result of one of the most fascinating development tales ever told. The finished product, *King Kong vs. Godzilla* (1962), has been seen by more people than any other Godzilla film ever made.

It was a fantasy pairing of the highest order: the two greatest and most memorable giant movie monsters of all time, in the same movie together despite each being owned by a separate production company. Such a thing was almost unthinkable at the time, and yet it came together after some byzantine behind-the-scenes wrangling. The 1962 monster mash-up has long been a dear favorite not only of fans of *kaiju eiga*, but of fans of science-fiction and fantasy films in general. The original 1954 *Gojira* may be undeniably the finest motion picture to come out of the *Showa* era, but a case can certainly be made that *King Kong vs. Godzilla* is the most beloved of all. It set the tone for the remainder of the *Showa* series, and some would even say, to a certain degree, it was more influential on the series as a whole than any other entry.

King Kong Meets Frankenstein?

It all began, suitably enough, in the mind of none other than Willis O'Brien, the special-effects genius responsible for creating the original stop-motion King Kong for Merian C. Cooper and Ernest B. Schoedsack's groundbreaking 1933 film from RKO Pictures. In the late 1950s, perhaps inspired by the astounding special-effects triumphs of his former protégé Ray Harryhausen and looking for something of a career renaissance, O'Brien began conceptualizing a potential project that would return his beloved creation Kong back into the spotlight. By 1960, O'Brien had worked up a full treatment for what was originally entitled *King Kong Meets Frankenstein*. His original idea was for Kong to square off not against the monster made famous by Boris Karloff for Universal Studios in the 1930s, but rather against a gigantic version of Frankenstein's monster put together with various animal parts. Needless to say, O'Brien intended to bring the whole affair to life using the famous stop-motion techniques he had perfected decades earlier.

Once he had a full treatment and some production sketches worked out, O'Brien went directly to his old friends at RKO Pictures, producers of the original *King Kong*, to pitch them on the idea. But there were many obstacles already rising up to impede the production. For one thing, the brass at RKO erroneously believed that Universal, producers of the classic *Frankenstein* films of the 1930s and '40s, owned the rights to the Frankenstein name (they only owned the rights to Jack Pierce's iconic makeup design; the character itself is in the public domain). To avoid any trouble, a new monster was envisioned to take the place of Mary Shelley's creation, and the project name was changed to *King Kong vs. the Ginko*. Even so, the glory days of RKO were long past, and the company was no longer a production studio, but simply a distribution house. Unable to back O'Brien, they put him in contact with John Beck, a small-time producer whose greatest claim to fame had been spearheading the whimsical James Stewart favorite *Harvey* (1950) for Universal.

Beck began to develop the concept into something he hoped to sell to a major studio. He brought in serial and science-fiction screenwriter George Worthing Yates, son of Republic Pictures founder Herbert Yates, to write the screenplay. The scripter of such fare as *It Came from Beneath the Sea* (1955), *Earth vs. the Flying Saucers* (1956), *The Amazing Colossal Man* (1957), and *Earth vs. the Spider* (1958), Yates transformed the treatment into something called *King Kong vs. Prometheus*, bringing it closer again to the original Frankenstein idea.

One of O'Brien's sketches for his proposed *King Kong Meets Frankenstein* movie.   *Author's collection*

Enter Toho

Also at this time, unbeknownst to O'Brien, Beck was maneuvering behind his back and gradually cutting him out of the process completely, taking his idea and running with it as his own. Without O'Brien's knowledge, Beck was shopping the script around to Hollywood studios, all of which turned it down due to the prohibitive expenses of stop-motion animation. Finally, Beck got a bite from Toho Company in Japan, a studio that had had great success making giant monster movies in recent years. The stop-motion issue would not present a problem, since Toho had long ago rejected the expensive technique in favor of using actors in costumes. Toho had long desired to make a King Kong movie, and now thanks to Beck's connections, they finally had the opportunity to obtain the rights to the character from RKO.

With the studio's thirtieth anniversary looming, it seemed like the perfect chance to do something special to commemorate the event. Rather than the Frankenstein monster, Toho decided to resurrect its own star monster, Godzilla, who hadn't been seen since 1955's *Godzilla Raids Again* (*Gojira no gyakushu*), and pit him against Kong in an ultimate international dream match of movie monster royalty. The project was renamed *King Kong vs. Godzilla* (*Kingu Kongu tai Gojira*); by this point it had been almost completely removed from the original concept of Willis O'Brien, who had had the project snatched right from under him and received no credit whatsoever for the finished product.

Toho's head of special effects, Eiji Tsuburaya, immediately shelved all other projects he had on tap in order to clear his schedule to work on what was a dream project for him. Tsuburaya had first been enraptured by the possibilities of movie effects after seeing *King Kong* as a young man back in 1933, so the giant gorilla was a Holy Grail of sorts for the master of Japanese monsters. Toho also recruited director Ishiro Honda, fresh off the science-fiction epic *Gorath* (*Yosei Gorasu*) (1962), to return to the Godzilla franchise for the first time since the original 1954 installment.

But this was destined to become a very different kind of Godzilla picture, and a very different type of *kaiju* film in general. In fact, it would set a new tone that would alter the course of Japanese *tokusatsu* for the remainder of the *Showa* era. After shelling out approximately $200,000 to RKO for the rights to their famous character, Toho took O'Brien, Yates, and Beck's already drastically altered concept and handed it over to their contracted screenwriter Shinichi Sekizawa, who had previously scripted such *tokusatsu* films as *Giant Monster Varan* (1958), *Battle in Outer Space* (*Uchu daisenso*) (1959), and *Mothra* (1961). This was Sekizawa's first crack at Godzilla, and to call his eventual script light in tone would be quite an understatement. Sekizawa's *King Kong vs. Godzilla* was to be an out-and-out comedy, toying with the *kaiju* tropes that had once struck such abject terror into the hearts of the Japanese. And although Honda was reportedly uncomfortable with the new direction, Sekizawa had an ally in Tsuburaya, who longed to tailor his films more directly to the children who were among their strongest supporters.

"The actual turning point [in the series] came in *King Kong vs. Godzilla*," says Steve Biodrowski, editor of *Cinefantastique Online*. "There's a scene in which one of the main characters is evacuating because Kong is coming to Tokyo, and she runs into one of her neighbors who has a little boy. Mom is trying to get the boy out to safety, and the boy keeps saying, 'Mom, I wanna see Godzilla!' Clearly this was a little nod to the audience, that we know this monster we created in the '50s that was supposed to be this scary harbinger of the atom bomb, is now this character that kids want to see, and they're not afraid of."

The Making of a Monster Mash-Up

Sekizawa's ingenious story line to combine the two monsters centered on the efforts of Pacific Pharmaceuticals, headed by the comically unscrupulous Mr. Tako (Ichiro Arishima), to obtain King Kong to be the company's mascot and public relations magnet. Tako dispatches employees Sakurai and Kinsaburo (played with great team chemistry by Tadao Takashima and Yu Fujiki, respectively) to the monster's island to wrangle him away from the wary natives. Meanwhile, as luck would have it, an American submarine accidentally frees Godzilla from the iceberg that had held him since the conclusion of *Godzilla Raids Again*. Kong is brought to Japan just in time to duke it out with the Big G, and when the Japanese military is unable to stop either of them, it's decided the best course of action is simply to pray that they will destroy each other.

The film features the first major appearance of series regular Kenji Sahara, as well as Akihiko Hirata (*Gojira*'s Dr. Serizawa) as the Prime Minister of Japan. Future Bond girl Mie Hama plays Sakurai's sister Fumiko, who becomes the object of Kong's fascination in what is clearly a tip of the hat to the original film's Ann Darrow, played by Fay Wray. The film balances homage to the original with new additions to the mythos, such as the red berries that have the power to put Kong to sleep, as well as the ape's ability to draw strength from electricity (a vestige from the film's original antagonist, the Frankenstein monster).

One element of O'Brien's *King Kong* that was jettisoned early on was the reliance on stop-motion effects. Although Tsuburaya had briefly contemplated mimicking O'Brien's methods, the lack of time and money once again necessitated the use of his tried-and-true suitmation technique. A brand-new suit was constructed for Godzilla veteran Haruo Nakajima, and Toho veteran supporting player (and *kaiju* newbie) Shoichi Hirose donned the King Kong costume. For many fans of monster films, the switch from stop-motion to man-in-suit is a major comedown, and Tsuburaya's Kong outfit is widely regarded as one of the special effect master's most lackluster efforts, despite his long-standing passion for the character. (Very telling is the fact that for its publicity materials, Toho opted to feature stills of O'Brien's 1933 creation and not the costume that actually appears in the film!) Nevertheless, Nakajima and Hirose tried their best to infuse the Godzilla/Kong dust-ups with a sense of fun, borrowing a great deal from the professional wrestling (*puroresu*) that was enormously popular in Japan at the time, particularly the styles of such mat superstars as Rikidozan and Toyonobori. With Tsuburaya's encouragement, they also incorporated more anthropomorphism than had ever been seen in giant monster films of any stripe up to that time.

Puppets and models were also employed by Tsuburaya's team to help bring the monsters to life. There was even a bit of stop-motion employed during an early scene in which Kong faces off against a giant octopus. In addition to the animated tentacles, real live octopi were also filmed for the sequence (Tsuburaya reportedly ate one of them for dinner following the shoot). Through it all, however, the one seemingly insurmountable conceit from the original *King Kong* that was utterly ignored was the fact that Kong had previously been established as approximately fifty feet in height, which would have placed him somewhere below Godzilla's knee. No explanation is given for why the Eighth Wonder of the World is now Godzilla's equal in size, and truth be told, any viewer who would require such an explanation in order to enjoy the film should clearly look to other movie genres for his or her pleasure.

Poster for the 1963 American release of *King Kong vs. Godzilla*.   *Movie Stills Database*

Eiji Tsuburaya coaches his two stars between takes.   *Movie Stills Database*

Kong Returns to America

One matter that has long been in dispute has been the ending of the film. In Honda's film, and Sekizawa's original script, King Kong, the more sympathetic monster of the story, as well as the more popular one at the time, emerges victorious in the end, swimming home while Godzilla is nowhere to be seen. A long-standing rumor that may have originated in the American fan magazine *Famous Monsters of Filmland* not long after the film was released has it that Kong only wins in the American cut of the film, and that Godzilla gets the duke in the original Japanese version. Although this urban myth has persisted for decades, it's just that, a myth, for there was no version of the story in which the big gorilla doesn't come out on top.

Nevertheless, there was indeed an American cut of the film put together shortly after its Japanese release on August 11, 1962, and it is this flawed, greatly altered edition that is the one most of the rest of the world outside of Japan is familiar with to this day. John Beck still retained the rights to produce an American version of the film for release in the United States, and lined up Universal-International, that purveyor of classic monster fare dating back nearly forty years, as his domestic distributor. Just as had occurred with the two previous Godzilla films, it was determined that changes would need to be made in order for the Japanese picture to play with American audiences.

Beck hired up-and-coming TV writers Paul Mason and Bruce Howard to tweak Sekizawa's screenplay, removing some of the satire of the Japanese media and corporate culture, and adding in completely new segments featuring an American spokesperson for the UN giving regular updates on the action. Tom Montgomery, future freelance director for such '60s TV fare as *Gilligan's Island* and *My Mother the Car*, was brought in to direct the scenes featuring stage actor Michael Keith as the spokesperson, as well as veteran TV actor Harry Holcombe as a paleontologist who laughably uses what appears to be a children's book about dinosaurs to help explain the monster phenomena. In addition to these changes, perhaps the most unfortunate of all was the removal of nearly all of Akira Ifukube's thrilling musical score (deemed "too Japanese") in favor of stock music from previous monster films including *Creature from the Black Lagoon* (1954) and *Frankenstein Meets the Wolf Man* (1943).

The American version of *King Kong vs. Godzilla* premiered in New York City on June 26, 1963, and went on to become a tremendous success (as of this writing, it remains the only Godzilla film that has never been released on home video in the U.S. in its original Japanese form). It received an A-picture release, which contributed to the film selling more tickets than any other Godzilla movie ever made. In Japan alone, it sold more than 12.5 million tickets, giving it the all-time attendance record for the entire Godzilla franchise. It also single-handedly injected new life into the King of the Monsters, bringing him out of a seven-year retirement; although there had been two previous *Showa* Godzilla films, the success of *King Kong vs. Godzilla* is really what kicked off the *Showa* era in earnest, as Toho, recognizing the box-office appeal of its original *kaiju*, would begin producing Godzilla movies on a regular basis from that point on.

The Legacy of KK vs. G

The movie would also set the tone for the remaining *Showa* pictures, giving audiences a widescreen, full-color Godzilla that was decidedly more fun and kitschy than the ultra-serious creature of horror that had first entered the public consciousness in 1954. It was a new type of *kaiju* film that would remain popular with audiences not only in theaters and drive-ins, but also on TV creature feature programs for decades to come, amping up the monster action and playing to the younger set (Godzilla's trademark battle cry was even permanently altered, going from a deep roar to more of a high-pitched whine).

As for Kong, he would make one more appearance in a Toho motion picture, namely 1967's *King Kong Escapes*, a co-production with American animation studio Rankin-Bass that was primarily based on the studio's successful Kong cartoon series and was in no way related to *King Kong vs. Godzilla* (and which also gave rise to Toho's first robotic *kaiju*, Mechani-Kong). As a final holdover of O'Brien's original concept, Toho would also eventually turn the Frankenstein monster into a *daikaiju*, featuring a new gigantic version of Mary Shelley's creation in *Frankenstein Conquers the World* (*Furankenshutain tai chitei kaiju Baragon*) (1965) and its sequel *War of the Gargantuas* (*Furankenshutain no kaiju: Sanda tai Gaira*) (1966).

There's a special place for *King Kong vs. Godzilla* in the hearts of monster movie fans everywhere. Of all the Godzilla films, it continues to enjoy a unique spot in the public's awareness. This has been most recently reaffirmed by the news that Legendary Pictures, the American production company responsible for the new American *Godzilla* (2014), plans to pit their own version of the giant lizard against a rebooted King Kong one more time in *Godzilla vs. Kong*, set for release in 2020. Nearly sixty years after they first collided, the two titans of the movie monster pantheon will once again have the opportunity to square off, to the delight of moviegoers worldwide.

Shinichi Sekizawa: Scripter of Monsters

Of all its many contributions to the development of the Godzilla franchise, perhaps *King Kong vs. Godzilla's* most valuable contribution was the introduction of the highly imaginative screenwriter Shinichi Sekizawa to the series. A perfect match for the more whimsical, even absurd turn the series was about to take, Sekizawa would go on to write eight of the remaining thirteen *Showa* pictures, making him almost as critical to the creative success of the Godzilla franchise in the 1960s and '70s as the likes of Ishiro Honda, Eiji Tsuburaya, and Akira Ifukube. The playful tone that helped make the Godzilla films of that era so beloved by generations of fans arose largely from the mind of this gifted writer.

He was born June 2, 1921, in Kyoto, Japan. His first love had been animation, and after high school he even studied it for a while, alongside Osamu Tezuka, the future "father of *manga*" most well-known for the *Astro-Boy* comic book series of the 1950s and '60s. Sekizawa even got his start in 1939 working on animated films. But as it did to many Japanese youth, World War II temporarily put Sekizawa's career on hold, as he was enlisted into the service of his country from 1941 through 1946.

Once he returned to Japan in his mid-twenties following the war, Sekizawa found work in occupied Japan with the small film outfit Beehive Productions, serving as an assistant director and screenwriter beginning with the film *Children of the Beehive* (*Hachi no su no kodomotachi*) (1948), the inspirational story of a group of war orphans who bond with a returning soldier. The following year, he would turn in his first script for Toho Company, for *Child of the Wind* (*Kaze no ko*). However, he wouldn't come to work steadily for Toho for some years, as he spent most of the next decade under contract to rival studio Shintoho.

While at Shintoho, Sekizawa penned his first *tokusatsu* script, for the science-fiction film *Fearful Attack of the Flying Saucer* (*Soratobu enban kyofu no shugeki*) (1956), now believed to be lost. This experience served him well for his eventual migration to Toho in 1958, where he would continue to work for the remainder of his screenwriting career. Although he would work on many different types of films for Toho, he would achieve his greatest renown working on *kaiju* and *tokusatsu* projects, and the studio would consistently put him to work on pictures of that nature, beginning with *Giant Monster Varan* (1958).

Over time, Sekizawa began to develop a lighter tone for the science-fiction projects he was given. He was often seen as the opposing counterpart of fellow Toho screenwriter Takeshi Kimura, known for his more serious-minded *tokusatsu* fare that was more in line with the original tone created by *Gojira* in 1954. But Sekizawa's interests lay along a different path. He wrote Toho's sweeping space opera *Battle in Outer Space* (1959) and the fantasy-tinged *Mothra* (1961), for which he also wrote the lyrics to the iconic song sung to the titular monster by her tiny fairy harbingers, the *shobijin*.

But that was all mere preparation for the most plum assignment of them all—the opportunity to direct the course of the prized Godzilla franchise starting with the enormously successful *King Kong vs. Godzilla* in 1962. Sekizawa's script for the monster throw-down fully embraced comedic elements that were soon to become staples of the series. He poked fun at the monsters, and parodied post-occupation Japanese culture as a whole. He would continue to do this in future installments of the series like *Mothra vs. Godzilla* (1964), with its cartoonish corporate villains; *Ghidorah, the Three-Headed Monster* (1964), and its almost human-like monster interactions; *Invasion of Astro-Monster* (1965), which combined *kaiju* and space opera; *Godzilla vs. the Sea Monster* (1966), with its secret society and giant shrimp; *Son of Godzilla* (1967), which gave us the infamous Minya; and *All Monsters Attack* (1969), the story of a daydreaming child's monster fantasies.

Sekizawa scripted many other films for Toho during the 1960s, including *Atragon* (1963), *Dogora* (1964), and *Latitude Zero* (1969). He even worked for Eiji Tsuburaya as the screenwriter for both pilots of Tsuburaya Productions' successful TV series *Ultraman* and *Mighty Jack*. In fact, the only Godzilla film of the 1960s that he didn't write was the 1968 *kaiju* summit *Destroy All Monsters*, which was given to Kimura.

Kimura also penned the script for the more politically and environmentally conscious *Godzilla vs. Hedorah* (1971), but that was by no means the end of Sekizawa's involvement with the King of the Monsters. He returned in 1972 with *Godzilla vs. Gigan*, in which he envisioned a giant cyborg chicken from space as the main foe, and also penned two original songs, "Godzilla March" and "Go, Go Godzilla!" (not to be confused with the later Blue Oyster Cult song). He would finish out his tenure on the franchise with the very kiddie-oriented *Godzilla vs. Megalon* (1973), for which he composed the lyrics to the fan-favorite song "Godzilla and Jet Jaguar," and finally *Godzilla vs. Mechagodzilla* (1974), the second-to-last film of the *Showa* era.

The task of writing the final *Showa* Godzilla film, *Terror of Mechagodzilla* (1975), would be given to young scripter Yukiko Takayama, a newcomer to the studio. *Godzilla vs. Mechagodzilla* would turn out to be Sekizawa's final screenplay, as he departed Toho at the age of fifty-three. He passed away in 1992 at seventy, leaving behind a memorable legacy of fun monster flicks that continue to be enjoyed by millions. His light sensibility and instinct for the ridiculousness inherent in the *kaiju* genre helped to make these movies the favorites they are today, and ensure that they never take themselves too seriously.

10

Franchise in Decline

The Late Showa Era

By the end of the 1960s, the Japanese film industry—and, for that matter, the entire nation of Japan—was in a very different place than where it had been at the beginning of the decade. The economic boom that had followed the American occupation was dying down, and an increasing industrialization was changing the face of traditional Japan. An oil crisis was looming in the near future, promising an even keener financial crunch.

Add to this the fact that television had supplanted the cinema as the primary form of entertainment for the Japanese people, and it's understandable that the fortunes of Toho Company and the other major Japanese movie studios were no longer what they once were. The masses of people who once flocked to every Godzilla film were shrinking, and those who did come were composed predominantly of small children. *Tokusatsu* cinema had always appealed to the young, but it seemed the audience had been growing steadily younger over the years, to the point that Godzilla movies had become a destination for parents to drop off their little kids while they went about their daily errands: Godzilla as babysitter, if you will.

As a result, the films of the later *Showa* era became even more juvenilized. In fact, many of the Godzilla films of the late 1960s and 1970s did not even receive a full, stand-alone theatrical release, but rather were included as part of theatrical packages known as Champion Festivals. An idea adapted from rival studio Toei's Manga Festival, the Champion Festivals were designed to maximize the appeal to children, combining feature films and the newly emerging phenomenon of Japanese animation, later known as *anime*, to create an all-day entertainment event for kids. Older *kaiju* films were even included in these twice- or thrice-a-year event releases, often edited down to fit the format. And all-new Godzilla films made between 1969 and 1975 were initially released in this way. The Champion Festivals did help sustain the popularity of Godzilla for a time, although they also had the consequence of helping to establish *anime* as the new premiere entertainment genre for the youth of Japan.

"Especially when we get to the late '60s and '70s, Japanese filmmakers were going for funny," says Dr. Bill Tsutsui, author of *Godzilla on My Mind.* "They knew who their audience was; their audience was kids. They were trying to amuse them. To say that all of them had some deep level of seriousness, even if they did have some elements of seriousness, would be going a little too far."

The so-called golden age of Japanese cinema was over, and the depressed economy meant that along with the smaller audiences, smaller budgets were also in place, meaning that the grand production design and ambitious special effects of Eiji Tsuburaya's earlier efforts for Toho could no longer be attempted, resulting in cheaper, more slapdash films that frustrate many devoted fans. However, there are also many who find a lot to love in the later *Showa* films, which fit so well into the kitschy, grainy landscape of 1970s grindhouse cinema.

All Monsters Attack

Japanese Title: *Gojira-Minira-Gabara: Oru kaijû daishingeki*
Literal Translation: *Godzilla, Minya, Gabara: All Monsters Attack*
Also Known As: *Godzilla's Revenge* (U.S. title)
Release Date: December 20, 1969

Originally, 1968's *kaiju* extravaganza *Destroy All Monsters* was envisioned as Godzilla's swan song—but the studio's greatest cash cow proved too attractive, especially in a time of diminished box office and struggling economy. Godzilla's popularity was not what it once was, but the decision was nevertheless made to go back to the well. The result was a film that is generally the most reviled of the *Showa* series, if not the entire Godzilla *oeuvre*. Yet even *All Monsters Attack* (later known in the U.S. as *Godzilla's Revenge*), an offbeat and often puzzling entry to be sure, contains more merit than its detractors are willing to give it credit for.

Ishiro Honda, the venerated director of the grim, original *Gojira* and so many other films in the franchise, returned one more time despite his increasing reservations regarding the more frivolous approach to the character. And it is indeed Shinichi Sekizawa's most kid-oriented script thus far, focusing on young Ichiro (Tomonori Yazaki), a little boy with working parents who fantasizes about hanging out with Godzilla's son Minya and

A decidedly odd-looking Godzilla presides over the Japanese lobby poster for *All Monsters Attack*.
Everett Collection

the other creatures on Monster Island, all while coping with real-life bully Gabara, as well as fending off a pair of bumbling bank robbers (Sachio Sakai and Kazuo Suzuki). Ichiro's difficulties with Gabara are mirrored by Minya's own bullying at the hands of a bizarre, almost feline *kaiju*, also named Gabara. The Monster Island scenes are presented as the daydreams of the imaginative Ichiro, stimulated by his contact with friendly toymaker Shinpei Inami (played by beloved character actor Hideyo Amamoto), and thus Godzilla and friends are no more than fictional constructs, just as they are in our world. This device makes *All Monsters Attack* truly unique amongst all Godzilla films.

Many have speculated that this film was inspired by the success of a new *kaiju* franchise at a competing studio: Daiei Film's Gamera series. Beginning in 1965 with *Gamera*, the exploits of the giant, flying, fire-breathing turtle had been gaining traction, and stood as the most successful attempt by another company to rival the prominence of Toho's Godzilla. And as the series continued in the late 1960s, it was quickly juvenilized to appeal more directly to children, emphasizing Gamera's outlandish battles with other monsters and spotlighting his special relationship with kids. Sequels such as *Gamera vs. Barugon* (1966), *Gamera vs. Gyaos* (1967), *Gamera vs. Viras* (1968), and *Gamera vs. Guiron* (1969) firmly established Gamera as a beloved good guy rather than a fearsome destroyer.

This influence is on full display in *All Monsters Attack*, as this is the first Godzilla film in which the creature is portrayed in an almost totally benevolent, child-friendly light. It can also be seen in Ichiro's bond with Godzilla, and especially with Minya, who in this film can shrink down to human size and actually speak. The fanciful feel of the movie is further emphasized by the childlike score composed by Kunio Miyauchi, composer for the very kid-friendly *Ultraman* TV series and a far cry from the brooding *sturm und drang* of Akira Ifukube. Still, despite the overall silliness of the picture, Honda manages to instill a certain amount of gravitas and purpose to the proceedings, highlighting the growing industrialization of Japan that was happening at the time and focusing on the new phenomenon of latchkey kids with two working parents, and the problems they must face. Through his relationship with his fantasy monsters, Ichiro learns to stand up for himself and be independent.

One of the reasons the film was a struggle to make and resulted in an uneven product was the serious illness of Eiji Tsuburaya at the time. Although he received credit for the movie's special effects out of respect, Tsuburaya was unable to work on the film at all, and effects duties were instead handled by Tsuburaya's assistant Teruyoshi Nakano, art director Akira Watanabe, and even director Honda himself, who stepped in during his old friend's time of need. Unfortunately, the compromised state of the visual effects department also necessitated the extensive use of stock footage from previous movies (another trick lifted from the Gamera franchise); and at a running time of less than seventy minutes, that means there's surprisingly little new monster footage.

Like previous Toho efforts such as *Invasion of Astro-Monster* (1965) and *War of the Gargantuas* (1966), *All Monsters Attack* was a co-production of Henry G. Saperstein's United Productions of America (UPA), and was finally brought to the States in 1971 by affiliated UPA distributor Maron Films under the perhaps misleading title *Godzilla's Revenge*. The blaring, abrasive (to Western ears) opening music was removed, and some unfortunate dubbing choices were made, with Ichiro voiced by what seems to be a young woman (as was common practice at the time) and Minya sounding something like Don Knotts. The result is a picture even more puzzling and annoying to some than the Japanese original.

Despite Toho's attempt to ape the success Daiei was having with Gamera, *All Monsters Attack* was not the rejuvenating hit the studio was hoping for. In fact, it was the first Godzilla picture to sell less than 2 million tickets—a dramatic decline from the more than 12.5 million tickets sold for *King Kong vs. Godzilla* merely seven years prior. There is no question the franchise was experiencing a lull both financially and creatively, becoming a follower in a subgenre in which it once had been the innovator. Some further retooling and reinvention was required, and for the first time in five years, the continual production of the series was put on a brief hiatus.

Godzilla vs. Hedorah

Japanese Title: *Gojira tai Hedora*
Also Known As: *Godzilla vs. the Smog Monster* (U.S. title)
Release Date: July 24, 1971

But for those who find even the bizarre *All Monsters Attack* a little too orthodox for their liking, there is always the single strangest and most surreal entry in the entire Godzilla canon, *Godzilla vs. Hedorah*. After taking all of 1970 off to regroup and to rethink the future of the franchise, it was determined not to put it in mothballs, but rather to inject some new blood and take things in a radically different direction. The result is a film that is a sentimental darling for many who grew up with it, but which leaves many others scratching their heads in utter puzzlement.

Moving away from the era of Ishiro Honda, producer Tomoyuki Tanaka was looking for someone with fresh ideas to take the helm, and he found him in forty-year-old Yoshimitsu Banno, who had worked his way up as an assistant director to Akira Kurosawa on such classics as *Throne of Blood* (*Kumonosu-jo*) (1957), *The Lower Depths* (*Donzoko*) (1957), *The Hidden Fortress* (*Kakushi toride no san akunin*) (1958), and *The Bad Sleep Well* (*Warui yatsu hodo yoku nemuru*) (1960), and most recently had turned heads as the director of *Birth of the Japanese Islands* (1970), which had been the talk of the 1970 Japan Expo.

Banno had radical ideas about what to do with the Godzilla series, and was given free rein to realize his vision. Seeking to move on from the antinuclear message that had been the monster's bread and butter since 1954, Banno took aim at the growing Japanese problem of environmental pollution, and together with Takeshi Kimura, crafted a tale in which the Big G tackles the threat of Hedorah, a hideous pile of sentient black goop formed from the accumulation of pollutants in Tokyo Bay and its surrounding waters. At long last, Godzilla had by this point completed the transition to superhero—no longer the fearsome death-dealer of years gone by, but now the benevolent defender of the planet and friend to children everywhere—specifically young Ken Yano as played by Hiroyuki Kawase in the first of two 1970s kid sidekick roles in the series.

To say the film is a drastic departure from what came before would be quite an understatement. Decidedly the product of the era of psychedelia, *Godzilla vs. Hedorah* features a funky score by Riichiro Manabe that is even more of a departure from the work of Akira Ifukube than was Kunio Miyauchi's score for *All Monsters Attack*, and which includes the cult favorite song "Return! The Sun," translated in the English-language version of the film as "Save the Earth!" It's punctuated by odd animated segments—a first for the Godzilla series—and even boasts an infamous scene in which Godzilla uses his atomic breath to propel himself through the air, as if flying backwards! Even the fight sequences—featuring Kenpachiro Satsuma, the future Godzilla of the *Heisei* series, in costume as Hedorah—are choreographed in a highly unorthodox manner, and shot in darkness for an eerie effect. With Eiji Tsuburaya gone, the duties of visual effects director now fell to Teruyoshi Nakano, who assumed the role for the remainder of the *Showa* series.

The artist for this Italian *Godzilla vs. Hedorah* poster seems to have never seen Godzilla before.

Toho Scope/Flickr

"It is just so wonderfully ludicrous," opines Dr. Bill Tsutsui. "They tried hard to make Godzilla timely and interact with the political debates of the day, such as pollution, and it's still a rollicking good time."

But in the end, Toho was most displeased with its wunderkind director and the direction in which he had taken its waning studio star. Tanaka was reportedly furious at the quirky, kooky, and very trippy *Godzilla vs. Hedorah*, and promptly removed Banno from directorial duties at Toho (his career at the studio was essentially over). The film was brought to the United States in February 1972 by American International Pictures (AIP), which had previously distributed *Mothra vs. Godzilla* (1964) and *Destroy All Monsters* (1968); and as *Godzilla vs. the Smog Monster*, it found a cult following with drive-in and grindhouse audiences thanks to its groovy, counterculture vibe.

Banno was just a little too far out for the conservative tastes at Toho, and when he reportedly continued to pitch ideas for Godzilla to the studio for later films, he was repeatedly turned down (although he'd get his vindication some forty years later when he helped spearhead Legendary Pictures' American *Godzilla*). His interpretation of Godzilla as a protector of the environment was a bold one, and resulted in the most unusual Godzilla film of them all. But in the end, the studio opted to stick with a more traditional approach to the aging franchise.

Godzilla vs. Gigan

Japanese Title: *Chikyû kogeki meirei: Gojira tai Gaigan*
Literal Translation: *Earth Assault Order: Godzilla vs. Gigan*
Also Known As: *Godzilla on Monster Island* (U.S. title)
Release Date: March 12, 1972

Reeling from what the studio considered a major misfire in *Godzilla vs. Hedorah*, Toho quickly rushed to secure the franchise with a more traditional return to form—in structure at least, if not in execution. With a full-on economic depression looming, Toho was cutting corners everywhere possible, and unfortunately, it really shows in *Godzilla vs. Gigan*. The heyday of the Honda-Tsuburaya team-ups of the 1960s was most decidedly over, and nowhere was it more evident than in this film, which despite Toho's valiant effort to rebuild, is a pale imitation of the grandeur of the early *Showa* period.

Following the departure of Yoshimitsu Banno, Toho lured back director Jun Fukuda, who hadn't helmed a Godzilla picture since 1967's *Son of*

Godzilla. Known for his fun, energetic approach, Fukuda was on a mission to make the new picture a great spectacle that would return the Big G to full form. Along for the ride as well was composer Akira Ifukube, the brilliant mind that had produced the score for the original *Gojira* and many other film in the series, but who himself had been absent from it since 1968's *Destroy All Monsters*. However, this time, Ifukube's cues for the new film were all stock pieces culled from previous installments (again, to save time and money); nevertheless, even in recycled form, his work is among the film's highlights for sure.

After the drastic experimentalism of *All Monsters Attack* and *Godzilla vs. Hedorah*, *Godzilla vs. Gigan*'s story line (a rare collaboration between Toho stable-mates Shinichi Sekizawa and Takeshi Kimura) hearkens back to the alien invasion plots of the 1960s, with a race of insectoid invaders (conveniently masquerading in human form) planning to conquer the Earth from their hidden base inside a Godzilla theme park, of all things, complete with a life-sized Godzilla statue that turns out to be a laser-firing weapon. However, unlike the elaborate costume and production design evident in the films overseen by Tsuburaya and Akira Watanabe in years past, the work on *Godzilla vs. Gigan* is decidedly low budget, often using ordinary wardrobe and plain settings, which would become a trend of 1970s Godzilla films.

The human characters of the film are among the series' most unusual, comprising disgruntled comic book illustrator Gengo Kotaka (Hiroshi Ishikawa), his banana-eating hippie sidekick Shosaku Takasugi (Minoru Takashima), and beautiful karate black belt Tomoko Tomoe (Yuriko Hishimi). When the trio uncovers the aliens' plot, Godzilla (portrayed for the final time by Haruo Nakajima) and his armadillo-like former enemy-turned-pal Anguirus (not seen since *Destroy All Monsters*) are called into action to save the day. To oppose them, the aliens call in another classic Toho *kaiju*, none other than the three-headed King Ghidorah. Joining forces with Ghidorah is a brand-new monster created for the film, and another of the film's creative triumphs: Gigan, the bird-like cyborg with a buzzsaw in his torso and massive hooks for hands—portrayed, just as Hedorah was, by future Godzilla actor Kenpachiro Satsuma.

Fukuda and his visual effects director Teruyoshi Nakano pulled out all the stops in creating some truly intense battle sequences for the film, filled with huge explosions. The fights are surprisingly violent, with Godzilla even being shown to bleed for the first time—something that would have been unheard of during the days of Tsuburaya and his very kid-friendly approach. But seemingly to counterbalance the heaviness of the violence, the film isn't without healthy doses of *Showa* silliness—including the decision to make Godzilla and Anguirus "speak" to each other! Although this monster "language" is made up merely of sound effects in the original version, the American cut of the film features the creatures speaking in English (albeit nearly unintelligible due to heavy sound distortion).

That American cut was picked up by a relatively new TV and movie distributor called Cinema Shares, a low-rent company known for grindhouse and exploitation fare that would work closely with Toho during the 1970s. Renamed *Godzilla on Monster Island* (inexplicably so, since very little of the movie actually takes place there), it was brought to the U.S. nearly five years later, in August 1977. This was mere months after the U.S. release of the original *Star Wars*, as Toho now found itself having to compete in a drastically different American genre film landscape. The stakes had been vastly raised, and the financially crippled studio was failing to keep up.

Even in Japan, *Godzilla vs. Gigan* was decidedly a B-picture, stuck in the Champion Festival ghetto unlike the much more high-profile entries of the previous two decades. Tanaka and Fukuda had tried valiantly to return Godzilla to greatness, but aside from the introduction of the popular foe Gigan, they had failed, hamstrung by an ever-dwindling budget. Sadly, this trend was not only to continue, but to worsen.

Godzilla vs. Megalon

Japanese Title: *Gojira tai Megaro*
Release Date: March 17, 1973

It's often difficult to pinpoint where the exact nadir of the *Showa* era truly was. The Godzilla films of the 1970s definitely have their fans, and even the more roundly criticized have their earnest defenders. However, it may be safe to say that the film with the smallest number of defenders would be *Godzilla vs. Megalon*. Although lovers of *tokusatsu* cinema, the author included, are usually loath to use the term "cheesy," if any film ever fit that description, it just might be this one, the product of a Japanese film industry in free fall.

The year 1973 was a financially devastating one for Japan, with a crushing oil crisis that tanked the economy, ensuring that fewer and fewer consumers were prepared to shell out their closely guarded cash for frivolous entertainment. Television had fully replaced the movies, thanks in no small part to its programs being free of charge, and *anime* (known in America at the time as "Japanimation") had become the subgenre of choice for the country's young people. Forced to get rid of whatever ballast it could to stay afloat, Toho dismissed every single one of its contracted actors, effectively ending the old-school studio system as most of its American counterparts had done a decade earlier. As a result, *Godzilla vs. Megalon* was the lowest of the low-budget *Showa* efforts.

Looking to the success of *tokusatsu* TV shows, and especially such super-hero/mecha fare as Tsuburaya Productions' *Ultraman*, Toho brought back Fukuda to direct his lightest, most juvenile project yet. When the Earth is threatened by the Atlantis-like lost kingdom of Seatopia and its giant insect guardian Megalon, Godzilla is once again called into service by a limitlessly spunky little boy (Hiroyuki Kawase, for a second time). In the ultimate *Ultraman* nod, the boy's father happens to be the inventor of the colorful robot Jet Jaguar, who joins forces with Godzilla after inexplicably growing to equal his size. The duo squares off against both Megalon and the returning Gigan, called in to even the sides.

More than ever, the battles are informed by the pro wrestling craze in Japan at the time, with Godzilla and Jet Jaguar taking the place of such popular in-ring tandems as Antonio Inoki and Giant Baba, complete with double-team maneuvers, and Godzilla even pulling off the world's longest sustained mid-air dropkick, not once, but twice. Unfortunately, one of those many contracted actors let go had been Godzilla suit-performer Haruo Nakajima, and the change is plain in the very different physical performance of the monster. Never before has the Big G been so anthro-pomorphized, striking battle poses and even shaking hands with his metallic partner. Even his facial design—which some have compared to a cute puppy—adds to the cartoonish bent of the proceedings. It's all part of Toho's all-out attempt to lure in as much of the child audience as it possibly could.

But the film failed to connect with a large audience, and the dire state of Toho can be clearly seen in its shoestring budget. The elaborate miniature city sets of the past were replaced by sparsely detailed pastoral scenes, with the exception of one impressive sequence in which Megalon destroys a dam. Megalon itself was far and away the least impressive of Nakano's creations, and indeed of the entire *kaiju* menagerie, appearing to have been slapped together in short order. And while Jet Jaguar was obviously introduced with the hopes of launching a new robotic superhero franchise of sorts (he even gets his own memorable theme song by screenwriter Shinichi Sekizawa and

GIANT AGAINST GIANT... the ultimate battle!

The very misleading poster for the 1976 American release of *Godzilla vs. Megalon*.

Everett Collection

score composer Riichiro Manabe), the lackluster box office of *Godzilla vs. Megalon* assured that it would be his only appearance.

Despite its creative shortcomings, *Godzilla vs. Megalon* wound up as arguably the most high-profile 1970s Godzilla film for American audiences. Just as it had with *Godzilla vs. Gigan*, Cinema Shares handled the U.S. distribution, and *Godzilla vs. Megalon* was released in America in April 1976, ironically over a year prior to the previously produced Godzilla movie. At the time, America was swept up in a new wave of King Kong-mania thanks to the Dino De Laurentiis–produced remake of the original RKO monster classic. Cinema Shares attempted to harness the monster madness to help its new release, even producing a hilariously misleading poster depicting Godzilla and Megalon fighting atop the World Trade Center, which also featured prominently in the new *King Kong.* Additionally, the film enjoyed a television premiere the following year on NBC that was hosted by *Saturday Night Live* superstar John Belushi in a Godzilla costume. In 1991, the film was even lampooned as part of *Mystery Science Theater 3000*, further highlighting the kitschy American fascination with the picture.

Godzilla vs. Mechagodzilla

Japanese Title: *Gojira tai Mekagojira*
Also Known As: *Godzilla vs. the Cosmic Monster* (U.S. title)
Release Date: March 21, 1974

After the last few entries in the series, it can be argued that there was really nowhere to go for Godzilla but up—and with *Godzilla vs. Mechagodzilla*, Toho managed to do just that. The final two films of the *Showa* series do represent something of a creative return to form, even if it wasn't enough to sustain the franchise in the long term. They also delivered the most memorable and enduring new *kaiju* of the decade, namely the titular mechanized version of the Big G, who, along with Mothra, Rodan, and King Ghidorah, has appeared in all three major eras of the franchise.

For once, the grindhouse aesthetic that permeated Toho's 1970s output seems to really click, as Fukuda's final Godzilla effort is a fun monster blowout that works well within the much smaller financial boundaries. For the first time since *Son of Godzilla* (1967), Masaru Sato returned to provide an exotic, jazz-inflected score reminiscent of his earlier 1960s work. Nakano's team constructs a unique new mammalian *kaiju*, King Caesar, to be Godzilla's latest tag-team partner (he too gets his own song, a Sato-composed ditty reminiscent of the much more well-known "Mothra Song").

But the *coup de grace* is most certainly Mechagodzilla, who starts out as an exact duplicate of Godzilla constructed by an invading race of aliens who turn out to be simian in nature—surely a nod to the very popular *Planet of the Apes* franchise then in full swing. When the aliens trick the world into thinking Godzilla has turned against them, it takes the real McCoy to show up and let everyone know what's what. During the fray, MechaG's "skin" is burned off to reveal the finest work of Nakano and his visual effects team, a simulated chrome exoskeleton bristling with high-tech weaponry.

Godzilla vs. Mechagodzilla was the third and final film in the series to be distributed in the States by Cinema Shares, who brought it over in March 1977 (also prior to 1972's *Godzilla vs. Gigan*, which might have been confusing to American audiences if there had been any chronological continuity to the films by this point, which there wasn't). Attempting to capitalize on the popularity of another American property, *The Six-Million-Dollar Man/Bionic Woman*, Cinema Shares and Toho sought to rename the picture *Godzilla vs. the Bionic Monster*. But when Universal (which owned that particular franchise) balked, the name was altered to *Godzilla vs. the Cosmic Monster*.

Containing interesting new creatures, colorful action, and even a musical interlude, *Godzilla vs. Mechagodzilla*, though maybe not the franchise turnaround Toho was hoping for, is perhaps the most popular Godzilla film of the 1970s. It certainly helped sustain the franchise just a little longer as the *Showa* era headed toward its inevitable conclusion.

Terror of Mechagodzilla

Japanese Title: *Mekagojira no gyakushu*
Literal Translation: *Mechagodzilla's Counterattack*
Release Date: March 15, 1975

There can be no doubt that by the middle of the 1970s, the Godzilla franchise was on its very last legs. Just as he had done in 1968 with *Destroy All Monsters*, producer Tomoyuki Tanaka was once again considering putting the big guy out to pasture, or at least on a long-term sabbatical. It was decided that one more entry would be produced, and the outcome would help determine whether it was time to draw the curtain on what would eventually be termed the *Showa* era of Godzilla. People just weren't coming out to see Godzilla movies anymore. Nevertheless, the studio had experienced a modest upturn with *Godzilla vs. Mechagodzilla*, and so Tanaka decided that the new film would be a continuation—the first time any substantial inter-film continuity had been attempted in close to a decade.

And yet *Terror of Mechagodzilla*, while a sequel, could not be more tonally different from its predecessor. A much darker film, it could only have been the product of the legendary Ishiro Honda, who was coaxed out of semi-retirement by Tanaka to return one final time and give his co-creation the send-off he deserved. Always a more serious-minded filmmaker than Fukuda, Honda infused his sequel with a grim sense of foreboding, accompanied by his longtime collaborator Akira Ifukube, whose work on the picture is some of the most memorable and dramatic of his entire career.

Also making his final series appearance is Akihiko Hirata, the original *Gojira*'s Dr. Serizawa, who here appears as Dr. Shinzo Mafune, a more stereotypical mad movie scientist in the script by newcomer Yukiko Takayama. Mafune is the discoverer of the latest new *kaiju* of the series, the fearsome Titanosaurus, a once-dormant dinosaur that the aliens from the previous film seek to use, with Mafune's help, as a partner-in-crime for the rebuilt Mechagodzilla in a two-pronged bid to destroy Godzilla and take over the world. Sandwiched among the monster action is one of Honda's typical romantic subplots, involving biologist Akira Ichinose (Katsuhiko Sasaki) and Mafune's android "daughter" Katsura (Tomoko Ai), which ends in Katsura's ultimate self-sacrifice—also very much in Honda fashion.

"Usually in Honda's films when we have the averted tragedy and the monster stopped, it's not a moment of triumph," explains Godzilla aficionado Miguel Rodriguez. "It's a moment of reflection and it's a little somber. If you just look at the difference between Fukuda's *Godzilla vs. Mechagodzilla* and Honda's *Terror of Mechagodzilla*, which is a direct sequel, the tonal differences between those films are pretty profound."

For what it's worth, *Terror of Mechagodzilla* is an example of Toho really making a solid effort to put a fitting cap on the Godzilla franchise. The miniature work is excellent, as is the fight choreography. Honda's more sober take makes for an interesting film, even if his attitudes and tropes were becoming a bit quaint and maybe even trite to the younger Japanese audience at the time. Nevertheless, despite the creative success, *Terror of Mechagodzilla* was a bust at the box office, reinforcing even more to Toho executives that they were making the right decision in finally pulling the plug on Godzilla.

"*Terror of Mechagodzilla* is a curious film in a lot of ways, because it's very much a Honda film," says Peter H. Brothers. "It's very sentimental, it touches

on a lot of things that audiences by the time of the '70s weren't very interested in. To some extent, Honda was losing his audience. They had moved
on to more gritty stuff. He just wasn't into making those kind of movies; he
was really incapable of doing that."

Meanwhile, back in the States, the film had one of the most convoluted
distribution journeys since the original *Gojira*. Longtime Toho associate Henry Saperstein had co-funded the picture and sold the American
theatrical rights to fly-by-night company Bob Conn Enterprises, which
heavily edited down the film, removing five minutes of footage to achieve
a G-rating from the MPAA. The resulting film, which was a narrative mess
thanks to all the cuts, was released in March 1978 as *The Terror of Godzilla*.
To make matters more muddied, Saperstein himself then took the original
cut of the film, redubbed it in English, and added an extended prologue
using footage from previous films. His version premiered on television in
the fall of 1978. For decades, only the butchered Conn edition was available
on home video, until the 2007 Classic Media DVD release restored both the
extended Saperstein version and the original Japanese cut, made available
in the U.S. for the first time.

Despite the enjoyment provided by the lower-budgeted Godzilla films
of the 1970s, there are many fans who believe that Toho should have called
it quits on the *Showa* series of Godzilla films a lot sooner than it did. As it
was, Godzilla was the only one of the many franchises Toho had popularized in the 1950s and '60s that was still going during those tough economic
times. But for even Toho's King of the Monsters, the time came to stomp off
into the sunset, at least for a while. The glory days of *daikaiju* and *tokusatsu*
cinema were long past, as was the boom period of Japanese cinema in
general. The interests of the public had moved on, and the world of special-
effects movies was on the verge of seismic change. And so, after a twenty-
year run, Godzilla was allowed to slumber, biding his time until he would
once again be reborn.

Dubbing and Drive-Ins

Godzilla as Baby Boomer Cheese

For an entire generation (or two) of American fans who grew up with Godzilla during the latter decades of the twentieth century, the character will always be associated with a certain type of poorly dubbed and, some might even say, hopelessly yet gloriously cornball entertainment. Thanks to American distribution companies such as UPA, AIP, and others, many of the *Showa* Godzilla films made their way first to American grindhouse and drive-in theaters, then Sunday afternoon syndicated television, and later still to basic cable bastions eager for cheap product. Although altered from its original Japanese form, this iteration of the Godzilla cycle is cherished by American fans to this day.

An important clarification: There can be no doubt, as this book hopefully attests, that the Godzilla films, and indeed all of Toho's *tokusatsu* output, were the products of vibrant, creative minds, and represent a subgenre of cinema that is rarely given its due as worthy of study and appreciation. Nevertheless, a book of this kind would also be remiss were it not to delve into a fully realistic appraisal of the general attitudes toward movies of this kind, particularly during the era in which they were being released. For while these motion pictures were quite successful and high profile in Japan, and particularly during the earlier years of the "*kaiju* boom" boasted what was at the time the state of the art in special effects, the fact remains that these films were simply never all that well regarded in the United States.

This was especially true during the 1950s through the 1990s, and to a lesser degree this bias has even persisted into the twenty-first century, though films like Guillermo del Toro's *Pacific Rim* (2013) and Gareth Edwards's *Godzilla* (2014) have helped "legitimize" the reputation of giant monster flicks with mainstream American audiences, much the same way George Lucas's *Star Wars* films did for sci-fi flicks and the current glut of comic book movies has done for the long-maligned superhero subgenre. Nevertheless, *kaiju* films have long enjoyed cult status in the United States, alongside such cinematic canons as the Italian zombie cycle, kung fu action movies, Hammer horror, and spaghetti westerns—many of which are hailed for their high quality by those who adore them despite being viewed askance by mainstream American filmgoers, especially in their own time.

Although part of that prevailing attitude may have been due to differing filmmaking techniques and such, it must also be stated that much of it may also be chalked up to casually racist and xenophobic views of the time. The first Godzilla film came to American shores a mere decade after the conclusion of World War II, a war in which Japan was not only the enemy, but which it had initiated by a direct attack on American soil. Needless to say, for many Americans, the wound was still raw. Many were predisposed to hold any Japanese exports in low regard, and this attitude was not at all helped by Japan's postwar reputation for producing shoddy, cheaply made goods—a reputation that endured into the 1980s. It wasn't much of a stretch for many Americans to assume that this reputation covered cinematic exports, as well. Quite frankly, anti-Asian stereotypes often sought to dismiss entire nations of people as outlandish laughingstocks worthy only of Caucasian ridicule, and this attitude certainly played a part in the default view of Japanese cinema in America.

Putting Words in Their Mouths

One major aspect of Godzilla films in America that the original Japanese did not share, and that will forever be linked to Japanese cinema in the minds of American audiences, was the practice of dubbing—replacing the original Japanese voices of the actors in the films with those of English-speaking voice-over actors. This was typically done via a postproduction studio recording process, in which new English dialogue was written—sometimes a direct translation of the Japanese, and sometimes a more "creative" reinterpretation—and matched up as well as possible with the mouth movements of the actors on the screen. As clumsy as it may have been, dubbing at least helped Godzilla movies to achieve notoriety in America at a time when it might have otherwise been impossible.

Needless to say, the process was usually far from perfect. Although there was some fine dubbing work done, much of it was also poorly synced, awkwardly written, and more awkwardly performed, which only did more to tarnish, or at least trivialize, the reputation of much of *tokusatsu* cinema in the States. An American practice that gained popularity in the early 1950s, not just for Japanese films but for any foreign-language films that got an

American theatrical release, dubbing certainly wasn't all that unusual to American audiences by the time of Godzilla's heyday. But whereas in most other countries when movies were dubbed into the native language, they didn't suffer from an expectation of perfection from audiences, who understood that the actors on screen were not actually speaking the dialogue they were hearing, for some peculiar reason, American audiences seemed to demand that dialogue and sound be flawlessly synced with the mouth movements they saw on screen; an expectation that was as unrealistic as it was unattainable.

Very often, dubbed dialogue would actually make the plot *more* difficult to understand, and the dramatic efforts of the original actors were reduced to laughable caricatures. Voice-over actors were sometimes even asked to put on a heavy accent deemed to be an appropriately "Japanese-sounding" voice to American ears. The thinking behind the practice was equally troubling, as American distributors lacked confidence that American audiences (read: white audiences) would have the desire to listen to Japanese dialogue while reading subtitles. And so, any time a foreign-language film deemed to have potential American appeal made it into the hands of an American distributor, the dialogue was routinely removed and dubbed over in English to increase the box-office appeal. And although dubbing is rarely done these days, it has been replaced with the even more elaborate practice of taking successful foreign-language films and completely remaking them with English-speaking, American actors. The reader may decide which practice is the more close-minded.

Among the most relied-upon recording companies responsible for the dubbing heard in Godzilla movies was the Titra Sound Corp., a 1960s New York–based facility used by many low-rent distributors of foreign films such as AIP and the Walter Reade Organization. Titra was known for being a highly professional outfit, and their clients included big-budget, major studio releases as well as B-pictures. Its Broadway facilities boasted skilled writers and directors, as well as many voice-over actors recruited from the New York theater world. Writers typically adapted the scripts directly from the original film dialogue, as opposed to using translated scripts provided by Toho, which often lacked a certain "American-ness" that was deemed necessary. Short loops of film would then be screened in the studio, as actors would do their best to match up their recorded dialogue with what they were seeing projected before them. Anywhere from fifty to seventy-five loops could be recorded during a given session, with little to no time to rehearse.

Other studios responsible for dubbing Godzilla films in America included Ryder Sound and Glen Glenn Sound, both Hollywood-based. Due to their location, these studios often used film and television actors looking for extra work, or those who regularly made a living in the movie and TV voice-over industry, then experiencing its golden age.

And then there was Frontier Enterprises, a company based in Tokyo that was utilized by Toho and other Japanese studios to create English-dubbed versions of their films prior to their American distribution. Unfortunately, this native-based process often resulted in the most slipshod and inconsistent dubs. These versions would be made available to U.S. distributors, some of whom would make use of them, while others would opt to create their own dubs. For this reason, several Godzilla films, including *Godzilla vs. the Sea Monster/Ebirah, Horror of the Deep* (1966), *Son of Godzilla* (1967), and *Destroy All Monsters* (1968), exist in more than one English-dubbed version, with differently adapted dialogue, which is often a source of frustration for fans. Another issue with the work of Frontier was that trained actors were usually unavailable, meaning that all that was required was knowledge of the English language.

Worst of all was the dubbing work done in the late 1960s and 1970s in Hong Kong, where many Japanese studios began sending their films to be prepped for international distribution, due to the very low cost. However, those studios definitely got what they paid for, as the work done in Hong Kong, particularly in the 1970s for films like *Godzilla on Monster Island/Godzilla vs. Gigan* (1972), and *Godzilla vs. the Cosmic Monster/Godzilla vs. Mechagodzilla* (1974), suffered from weakly translated scripts and hack voice-over work done by actors whose accents often ran the gamut of the English-speaking world. It was this level of work, seen not only in *kaiju* films but also in popular martial arts and kung fu movies of the period, that largely helped nourish the stigma and generate the modern stereotype of badly dubbed Asian cinema in America. Hong Kong dubbing continued to be used well into the *Heisei* era of the 1980s and '90s, and has resulted in what many fans consider to be even worse dubs than those of the *Showa* era.

English-dubbed versions of Godzilla films are also known for utilizing the voices of some renowned actors over the years. In the earlier years, it was often considered preferable to include Asian actors for "authenticity" (even if they weren't Japanese), and so the voice of beloved Chinese American actor James Hong can be heard in *Godzilla, King of the Monsters* (1956), the American version of the original *Gojira*. Keye Luke, known in his younger years as Charlie Chan's "Number One Son," is featured in *Godzilla Raids*

Again (1955) (originally known in the U.S. as *Gigantis: The Fire Monster*), as is a young George Takei, later to gain fame as *Star Trek*'s Mr. Sulu. Hal Linden, later star of *Barney Miller*, was often employed by Titra in the 1960s. Glen Glenn made use of voice-over legend Marvin Miller, best known as the voice of Robby the Robot in *Forbidden Planet* (1956)—he can be heard, for instance, as the voice of Akira Takarada's character Fuji in *Invasion of Astro-Monster* (1965), known in the U.S. as *Monster Zero*. Paul Frees, perhaps the king of the voice-over actors of the 1950s–70s, lent his voice to several Japanese productions, most notably in the role of Dr. Hu in *King Kong Escapes* (1967)—a film that happened to be a co-production of Rankin-Bass, the very company that had famously featured Frees in such animated 1960s TV specials as *Rudolph the Red-Nosed Reindeer*, *Frosty the Snowman*, and *Santa Claus Is Comin' to Town*.

Godzilla Goes Hollywood

The alteration of Godzilla films for American consumption can be traced back to the franchise's earliest contact with U.S., back in the mid-1950s when the original *Gojira* was snatched up by colorful showman and producer Joseph E. Levine and transformed into *Godzilla, the King of the Monsters*. In addition to some limited dubbing (unlike with later films, much of the Japanese dialogue was left in), certain scenes were cut and other new footage, directed by Terry Morse, was shot and added to the film, resulting in a more "American-friendly" product. This practice continued through later installments like *Godzilla Raids Again* (1955) and *King Kong vs. Godzilla* (1962), often with decidedly mixed results. Nevertheless, although mainstream critics may have laughed in disdain, filmgoers ate them up, especially baby-boomer kids and teens, most of whom didn't even realize that the original Japanese versions had been different.

With the growing success of Toho's releases on American soil, interest began to grow among American producers and distributors to do business with the Japanese film studio. Not only were these American businesses agreeing to distribute Toho's product in the U.S., they were actually investing their own capital, effectively co-producing several important Toho releases during the 1960s and '70s. This would ensure that the films continued to gain great exposure in the United States, and would also continue to be made in part with the need to appeal to an American audience firmly in mind.

Although a Japanese creation, Godzilla has been a figure in American
pop culture since the release of *Godzilla, King of the Monsters* in 1956.
Tom/Flickr

In the grand tradition of Levine, other enterprising American producers stepped into the picture to do business with Toho starting in the mid-
1960s, at a time when it seemed like the American appetite for monster
movies was insatiable. Samuel Z. Arkoff of AIP, which had experienced great
success distributing *Mothra vs. Godzilla* (1964) in the U.S. as *Godzilla vs. the
Thing*, partnered with Toho on such pictures as *Dogora* (1964), *Frankenstein
Conquers the World* (1965), and *Godzilla vs. Hedorah* (1971), known in America
as *Godzilla vs. the Smog Monster*. Don Sharpe, a prolific TV producer of the
1950s, joined with Toho on the production of *Latitude Zero* (1969), a project
so financially plagued that it soured Toho greatly on working with American
companies, and was the last film Sharpe would ever produce.

But no American producer experienced as much success working with
Toho as Henry G. Saperstein, head of UPA. Saperstein funded the productions of *Invasion of Astro-Monster/Monster Zero* (1965), *War of the Gargantuas*
(1966), and *All Monsters Attack/Godzilla's Revenge* (1969). He was instrumental
in the making of *Frankenstein Conquers the World* (1965), brokering the deal
between Toho and AIP (and receiving a chunk of the profits). He was also
involved in the American distribution of *Terror of Mechagodzilla* (1975), as
well as that film's adaptation for American television. He worked with Toho

on several other projects, becoming an instrumental part of that studio's American business during the 1960s and '70s.

The intermingling of Toho with American production partners during this period also led to the memorable participation of several American actors and actresses in Toho productions. Whether they were faded American stars that had lowered their standards to keep their careers going or struggling newcomers desperate for work, they were able to carve out a special niche for themselves that has made them lauded and remembered by fans all over the world to a degree that was probably unimaginable to them at the time.

An example of an American who made his entire living as an actor in Japan, Robert Dunham started as a voice-over actor for Frontier Enterprises, but would later go on to appear in such films as *Mothra* (1961), *Dogora* (1964), and *Godzilla vs. Megalon* (1973). Rhodes Reason, lantern-jawed supporting player in countless cowboy and cop shows of the 1950s and '60s, starred in *King Kong Escapes* (1967), an experience he laughed off every chance he could. Saperstein, as part of his dealings with Toho, persuaded the studio to include name American actors in their films to increase the international appeal. Thus, James Dean cohort and Oscar nominee Nick Adams starred in *Invasion of Astro-Monster* and *Frankenstein Conquers the World*. When Adams couldn't appear in *War of the Gargantuas*, Saperstein obtained the services of the far less enthusiastic Russ Tamblyn, best known as Riff in *West Side Story* (1961). Perhaps the most American-heavy of all the U.S./Japan co-productions was *Latitude Zero*, which featured Cesar Romero, Patricia Medina, and even Oscar-winning co-star of *Citizen Kane* (1941), Joseph Cotten. It was partly the hefty payroll required by such marquee names that led to the financial disaster of that project.

Growing Up Godzilla

Growing up a fan of horror and/or science-fiction cinema in the America of the latter half of the twentieth century, one could not avoid exposure to Godzilla films. For the baby-boomer generation and Generation X, they were something of a rite of passage—along with things like the monster movies of Universal Studios and Hammer Films, the B-horror flicks of Bert I. Gordon and William Castle, kung fu movies and the *Planet of the Apes* franchise. The boomers even developed a particular label for those very young fans who grew up obsessed with all things creepy and never lost their kitschy sensibilities later in life: "monster kids."

Even though the earliest Godzilla films received A-level releases through major American studios like Warner Bros. and Universal, as time marched on and the appeal of the films skewed younger and younger, they became relegated to B-movie status. By the mid-1960s, many Godzilla films made it to the U.S. as part of double features. In those pre-multiplex days, there was a definite hierarchy amongst theaters, and most Godzilla films never made it to the big, prestige establishments, but were rather shown in the smaller venues that specialized in lower-profile material (colloquially known as "grindhouses") as well as drive-in theaters, where B-movies were generally more welcome.

Plenty of American kids grew up seeing Godzilla movies for the first time in these grindhouses and drive-ins, and once they left the theaters, they made their way to a medium where more youngsters than ever would get their first *kaiju* exposure: television. In fact, some Godzilla films, including *Godzilla vs. the Sea Monster* and *Son of Godzilla*, were released directly to TV. Independent and syndicated TV outlets, always on the lookout for cheap material to fill their schedules, snatched up all manner of B-movies, including Godzilla and other monster features. Late-night television became known for such flicks. In many markets, the local channels boasted weekly features that specialized in these types of films, such as WNEW Channel 5 in New York City, which ran "Drive-In Movie" throughout the 1980s, as well as New Jersey bastion WWOR Channel 9, which was known for showing a Godzilla marathon each year during Thanksgiving weekend. These and many other showcases across the nation introduced Godzilla and friends to legions of new fans.

Even into the 1990s, while the *Heisei* era of Godzilla movies was in full swing in Japan, American fans were still thrilling to the classics of the 1950s–70s *Showa* era thanks to basic cable, which picked up the B-movie mantle after the syndicated TV channels decided to fill up their slates with paid infomercials. Basic cable stalwarts such as TBS, TNT, and the newly formed Sci-Fi Channel (later known as Syfy) included Godzilla in their regular lineups, often showing many that were rarely seen on TV in the earlier days, such as the American edit of *Godzilla, King of the Monsters* (1956).

But eventually, even the basic cable outlets would abandon Godzilla. By the turn of the twenty-first century, a shift began to take place in the cable TV industry that put a premium on new, original programming as the

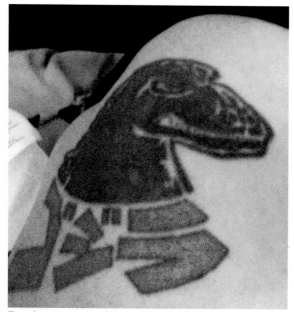

Fans have proven willing to go to any length to show their devotion to the Big G!   *James Bridge*

packages of older TV shows and movies that were their bread and butter for so long began to be phased out. Ironically, this was in part due to the belief that they only appealed to an older fan base—the very folks who had once been the youngsters watching the same stuff during the 1960s, '70s, and '80s. There was also a desire to own newly produced in-house content rather than pay for someone else's content; plus, the old stuff was more difficult to monetize through merchandising.

Whatever the reasons, the Godzilla movies and many other subgenres with which they had once shared the American airwaves are now rarely to be found on television. Younger generations must work a bit harder to seek them out, but there are many who do, turning to home video and streaming services. This takes a bit more legwork, and is not as organic as the exposure that created the "monster kid" phenomenon. Besides, some would argue that today's genre fans have a less campy disposition than their forebears, and in fact, the Godzilla movies made in more recent years are much more serious and less whimsical in tone. But to countless American fans, the Godzilla movies still represent a moment in time; memories of a youth well spent watching men in rubber suits topple miniature wooden buildings, and loving every minute of it.

Although vinyl action figures are the most sought after of all *kaiju*-related toys, Godzilla trinkets of all kinds abound. *Photo by author*

Henry G. Saperstein: Godzilla's American Uncle

If there is anyone Americans can be most thankful to for their initial exposure to Godzilla, it just might be Henry G. Saperstein, chairman of UPA. The quintessential fast-talking, cigar-chomping philistine producer, Saperstein was responsible for bridging the gap between Toho and the United States better than anyone, and bringing the studio's output to a wide U.S. audience. It was a unique partnership that played a major role in weaving Godzilla's *Showa*-era pictures into the fabric of American popular culture.

Born in Chicago on June 2, 1918, Saperstein got his first taste of the movie business as the manager of a chain of theaters in the 1940s and '50s, which he had partly inherited from his father. His earliest experience in film production came during this time as well, as he made some training films for the U.S. Air Force. But it wasn't until 1960 that, at the age of forty-two, he embarked fully on a career as a mover and shaker in Hollywood's production and distribution business.

It all started with Saperstein's purchase of United Productions of America, a once acclaimed and prestigious animation studio that had revolutionized the way cartoons were made in the late 1940s and '50s, and created the popular characters Mr. Magoo and Gerald McBoing-Boing. When *1001 Arabian Nights*, the feature-length cartoon in which the studio had invested most of its hope and money in 1959, was a total flop, bankrupt company founder Stephen Bosustow was forced to sell to the highest bidder, which turned out to be Saperstein.

More of a pragmatist than the artistically ambitious Bosustow, Saperstein set to work making UPA profitable again. Seeing the potential in the largely untapped world of TV animation, he immediately launched UPA's biggest cash cow, the myopic Mr. Magoo, into his first TV series. With an entire animation house already at his disposal, he continued with what UPA was known for at first, producing a cartoon series based on the popular comic strip *Dick Tracy*; the Disney-like animated feature *Gay Purr-ee* (1962), featuring the work of animation legends Chuck Jones and Abe Levitow, as well as the voices of Judy Garland, Robert Goulet, Hermione Gingold, Red Buttons, and Mel Blanc; as well as the beloved TV special *Mr. Magoo's Christmas Carol* (1962).

But after a second Magoo series in the mid-1960s, Saperstein began looking beyond the world of animation to boost UPA's bottom line—uncharted waters for the studio. Specifically, he was looking for popular fare from the world of action, horror, and science fiction that he could cheaply produce and distribute, particularly on television, where he already had a distribution system set up. Without sufficient capital, he needed a studio with which to partner, and began looking beyond American shores for a foreign product he could potentially bring to the U.S. as a novelty. Initially considering Britain's Hammer Films, makers of suspense and monster movies, he instead turned to Toho Company in Japan, which had already had some American success with films like *Godzilla, King of the Monsters*, *Rodan* (1956), and *Mothra*.

After taking in a screening of the original *Godzilla*, Saperstein was impressed, particularly with the monster's potential as a heroic figure, something Toho had only been mildly toying with by that point. Putting his best foot forward, he took a night course to familiarize himself with Japanese culture and set up a meeting with Toho's brass. The result was something unprecedented: a full partnership between a Japanese film studio and an American production company. In exchange for investing 50 percent in a series of Toho productions, Saperstein would enjoy significant creative and casting input, and establish American distribution in theaters and on television.

Immediately, Saperstein began having a direct influence on Toho's output. He was a strong proponent of Godzilla becoming more of a "good guy" to directly appeal to the kids who were already cheering for him. He pushed for white actors to be included in order to increase international appeal. The first of these was Nick Adams, an intense method actor with a strong New York accent, who had alienated much of Hollywood with his eccentric behavior and rumored romantic escapades, and was frankly desperate for work. Saperstein got him hired for his first Toho co-production, *Frankenstein Conquers the World* (*Furankenshutain tai chitei kaijû Baragon*), a film that pitted a giant, mutated human with the heart of the original Frankenstein monster against the reptilian *kaiju* Baragon. For added excitement, Saperstein insisted on the inclusion of a battle with a giant octopus (similar to a scene he had enjoyed in *King Kong vs. Godzilla*), but the scene never made it to the finished film. Saperstein released the English-dubbed version of the film in America on July 8, 1966, eleven months after its initial Japanese release.

Adams turned out to be a great fit, loved working in Japan, and got along great with cast and crew—some might say a little too great, as he was rumored to have begun an affair with co-star Kumi Mizuno that contributed to the breakup of his marriage. Saperstein used him again in his next contracted project with Toho, which turned out to be the sixth Godzilla movie. Known in Japan as *The Great Monster War* (*Kaiju daisenso*), the film was rechristened by Saperstein as *Monster Zero* for American release (later lengthened to *Godzilla vs. Monster Zero* for increased appeal on television). Adams starred as Astronaut Glen alongside Toho headliner Akira Takarada as Astronaut Fuji, and once again got to live out his real-life romance on screen alongside Kumi Mizuno as the mysterious Miss Namikawa. Saperstein's influence is felt in the film's decidedly campier vibe and colorful science-fiction theme.

But Saperstein would have a tougher time getting theatrical distributors in America interested in *Monster Zero*, as well as in his third Toho co-production, *War of the Gargantuas* (*Furankenshutain no kaijû: Sanda tai Gaira*). Unable to secure Adams a third time, Saperstein instead brought in Russ Tamblyn, star of *West Side Story* and *The Haunting* (1963). Unfortunately, Tamblyn's experience in Japan was not as warm and positive as Adams's; he had a hard time adjusting to Japanese culture, and was notoriously contentious with Saperstein and difficult to work with. In the end, it took Saperstein five years to finally land a distributor for the

English-dubbed versions of both *Monster Zero* and *War of the Gargantuas*, running them as a drive-in double feature in 1970.

Meanwhile, Saperstein continued to diversify UPA's releases further away from the company's origins in animation, co-producing the rock 'n' roll documentary *The Big TNT Show* (1966); *Turn On, Tune In, Drop Out* (1967), a psychedelic anthology film starring counterculture guru Timothy Leary; and a German TV production of *Swan Lake* (1966). As part of his distribution agreement with Toho, he found himself saddled with an espionage picture called *International Secret Police: Key of Keys* (*Kokusai himitsu keisatsu: Kagi no kagi*) (1965). Deeming it completely unmarketable to American audiences, he went completely outside the box, hiring comedian Woody Allen (after Lenny Bruce turned him down) to come up with a completely different, comical script and fit the words into the mouths of the original actors using the voices of Allen, his wife Louise Lasser, and other American actors. The result was the bizarre parody film *What's Up, Tiger Lily?* (1966). Using his influence with Toho, Saperstein borrowed the acclaimed Japanese actor Toshiro Mifune, star of countless Akira Kurosawa films, for an American production called *Hell in the Pacific* (1968), a World War II picture co-starring Lee Marvin that was one of the earliest efforts of British director John Boorman.

The last release of Saperstein's original five-picture deal with Toho was the tenth Godzilla film, *All Monsters Attack* (*Gojira-Minira-Gabara: Oru kaijū daishingeki*) (1969), which Saperstein retitled, in typical reductive fashion, *Godzilla's Revenge*, and brought to the U.S. in 1971. By now, Saperstein's influence had been fully realized, as Godzilla was portrayed as a friend to children, in a film targeted completely at a child audience. Even after the completion of his initial deal, Saperstein continued to play a part in getting Godzilla movies distributed in the United States, joining forces with fellow schlockmeister Samuel Z. Arkoff at AIP for the release of *Godzilla vs. the Smog Monster* in February 1972, and financing an alternate cut of the final *Showa* Godzilla film, *Terror of Mechagodzilla*, for TV release in the fall of 1977.

By now Saperstein was extremely comfortable working with Toho, and Toho executives found him to be the American producer with whom they most preferred to collaborate. He co-produced *The Last Days of Planet Earth* (*Nosutoradamusu no daiyogen*) (1974), a film capitalizing on the popularity of the prophet Nostradamus that he brought to America in July 1979, as well as *ESP* (*Esupai*) (1974), made by frequent Godzilla director Jun Fukuda to cash in on the psychic craze of the 1970s, which Saperstein was never able to successfully distribute in the U.S. His final Toho collaboration was the vampire film *Evil of Dracula* (*Chi o suu bara*) (1975), which he distributed directly to American TV in 1980.

In his latter years, Saperstein continued to cash in on the enduring popularity of UPA's most beloved character, producing one more Mr. Magoo animated series, *What's New, Mr. Magoo?*, in 1977. Twenty years later, at the age of seventy-eight, he made one last payday off the character when he leased it to Walt Disney Pictures for a live-action feature film starring funnyman Leslie Nielsen as the bumbling Magoo. The following year, on June 24, 1998, just three weeks after his eightieth birthday, Henry G. Saperstein died of cancer in Beverly Hills, California. Although he accomplished much during his unique career in show business, he will best be remembered as one of the guiding figures of American grindhouse cinema during the 1960s and '70s. A capitalist through and through, his motives may have been much more financial than artistic, but through his efforts millions of American fans were converted to the cult of Godzilla, and gained a lifelong affinity for the character.

12

No More Mr. Nice Guy

The Heisei Era

Even Godzilla is entitled to a second chance. Although most agree that the monster's heyday was the *Showa* era, in particular the 1950s and '60s, the monster experienced a full-scale renaissance during the 1980s and '90s that is remembered fondly by many who first discovered him during this period, and that took the franchise in some bold, new creative directions (as well as some safe and obvious retreads). Produced during a renaissance of sorts for the Japanese nation as a whole, the *Heisei* series took things in a darker direction, returning Godzilla to his destructive roots and returning Toho Company to prominence in the process.

Just as the *Showa* era took its name from the reign of Emperor Hirohito, *Heisei* refers to the current Japanese era, which began January 8, 1989, the day Akihito took over as emperor from his father, who had died the day before. Six of the seven films of the *Heisei* era were made during the reign of Emperor Akihito; despite the fact that the first of the *Heisei* films, *Godzilla 1985*, was actually made at the end of the *Showa* era, in order to make a clear distinction between the original series and the rebooted series, *Godzilla 1985* is labeled a *Heisei* film in hindsight.

Both philosophically speaking and in terms of production, the films of the *Heisei* era could not be more different from the majority of their *Showa* predecessors. In a sense, there was an attempt to remedy what many considered to be missteps of the *Showa* era with the relaunched franchise. Experiencing regret over how Godzilla had been turned into a sympathetic and heroic figure over the course of the 1960s and '70s, executive producer Tomoyuki Tanaka sought to make the monster fearsome and evil once again, in order to recapture the original terror and the original social message that had helped *Gojira* make such an impact with audiences back in the 1950s. The silliness and whimsy that had only increased as the *Showa* era progressed was unceremoniously dumped in favor of a grittier, more serious approach that was very much in keeping with what genre fans seemed to be looking for in the 1980s (as the similar transformation of Batman, for example, would confirm).

However, the cinematic landscape had changed quite a bit since the Big G had taken his last bow in 1975's *Terror of Mechagodzilla*. George Lucas's ultimate game-changer, *Star Wars*, had hit theaters in 1977, and nothing would ever be the same. The American science-fiction and fantasy films that followed, including the likes of *Close Encounters of the Third Kind* (1977), *Alien* (1979), *Raiders of the Lost Ark* (1981), *Blade Runner* (1982), and *Ghostbusters* (1984), had taken movie special effects to a level light years beyond what had been seen before. For the first time, American films were dominating the Japanese market every year, as the Japanese film industry shrank to a shell of its former self. Toho Company, which had once been at the forefront of visual effects back in the monster heyday of the 1950s and '60s, now found itself far from the cutting edge, having been left behind by a competitive foreign marketplace, its genre output perceived as second-rate B-pictures even by its native audience.

It was perhaps for this reason that the films of the *Heisei* era received so much less American exposure than earlier Godzilla films. Only the first of them was ever released theatrically in the U.S., and they were virtually nowhere to be seen on television, even taking years in most cases to achieve home video release stateside. For most rabid *kaiju* fanatics outside Japan at the time, keeping up with the latest Godzilla movies in a pre-Internet world meant diligently tracking down bootleg VHS copies, which were often of very low quality and sometimes not even subtitled in English, let alone dubbed. It is only in the current century that the Godzilla films of the 1980s and '90s have been made readily available to American audiences, even if they are decidedly less prominent in popular culture than the *Showa* classics. Nevertheless, in Japan the *Heisei* Godzilla films represented a major financial upturn for the franchise—in the case of Godzilla, absence did indeed make the heart grow fonder, as Japanese flocked to theaters to catch the new movies in numbers not seen since the 1960s.

One interesting change that Toho made with the *Heisei* films was the establishment and maintenance of a fixed, definable continuity among the movies in the series. Whereas during the *Showa* era the inter-movie continuity was vague and tenuous at best, and all but abandoned after the 1960s, beginning with *Godzilla 1985* and culminating a decade later in *Godzilla vs. Destoroyah*, the series boasts a coherent, ongoing structure, with recurring characters, where plot elements are carried over from one film to another. Still, even though Toho had opted to eliminate from continuity all *Showa* films besides the original *Gojira*, that didn't prevent the studio from resurrecting all the major monsters from the *Showa* era such as Mothra, Rodan, King Ghidorah, and Mechagodzilla, choosing safe bets for audience appeal over new innovation.

Where the innovation came in was in the eschewing of the fun and fantastical for the technological and the militaristic. There is little magic or aliens to be found in the *Heisei* era, as the films prefer to ground their plots as much as possible in more "plausible" (a relative term!), reality-based elements. While the Japanese film industry may have contracted, Japan as a world power had actually grown since the depressed days of the 1970s, and the nation had become known as a leader in technology and a strong economic force that many believed even threatened the dominance of the United States at the time. If Japan's adolescence as a modern nation had been the 1950s through the 1970s, it was now a mature adult, and this confidence in technology and overall national maturity can be observed throughout the films that represent Godzilla's late-twentieth-century rebirth.

"That's about the time that Japan seemed to be taking over the technology world," says Miguel Rodriguez, organizer of the highly popular Horrible Imaginings Film Festival. "Japan in the '80s and '90s was completely different than Japan in the '60s and '70s, and that's reflected in the *Heisei* series. They always have to have some kind of crazy tech that they're using. The tech aspect in the *Heisei* series seems to take center stage, even ahead of Godzilla."

Godzilla 1985

Japanese Title: *Gojira*
Also Known As: *The Return of Godzilla* (international title)
Release Date: December 15, 1984

Despite Toho's decision to cancel the Godzilla series in 1975, producer Tomoyuki Tanaka had never given up hope of keeping the character alive, and in fact continued laboring to bring a reboot concept to fruition for close to a decade. There were several false starts over the years, both real and rumored. One unsubstantiated story had it that in 1978 Tanaka was working with old associate Henry Saperstein at UPA on a project called *Godzilla vs. the Devil*. Two years later, Tanaka developed a treatment for a film in which Godzilla would return to take on a shape-shifting monster called Bagan.

Although Bagan never made it to the screen, that treatment became the basis for the eventual relaunch that happened in 1984.

When he finally got his green light from Toho, Tanaka went straight to Ishiro Honda, his most trusted director from the *Showa* days. But Honda, still bothered by the puerile turn the series had taken in the 1970s, as well as opposing the very notion of continuing after the death of special-effects master Eiji Tsuburaya in 1970, strongly declined the offer to helm the project. And so Tanaka instead turned to Koji Hashimoto, who had served as an assistant director on such *tokusatsu* favorites as *King Kong vs. Godzilla* (1962), *Ghidorah, the Three-Headed Monster* (1964), *Frankenstein Conquers the World* (1965), *Invasion of Astro-Monster* (1965), *Latitude Zero* (1969), and *All Monsters Attack* (1969), and had just finished his own directorial debut on the brand-new science-fiction project *Bye, Bye Jupiter* (1984).

Intending it to be an "event film" of the type that Hollywood had been churning out for the previous decade, Toho invested quite a bit in the new picture, which they simply titled *Gojira*, sometimes called *The Return of Godzilla* to avoid confusion with the 1954 original. Part of the reason for the simple title was that the movie was intended as a direct sequel to the original, disregarding completely the fourteen sequels that had come after it. Going for a more streamlined approach, the film once again presented Godzilla as a destructive force of nature, and for the first (and only) time other than the original film, there was no *kaiju* opponent; rather, all the focus was once again on the King of the Monsters and humanity's struggle to defeat him. Thirty years after the first rampage in Tokyo, a new Godzilla emerges from the Pacific to wreak havoc, this time bringing the United States and the Soviet Union to the brink of nuclear war when each side initially believes the other is responsible for the carnage. Japan then steps in, putting into action the impressive Super-X combat vehicle to take the creature down once and for all.

Bringing all the mayhem to life once again was Teruyoshi Nakano, this time with a far greater budget to work with than he had on his 1970s Godzilla projects. A brand-new Godzilla suit was designed, this time with a brand-new actor inside: Kenpachiro Satsuma, who would remain the man behind the monster for the entire *Heisei* era. In addition to the suit, for the first time, a twenty-foot-tall animatronic replica known as "Cybot Godzilla" was also used for certain close-ups, although the machine did not fully function as expected and couldn't be used as extensively as first planned. Although the effects were certainly more impressive than much of what had been seen in Godzilla films up to that point, they still were not close to the level being produced in the U.S. by the likes of George Lucas's Industrial Light and Magic studio.

The film was picked up by New World Pictures, the company owned by legendary B-movie producer Roger Corman, and prepped for a full-scale American release. Retitled *Godzilla 1985*, it was ironically handled very much like the 1954 film had been, with extensive editing and newly shot American scenes added with English-speaking actors in order to increase the film's marketability in the U.S. This meant even bringing back Raymond Burr, who had played reporter Steve Martin in the re-edited original, *Godzilla, King of the Monsters* (1956). The new scenes added little to the film, but rather muddied the plot more than anything, and the shameless product placement (anyone for a Dr. Pepper?) made matters even worse. The film was released in the U.S. on August 23, 1985, but languished in a summer that included the likes of *Back to the Future*, *Rambo*, and *The Goonies*. The movie's lackluster American box office would mean no more stateside theatrical releases for Godzilla; but on the other side of the Pacific, the film had been a modest success, ensuring that the monster would be back for more, if only in his home country.

"They could've used Honda on that picture, because there were some directorial missteps," opines Peter Brothers. "When Godzilla is attacking the city, which is supposed to be the set piece of any Godzilla movie, he comes upon the bullet train, hearkening back to that scene from the first one. All you have to do is play the two of them to see the difference of how they were handled. There's just no comparison."

Godzilla vs. Biollante

Japanese Title: *Gojira tai Biorante*
Release Date: December 16, 1989

The limited success of the previous film led to a few false starts before work began on the next installment in the series. Toho had decided a full-scale continuation of the franchise was a good idea, but believed it could be done better this time. The failure of *King Kong Lives* (1986), the sequel to Dino De Laurentiis's 1976 *King Kong* remake had given Tanaka pause as to the potential of modern-day giant monster movies, but when *Little Shop of Horrors* (1986) scored a major hit, he not only decided to push ahead, but he would even take a cue from that film's Audrey II plant monster for Godzilla's newest and most unique foe.

The origins of the film's plot came from a national story contest held by Toho that was won by a dentist named Shinichiro Kobayashi. That story was handed by Tanaka to Kazuki Omori, a maverick independent film director who had agreed to work with a studio for the first time. Although Omori was initially skeptical of the project due to his disapproval of the creative choices Tanaka had made with the franchise back in the 1970s, Omori was determined to help return the character back to prominence, and fashioned a script that is truly one of the most creative and unusual in the entire Godzilla canon. It took three years for the script to be developed and reworked before the picture was finally made in 1989.

Of all the creatures Godzilla ever faced, perhaps none was as bizarre as Biollante, a genetic monstrosity created from a combination of Godzilla DNA, human DNA, and rose DNA, resulting in a strange sentient plant that seems to be part lizard and part flower. Omori's script fuses the traditional antinuclear message of Godzilla with a new warning against the abuses of biotechnology, and also introduced the character of Miki Saegusa, a young telepath who would form a bond with Godzilla and continue to pursue the beast for the remainder of the *Heisei* series. Most importantly, it returned the series to the monster vs. monster format that had worked well in the past, which Toho believed would lead to even greater success than *Godzilla 1985* had achieved.

To pull it off, Tanaka hired a brand-new visual effects director who had previously been an employee of Tsuburaya Productions and had done fine work for Toho on the sci-fi action film *Gunhed* (1986), Koichi Kawakita. As Tsuburaya himself had done during the early *Showa* era, Kawakita remained visual effects director for the remainder of the *Heisei* era, and crafted a whole new look for the monster and for the series that really helped to define the new era and make it stand out from what had come before. In fact, the new Godzilla suit design introduced for *Godzilla vs. Biollante* would remain in place with little change for the next five films. Kawakita's realization of Biollante was equally impressive, if not more so, using more than thirty-two technicians to operate the complex structure.

Initially, Miramax, an American studio dedicated to distributing independent and foreign films, had agreed to release *Godzilla vs. Biollante* in America, but there were doubts about its American marketability; Miramax balked, prompting a lawsuit that led to Miramax finally releasing the movie in 1992, albeit as a direct-to-home-video release. The film was received quite well by avid Godzilla fans in both Japan and North America, although Toho was disappointed that it not only didn't surpass *Godzilla 1985*, but actually failed to perform as well as its predecessor. It was decided that the film had been too unorthodox for mainstream audiences, and a return to the more traditional formula (and more traditional *kaiju*) was the answer—which is a shame, because *Godzilla vs. Biollante* represents one of the few times that Toho took a thoroughly bold and original creative chance with its cash cow.

Godzilla vs. King Ghidorah

Japanese Title: *Gojira tai Kingu Gidora*
Release Date: December 14, 1991

After the box-office failure of *Godzilla vs. Biollante*, Toho decided to be more conservative and play it safe with its next installment. Initially, Tanaka and Omori had planned a more direct sequel, but when the eighty-year-old Tanaka took ill, his assistant Shogo Tomiyama took over day-to-day production duties, which he'd continue to hold for the remainder of the *Heisei* era. Tomiyama was most skeptical of *Biollante* of all, believing the film failed to connect with young audiences and was overshadowed by the modern American blockbusters that had infiltrated Japan. As a result, the next film would be both a return to traditional roots and a fiercely jingoistic enterprise intended to stir audience support.

Rather than take a chance on another unknown monster, Toho brought back Godzilla's most memorable foe from the *Showa* era, the three-headed golden dragon Ghidorah. Akira Ifukube, whose music had defined the classic Godzilla films, was lured back for the first time since 1975 to create a whole new score. More than in the previous two films, the fantastical elements were amplified, although admittedly not to the extent of the more outlandish *Showa* pictures.

Omori was kept on as writer and director, and influenced by the success of American franchises like *The Terminator* and *Back to the Future*, he crafted a tale that was heavy on the sci-fi action and time-travel antics. Godzilla's origins would even be revisited, as visitors from the future warn the Japanese that the monster will destroy their nation in the twenty-first century, and must be wiped from existence by going back in time to World War II and preventing the nuclear accident that originally mutated him from normal dinosaur form. However, the visitors have ulterior motives, as their real plot involves replacing Godzilla with the much more devastating

King Ghidorah, who will prevent Japan from rising to become the world's most powerful nation in the twenty-first century.

Time-travel paradoxes abound, and it's advised that one watch the film without too analytical an eye (if Godzilla is erased from existence, for example, how is it that the characters in the present continue to remember him?). The *Terminator* influence also extends to the presence of future android M-11, played by Caucasian actor Robert Scott Field with more than a slight nod to Arnold. The monster action is pleasing, and the film appealed to a much wider audience, proving that perhaps Tomiyama's decision to make it more derivative and less risky had been a financially sound, if creatively stunted one.

"They realized Godzilla was more interesting when he was the bad guy, but at the same time, the audience wanted to see Godzilla beat up other monsters," explains Steve Biodrowski, editor of *Cinefantastique Online*. "So they became experts at talking out of both sides of their mouths. In *Godzilla vs. King Ghidorah*, for example, the movie keeps flip-flopping on Godzilla. Which is the worst evil, which one are we going to choose? He became this angry junkyard dog who was really dangerous and you wouldn't want him to be your pet, but when the other monsters came invading, it was kind of nice that he was there."

With a plot involving a conspiracy to prevent Japan from achieving its grand destiny, the film has a patriotic confidence that is rare in *tokusatsu* cinema, and reflects Japan's position at the time as a leader in technology and a growing economic force in the world. No longer the timid nation neutered after the war by America, Japan had grown to resent its Western ally/rival a bit, and many believe this attitude is reflected in the way in which Allied American troops are portrayed as the enemy and Imperial Japanese sailors are portrayed in a heroic, sympathetic light. In fact, it was reported at the time that Japanese audiences cheered at the scenes in which the pre-radiation Godzillasaurus comes to the aid of the Japanese sailors, squashing the inept American forces underfoot.

The perceived anti-American slant of the film made U.S. headlines at the time, but the controversy was not quite enough to score *Godzilla vs. King Ghidorah* a prompt American release (in fact, it may have delayed it). The film did not officially make it to the U.S. until 1998, when Columbia/TriStar issued it on home video as part of a distribution deal with Toho that came with the rights to make their own American *Godzilla* movie that same year.

King Ghidorah returns from the dead as Mecha King Ghidorah to carry on the fight.

Everett Collection

Godzilla & Mothra: The Battle for Earth

Japanese Title: *Gojira tai Mosura*
Also Known As: *Godzilla vs. Mothra* (international title)
Release Date: December 12, 1992

The success of *Godzilla vs. King Ghidorah* encouraged Toho to continue in the same direction, and the next *Heisei* Godzilla film brought back another very popular classic *kaiju* from the 1960s, Mothra—not seen since *Destroy All Monsters* some twenty-four years prior. Along with Mothra came the tiny, beloved *shobijin* fairies once played by the Peanuts pop duo, as well as a new, evil counterpart to the giant moth goddess, the menacing Battra. The result was one of the biggest smash hits in Toho's history—the highest-grossing film in the entire Japanese franchise and second only to the venerated *King Kong vs. Godzilla* (1962) in ticket sales. In fact, in 1993, the film was number two behind *Jurassic Park* at the Japanese box office.

Although Kazuki Omori stepped out of the director's chair this time around, he did contribute the script, as he continued to shape the development of the new Godzilla. Helming the project this time out would be Takao Okawara, who had just come off his directorial debut for Toho in *Reiko, The Psyche Resurrected*, and would go on to direct more *Heisei* Godzilla films than anyone else. The most fanciful *Heisei* picture to date, *Godzilla & Mothra* follows the exploits of adventuring explorer Takuya Fujita (Tetsuya Bessho), his ex-wife Masako Tezuka (Satomi Kobayashi), and bumbling corporate stooge Kenji Ando (Takehiro Murata) as they uncover a threat posed to humanity by Battra and must summon Mothra from Infant Island to combat both the new threat and the recently reawakened Godzilla.

There is more than a little touch of Indiana Jones to the proceedings, and this was entirely Omori's doing as he attempted once again to infuse elements from American blockbusters into the Godzilla franchise. This is just as much Mothra's movie as it is Godzilla's, and it contains several references to the film they last headlined together, 1964's beloved *Mothra vs. Godzilla*. Initially hesitant to bring back Mothra due to a belief that her appeal was limited outside Japan, it was decided to go ahead once Toho learned of Mothra's enormous popularity with the majority female population of Japan.

Although rushed into production to keep the momentum going from *Godzilla vs. King Ghidorah*, *Godzilla & Mothra* is nevertheless a thrilling romp, with some unique fight choreography and impressive effects from Kawakita. Audiences responded well to the return of Mothra, the second most popular *kaiju* after Godzilla himself. Not since the 1960s had Toho experienced so much success with the Godzilla franchise, and installments once again went into consecutive production, just as they had in decades past. It was eventually released on home video in the U.S. by Columbia/TriStar in 1998 as a double feature with *Godzilla vs. King Ghidorah*.

Godzilla vs. Mechagodzilla II

Japanese Title: *Gojira tai Mekagojira*
Release Date: December 11, 1993

The reintroduction of memorable *Showa* characters continued the following year, when Toho brought back not only Mechagodzilla, perhaps Godzilla's most popular 1970s foe, but also the giant pteranadon Rodan, which, like Mothra, had not been seen since the 1960s and *Destroy All Monsters*. Even more ambitiously, Toho at first had striven to bring back none other than King Kong to once again duke it out with the Big G, but was unable to secure the very expensive rights to the character from Universal Studios (even getting permission to use Mechani-Kong, a robotic version Toho itself had created for *King Kong Escapes* [1967], proved impossible).

Koichi Kawakita's controversial yet cute design for Little Godzilla.
Everett Collection

The film was called *Godzilla vs. Mechagodzilla II* for international release only, in order to avoid confusion with the original 1974 film of the same name, to which the new movie was not connected in any way (apparently Japanese audiences have an easier time handling such ambiguities). In fact, even the nature of Mechagodzilla was completely revamped by screenwriter Wataru Mimura, who contributed his first of an eventual five Godzilla movie scripts. This time, since Godzilla had been firmly reestablished as the bad guy, MechaG was introduced as the good guy—no longer a creation of aliens bent on world domination, but rather the terrestrial product of the Japanese military in an effort to repel the perpetual menace of Godzilla once and for all.

In addition to Mechagodzilla and Rodan, also returning to the fold, though not in quite the same form, was Godzilla's son. No longer the goofy and juvenile Minya of the late 1960s *Showa* films, which were deplored by returning director Takao Okawara, this time Baby Godzilla (as he is called) is a more realistically depicted baby dinosaur, and the size of a human. Putting a sympathetic dinosaur center stage seems to have been the result of the influence of the highly successful *Jurassic Park* (1993), and Baby's bond of friendship with the psychic Miki Saegusa only strengthens the comparison.

Godzilla vs. Mechagodzilla II is fondly remembered for its tremendous action, arguably the best executed of the *Heisei* era, or possibly any era of Godzilla. For a brief moment, it was considered as the final film of the *Heisei* series, in part as a show of respect for the recently passed Ishiro Honda, and also due to the rumblings of an American-made Godzilla film on the horizon. However, that American version would turn out to be several years away, and respect for the dead was not enough to deter Toho from continuing to go to the well on what was once again a very lucrative franchise. *Godzilla vs. Mechagodzilla II* reached America in 1998 first as a pay-per-view satellite television release through Sony Pictures, the parent company of Columbia/TriStar.

Godzilla vs. Space Godzilla

Japanese Title: *Gojira tai Supesugojira*
Release Date: December 10, 1994

Widely regarded as the greatest misstep of the *Heisei* era, *Godzilla vs. Space Godzilla* is an odd film that derails much of the momentum of the previous few entries in the series, with an entirely different creative team that appeared to have a very different philosophy from the likes of Kazuki Omori, Takao Okawara, and Wataru Mimura. With a strange premise, subpar creature design, an uneven plot, and even more uneven performances, it may just be a contender for the least popular film in the entire Godzilla franchise.

The director, Kensho Yamashita, had been an assistant director on *Terror of Mechagodzilla* (1975), but had not directed a major motion picture in fifteen years, and *Godzilla vs. Space Godzilla* would turn out to be his second and final major feature film. The screenwriter, Hiroshi Kashiwaba, was a veteran of television best known for teenybopper movies. Together, they opted to take Godzilla in a more lighthearted direction, resulting in a film that is closer to the more silly entries in the *Showa* series than anything else produced in the 1980s and '90s.

Space Godzilla turns out to be one of Godzilla's most bizarre foes, a warped clone of Godzilla resulting from cells from the monster that are somehow sucked into a black hole in space and blasted with cosmic radiation (it is hinted that the cells may have gotten there as a result of Big G's battle with Biollante). When Space Godzilla makes his way to Earth and begins siphoning energy from the planet's core, Godzilla comes the closest he had come since the 1970s to being the defender of humanity—albeit still a very dangerous defender. Assisting Godzilla in the fight against his space doppelganger is the giant robot MOGUERA, lifted from Ishiro Honda's classic *tokusatsu* picture *The Mysterians* (1957) and taking the place of the destroyed Mechagodzilla.

Godzilla steps up to the heroic plate in large part due to the fact that Space Godzilla has threatened his son, now known as Little Godzilla. Disappointed in the young *kaiju's* dinosaur-like appearance in the previous film, effects director Koichi Kawakita redesigned him in a more cartoonish fashion, with an almost *anime*-like appearance that made him look more similar to Minya than anything else. This only further added to the kiddie appeal of the film, and may have even been an attempt to launch a children's TV series starring Little Godzilla, which never got off the ground.

Godzilla vs. Space Godzilla made it to America in January 1999 as a home video release by Columbia/TriStar. By that point, the American version of Godzilla had already reared its iguana-like head, and Toho had shuttered the Japanese franchise. However, before it did so, there would be one final picture to be made, which was a good thing, since this particular entry would have been a less-than-stellar way to send the big guy off into the sunset.

Godzilla vs. Destoroyah

Japanese Title: *Gojira tai Desutoroia*
Literal Translation: *Godzilla vs. Destroyer*
Release Date: December 9, 1995

By 1995, TriStar Pictures had officially secured the rights from Toho to make the first-ever American Godzilla film. For this reason, and to avoid confusion in the marketplace, Toho decided it was time to take its own Godzilla out of commission. At the time, the belief was that TriStar would be permanently taking over the Godzilla mantle, as Toho graciously passed the torch to the Americans. And while this did not turn out to be the case, *Godzilla vs. Destoroyah* would be the final film of the *Heisei* era, and would mark the death of the *Heisei* version of the monster.

Toho made no attempt to keep it a secret, either; rather, the new film was completely marketed around the promised death of Godzilla, which gained it more international publicity than any release in years. Wanting to do things the right way, Toho brought back the proven commodities of Kazuki Omori to pen the script, Takao Okawara to direct, and for the final time, the great Akira Ifukube to write the score. Japanese audiences flocked to witness the demise of the beloved/dreaded King of the Monsters, making *Godzilla vs. Destoroyah* the number-one film in Japan for 1996.

In the ultimate tip of the hat, the film drew direct connections to the original *Gojira* (1954), as young Kenichi Yamane (Yasufumi Hayashi), grandson of the original Dr. Yamane (Takashi Shimura) and son of Emiko Yamane (Momoki Kochi, reprising her 1954 role in her final film appearance), is recruited to help the Japanese military's G-Force to neutralize the threat of Godzilla. After absorbing massive amounts of radiation in his battle against Space Godzilla, a glowing-red Godzilla appears to be on the verge of a literal meltdown. And to make matters worse, at the bottom of Tokyo Bay, the remnants of Dr. Serizawa's Oxygen Destroyer, which killed the original Godzilla forty years prior, have now mutated dormant, fossilized trilobites into large, extremely hostile monsters, which naturally come ashore and terrorize the populace.

In another nod to American blockbusters, the attack of the enlarged trilobite-creatures is very reminiscent of action seen in the *Aliens* franchise, adding a rare element of horror to the proceedings. Once the creatures merge into one gigantic *kaiju*, matters become far worse, as the new monster tangles with both Godzilla and the now nearly full-sized Godzilla Junior

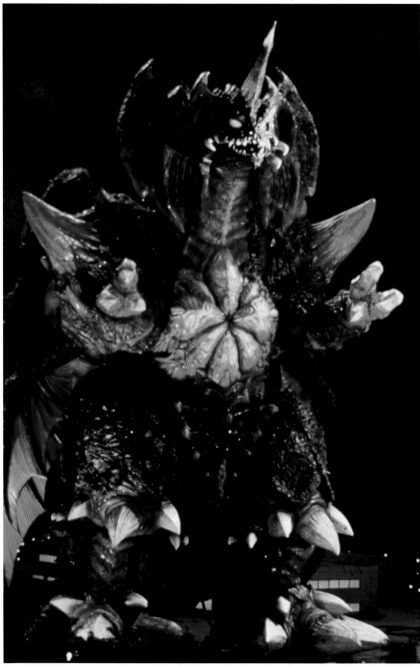

Destoroyah was one of the most ambitiously designed *kaiju*, and perhaps Kawakita's crowning achievement.

Everett Collection

(as he is now called, with his strong resemblance to his father). Known as Destoroyah (Toho was going to translate the name as Destroyer, but decided that name would be too difficult to effectively copyright), the creature is the living embodiment of the very technology that destroyed the original version of Godzilla.

After a fierce battle with Destoroyah in which he is aided by G-Force, Godzilla at last succumbs to the radiation poisoning, and melts away in a final death scene that is surprisingly tasteful and poignant, magnified by Ifukube's magnificent musical contribution into what may be the series' single most moving moment. Toho delivered on its promise to kill off Godzilla, although we are left at the end with the notion that Godzilla Junior just may be following in his father's rather large footsteps.

Columbia/TriStar released the film to home video in America alongside *Godzilla vs. Space Godzilla* in January 1999, mere months after TriStar's own American *Godzilla* had been released to theaters worldwide. The failure of that film would eventually prompt Toho to take back the reins and reintroduce Godzilla to audiences once again, but for now the monster was at last at peace, humanely put out to pasture in what turned out to be one of the strongest, if not the single strongest, entry in the entire *Heisei* series.

The *Heisei* era had taken Godzilla in a very different direction than the *Showa* era, and those films of the 1980s and '90s were enjoyed by a whole new generation of fans for whom they represented an introduction to something completely new. Ironically, the very qualities of the *Heisei* films that make them stand out as unique—their serious tone, their emphasis on military action, their minimizing of fantastical elements—are often derided by fans of the earlier, lighter films, just as they are lauded by those who prefer their Godzilla lean and mean. But polarizing though they may be, they are commendable for their effort to recapture what originally made Godzilla work so well when he first trampled his way onto the screen in 1954. Their success in doing that may have varied, but they stand as an impressive, self-contained achievement in continuity, as well as a return to box-office dominance for Toho's *Godzilla*.

"They were trying to go back to some of the spirit of that original movie and make them more relevant, make them more adult-oriented," offers Dr. Bill Tsutsui, author of *Godzilla on My Mind*. "In some ways they succeeded . . . but in the 1980s, Japan just didn't have that big bogeyman out there to get audiences to leave the theater in tears like they did in 1954."

Kim Jong's Kaiju: The Strange Story of Pulgasari

At the same time that Godzilla was experiencing his *Heisei*-era rebirth in 1985, across the Sea of Japan, the most unlikely *daikaiju* film of all time was being made in, of all places, the communist dictatorship of North Korea. In the history of Asian *tokusatsu* cinema, there is perhaps no tale as odd and fascinating as that of *Pulgasari*, the giant monster movie produced by none other than Kim Jong-Il. It's a tale of kidnapping, international intrigue, and political propaganda that would make for a fine movie screenplay in its own right, if it didn't all actually happen in real life.

Few Westerners could have conceived of the fact that Kim Jong-Il, then son of North Korea's dictator Kim Il-Sung and future megalomaniacal ruler in his own right, also happened to be an enormous film aficionado. Naming *Gone With the Wind* (1939) as his favorite movie, and Elizabeth Taylor as his favorite actress, Jong-Il thrilled to the slick productions of Hollywood, and longed to have a thriving film industry in North Korea, which would, of course, be fully controlled and manipulated by the North Korean government. However, North Korea's film industry, such as it was, lacked the creative spark that he desired, and so he decided that if he couldn't grow his own visionary director, he would have to steal one.

Sang-ok Shin had been one of the most successful and prolific directors in neighboring South Korea, with a career reaching back to the early 1950s and including more than sixty films. He also happened to be married to one of South Korea's top leading ladies of the screen, Eun-hie Choi. While visiting Hong Kong in 1978, the power couple was abducted by North Korean secret police and brought to Kim Jong-Il, who explained that he wanted Shin to be the face of the North Korean film industry, with Jong-Il as his benevolent benefactor/producer. Shin refused, and he and his wife were jailed for five years before finally relenting and agreeing to make a series of pictures for North Korea.

There would be films such as *The Emissary Who Did Not Return* (1984), which he directed under his wife's name; as well as the Soviet co-production *Sogum* (1985), and *Sarang sarang nea sarang* (1985), both of which featured his wife in a starring role. But the project that would live on forever in cinematic infamy would be his last North Korean project, a culmination of years of longing on the part of his bespectacled jailor and boss. For years, Jong-Il had admired the *kaiju* films made in nearby Japan, and Godzilla in particular. His idea was to make a *kaiju* film for North Koreans, based on a popular Korean folk tale about a metal-eating monster that helped downtrodden villagers fight back against an oppressive king.

In order to get the job done right, Shin and Jong-Il struck an improbable deal with Toho to bring in some key creative personnel. They included visual effects director Teruyoshi Nakano, who had worked on countless *tokusatsu* projects in the 1960s, '70s, and '80s, including thirteen Godzilla movies; as well as Kenpachiro Satsuma, who had just finished playing Godzilla for the first time in *Godzilla 1985* and would don the metallic suit Nakano had designed for the titular creature in the film, which would be known as *Pulgasari* (sometimes spelled *Bulgasari*). They would even recruit Little Man Machan, the aging midget wrestler who had played Godzilla's son Minya in the 1960s, to portray the diminutive early version of Pulgasari.

The resulting film is a surreal blend of folklore and propaganda, featuring a jailed blacksmith in medieval Korea who fashions a tiny figurine out of rice, which comes to life when doused with his daughter's blood. The creature befriends nearby peasants and helps them fend off attacks from feudal lords, in exchange for various metal objects that it consumes to grow larger and larger. In the end, once the oppressors are defeated, Pulgasari himself becomes an unchecked menace that must be neutralized to restore balance and order. Some have called it a commentary on the dangers of capitalism, while others suggest it even contains subtle criticisms of the North Korean government that its director may have incorporated. There are none, however, who have suggested that it is a good movie.

Pulgasari received little exposure outside North Korea, other than places like the Soviet Union and Pakistan, where it was released to television under the inexplicable title, *Zombi 34: The Communist Bull-Monster.* However, Shin and Choi never stuck around long around to see how the film was received, because while on a business trip to Austria in 1986, they managed to give their North Korean captors the slip at last and return to their home in South Korea. Jong-Il immediately had Shin's name removed from all prints of *Pulgasari*, which likely only served to elate the emancipated director even further.

After convincing the South Korean authorities of the verity of their story thanks to some fortunate secret audio recording he had done, Shin went back to making movies in 1990. Four years later, he made his way to America to finish out his career in Hollywood, making his U.S. debut under the pseudonym Simon Sheen by writing, producing, and directing, of all things, *3 Ninjas Kick Back* (1994), a sequel to the kids' martial arts movie *3 Ninjas* (1992). He would go on to executive produce the next two sequels in the series, *3 Ninjas Knuckle Up* (1995) and *3 Ninjas: High Noon at Mega Mountain* (1996), starring Hulk Hogan. And in the ultimate revenge against Kim Jong-Il, in 1996 he wrote the script for an American remake of *Pulgasari* called *The Legend of Galgameth.*

The following year, Kim Jong-Il ascended to power in North Korea. Perhaps it was no coincidence that it was then that *Pulgasari* finally got a Japanese release, putting it head-to-head with the American *Godzilla* at the box office there. American audiences had no opportunity to experience the film until a very limited New York engagement was finally arranged in 2005 using one of the rare remaining prints, just one year prior to Shin's death from liver failure at the age of seventy-nine (no one had thought to invite him to the premiere). The film was finally released to home video in the U.S. and Europe in 2015, allowing the rest of the world the chance at last to witness the product of the weirdest collaboration in the history of the *kaiju* genre.

13

March of the Monsters

The Music of Akira Ifukube

In cinematic history, there have been many composers whose work becomes forever linked with that of a specific director, a specific genre, or a specific franchise. In some cases, it would be hard to imagine certain films or characters without their famous music, and we can honestly say that the music is inextricably linked, and in fact a large part of why a film works as well as it does. What would the late films of Alfred Hitchcock be without Bernard Herrmann? What would the spaghetti westerns of Sergio Leone be without Ennio Morricone? Or *Star Wars* (1977) without John Williams? *The Godfather* (1972) without Nino Rota?

These films are unbreakably tied to the music of specific composers; such is the case with Godzilla and Akira Ifukube. As crucial as Monty Norman's thrilling James Bond theme, Max Steiner's sweeping *Gone with the Wind* (1939) suite, or Maurice Jarre's awesome theme for *Lawrence of Arabia* (1962), Ifukube's Godzilla themes are not only instantly recognizable, conjuring up mental images of the mighty monster on an uncontrollable rampage, but they also helped without a doubt to make Godzilla such a massive success, beginning with his stunning work on the original *Gojira* (1954), on through the many other entries in the series that he scored. Amongst the key central figures in the establishment of Godzilla, Ifukube deserves a place right alongside producer Tomoyuki Tanaka, director/writer Ishiro Honda, and special-effects master Eiji Tsuburaya. If a Mount Rushmore of *daikaiju eiga* were to be sculpted, those would the four faces that adorned it.

"Ifukube's music is as much a part of Godzilla's 'signature' as anything else," says prolific *kaiju* scholar Stuart Galbraith IV. "Ray Harryhausen liked to say that Max Steiner's music for *King Kong* was something like 60 percent of the reason for that film's greatness. I think something similar could be applied to Ifukube's music."

And yet Akira Ifukube accomplished much beyond the confines of the King of the Monsters. He produced countless scores, not only for other Toho *tokusatsu* pictures, but for many other films of other types over a movie career that lasted decades. And even if he never composed a single film score, Ifukube would have been long remembered as a serious composer of classical music; one of the most prominent Japanese composers of the twentieth century, as a matter of fact. Ifukube was highly respected before he had written a single movie score, and it was considered a major coup at the time when Toho lured him into the movie business.

A Musical Birthright

He was born May 31, 1914, in Kushido, the biggest city on the northern-most Japanese island of Hokkaido, the third son of a chief constable and the grandson of a Shinto priest. His link to the local Ainu population, an indigenous Japanese people who predate the modern ethnic Japanese and were a sizable demographic in the rural Tokatsu Plain area where he was raised, shaped his upbringing and cultural awareness from an early age, and would contribute to his lifelong fascination with ancient Japanese folk musical styles. As a youth, he studied both the violin and the shamisen, a traditional Japanese stringed instrument.

Ifukube attended high school in the Hokkaido capital of Sapporo, where, at the age of fourteen, he was first exposed to Western classical music in the form of a radio broadcast of Igor Stravinsky's *The Rite of Spring*. His interest piqued, the adolescent Ifukube decided to combine his fascination with Japanese and European classical music and become a composer. Ever the pragmatist, when he began studies at Hokkaido University, his main focus was forestry, which he intended to pursue as a full-time career while composing on the side as much as possible. At nineteen, he completed his first composition, a piano solo entitled *Piano Suite*, which he dedicated to American classical pianist George Copeland, an associate of Claude Debussy with whom he enthusiastically had been corresponding until civil war erupted in Spain, where Copeland was living at the time.

A major break occurred in 1935, when Ifukube's first full orchestral piece, *Japanese Rhapsody*, was unanimously voted first-prize winner in an international competition for young composers promoted by Russian composer and pianist Alexander Tcherepnin. This led to a brief apprenticeship with Tcherepnin himself during the Russian's visit to Japan the following year, which further sharpened Ifukube's grasp on Western music. The young Japanese composer, fresh out of university, was getting a name in classical music circles, and before long, his compositions were even being played in European concert halls by the late 1930s.

Still wishing to be practical and earn a dependable living outside of the notoriously undependable arts, Ifukube entered the forestry field after graduation, working as a lumber processor. During World War II, he was drafted by the Imperial Japanese Army to study the elasticity and vibratory strength of wood for the war effort. Fate stepped in when, while conducting X-ray testing without proper protection due to a wartime lead shortage, Ifukube suffered radiation burns that caused permanent physical damage and effectively ended his forestry career, compelling him to delve full-time into the world of music, both as a composer and (once again, pragmatically) as a teacher. Ironically, at the conclusion of the war, as Ifukube was recovering from his injuries and preparing to embark on his new career path, one of his own marches would be played for Gen. Douglas MacArthur when he arrived in Japan to formalize the nation's surrender to the Allied forces.

Learning the Score

In 1946, Ifukube began teaching music at Nihon University's College of Art, a post he would hold for seven years. During that period, his professional horizons would be further expanded by an entry into the field of film music. Although initially hesitant, he was persuaded by Fumio Hayakasa, a former university classmate who was experiencing success in the movies as a composer for director Akira Kurosawa. Hayakasa brought Ifukube to Tokyo and introduced him to the brass at Toho Company, where he would wind up contributing the most memorable musical work of his life.

The very first score Ifukube composed was for the Toho film *Snow Trail* (*Ginrei no hate*) (1947), sometimes known as *To the End of the Silver Mountains*. Directed by Senkichi Taniguchi from a Kurosawa screenplay, it would also mark the debut of future Japanese movie mega-star Toshiro Mifune, and also featured Takashi Shimura, eventual star of *Gojira* (1954). From the beginning, Ifukube was treated with great respect due to his existing reputation as a classical composer; often, he would use this reputation and the respect it brought to take an assertive creative role in the films he worked on, even if it meant butting heads with directors and producers over artistic decisions. Over the years, some would accuse Ifukube of looking down on the work he did in film, which may be in part due to the fact that when he first started, movie music was not taken very seriously; in fact, what little preparation Ifukube gave himself came not from previous film composers, but rather from the realm of opera, where rich character motifs and evocations of mood were the norm. In this way, he would prove to be ahead of his time.

With a philosophy that film music should only exist to serve the dramatic functions of the film that it's written for, Ifukube threw himself into it full-bore, composing eighty-two feature film scores in his first seven years in the business, all before taking on the project that would change his life forever. He composed for Kurosawa on the film *A Quiet Duel* (*Shizukanaru ketto*) (1949), as well as for other prominent Japanese directors such as Kon Ichikawa and Hiroshi Inagaki. By the early 1950s, he was one of the most sought-after composers on the Japanese movie scene. It was no surprise, therefore, that in 1954 when Tomoyuki Tanaka and Ishiro Honda were looking for the perfect musician to create the ultimate soundscape for their rampaging, titanic, radioactive terror, they would turn to Akira Ifukube.

Godzilla Comes Ashore

Just as he had been hesitant to become a film composer, so too did Ifukube initially hesitate when warned by some of his colleagues that making music for monster movies was beneath his talents as a serious musician and composer. Nevertheless, he took the assignment, and even though he was indeed typecast to a certain extent as a horror/science-fiction composer from that point on, he continued to compose for many other projects, including "serious" assignments outside the movie business. But make no mistake—Ifukube relished the chance to score *Gojira*, which gave him a chance to depart from his typically more melodic and subtle work into the realm of bombast and overt theatricality.

"Part of what he was going for was the bigness of Godzilla himself, and the idea that he supposedly was caused by atom bomb testing," explains Larry Tuczynski, whose website *Godzilla Monster Music* is considered the Internet's foremost reference on the subject. "In 1954 when it first came out, it wasn't that long removed from when Japan had lost World War II and had two atomic bombs dropped on it. That definitely had an influence on what he was doing."

Starting with *Gojira* and continuing into the multitudinous *daikaiju* film scores he would create over the ensuing two decades, Ifukube established a reliable pattern of interconnected themes. This pattern included a thrilling march or battle theme, such as the one included in *Gojira* and later films

The 1950 war drama *Listen to the Voices of the Sea* was one of the first films to be scored by Ifukube.

Public domain

like *Invasion of Monster Zero* to accompany the valiant efforts of humans to fight back against the enemy—this was a concept very familiar to Ifukube, who had composed many military marches during the war. Also falling into this category would be the main title theme of *Gojira*, with its fervent, frantic strings and brass over driving drums that, although originally intended as a military march, has come to be regarded as the official theme music of Godzilla himself, inevitably heralding his appearance and as inextricably linked to the monster as Williams's *Superman* theme to the Man of Steel, or Morricone's *The Good, the Bad and the Ugly* theme to the Man with No Name. There was also usually a dark, brooding theme meant to encapsulate unspeakable horror, such as the iconic cue "Godzilla Comes Ashore" from the original film, which hits when the monster begins his first assault on Tokyo. And finally, there would be a melancholy "requiem" theme of sorts, usually meant to convey intense sorrow or loss—in sharp contrast to the more upbeat American monster movies, which typically ended on a more positive note.

"His contribution is two-fold," explains Miguel Rodriguez. "First of all, it lends a certain *gravitas* to the monster, because there are some themes that are extremely somber. Some are among the best pieces of movie music ever made. And then some are a little more upbeat. It's not like this crazy action movie kind of score—it's very different. I think he thought a lot about the mood, and it was so strong that they just kept using it."

Some have pointed to what they see as a poverty of ideas in Ifukube's repeated use of this trio of themes, and it is a fact that he even recycled pieces wholesale from time to time, such as the theme from *Giant Monster Varan* (1958), which was later retooled as the main theme for *Ghidorah, the Three-Headed Monster* (1964). But it must be understood that the Japanese film industry at the time operated very differently from Hollywood, and Ifukube enjoyed none of the luxuries of his American contemporaries like Herrmann, Alfred Newman, John Barry, and Henry Mancini. Often given mere weeks, sometimes even days to turn around a new score, including composition time, arranging, recording, and mixing, he sometimes didn't even have the opportunity to view the film footage prior to composition, instead having to rely on the directors' descriptions of scenes, as he did for the original *Gojira*, for which he didn't even know what the monster would look like. At his height, it was not uncommon for him to score up to twenty films in a given year.

In addition to creating the music for these films, Ifukube was also responsible for creating many of the sound effects. Unlike in America, where the sound editing department was completely separate, the more bare-bones and streamlined system in Japan meant that most on the crew wore several hats, and since Ifukube was so familiar with musical instruments, he would use them to create unique sounds for the monsters. For instance, the original roar of Godzilla (Honda was adamant that the monster have a roar, despite the fact that reptiles typically make no sound) was created by Ifukube by taking a resin-coated glove and rubbing it along the loosened strings of a contrabass, then slowing down the sound in post-production. He also created the sound of Godzilla's booming footsteps, by using a thick, knotted rope to strike either an amplifier box or a kettle drum, according to different sources. Later, for King Ghidorah's trademark cry, he used an electronic organ, very much in vogue in the mid-1960s.

"There's a musical quality to the monsters that gives them a character all their own," says Miguel Rodriguez. "That was all Ifukube. There's nothing as recognizable as that Godzilla roar; it's so unique."

A Career in Kaiju

Ifukube's formula served him very well in a series of science-fiction and monster movie scores unparalleled in the history of genre cinema. His next *tokusatsu* score after *Gojira* would be *Rodan* (1956), followed by *The Mysterians* (1957), *Giant Monster Varan* (1958), and *Battle in Outer Space* (1959). In 1962, he returned to the Godzilla franchise for *King Kong vs. Godzilla*, and even though much of his brilliant score was excised for the American edit, even that version retains his powerful tribal theme, meant to evoke some of the original 1933 *King Kong*.

He would go on to score a string of Godzilla films in the 1960s. For *Mothra vs. Godzilla* (1964), he composed the haunting song "Sacred Springs" ("Seinaru Izumi"), a follow-up to the classic original, "Mothra's Song." That was followed by scores for *Ghidorah, the Three-Headed Monster* (1964) and *Invasion of Astro-Monster* (1965). He had formed a strong creative bond with director Ishiro Honda, which continued on other films such as *Atragon* (1963), *Dogora* (1964), *Frankenstein Conquers the World* (1965), *War of the Gargantuas* (1966), and *King Kong Escapes* (1967). In addition to the incredibly fruitful Honda collaboration, Ifukube also found time to score a wide range of other films, including the *Zatoichi* series of samurai films for Daiei Studios, as well as Daiei's dark fantasy *Daimajin* trilogy.

His thrilling music often enhanced films that were admittedly lackluster or clumsily executed, giving them a sense of weight and sweeping drama despite the low-budget special effects. As the Godzilla films became more juvenile and less serious, Ifukube's brooding music was no longer a perfect fit, and so other composers like Masaru Sato, Kunio Miyauchi, and Riichiro Manabe were brought in. However, all agreed that it was Ifukube's music that was still most associated with the monster, and when Toho wanted to create the ultimate badass monster mash-up in 1968 with *Destroy All Monsters*, they would turn once again to Ifukube, who composed a driving, utterly breathtaking march theme that remains one of his finest pieces of work.

Coda

By 1974, Ifukube was winding down his film career. He returned to teaching at the Tokyo College of Music, where he was named president in 1976. In the meantime, he was invited back to contribute one more score for what was to be the last of the original *Showa* Godzilla series, *Terror of Mechagodzilla* (1975) (As a testament to his importance, Toho had used his music for 1972's *Godzilla vs. Gigan*, but in a typical cost-cutting measure, only cues from previously released films were used in order to avoid having to pay him.) Three years later, he retired fully from film score composition at the age of sixty-four, choosing to focus on his great love, serious classical composition.

Still, it was difficult for Ifukube to escape the shadow of the King of the Monsters. For years, fans of his music had been hoping he would orchestrate some of his themes for live performance, but he had resisted, believing that film music was without value when not paired up with the drama on the screen. Finally, he relented in 1983 when he unveiled his *Symphonic Fantasia*, a sweeping overture containing many of his popular movie motifs, which he would include in his live concert performances (it was later retitled *Godzilla Fantasia* for even greater fan recognition). He put together a second film music suite, *Ostinato*, in 1986. By that time, the Godzilla movie series had started up again, but Ifukube remained on the sidelines, preferring to stay retired.

This would have been the perfect cap to a legendary career, but Ifukube was about to experience a renaissance while pushing eighty. Because he had refused to return to film scoring, Toho had brought in new composers to score the Godzilla films of the second wave. As part of his score for *Godzilla vs. Biollante*, Koichi Sugiyama had asked permission to incorporate some of Ifukube's iconic music, but in the end the maestro was very unhappy with the finished product, feeling his music had been modified to sound more like pop music, which he disliked. With the encouragement of his daughter, and to prevent further alteration of his work, Ifukube agreed to return to the Godzilla series for one last run.

"He had quite a bit of new music, but for continuity's sake he would also reuse some of the music," says Larry Tuczynski of the maestro's return to the series. "Kind of like in the James Bond films, somewhere in there you always hear that Bond theme, no matter who's actually doing the score. When Toho brought him back, he wanted some continuity from the early films."

His first *Heisei* score was for *Godzilla vs. King Ghidorah* (1991). He would go on to score *Godzilla & Mothra: Battle for Earth* (1992), and then what is often considered his finest latter-day work, *Godzilla vs. Mechagodzilla II* (1993). He had intended that one to be his last, but when Toho elected to kill off Godzilla in 1995 with *Godzilla vs. Destoroyah*, Ifukube could not resist the opportunity to set such a momentous occurrence to music, ending his long-standing relationship with the monster in grand fashion, with the greatest of all his requiem-style themes. Emphasizing the intrinsic link to the character that had defined his career, he declared that it felt like he was writing music for his own funeral. Even though he would never again compose new music for Godzilla (or for any film), when the monster was brought back once again in the 2000s for the Millennium series, those films routinely reused his music to instantly invoke the majesty of the Big G.

After enjoying a decade of full retirement, Ifukube was diagnosed with cancer and passed away on February 8, 2006, at the age of ninety-one. One of his nation's most revered composers, his career will always be best remembered for his work in the movies, particularly the essential contribution he made in cementing Godzilla as one of popular culture's most enduring and memorable creations. And although some musical purists bemoan the manner in which such allegedly lowbrow work overshadowed much of his other very fine achievements in music, perhaps the maestro himself put it best in an interview he gave for the liner notes to his 1978 musical compilation *Works of Akira Ifukube*: "When people tell me that I might have written something serious if I had not gotten into the movies, I tell them it is possible, but I might have starved also."

Setting Mayhem to Music

Although it was Akira Ifukube who composed the definitive theme music for Godzilla, there have been several other composers over the years who have also made significant contributions to the *kaiju* musical canon. Here is a trio of the best and brightest lights in Godzilla's film score firmament.

Masaru Sato

Second only to Akira Ifukube himself in terms of how many Godzilla films he scored, Masaru Sato was also a very different composer from Ifukube, preferring more Western jazz- and pop-influenced styles, in contrast to Ifukube's interests in European classical and traditional Japanese forms of music. Nevertheless, he idolized the maestro, as well as his longtime associate, Fumio Hayasaka, who would take the young Sato under his wing at the start of his film career.

Like Ifukube (and Hayasaka, for that matter), Sato was a native of the Japanese island of Hokkaido, and was born May 28, 1928, in the town of Rumoi, although he was raised in the Hokkaido capital of Sapporo. The youngest of six brothers, he was born into a very musical family, which made it easy for him to choose music as his career from an early age. At the age of twenty-two, he heard Hayasaka's new score for the landmark Akira Kurosawa film *Rashomon* (1950) and immediately sought out Hayasaka to become his pupil.

Hayasaka introduced Sato to Kurosawa, and in just a few short years, the young composer found himself working with the legendary director, beginning in 1954 when he served Hayasaka as an assistant orchestrator on *Seven Samurai*. When his mentor died suddenly the following year, Sato stepped in as direct collaborator with Kurosawa, and would continue on as his go-to composer for the next decade. Among the classic Kurosawa films Sato scored are *Throne of Blood* (1957), *The Hidden Fortress* (1958), *The Bad Sleep Well* (1960), *Yojimbo* (1961), *Sanjuro* (1962), *High and Low* (1963), and *Red Beard* (1965).

But Sato's first original score for Toho would actually be for *Godzilla Raids Again* (1955), the sequel to the smash hit *Gojira* that the studio had rushed into production. Although it is a drastic departure from Ifukube's music for the original film, and is not often fondly remembered among the Godzilla musical canon, it marked the beginning of a fruitful association with Toho's most popular franchise. He contributed the jazzy, hard-boiled score to Ishiro Honda's noirish horror picture *The H-Man* (1958), but ironically he would never work with Honda on a Godzilla movie. Instead, his next three Godzilla scores would be for director Jun Fukuda, whose lighter approach was more congruous with Sato's own take on the material. These included *Godzilla vs. the Sea Monster* (1966), *Son of Godzilla* (1967), and later, *Godzilla vs. Mechagodzilla* (1974).

"A fair amount of his work on Godzilla films doesn't seem to fit the films the way Ifukube's music did," opines *tokusatsu* music expert Larry Tuczynski. "His style was completely different, and instead of propelling the film, to me it took a little bit away from what was happening on screen. Ifukube's stuff sticks in your memory, where you can't really say that so much about Sato's music."

Sato's score for *Godzilla Raids Again* helped distinguish the sequel from its original predecessor.

Public domain

Beyond his work in *tokusatsu*, Sato was among the most prolific Japanese film composers of his day, with more than three hundred film scores to his credit, the lion's share of them for Toho Company, over the course of a career that spanned nearly half a century. He wrote his final score in 1999 for the samurai epic *After the Rain* (*Ame agaru*), directed by Takashi Koizumi from a script that had been written by Sato's longtime associate Kurosawa shortly before his death. Sato himself passed away later that year at the age of seventy-one. Unlike Ifukube, he never composed for the concert hall, but instead devoted all his prodigious energies to movie work.

Riichiro Manabe

By the 1970s, the Godzilla series had taken a drastic shift away from the sober tone of its origins, and Ifukube's music simply was not appropriate for encapsulating the more fun and upbeat vibe that went along with the monster's more heroic adventures. New blood was brought in by Toho to help freshen things up, and among the new wave of musicians was veteran composer Riichiro Manabe, who had enjoyed a varied career as something of a mercenary for Japanese film studios that included Nikkatsu and Shochiku. Manabe's work is often derided by those who abhor the more whimsical films of the late *Showa* period, and in fact the composer himself was often loath to discuss his *kaiju* work in later years; nevertheless, his contributions are important, and bridged a crucial gap in the history of the Big G.

Born November 9, 1924, in Tokyo, Manabe was working as a film composer from the tender age of twenty-one, when he contributed the score to the Nikkatsu picture *Aijo* (1956). He worked consistently through the 1950s and '60s, lending his talents to a wide range of material, from cinematic treasures like Nagisa Oshima's *A Town of Love and Hope* (*Ai to kibo no machi*) (1959), to sordid exploitation fare like *Naked Youth* (*Seishun zankoku monogatari*) (1960) and *The Sun's Burial* (*Taiyo no hakaba*) (1960).

By the time he was hired to score Yoshimitsu Banno's utterly bizarre *Godzilla vs. Hedorah* (1971), Manabe already had fifteen years of composing under his belt. Taking a unique approach to the material, Manabe put together a suitably strange score for a strange film. The work is admittedly uneven; funky in parts, incorporating electric guitars, synthesizers, and other unorthodox instrumentation; jarringly switching gears into a triumphant march worthy of a college football team, as Godzilla inexplicably flies backward through the air, propelled by his own atomic breath. And then there is his blaring trumpet theme, nearly as instantly identifiable with late *Showa* Godzilla as Ifukube's classic theme is with early *Showa*

Godzilla. Manabe even composed the music for the film's notorious pop number, "Return! The Sun" (aka "Save the Earth").

Often maligned, *Godzilla vs. Hedorah* is certainly nothing if not unusual, and Manabe's score is oddly suited to it. And despite Tomoyuki Tanaka's reported displeasure with the film, he brought Manabe back two years later to score the less odd but even more juvenile *Godzilla vs. Megalon* (1973). The epitome of '70s-style light jazz and esoteric funk, the score also includes another pop ditty by Manabe, the infectious "Gojira and Jaguar, Punch Punch Punch," as well as the lesser-known "Beat Megalon," both of which were released in Japan as singles.

Manabe composed through the 1970s and '80s, including for the films of horror director Michio Yamamoto, such as *The Vampire Doll* (*Chi o suu ningyo*) (1970), *Lake of Dracula* (*Noroi no yakata-Chi o su me*) (1971), and *Evil of Dracula* (*Chi o suu bara*) (1974). He initially retired in 1980 at the age of fifty-five, but came out of retirement twice: first in 1991 for the television movie *The Village of the Eight Tomb*, and finally in 2010 at the age of eighty-five for the documentary *The Oshima Gang*, which chronicled the making of the UK/Japanese co-produced David Bowie vehicle *Merry Christmas Mr. Lawrence* (1983). Riichiro Manabe passed away at age ninety on January 29, 2015.

Michiru Oshima

The history of Godzilla is largely populated by creative and visionary men, but if one had to choose the woman whose behind-the-scenes contribution to the Godzilla franchise was the greatest, Michiru Oshima would certainly be an excellent choice. A composer of three acclaimed scores during Godzilla's most recent Millennium phase, she was a musical force not seen in the series since the *Showa* days, defining Godzilla's character like none had done since the likes of Ifukube and Sato.

Oshima was born March 16, 1961. in Nagasaki, Japan, and attended Tokyo's prestigious Kunitachi College of Music, where she studied composition. Much like Ifukube, she began in her school days as a composer of orchestral music, including her "Orasho" symphony. After spending much of her twenties thusly, she entered the film industry in 1990 with a score for Taku Furukawa's *anime* short *Tarzan*. Her first feature film score would come the following year, for the gangster movie *Don ni natta otoko* (1991).

Anime would continue to be fertile ground for Oshima's creative efforts, and her career includes work on such popular franchises as *Sailor Moon*, *Fullmetal Alchemist*, and *Arc the Lad*. She has also worked extensively in the field of video games, producing music for such popular titles as PlayStation's *Legend of Legaia*

(1998) and Nintendo's *The Legend of Zelda: Twilight Princess* (2006). With such an unorthodox resume, it's easy to see how she was able to hone such an unusual style, incorporating synthesizers and other electronic instruments along with traditional instruments, resulting in a new and fresh sound that would have been unthinkable for an earlier generation of composers.

This groundbreaking approach is what brought her to the attention of Toho, and in 2000 she was commissioned to write the score for *Godzilla vs. Megaguirus*, the second film in the Millennium series. In keeping with the completely new approach to the franchise, Oshima created a totally different musical landscape for Godzilla, including a theme for the monster that is easily the most memorable since Ifukube's compositions. Understandably, she was brought back to score the fourth and fifth Millennium films, *Godzilla Against Mechagodzilla* (2002) and *Godzilla: Tokyo S.O.S.* (2003), lending a sense of musical continuity to those two closely related sequels.

"She was kind of a throwback to the Ifukube style," says Larry Tuczynksi. "Her scores were better than some of the one-off and two-offs that other composers did. I don't think they took it as seriously as Ifukube did, but it seemed to me that she really got into it and was serious about trying to make some memorable music. She went back to his type of roots."

Oshima's lush sense of melody and dramatic orchestrations have made her a favorite amongst Godzilla fans—even those who are often critical of the Millennium series as a whole. She continues to compose for the screen, and in recent years has switched much of her focus to television work. In 2016, she received her eighth Japanese Academy Award nomination, for her score to the nineteenth-century period picture *Kainan 1890* (2015).

14

Lost in Translation

The Disastrous American Version

After "killing off" their Godzilla in 1997, Toho Company cleared the way for TriStar Pictures, an American studio that desired to create an interpretation of the King of the Monsters for the U.S. The result was one of the most notorious misfires in movie history. The 1998 American *Godzilla* nearly destroyed a franchise that had existed for over forty years, and is viewed by fans today as the ultimate aberration in the series. Filmmakers Dean Devlin and Roland Emmerich had little regard for their source material, and their condescending contempt is clearly evident in the bitter fruit of their labors. Rarely has such a valuable property been so utterly mishandled, and to this day, longtime fans insist on referring to the iguana-like creature that appeared in the film as "Godzilla in Name Only," or simply GINO.

A critical disaster of epic proportions that stands alongside such films as *Howard the Duck* (1986), *Ishtar* (1987), *Waterworld* (1995), and *Gigli* (2003), the film nevertheless did make a profit at the box office, but fell so far short of projections, met with such a vociferous public backlash, and was such a merchandising flop that all plans for sequels were abandoned. Careers were damaged and even ruined, licensees went out of business, and Toho quickly distanced itself from the project, choosing instead to reboot its own franchise in an attempt to return its greatest creation to his former glory. And yet, what eventually became one of Hollywood's greatest failures took nearly a decade to bring to the big screen. A great deal of work and planning led up to that infamous moment in cinematic history when Godzilla faced Ferris Bueller.

Godzilla in Developmental Hell

As with many great catastrophes, it all began with the greatest of intentions. And in this case, those intentions initially came from an American who had been dealing with Toho and influencing the Godzilla franchise for decades—namely Henry J. Saperstein, the producer and distributor who had been responsible for much of the series' popularity in the United States during the 1960s, '70s, and '80s. For years, Saperstein had been trying to convince Toho to license a 100 percent American version of Godzilla to be produced by a Hollywood studio. He was finally given leave to try around 1990; but by this point he was in his early seventies, and his producing days were behind him. Instead, he began pitching the concept around Tinseltown, in an effort to sell off the lucrative rights to the American version (ironically, Saperstein would pass away a mere five weeks after the eventual film was finally released in 1998).

Initially meeting with Sony producers Cary Woods and Robert Fried circa 1991 about the possibility of a live-action movie based on Saperstein's famous Mr. Magoo character (a project that eventually came to fruition in 1997), Woods and Fried instead came away with the American rights to a property that intrigued them even more, Godzilla. Nevertheless, when both of Sony's major film studios, Columbia Pictures and TriStar Pictures, turned the project down, Woods and Fried went directly to notoriously eccentric Sony CEO Peter Guber (who had been involved in the lucrative Batman film franchise), who loved the idea and foisted the project onto TriStar. By the following year, the studio had gotten Toho's official blessing.

As it began to take shape in the early '90s, a few different directors were courted, with the project originally offered to James Cameron of *Terminator* (1984) and *Aliens* (1986) fame; then attached for a couple of years to Tim Burton, who was in the midst of reinventing the *Batman* franchise; followed by Joe Johnston, director of *Honey, I Shrunk the Kids* (1989) and *The Rocketeer* (1991); and even Paul Verhoeven, edgy director of *Robocop* (1987) and *Total Recall* (1990), who passed outright on the project.

The movie biz began to buzz as TriStar went into preproduction in 1994, hiring Ted Elliott and Terry Rossio, the screenwriting team responsible for Disney's *Aladdin* (1992), to pen a script to be directed by Jan de Bont, the Dutch auteur whose first feature, *Speed* (1994), had been a successful action blockbuster. Thematically, the reboot was to be a bold one: Godzilla would not be the product of nuclear experimentation gone amuck, but rather the creation of a secret race of Atlanteans, engineered to protect Earth from an extraterrestrial monster called the Gryphon, with both behemoths to be designed by the late practical effects master Stan Winston. And while this clear homage to 1970s-style *Showa* Era outrageousness might have been interesting to see, it was not meant to be, as TriStar refused to approve the massive budget de Bont deemed necessary, and the director abandoned the project.

Enter Devlin and Emmerich

Next, TriStar approached the creative team of producer Dean Devlin and director Roland Emmerich, a very hot commodity at the time (this film would change that). Responsible for the 1994 sci-fi thriller *Stargate* and fresh off what was to be a mammoth success in the alien invasion epic *Independence Day* (1996), Devlin and Emmerich needed some cajoling to take an interest in Godzilla, a property they considered campy and ridiculous right from the start. They only agreed to do it once they received total autonomy, which meant jettisoning Elliott and Rossio's script, as well as nearly anything having to do with the original Toho Godzilla, which they made it clear they wanted absolutely nothing to do with. As they co-wrote a new screenplay from scratch, they equated what they had in mind, in terms of making a "serious" Godzilla that broke ties with its campier roots, with what Tim Burton had done the previous decade by reinventing Batman as a more mature take on what had once been a much campier TV property in the 1960s.

Devlin and Emmerich's drastic reimagining would require a drastic creature redesign, and for that task the duo brought in visual effects and production designer Patrick Tatopoulos, who had worked with them previously on *Stargate* and *Independence Day*, and was also known for his work on *Bram Stoker's Dracula* (1992). With marching orders from Devlin and Emmerich, who found the look of the original Godzilla to be too implausible, Tatopoulos envisioned a Godzilla that was decidedly a living, breathing, functioning animal, structured closer to the dinosaurs of *Jurassic Park*, a sleek reptile with great agility and speed. It was also much smaller in size, and its more "realistic" design meant that it would lack two of Godzilla's most essential qualities: invulnerability to human weapons, and worst of all, atomic breath—the absence of which would eventually be enough to send Godzilla fanatics into fits of apoplexy.

"Devlin and Emmerich did their research, and they said, 'We watched all the Godzilla movies, and we can't in any good conscience do an exact translation,'" says August Ragone, the Walter Winchell of Godzilla fandom and author of *Eiji Tsuburaya: Master of Monsters*. "Toho was saying, this is what Godzilla is, and they looked at these movies and they thought they were

Godzilla in Name Only: The creature as designed by Patrick Tatopoulos.   *Movie Stills Database*

all trash. So they just decided to do their own thing, which was basically to remake *The Beast from 20,000 Fathoms* without paying for the rights."

Tatopoulos's Godzilla bore almost no resemblance whatsoever to Toho's creature, which was exactly what Devlin and Emmerich wanted. And with the digital effects revolution in full swing, practical effects would be largely abandoned in favor of a completely CGI creation, yet another blasphemy for fans of Japanese suitmation. Legend has it that when Tatopoulos and Emmerich brought a miniature maquette of the newly designed creature to the Toho offices in Japan for approval, studio chairman Isao Matsuoka, Godzilla producer Shogo Tomiyama, and special-effects designer Koichi

Kawakita were stunned into silence. Tomoyuki Tanaka, executive producer of Toho's Godzilla series since day one, was unable to attend the meeting due to failing health (he would, in fact, pass away mere months later), and had to be informed secondhand by a reluctant Tomiyama. Under pressure to preserve the lucrative relationship with TriStar, Toho execs cautiously gave their blessing, but the seeds of their doubt in the project had been planted.

King of the Iguanas

Devlin and Emmerich co-wrote an entirely new script, which returned Godzilla to his original nuclear origins, but kept little else that was recognizable. No connection to Japan was made whatsoever, with this new creature being derived from iguanas exposed to atomic testing in French Polynesia. The beast travels to New York City, followed closely by biologist Nick Tatopoulos, played by Matthew Broderick, an actor known mainly for light comedy. In New York, Tatopoulos (whose name was an obvious rib on the film's production designer) joins forces with plucky news reporter Audrey Timmonds (ingénue Maria Pitillo, whose promising career was decimated by the film's notorious failure) and French Secret Service agent Phillipe Roache (Jean Reno) to help the military put a stop to the creature's rampage.

Longtime fans of Godzilla would find little in this monster that they either expected or liked. A far cry from the methodical force of nature that had demolished Japan time and again, this Godzilla trotted down city blocks at top speeds, dwarfed by Manhattan skyscrapers and cleverly evading army artillery, unlike the original Big G, for whom bullets and shells were mere annoying distractions. This Godzilla also turned out to be pregnant, burrowing under Madison Square Garden to lay its multitude of eggs. This leads to a puzzlingly long sequence in which Tatopoulos and company are stalked throughout the Garden by Godzilla's man-sized hatchlings, who look for all the world like the velociraptors of *Jurassic Park*. Just when you might forget you're watching a Godzilla movie, the monster shows up one last time, just long enough to become entangled in the cables of the Brooklyn Bridge and get killed by a single missile barrage. An ignominious end to an ignominious adaptation, which made it hard to dispute the label of "Godzilla in Name Only."

"They were trying to make a more Hollywood kind of product," explains Dr. Bill Tsutsui, author of *Godzilla on My Mind*. "But in the process, they lost

Although one of America's most likable actors, Matthew Broderick was simply the wrong choice for a Godzilla movie. *David Shankbone/Wikimedia*

the soul of Godzilla, and really just created an animal, a reptile running through Manhattan, rather than creating a heroic figure . . . They really tried to separate Godzilla from his Japanese origins, and that just doesn't work. No matter where you go in the world, Godzilla and Japan are of a piece."

Dropping the Bomb

In the months leading up to the film's May 20, 1998, release, TriStar's hype and marketing machine was cranking at full power, prepping the moviegoing public for what was to be one of the biggest letdowns of Hollywood's modern blockbuster era. The decision was made to not reveal what the creature looked like (in hindsight, it's easier to understand why), which only made fans all the more curious. Posters of the creature's giant foot, with the infamous tagline "Size Matters" became ubiquitous. Fast food chain Taco Bell became a major part of the campaign, and to this day, the phrase, "Here, lizard, lizard, lizard!" will register instant recognition with just about anyone who grew up in the 1990s. Trendmasters, the toy company that in 1994 had produced a coveted line of action figures based on the *Heisei* Era Toho monsters, prepared an ambitious line of toys based on the new movie, the utter lack of consumer interest in which would lead to the company's eventual demise in 2002.

As expected, the film opened big, as it was the most anticipated movie of the summer. However, critics mercilessly lambasted it, with many calling it the worst big-budget summer blockbuster ever made, and negative word of mouth spread very quickly. For its opening weekend, it made a little over half what was projected, and suffered a 59 percent drop in its second week. In the end, the film actually made a small profit, its domestic gross just barely exceeding its $130 million budget (ironically greater than the one de Bont had previously requested). Interestingly, the film would do noticeably better in the international market, playing well in nations that were unfamiliar with Toho's original Godzilla series. In fact, to this day in many of those countries, the American TriStar *Godzilla* is considered far superior to the low-budget Japanese version.

However, that international opinion would prove to be somewhat of an anomaly, and many fans in foreign lands remained puzzled when no follow-up sequels were ever made, unaware of what a colossal disaster the picture had been in America. Initially bitter and angry at the fans that had rejected their work, Devlin and Emmerich would later come to admit the film's egregious faults, largely stemming from their own insistence on abandoning the very things that had made the original series so beloved in the first place. Indeed, the film had originally been envisioned as a tentpole franchise for Sony, but any plans for sequels were quickly shelved after the massive backlash. And while in the end *Godzilla* was a moneymaker for the studio, its notorious reputation made it box-office poison nonetheless.

"Devlin and Emmerich had zero respect for the franchise, for the character, and for the creations of Honda and Tsuburaya," says Miguel Rodriguez. "They were quoted as saying, this is going to be a real special effects thing, not a bunch of guys in suits knocking over Lego buildings. There's another comment from someone at Toho that sums it up really well: Americans don't understand something they can't destroy . . . They clearly just wanted to make it *Jurassic Park*, and that is a complete misunderstanding of what Godzilla is. Godzilla is more like a Shinto god, not just some big lizard."

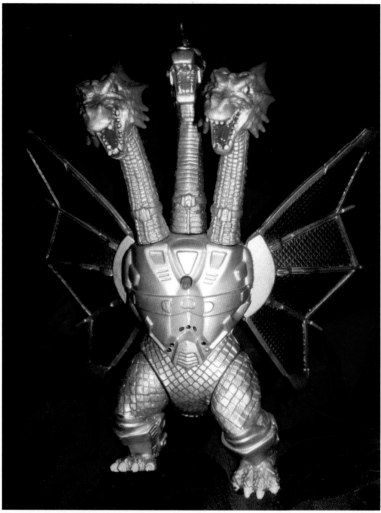

Trendmaster's Mecha King Ghidorah action figure, part of the company's 1990s *Heisei*-inspired line.   *Al Pavangkanan/Flickr*

Aftermath

Flawed interpretations and unfaithfulness to the source material aside, Devlin and Emmerich's *Godzilla* remains an eminently bad film. From the shoddy, nearly logic-free script, to the cringeworthy on-screen performances, to the soulless special effects, it came to be seen as the embodiment of all that is wrong with the American film industry's obsession with big-budget "event" pictures—an obsession that continues stronger than ever to this day.

Almost inconceivably, TriStar had completely bungled what, on paper, was one of the most appealing, slam-dunk, established movie properties in existence. Toho was aghast at the finished product, instantly regretting the decision to hand the franchise over to an American studio. Taking back the rights, Toho execs immediately decided to reboot their own Godzilla series, unwilling to allow Devlin and Emmerich's film to be the last word on the iconic character. In a further maneuver to disown the American incarnation, they would even include TriStar's monster, which they renamed "Zilla" (since, as they explained, the Americans had removed the "God" from the character), in 2004's *Godzilla: Final Wars*, in which the beast is unceremoniously dispatched with ease by Toho's King of the Monsters.

"The basic mistake TriStar and others like them almost always make is that they almost never do the very thing they should do first: Carefully study the original films and try to get a handle on their appeal," says Stuart Galbraith IV. "Why has Godzilla as a series and as a character lasted so long? What is it about those old movies that keep people coming back to them? It's fine to start with that but then go off in an entirely different direction, but that's not what they did at all."

The TriStar *Godzilla* remains to this day one of cinema's most infamous punchlines, and helped to sour American audiences on the giant monster subgenre. In fact, it would take more than a decade and a half for another American studio to even consider making an American version of Godzilla. Mishandled on every level, from its misguided conceptualization to its hopelessly bloated marketing budget, it is a cautionary tale of the worst-case scenario that can arise from studio hubris and the unwillingness to at least take into consideration the desires of the built-in audience so coveted by those who choose to endlessly adapt and reboot previously established properties. In the end, its failure would prove to be one of the most damaging assaults the mighty Godzilla ever faced. And yet, just like all the other times, he would somehow find a way to survive.

15

Third Wave

The Millennium Era

B y the dawn of the current century, Godzilla had been finally showing some signs of his age, after nearly half a century in the public eye. Two whole generations had come of age with the giant lizard, and it seemed that just about everything that could be done, had been done. On top of all that, Godzilla had recently taken an unfortunate pounding in the form of a one-two punch: First, he was killed off in *Godzilla vs. Destoroyah* (1995), the last of the *Heisei* era Godzilla films, and then his image was grossly tarnished by the creative failure and box-office disappointment of the 1998 American reboot movie. The monster was certainly in need of a massive shot in the arm, and Toho sought to administer exactly that with what came to be aptly known as the Millennium series.

Toho studio executives were reeling from the TriStar Pictures disaster, and vehemently reclaimed the rights to their very valuable character. After shepherding the franchise for nearly half a century, executive producer Tomoyuki Tanaka had passed away in 1997, shortly after handing over the reins to his former assistant, Shogo Tomiyama. All plans to turn the American film into a franchise were promptly scrapped, and Tomiyama announced that Toho would instead reboot the character and the franchise themselves, something that would have seemed unthinkable when they passed the torch to the Americans a mere four years prior. Some serious damage control was in order if the King of the Monsters could ever be expected to be taken seriously again.

Just as in previous eras, the Millennium series represented yet another shift in philosophy, and in approach. Some of it was a reaction to the American movie, and some was a desire to change with the times and to meet perceived audience expectations. Whereas the *Heisei* series had maintained a cohesive continuity from film to film, the Millennium series would, with one exception, be conceived as a series of stand-alone films, even more so than the original *Showa* series had been. Unlike with the indelible legacies created by the likes of Ishiro Honda and Kazuki Omori, Toho developed an anthology approach, planning to spotlight a different director with each Millennium installment, so that each film would emerge as the unique vision of that individual, many of whom had grown up as Godzilla fans.

More than ever before, the emphasis would be put on action, with the human story lines, occasionally criticized for slowing down earlier films, moved to the background and wall-to-wall monster mayhem emphasized. This attitude led to one major shortcoming of the Millennium series: By the new century, digital special effects were the order of the day in genre motion pictures, and Toho was struggling mightily to keep up. Whereas during the 1950s and 1960s, the studio had been known for being on the cutting edge of special effects thanks to the efforts of Eiji Tsuburaya, their status had slipped dramatically in the intervening decades. This was no more apparent than during the Godzilla films of the 2000s, which relied heavily on CGI that was often of low quality, and certainly far behind the standard of the time, on display in films from the *Matrix*, *Harry Potter*, and *Lord of the Rings* franchises.

The newly redesigned Millennium Godzilla faces off with Orga.   *Everett Collection*

The Millennium series also struggled to find an audience. Whereas Godzilla had once been Toho's cash cow—the dependable, go-to franchise that would always attract sizable returns—times had changed in Japan. The character had been less visible in recent years, and with the huge influx of American movies continuing at an ever-greater pace, audiences were opting for Hollywood's versions of cinematic spectacle over the home-grown, traditional kind. Although the films in the Millennium series are enjoyed by many Godzilla fans—in fact, even preferred by some—at the time, they were considered box-office disappointments for Toho, and evidence that perhaps the character had worn out his welcome and should have stayed dormant.

In the end, the Millennium era represents a valiant effort on Toho's part to right the ship and return Godzilla to iconic status. For all its faults, it also boasts many fine moments, and some of the most exciting monster battles seen in the entire series. It introduced Godzilla to the twenty-first century, and even though it is the shortest-lived of all the eras, it helped ensure that the scaly juggernaut would keep on going, if even for just a few more years. And every one of the Millennium films is preferable to Roland Emmerich's *Godzilla* (1998), anyway.

Godzilla 2000

Japanese Title: *Gojira ni-sen mireniamu*
Also Known As: *Godzilla Millennium* (international title)
Release Date: November 6, 1999

For its first Godzilla film in four years, and the first to be made since taking back the franchise, Toho really looked to thoroughly reboot the franchise, as they had done with *Godzilla 1985* at the start of the *Heisei* era. All previous continuity was thrown out the window, with the exception of the original 1954 film (this would become a recurring pattern in the Millennium series, with each installment completely wiping the slate clean). Despite the desire to make each new film the stand-alone vision of a different director, for this first film in the Millennium series, Toho turned to Takao Okawara, who had directed three of the best of the *Heisei* films (*Godzilla 2000* would be his final film to date). In partnership with TriStar, which had retained American distribution rights to Godzilla, Toho made a full-court press to publicize the

(Left to right) Takehiro Murata, Mayu Suzuki, and Naomi Nishida witness the destruction in *Godzilla 2000*.   *Everett Collection*

film in the States like no Toho production had been in decades—it would even get the first U.S. theatrical run of any Toho export in fifteen years.

Perhaps in an effort to erase memories of the very vulnerable, animal-like creature of TriStar's *Godzilla* (1998), *Godzilla 2000* presents the big guy as an unstoppable force of nature, further emphasized by the fact that he is being tracked and studied like a natural disaster by an intrepid scientist, played by Takehiro Murata (previously seen in *Heisei* films *Godzilla & Mothra: Battle for Earth* and *Godzilla vs. Destoroyah*). This is certainly more like the Godzilla of old, even if he looks quite a bit different, boasting a drastic, reptilian redesign and played for the first time by veteran stunt performer Tsutomu "Tom" Kitagawa.

Unlike the previous Toho reboot, *Godzilla 1985*, as well as the recent American reboot, *Godzilla 2000* doesn't spotlight only the monster by himself, but rather boasts a brand-new *kaiju* foe, the ancient alien life form known as Orga. Nevertheless, this is where much of the CGI work on the film truly shows its age, as the monster is sometimes rendered quite weakly.

And speaking of CGI, this film also features the first-ever digital version of Godzilla, as the monster is shown, for the first time, swimming underwater. What the effects work may lack in execution on this picture, it makes up for in ambition. The monster is always presented in an awe-inspiring light, including a truly memorable first appearance worthy of the King of the Monsters.

In their efforts to publicize the film in the United States, Toho and TriStar even created a poster showing Godzilla towering over the Brooklyn Bridge—a direct knock at the '98 American film, in which the monster is small enough to become tangled in the cables of the very same bridge, and meekly dies there after being hit with a mere three missiles. But despite the effort to market the film stateside, it did not fare terribly well when released to American theaters at the end of the 2000 summer movie season. Presumably, audiences may have been confused, having just seen the radically different TriStar film just two years prior, and they roundly rejected the much smaller-budgeted Toho product. *Godzilla 2000* would be the only Millennium installment to receive a U.S. theatrical release—all future films would go directly to home video in America.

Godzilla vs. Megaguirus

Japanese Title: *Gojira tai Megagirasu: Jî shômetsu sakusen*
Literal Translation: *Godzilla vs. Megaguirus: The G Annihilation Strategy*
Also Known As: *Godzilla X Megaguirus: The G Extermination Command*
Release Date: December 16, 2000

A bold film that attempts several new and interesting things, *Godzilla vs. Megaguirus* introduces yet another brand-new *kaiju* opponent, and strikes some tonal chords that were fairly unique for the Godzilla franchise. Masaaki Tezuka, who had recently worked as an assistant director on Toho's *Rebirth of Mothra* series, was recruited to make his official directorial debut on the picture, working with an interesting script from veteran *Heisei* screenwriters Hiroshi Kashiwabara (*Godzilla vs. Space Godzilla*) and Wataru Mimura (*Godzilla vs. Mechagodzilla II*), who had just finished working together on the *Godzilla 2000* screenplay.

A striking feature of the film is its horrific overtone, rarely seen in latter-day *kaiju* cinema. But after all, *kaiju* movies are monster movies, and have their roots in horror, so it made sense for *Godzilla vs. Megaguirus* to stretch back a bit to embrace those roots. The plot is an odd and convoluted one, centering on time travel and a weapon that can generate wormholes. When a particular wormhole opens a rift to the prehistoric era, a giant dragonfly sneaks into the present day and lays a mass of eggs, which hatch into dangerous larvae known as Meganulon. This reference certainly tickled longtime *kaiju* aficionados, as the Meganulon hadn't been seen since the original *Rodan* (1956). The terrifying creatures prey on humans in a manner more typical of a Wes Craven or John Carpenter film than to anything usually seen in a Godzilla movie.

Later, the Meganulon metamorphose into flying Meganula, and a swarm of them engage in a particularly impressive and unusual battle with Godzilla, which takes place on a tropical island, hearkening back to the "island" films of the 1960s. It's one of the most impressive uses of CGI in the Millennium era, and is a precursor to Godzilla's upcoming city-stomping confrontation with the titular adversary Megaguirus herself, who emerges as the queen of the Meganula. The fight scenes, some of which are staged in broad daylight, have a different look than many other similar scenes from other films, usually shot with dim lighting and on interior soundstages. While this film also has plenty of that, its action sequences are breaths of fresh air, as is the brand-new monster competition.

After the lackluster American showing of *Godzilla 2000*, Sony (parent company of TriStar Pictures) scrapped plans to release *Godzilla vs. Megaguirus* theatrically in the U.S. Instead, it had its American premiere on television, making its debut on the Sci-Fi Channel on August 31, 2003. It was released to DVD the following February.

Godzilla, Mothra and King Ghidorah: Giant Monsters All-Out Attack

Japanese Title: *Gojira, Mosura, Kingu Gidorâ: Daikaijû sôkôgeki*
Literal Translation: *Godzilla, Mothra, King Ghidorah: The Giant Monsters' General Offensive*
Also Known As: *GMK* (promotional abbreviation)
Release Date: December 15, 2001

One of the most original and daring Godzilla films of any era, *GMK* (as it is known to hardcore fans worldwide) stands completely on its own to an even greater degree than the other Millennium films. Along the way, it made over Godzilla in a quite dramatic fashion, retooled his entire origin, and even redefined the nature of the *daikaiju* themselves. It is widely regarded as the very best entry in the Millennium series.

The concept was the brainchild of writer-director Shusuke Kaneko, who had reinvented and reinvigorated Daiei Studios' Gamera franchise in the 1990s with the *Heisei* trilogy of *Gamera: Guardian of the Universe* (*Gamera daikaiju kuchu kessen*) (1995), *Gamera 2: Attack of the Legion* (*Gamera 2: Region shurai*) (1996), and *Gamera 3: Revenge of Iris* (*Gamera 3: Jashin kakusei*) (1999). Just as Kaneko had made Godzilla's chief box-office rival into a more serious character of deeper gravitas, so he also approached Godzilla and his cronies with more of a reverent and mythic attitude, emphasizing their folkloric aspects and the manner in which the original conception of the *daikaiju* had drawn from ancient Japanese legends.

In Kaneko's vision, Godzilla is not a mere physical being, created via nuclear radiation. Rather, the creature for the first time takes on an overtly supernatural tone, being animated in part by the vengeful souls of those killed during the Pacific theater of World War II. These souls, in the form of Godzilla, seek the destruction of Japanese civilization, and the only force that can stop them are the ancient Sacred Guardian Beasts of Yamato, whom Godzilla fans will recognize as none other than Mothra, Baragon, and also King Ghidorah, here portrayed for the first and only time as a force for good, not evil. These *kaiju*, reimagined by Kaneko as Earth's mystical protectors, unite to fend off Godzilla in a series of epic encounters.

And this Godzilla is decidedly the most vindictive, sadistic, and outright evil of any incarnation committed to the screen. This is the only entry in the Millennium series in which the new reptilian suit designed by Shinichi Wakasa was not used, but rather, an entirely different design created to more closely resemble the traditional, 1954 Godzilla suit. Yet this is a more demonic take on that classic look, featuring all-white, zombie-like eyes and a more defined musculature. This is also the only Millennium film in which Tom Kitagawa does not don the suit, but rather, it is worn by the much taller stunt actor Mizuho Yoshida. Fans may also be shocked to see this Godzilla specifically targeting human victims with a wrathful fury, rather than the more general, wholesale property destruction he typically engages in.

If the Millennium series was indeed devised to give different directors the chance to shine and to exhibit their own unique take on the King of the Monsters, then *Godzilla, Mothra and King Ghidorah: Giant Monsters All-Out Attack* is certainly the film that most lives up to that promise. Kaneko's take on Godzilla and his cohorts is a fresh and fascinating one, and the most loved by fans. For its American release, it was paired with the previous entry, *Godzilla vs. Megaguirus*, as a double feature on both the Sci-Fi Channel in August 2003 and on the ensuing DVD release in February 2004.

Godzilla Against Mechagodzilla

Japanese Title: *Gojira X Mekagojira*
Release Date: December 14, 2002

You just can't keep a good robot down, and so it was inevitable that Mechagodzilla, one of Godzilla's most enduring foes, would eventually take his Millennium era bow. This is technically the third film to bear the moniker *Godzilla vs. Mechagodzilla*, following previous entries in 1974 and 1993, and so to avoid confusion internationally, the movie was given the slightly altered title *Godzilla Against Mechagodzilla*. It also bears mentioning that this interpretation of Mechagodzilla is quite different from the ones that came before. But one thing remains constant: Just as with all other Mechagodzilla appearances, this one is a crowd-pleaser that delivers in both the action and drama departments.

Breaking the unwritten rule to spotlight a new director with each Millennium film, Toho instead brought back *Godzilla vs. Megaguirus* director Masaaki Tezuka to helm Mechagodzilla's return, with a script by his *Megaguirus* collaborator, Wataru Mimura. Their version of Mechagodzilla, however, would not be the creation of invading aliens, as it had been in the 1974 film, nor was it merely a giant robot created by the Japanese military, as it had been in the 1993 film. This time, Mechagodzilla is a cyborg, made from robotic machinery grafted onto the skeleton of the original Godzilla, supposedly lying at the bottom of Tokyo Bay since 1954. To further differentiate it from previous versions, this Mechagodzilla is given the name "Kiryu," meaning roughly "mechanical dragon."

Just as it had in the 1993 *Heisei* film, Mechagodzilla (Kiryu) is here created to beat back the onslaught of the destructive Godzilla. This film has some impressive *kaiju*-on-mecha action, including a nightmarish sequence in which we discover that the spirit of the original Godzilla is still somehow inhabiting the mechanized Kiryu, and it causes the robot to turn on its masters and go on its own destructive rampage through the city.

But aside from all the action, the film is also marked by some of the most interesting and endearing human characters and story lines to be found in recent Godzilla fare. The story has decidedly militarized overtones, with newcomer Yumiko Shaku starring as Lt. Akane Yashiro, a soldier with a score to settle after losing several friends in a previous battle with the Big G. Later, she must pilot Kiryu along with a subordinate (Yusuke Tomoi) who holds her responsible for the death of his brother during the aforementioned battle. Along the way, she crosses paths with the awkward scientist Tokumitsu Yahara (Shin Takuma), one of the designers of Kiryu, and his daughter Sara (Kana Onodera). Yahara, a single father, clearly has a crush on the much more assertive Yashiro, and in a sweet post-credits scene, finally works up the courage to ask her out.

Godzilla Against Mechagodzilla was the most successful film in the Millennium series to that point, and eventually made its way to home video in the U.S. in March 2004, just one month after the *Godzilla vs. Megaguirus/GMK* double-feature disc had been released. The film was such a hit, in fact, that Toho broke another self-imposed rule by ordering a direct sequel.

Godzilla: Tokyo S.O.S.

Japanese Title: *Gojira tai Mosura tai Mekagojira: Tokyo SOS*
Release Date: December 13, 2003

The only direct sequel in the entire Millennium series, *Godzilla: Tokyo S.O.S.* also marks Masaaki Tezuka's third and final effort as director. Having introduced the Godzilla/Kiryu story line in the previous film, Tezuka took even further ownership this time around, rejecting the proposed story treatments presented to him by Toho, and opting instead to write the screenplay himself (something he had never done before). In addition to Mechagodzilla's fifth appearance in the series, Tezuka also brought back the beloved Mothra and her larvae as integral parts of the plot.

As the military scrambles to rebuild Kiryu after the robot's clash with Godzilla in the previous film, the Big G returns to Japan to dish out even more damage. This is where Mothra and her trusted *shobijin* fairies return to action, not seen in this particular continuity since their first appearance in the original *Mothra* (1961). The fairies warn that the reason Godzilla keeps attacking is that the bones of the original Godzilla have been defiled by being used to construct Kiryu in the first place, and they must be returned to the ocean floor to banish Godzilla for good. Naturally, the military doesn't heed their words, and what follows is a three-way battle involving Kiryu, Godzilla, *and* Mothra that threatens to flatten Japan for good.

Toho veteran actor Hiroshi Koizumi, first seen by Godzilla fans in *Godzilla Raids Again* (1955), reprises his role of Dr. Shinichi Chujo, the scientist who discovered Mothra in the 1961 film more than forty years prior. Also thrown in for longtime fans is a brief appearance by, of all things, the giant sea turtle Kamoebas, previously seen in Ishiro Honda's *Space Amoeba* (1970).

In an attempt to broaden Godzilla's appeal to younger fans, who had largely abandoned *tokusatsu* cinema in favor of the hottest latter-day trend in Japanese entertainment, *anime*, *Godzilla: Tokyo S.O.S.* was released in Japan as part of a double bill with the *anime* feature *Hamtaro: Miracle in Aurora Valley* (*Gekijo ban Tottoko Hamutaro: Orora no kiseki*), part of the Hamtaro animated franchise that was all the rage in the early 2000s. The results were less than stellar, however, and it was decided that the Kiryu story line would not be continued beyond this film. In December 2004, *Godzilla: Tokyo S.O.S.* was released in the U.S. on DVD—the fourth Godzilla film brought to American home video that year.

Godzilla: Final Wars

Japanese Title: *Gojira: Fainaru uôzu*
Release Date: December 4, 2004

By 2004, with five new Godzilla films in the rearview mirror, it was clear to many within Toho that the Millennium series had not quite lived up to the hopes they had for reinvigorating the franchise. They had certainly kept it going, but the returns were dwindling, as were the audiences. It was decided that the next Godzilla film would also be the last, at least for the foreseeable future. But Toho wasn't about to send their favorite monster off into the sunset (again) without the proper goodbye—an all-out, balls-to-the-wall monster rally of epic proportions. *Godzilla: Final Wars* was like no other Godzilla film that had come before it, and this left some fans scratching their heads in confusion. Nevertheless, it is a fun-filled romp that contains everything but the kitchen sink, and succeeds at entertaining, even as sense and logic are cast to the four winds.

Stylish auteur Ryuhei Kitamura was not the usual type of director tapped by Toho to make a Godzilla film, but he had been a die-hard fan as a kid during the *Showa* era, and campaigned hard for the chance to put his definitive mark on the franchise for its fiftieth anniversary, and possibly final, film. Teaming with previous screenwriting partner Isao Kiriyama, Kitamura also contributed the script for the film. The result was a director's vision that truly took Godzilla in a completely different direction, specifically from a tonal point of view. *Final Wars* is an outrageous film, filled with mutants, aliens, outlandish action set pieces, and a virtual who's who of classic *kaiju*.

Drawing on his love of *Showa*-era wackiness, Kitamura filled the picture with countless homages to the films of his youth. Godzilla goes through a gauntlet of past opponents, doing battle with one after another in various corners of the globe, including Rodan, Mothra, and King Ghidorah, as well as creatures not seen since the *Showa* era, such as Anguirus, Gigan, Kamacuras, Kumonga, King Caesar, Ebirah, and even Hedorah the Smog Monster. The sinister Xiliens, not seen since *Invasion of Astro-Monster* (1965), figure prominently into the plot, and two of them are even played by franchise veterans Akira Takarada and Kumi Mizuno. Concepts and set pieces are "borrowed" liberally from everything from *X-Men* to *The Matrix.* Godzilla's son Minya, not seen since *Destroy All Monsters* (1968), shows up, smoke rings and all. Even the 1998 CGI American Godzilla, here known as "Zilla," shows up to get summarily trounced in record time by the real deal.

"I'm in the great minority who felt that one was actually a big improvement over the other Millennium films," says Japanese film scholar Stuart Galbraith IV, generally not what one would call a fan of the Millennium series. "It's not good, exactly, but it was the only entry from that period that had a real vision and a vastly different look. Not a *good* vision, not a *good* look, necessarily, but I admired and still admire its *chutzpah.*"

Godzilla: Final Wars was a polarizing film. For some, it was a delightful romp that threw out all the rules and delivered wall-to-wall monster action and fanciful science-fiction adventure. Others found it to be a disappointing disaster, often citing the very things considered positives by the fans that loved it. Fun as it is, it can't be denied that it's also a bit uneven and most definitely doesn't take itself too seriously. Of course, at the end of the day, it is a movie about a giant irradiated dinosaur pitted against a race of aliens, so maybe it doesn't need to.

"We're at a point where very often people seem less concerned with making a good movie as they are with fan service, with doing something 'for the fans,'" offers Steve Biodrowski, longtime *kaiju* lover and editor of *Cinefantastique Online.* "And I think people were expecting to get fan service with that last Godzilla movie, and they didn't get it. They just did something radical and weird with all those ideas, and turned it into something else."

In the ultimate publicity stunt for Godzilla's big send-off, Toho arranged for the film to make its official premiere at the historic Grauman's Chinese Theatre in Hollywood, following a ceremony celebrating Godzilla's very own star on the Hollywood Walk of Fame. Unfortunately, that wasn't enough to energize the Japanese audiences: When the film opened in Japan five days later, it did only tepid box office, confirming executive producer Shogo Tomiyama's initial decision that the series should be put into mothballs for the foreseeable future. It was released on DVD in the U.S. one year later, in

December 2005. As for the ambitious director Ryuhei Kitamura, he seemed to take a liking to Hollywood, and remained there to make a number of genre pictures, including the horror film *The Midnight Meat Train* (2008) starring Bradley Cooper.

In hindsight, the Millennium series is judged by some to have been a failure. It certainly didn't attract the big-time box-office numbers that many films during the *Showa* and *Heisei* eras had. Some take issue with the overabundance of action and a perceived heightened militarism in the pictures. What the series does represent is an effort on Toho's part to do something different, even if that effort didn't quite succeed. Shogo Tomiyama may not quite be up to the mantle of Tomoyuki Tanaka as stewards of the Godzilla franchise go. But with well over a decade since *Final Wars* led to the longest drought in the history of the franchise, divorced from box-office figures, the films can be enjoyed on their own merits, as the interesting experiments they are.

"The problem now is that Toho as a company is very much a great hindrance to the Godzilla series," says Stuart Galbraith IV. "Good artistic choices are simply impossible at the corporate level. You need a compact team of several screenwriters, an imaginative director and a supportive producer and, sadly, Toho hasn't had anything like that combination for many years."

16

Monster Factory

A History of Toho Company

One of the most successful production houses in the world, Toho Co., Ltd., has been in business since the 1930s, and in the 1950s became home to its most internationally famous creation, Godzilla. Over the course of a history spanning more than eighty years, Toho popularized the *kaiju* phenomenon with films like *Rodan* (1956), *Mothra* (1961), and *War of the Gargantuas* (1966); produced Akira Kurosawa classics like *Seven Samurai* (1954), *Throne of Blood* (1957), and *Yojimbo* (1961); as well as *anime* landmarks like *Akira* (1988) and *Princess Mononoke* (1997), and horror favorites *Kwaidan* (1964) and *Ringu* (1998).

In fact, Toho did far more even than that. One of a handful of major Japanese film companies, it held sway over a huge portion of the market, and commanded faithful audiences of millions who would flock to see their most popular pictures. Beyond even the aforementioned standouts that are best known to Western audiences, in Japan Toho was known for much, much more, with a filmography that includes light comedies, historical epics (*jidai-geki*), and other genres. Just as Hollywood had its studio system that reigned supreme for decades, so too did the Japanese film industry, and Toho was a major part of that system.

The studio system in Japan, in fact, lasted a good decade longer than it did in America. During that time, Toho was known for producing some of the most polished motion pictures around, similar to the reputation M-G-M enjoyed during the height of Hollywood's studio system. In more recent decades, the company has certainly lost some of that prestige, with the demise of the Japanese studio system, heated competition from television, and most recently the utterly dominating inroads made by the American movie industry. Toho may not be the sterling giant it was in those glory days, but it still continues to produce filmed entertainment at a vigorous pace, and is very much alive and well. In the history of Japanese cinema, it stands out as an important force, both commercially and artistically.

Photo Chemical Laboratories

The company that would eventually come to be known as Toho grew out of Photo Chemical Laboratories (PCL), an outfit founded in 1929 by photographer Yasuji Uemura, originally for the purpose of developing film for the new movie studios that were cropping up throughout Japan. Sound technology arrived in Japan just a few years later than it did in the States, but by the early '30s, Japanese studios were looking into it, and PCL expanded its operations to include sound recording equipment, and even soundstages for filming. Although originally intended to be rented out, before long Uemura recognized the profitability of actually making his own films, using his own equipment.

At first, these films were commercial, advertising products like beer and candy. By the mid-1930s, PCL was making about fifteen pictures a year. Just like many of the early Hollywood studios, PCL started specializing in musical comedies, which helped them to show off their sound capabilities, and also helped to introduce new popular songs that could later be marketed to the public. And despite the modern-day association of the studio with science-fiction and monster movies, musicals and comedies would remain its bread and butter for decades.

Several of the major Japanese movie studios grew out of an already existing and thriving industry in that country, railroads. Wealthy and powerful railroad magnate Ichizo Kobayashi, founder of Hankyu Railway, took notice of PCL and officially acquired it in 1935. He had already expanded his interests into the ownership of theaters stretching back a decade prior, and the growth of sound pictures made him interested in generating his own movies to be exhibited by the Tokyo Takarazuka Theater Company, the theater chain he owned—a very common practice in America as well at that time, although it was later deemed monopolistic. Under Kobayashi, PCL absorbed JO Studios, another small film company that had once been a film laboratory.

Studio System Conglomerate

PCL was becoming a powerhouse operation by this point, and began competing with the major studios of Japan. In 1935, it began both producing and distributing its own pictures, boasted state-of-the-art equipment, and was even luring away major talent from other companies. Two years later, Kobayashi merged PCL, JO, and other small distribution companies he had acquired to create one giant entity known as Toho Company—which was poised to dominate the Japanese film industry along with a handful of other major studios that included Nikkatsu and Shochiku.

Long before the era of *daikaiju eiga* and *tokusatsu*, the late 1930s became what was later known as Toho's first golden age. Films made during this period, including Eisuke Takizawa's *Saga of the Vagabonds* (*Sengoku gunto-den*) (1937) and Kajiro Yamamoto's *Enoken's Chikiri Kinta* (1937) (one of a series of comedy vehicles for the popular comedian Kenichi "Enoken" Enomoto) began to attract notoriety for the relatively new studio, as well as growing audiences. Much like its American counterparts, Toho also began an impressive in-house apprenticeship program, designed to prepare future on-screen talent, directors and other personnel, and thereby ensure that the studio would continue operating like a well-oiled machine.

Propaganda Machine

With the onset of the Second World War, Toho Company, which had newly emerged as a major studio, took a dark turn that stands as an unfortunate— if somewhat understandable—blemish on its history. As the militaristic Japanese government sought to justify its invasion of China, and further glorify its other acts of imperialistic aggression, Toho was pressured to create propaganda films, and even worked cooperatively with filmmakers from Japan's Axis ally, Nazi Germany. And although several studios were pressed into similar service, Toho was the most complicit of all, and became even more enthusiastic a collaborator following Japan's attack on Pearl Harbor and the entry of the United States into the war.

Although propagandistic in theme, the quality of Toho's output remained of the highest caliber, as could be seen in the pinnacle of Japanese war-era films, *The War at Sea from Hawaii to Malay* (*Hawai Mare oki kaisen*) (1942), which showcased the stunning miniature work of budding special-effects mastermind Eiji Tsuburaya. Patriotic films continued to be churned out throughout the war years of the early 1940s, and by 1942, the Japanese government had even seized direct control of the studio's distribution network. It was a tough time not only for Toho, but for the entire Japanese movie industry. Film stock was being donated to the war effort, resulting in cheaper-quality film being used; budgets were being slashed as the economy of the country contracted, and by the latter years of the war, Toho's output was barely a fifth of what it once was; also, much of the physical infrastructure was being devastated by Allied bombing raids.

But Toho survived the war, and after Japan's surrender in August 1945, the studio was reorganized under the American occupation. The occupiers did not look kindly upon those in the film industry who had collaborated with the Japanese government, and so things were shaken up a bit within Toho. This led to some internal turmoil, as Communist Party members within the company gained an inordinate amount of power, and the trade unions began to rebel. The resulting strikes in 1946 threatened to tear the studio apart. In fact, a total of approximately 450 studio workers walked off the job, including some of the most talented actors and directors. They would form a company called Shintoho ("New Toho") that was initially affiliated with Toho, but eventually broke off completely on its own by 1950.

Postwar Turmoil

A new studio head, Tetsuzo Watanabe, attempted to free the company from the choking influence of the Communist faction, but this only resulted in further in-house hostilities, which shut the studio down completely for nearly half a year. Growing Cold War tensions, inflamed by the continued American presence and the accompanying Red Scare paranoia, only made matters worse. With the studio's talent pool in shambles, Toho began relying more and more on its training program to help introduce a new generation of directors and actors into the spotlight. In the long run, this would prove most fortuitous for the studio, as it wound up ushering in what would become Toho's most memorable golden age of all.

The conclusion of the American occupation in 1952, combined with the rebuilt Japanese economy and the tremendous influx of new blood, led to a halcyon period for Toho, which saw dramatic growth both in output and in quality. The Japanese studio system was in full swing, and although Toho couldn't boast the kind of production values enjoyed by top American studios like M-G-M or Paramount, they were pretty much the closest thing outside the borders of the United States, and at the forefront of a Japanese film industry that was leading the world in sheer volume. The 1950s saw the emergence of innovations like color and widescreen presentation, and Toho films took on a polish never seen before (or since).

The growing popularity of double features added to the evolution of B-movies, many of which were of a genre variety. Toho began to specialize in launching film series—franchises that proved themselves tried and true, and were sure to bring in major returns every time. Often, these were light comedies with a very contemporary setting—an approach that set Toho apart from other studios that specialized in period films, for example. The *Ekimae* and *Shacho* comedies were particularly prolific, and helped kickstart the careers of stars like Frankie Sakai and Hisaya Morishige. Especially beloved were what came to be known as "salaryman comedies"—comic films designed to appeal to Japan's white-collar workforce, not unlike the workplace sitcoms that gained especial popularity on U.S. television.

Golden Age

The 1950s was the period in which Toho's most celebrated director, the legendary Akira Kurosawa, emerged as one of the finest auteurs not only in the history of Japanese cinema, but of cinema worldwide. Starting with films like *Ikiru* (1952), *Seven Samurai* (1954), and *Throne of Blood* (1957), Kurosawa arose from the studio's director mentorship program and established himself as a filmmaker of formidable talents. Along the way, he made a household name out of a young actor named Toshiro Mifune, who became an action hero akin to the likes of John Wayne and Clint Eastwood in America.

Large-scale dramas and big-budget musicals enriched Toho's fortunes during this period. Even the West began to take notice, with Kurosawa and other directors like Hiroshi Inagaki drawing great prestige worldwide. In 1956, Inagaki's *Samurai: The Legend of Musashi* (*Miyamoto Musashi*) landed Toho its first Academy Award for Best Foreign Film. Emerging actors like Akira Takarada, Akihito Hirata, Hiroshi Koizumi, Mariko Okada, Chikage Awashima, and many others became bona fide movie stars in the Hollywood mold. In addition to Kurosawa and Inagaki, newer directors included Jun Fukuda, master of the crime drama, and Ishiro Honda, a quiet but passionate craftsman who would step into the forefront of Toho's newest and most lucrative craze.

Honda's *Gojira* (1954) was more than just a major hit for Toho Company. It literally redefined how the company would do business, reshaped its slate of future content, and influenced how Toho would be viewed by the rest of the world, particularly the United States. Overnight, giant monster-mania took hold of Japan, and before long, Toho was cranking out more *daikaiju eiga* to meet the overwhelming demand, and to try and replicate the success of that first Godzilla movie. With *Rodan* (1956), *kaiju* films started to be made in bright, full color, only further adding to their appeal. More than just giant monsters, the new interest of the public extended to all kinds of science-fiction cinema. Honda became pigeonholed as the go-to director for such pictures, and the man who made all the dazzling special effects possible was Eiji Tsuburaya.

"They were extremely well-made movies," says Peter H. Brothers. "They certainly tapped into something. Just compare them to the American ones that were so low-budget—they did *Rodan*, we did *The Giant Claw*. They did *Battle in Outer Space*, we did *Plan 9 from Outer Space*. A little different."

Over the course of the 1950s, *tokusatsu* films, especially of the *kaiju* variety, grew to a sizable percentage of Toho's product, and were clearly becoming their biggest moneymakers, especially in the overseas markets. Americans wanted more and more giant monsters, and Toho was only too happy to provide them. The appeal was further enhanced when Toho jumped on the widescreen bandwagon initiated by Hollywood in the early '50s as a ploy to compete with television. Toho's first widescreen release, using a format the company branded as "Toho Scope," was the romantic comedy *On Wings of Love* (*Oatari sanshoku musume*) (1957), and by the end of the decade, nearly every single Toho release was being filmed in Toho Scope.

Lobby poster for the 1959 American release of *The Mysterians*, one of Toho's earliest international hits.   *Movie Stills Database*

"The Japanese were producing these movies, and they were very successful in Japan," says *tokusatsu* historian August Ragone. "Foreign movie distributors were coming to Toho and saying, 'We want more of these movies. What sci-fi monster pictures do you have?' So Toho started producing pictures with the foreign market in mind very early out of the gate."

International Phenomenon

The *kaiju* craze continued unabated into the '60s, but was only part of Toho's explosive success during the early portion of the decade. Unlike in Hollywood, where the factory-like studio system was disintegrating under the pressure of anti-monopoly legislation and decreased ticket sales due to television, Japan's studio system was thriving more than ever. Toho was a veritable engine of film production, making about eighty movies per year, and had a legion of stars under contract. The lion's share of its most popular releases continued to be musicals and comedies, and if the two genres intersected, all the better.

"You have to keep in mind that Toho, back in the '50s and '60s, was producing lots of movies of all kinds," says Stuart Galbraith IV. "Dozens and dozens of features every year, of which Godzilla was an important, but by no means all-important part of the equation. The studio was carefully monitoring audience trends with each new release, and trying to cater to that same audience for the next picture."

The seven-man comedy troupe/jazz ensemble known as the Crazy Cats (*Kureji kyatsu*) starred in a series of large-scale, big-budget comedies, including *Crazy Cats Go to Hong Kong* (*Honkon kureji sakusen*) (1963), *Las Vegas Free-for-All* (*Kureji kogane sakusen*) (1967), and many others. And Toho's most popular new star turned out to be the young and handsome Yuzo Kayama, who topped the box office with his prolific *Young Guy* (*Wakadaisho*) series, in which he starred as the jet-setting college student Yuichi Tanuma. Kayama was equally adept at drama, and even appeared with fellow mega-star Toshiro Mifune in Kurosawa pictures like *Sanjuro* (1962) and *Red Beard* (1965). Like American counterparts of the era such as Frankie Avalon and Pat Boone, Kayama was also a musician, and released several hit pop songs, making him a bona fide multimedia sensation for Toho.

"Toho was doing Kurosawa films, and like a lot of companies did, they were diversified, so they did their high-class movies and their pop culture fun entertainment," says science-fiction cinema pundit Steve Biodrowski. "There's a lot of back-and-forth; a lot of the same actors in Kurosawa samurai

Columbia Pictures brought *Mothra* to America in 1962, adding prestige to Toho in the process.
Movie Stills Database

movies turn up in Godzilla films, and they're pretty good actors. Here in the U.S., they have a reputation for being cheap movies, but when you look at the movies in the '60s, there are a lot of locations, a lot of detailed sets filled with extras. They look like big, lavish movies."

And speaking of Kurosawa, the master's successes continued in the 1960s. In addition to *Sanjuro* and *Red Beard*, he also scored a major hit with *Yojimbo* (1961) and others, and was a classic example of a director who was able to please both audiences and critics in equal measure. As part of an international wave of directors, his work became instrumental in firmly establishing film as a respected art form in the mainstream consciousness, and in turn influenced the growing *auteur* movement in American cinema, as well.

Honda and Tsuburaya remained busy with their *tokusatsu* epics, and the first half of the 1960s was dominated by their astounding collaborations. The originator of the trend, Godzilla himself, was brought back with *King*

Kong vs. Godzilla (1962), Toho's most lucrative *kaiju* picture and the one that kicked off an ongoing string of highly successful Godzilla films in the 1960s. Hollywood was definitely taking notice, and Toho earned a reputation as a cutting-edge creator of top-of-the-line movie special effects, which was even more impressive given the relatively limited budgets Tsuburaya often had to work with. Unlike in America, these films were viewed not as B-pictures but as A-pictures, and featured some of Toho's brightest stars, including the beautiful new actresses Kumi Mizuno and Mie Hama, who would go on to appear as a Bond girl in the Toho co-produced *You Only Live Twice* (1967).

"The Americans were offering them money they had never seen before," says August Ragone. "But even in those days, if the Japanese had known better, they would've known they were getting only a pittance. Which kind of reflects on why [Toho] is so harsh nowadays. They were selling worldwide rights in perpetuity for some films for $10,000. Part of it was the prestige of their films getting picked up, for example, by Columbia Pictures, which picked up *Mothra*."

An Industry on the Wane

Toho was moving full-speed ahead with its many successful franchises and genres: Godzilla films and other *tokusatsu*, spy and crime thrillers, historical epics and musical comedies, and of course the Kurosawa juggernaut. The company had streamlined production to a degree equal to that of the greatest old-time Hollywood studios. But fortunes began to change as the 1960s drew to a close. The phenomenon of television took off in Japan about a decade later than it did in America, and the new technology was taking a serious toll on movie ticket sales—even more of a toll than it had taken in America. Part of the cause for Toho's troubles was also due to audiences getting tired of stale product as well—most of the top stars had been in place for close to a decade, and many of the company's moneymaking franchises—Godzilla included—were being continued far longer than audience demand seemed to indicate was wise.

"Japanese kids started saying, 'I don't have to go to the movies to see these pictures, I can watch them on TV for free,'" explains Ragone. "Other studios were putting crazy monster stuff on TV. Audiences really had to be lured. By the late '60s, there was a big push for sex and violence to get butts in seats."

Godzilla films and other series plodded on into the 1970s, despite the company going into financial freefall due to contracting revenue. Even much of the film crews under contract to Toho were starting to age due to a dearth of new incoming staff. The quality of the pictures had suffered dramatically, and it was clear from what appeared on the screen that the days of glossy, Hollywood-style productions had reached an end. The *tokusatsu* pictures were now treated as B-picture fare for children, and it showed.

An oil crisis in Japan added to the financial ruin of the entire Japanese film industry. Some companies, like Daiei Film, producer of the Godzilla competitor *Gamera*, went bankrupt. The stalwart warhorse Nikkatsu Corporation resorted to making softcore pornography (*roman porno*) in order to stay afloat. Toho soldiered on, but the once-mighty studio system had to be abandoned in much the same way Hollywood's studios had abandoned it in the 1960s, relegating themselves to distribution, and leasing out an ever-dwindling production space for filming of productions often financed by outside parties. Without the ability to hold actors and crew under long-term contracts, all of the company's film franchises, with the exception of Godzilla, were finished with by 1971—and even the Big G himself was put on extended hiatus by 1975.

Toho's contracted players were scattered to the four winds, and several formerly contracted directors, including Honda and his mentor Kajiro Yamamoto, had their careers cut short for lack of work. Newer directors like Jun Fukuda and Kon Ichikawa had to take work where they could find it, whether with Toho or elsewhere, and be far less discriminating in the assignments they took on. Toho even got in bed with the enemy and began taking production money from TV companies like the Tokyo Broadcasting System and Fuji Television, often settling merely for distribution rights. The company was even broken up to a degree, with new divisions such as Toho Pictures and Toho-Eizo watering down its unified image in the eyes of the public.

The Anime Boom

In the search for revenue, Toho began to turn more and more to children as its primary audience, and this was one of the reasons it began tapping into what had become Japan's biggest craze since the *kaiju* hysteria of the 1950s and '60s: *anime*. Unlike *kaiju*, however, the *anime* fad didn't seem to be going away, and history would show it was indeed much more than a fad, as its popularity both in Japan and abroad continues to this day. Emerging in the '60s with internationally popular properties such as *Astro Boy* (*Tetsuwan Atomu*) and *Speed Racer* (*Mahha GoGoGo*), as well as the many works of the

Toei Animation Studio, by the 1970s *anime* had become the most popular genre of filmed entertainment among Japanese children.

With the beginning of the so-called Champion Festivals—summer programming blocks designed to appeal to kids—Toho began distributing *anime* as part of the bill. Through a deal with Disney that lasted from the mid-1970s through the mid-1980s, Toho even acquired Japanese distribution rights to American animated films, which were just as popular, if not more so. Eventually, Toho took the plunge and began creating animated content of its own, most prominently the Doraemon series, a film franchise based on a highly successful and equally long-running *anime* TV series and comic book series, which has been generating profits for the company through a continuous series of releases that has gone on for nearly four decades, with a total of thirty-seven films to date.

The major success of both the imported Disney movies and original *anime* like *Doraemon* helped to refill Toho's coffers after the disastrous 1970s, and although the company would never again reach the heights of its 1950s and '60s glory days, it was back to being a healthy, fully functioning movie production house by the early 1980s. For the first time in over a decade, Toho began attempting big-budget, large-scale pictures again, and even rebooted their heaviest hitter in 1984 with the release of a new *Gojira*, later to reach American shores as *Godzilla 1985*. Eventually, the success of the film would lead to a second spate of Godzilla films that continued well into the 1990s.

American Occupation of a Different Kind

Kurosawa, now a worldwide legend, returned to moviemaking in 1980 with *Kagemusha*, a picture partially financed by his old employers at Toho. However, for the most part Toho was now in the business of making smaller films, not willing to take the risks it had taken in earlier days. The Japanese film industry had changed drastically, and American films were now what the Japanese public wanted to see, rather than its own domestic productions (as an example, in 1982, *E.T. The Extra-Terrestrial* became the highest-grossing film in Japanese history, and held the record for fifteen years, until it was broken by *Titanic*). Nevertheless, now and then an original Toho film could still pack them in, as happened in 1986 with the endearing animal buddy film *The Adventures of a Kitty* (*Koneko Monogatari*), which was such a hit that it got a U.S. theatrical release as *The Adventures of Milo and Otis*.

"In the '70s and '80s it was cheaper to buy the rights to American films, or films from Hong Kong and Europe, and release them in Japan," Ragone says. "They had a bigger turnaround for foreign films. And they basically started to dominate the Japanese box office."

The Godzilla franchise continued to do impressive numbers for Toho through the mid-1990s, and in fact, by that point *kaiju eiga* were among the only releases Toho was producing in-house. The company that had once released eighty movies per year was now down to about two or three per year, with the rest being distribution deals on outside productions. Godzilla and Mothra continued to appear in films of their own throughout the decade, and were just about the only dependable properties Toho had left. In 1995, Toho made a profitable deal with Sony/Columbia in the United States for the rights to make an American version of Godzilla, and would not mount another Godzilla production until 1999.

Studio Ghibli

Among the companies that Toho enjoyed distribution deals with was an animation house called Studio Ghibli. Similarly to Disney's early relationship with Pixar Animation, Toho released most of the very popular and very high-quality animated features produced by Studio Ghibli beginning with Isao Takahata's *Grave of the Fireflies* (*Hotaru no haka*) in 1986. Just as Kurosawa's work had done, the animated films of Studio Ghibli brought Toho a great deal of prestige, especially those of acclaimed director Hiyao Miyazaki, who was responsible for such international successes as *My Neighbor Totoro* (*Tonari no Totoro*) (1988) and *Princess Mononoke* (*Monoke-hime*) (1997), the film that put Studio Ghibli on the map internationally. The relationship between Toho and Ghibli continues to this day, and has included further Miyazaki projects like *Spirited Away* (*Sen to Chihiro no Kamikakushi*) (2001) and *Ponyo* (*Gake no Ue no Ponyo*) (2008). *Spirited Away* was a major windfall for Toho, winning the Academy Award for Best Animated Feature (the only hand-drawn animated film and only foreign-language film ever to do so), and also grossed ¥30.4 billion (approximately $300 million), making it the highest-grossing film ever in Japan, a distinction it still holds.

In addition to the Studio Ghibli releases, Toho has distributed many other prominent *anime* productions, including Katsuhiro Otomo's *Akira*, the dystopian science-fiction piece that helped establish *anime* as serious entertainment for people of all ages. And then there is the undying *Pokemon* franchise, popular with at least two different generations of toy-buying kids all over the world for the past twenty years. Based on a successful video game, which later branched into an interactive card game and still later the world-dominating app *Pokemon Go*, *Pokemon* is a pop culture sensation that is virtually unrivalled; and although owned by the Pokemon Company, its releases have been distributed by Toho in various incarnations as both animated TV series and animated motion pictures on a regular basis since 1997.

Toho Today

In the twenty-first century more than ever, Toho Company has been relegated to the status of a corporate entity more than a motion picture production company. Although new films are produced now and then, including a handful of new Godzilla pictures in the 2000s, Toho is now involved primarily in the distribution of films, much like its American counterparts. Also like its American counterparts, it has diversified into a great many other divisions and businesses as a means to stay profitable. Toho owns and operates theaters, a record label, a film laboratory, and many other interests. It has even gotten involved directly in TV distribution. These changes have become necessary during a time when the Japanese public, particularly the young people media companies crave, no longer regularly attends movies at the theater, preferring TV and streaming or on-demand services. And when they do attend the cinema, they are much more likely to be seeing American blockbusters than the more humble domestic fare, often viewed as vastly inferior.

The Toho Company of today is a shadow of its former self, with even the physical studio space whittled down to a tiny fraction of what it once was, the rest sold off or leased out. Ironically, much of the attention and prestige the company receives these days is due to its glorious past, as film buffs have begun to rediscover many of the pictures of earlier decades not typically seen outside of Japan. The home video market is still a thriving one in Japan, and old Toho movies now enjoy an audience on various media platforms.

Once dominating the movie industry in its native country, Toho is now something of an outmoded relic; a reminder of Japan's former cinematic triumphs. Much of the clout and recognition it still holds is thanks to the enduring popularity of Godzilla, and even that is mainly outside of Japan. Returning to the well once again in 2016, Toho got back into the Godzilla business with *Shin Godzilla* (aka *Godzilla Resurgence*), presumably the kickoff of a whole new series of exploits for the giant dinosaur. Seemingly, Toho has willingly embraced its destiny as the caretakers of Godzilla *ad infinitum*. It may not ever be able to recapture the majesty of its former status, but through the continued presence of the unstoppable King of the Monsters, perhaps Toho can vicariously enjoy a certain modicum of relevance, assured of a place in the pop culture landscape for the foreseeable future.

The Legacy of Toho Company (Besides You-Know-Who)

If we can ignore the 328-million-pound radioactive dinosaur in the room for just a moment, it becomes clear that Toho is responsible for a whole lot of other highly entertaining and critically acclaimed cinema over the past eighty-plus years. Here's a rundown of fifteen of the most important and most popular pictures produced and/or distributed by Toho that have absolutely nothing to do with Godzilla . . .

Drunken Angel (1948) (Yoidore tenshi)

A startling picture that helped put Toho back on track after being freed from the yoke of government control and helped establish Akira Kurosawa as Toho's finest young director, this tale of the *yakuza*—Japan's most powerful organized crime syndicate—was also the first collaboration between Kurosawa and the actor who would become the John Wayne to his John Ford, Toshiro Mifune.

Seven Samurai (1954) (Shichinin no Samurai)

Akira Kurosawa's seminal masterpiece of medieval Japan influenced everything from American westerns like *The Magnificent Seven* (1960) to science fiction like *Star Wars* (1977). Starring action icon Toshiro Mifune and Takashi Shimura (*Gojira*'s Dr. Yamane), it is typically ranked among the finest motion pictures ever made, in any language.

The Mysterians (1957) (Chikyu Boeigun)

The first of Toho's "space opera trilogy" (along with *Battle in Outer Space* (1959) and *Gorath* [1962]), *The Mysterians* was Toho's first *tokusatsu* release to feature the Toho Scope widescreen format, as well as their Perspecta stereo sound system. A dazzling showcase of Eiji Tsuburaya's special-effects genius, it ranks alongside *War of the Worlds* (1953) and *Forbidden Planet* (1956) as one of the best science-fiction films of the 1950s.

The H-Man (1958) (Bijo to Ekitainingen)

A bold entry in the *tokusatsu* genre, *The H-Man* is cited by many lovers of Japanese genre cinema as perhaps the finest non-Godzilla picture of the Ishiro Honda/Eiji Tsuburaya team. With no giant monsters or sprawling miniatures in sight, this film instead combines elements of crime drama and even film noir to tell a terrifying story that's part *The Blob* (1958) and part *Invasion of the Body-Snatchers* (1956).

Matango (1963)

Saddled with the awful title of *Attack of the Mushroom People* in the United States, *Matango* is nonetheless considered one of Honda and Tsuburaya's finest pieces of *tokusatsu* cinema, combining elements of horror and science fiction to tell a decidedly sober tale that is unlike most other *tokusatsu* pictures of the period.

The Elegant Life of Mr. Everyman (1963) (Eburi manshi no yûga-na seikatsu)

An example of Toho's highly successful "salaryman comedies," Kihachi Okamoto's *The Elegant Life of Mr. Everyman* tells the poignant-yet-funny story of a put-upon adman who decides to write a novel about his own life. An ingenious piece of work combining live action, animation, and elements of comedy and drama, this is one of Toho's greatest films of the 1960s—and least known to Western audiences.

Atragon (1963) (Kaitei Gunkan)

A thrilling tale of submarine adventure based on Shunro Oshikawa's popular young adult fiction series, *Atragon* boasts the drill-nosed undersea battleship the Gotengo, as well as the serpentine *kaiju* known as Manda, and is a perfect example of Honda and Tsuburaya working on all cylinders to produce a fantasy film appealing to viewers of all ages.

Sanda and Gaira strike a pose in a publicity shot for *War of the Gargantuas*.   *Movie Stills Database*

Kwaidan (1964)

When the greatest international horror films are ranked, this chilling anthology of Japanese cautionary folktales is invariably included high on the list. Based on the stories of European writer Lafcadio Hearn, director Masaki Kobayashi's collection of frightful vignettes won the Special Jury Prize at Cannes Film Festival, and was nominated for the Oscar for Best Foreign Language Film.

War of the Gargantuas (1966) (Furankenshutain no kaijû: Sanda tai Gaira)

Although in Japan it was made as a direct sequel to *Frankenstein Conquers the World* (1965), in its international release *War of the Gargantuas* was made to stand on its own, and as such it stands as perhaps the most popular one-off *kaiju* film. Featuring the Oscar-nominated American actor Russ Tamblyn, this was a co-production of American distributor UPA.

Akira (1988)

Often cited as the film that helped "legitimize" *anime*, Katsuhiro Otomo's *Akira*, based on his popular futuristic *manga*, is usually listed alongside such films as Fritz Lang's *Metropolis* (1928), Stanley Kubrick's *2001: A Space Odyssey* (1968), and Ridley Scott's *Blade Runner* (1982) as one of the most impressive science-fiction films of all time.

Gunhed (1989) (Ganheddo)

A rare example of a science-fiction film that was later adapted into a *manga* instead of the other way around, Masato Harada's influential picture tapped into the fascination with cybernetics and other computer technology at the time, also seen in American films like *The Terminator* (1984), as well as in games like *BattleTech*. Its concept of mechanized warfare is still popular in Japanese sci-fi today.

Ringu (1998)

Later remade in the United States by Gore Verbinski as *The Ring* (2002), Hideo Nakata's iconic classic is perhaps the most beloved example of the Japanese brand of modern psychological horror (or "J-horror"). At the forefront of a slew of similarly remade J-horror gems, it also spawned several sequels, and its imagery remains haunting nearly two decades later.

Spirited Away (2001) (Sen to Chihiro no Kamikakushi)

Celebrated animator Hiyao Miyazaki delighted worldwide audiences throughout the '80s, '90s, and 2000s with his groundbreaking works, but *Spirited Away* stands as his finest hour, a brilliant fantasy that captured the Academy Award for Best Animated Feature and became the highest-grossing Japanese film of all time.

Howl's Moving Castle (2004) (Hauru no Ugoku Shiro)

Hiyao Miyazaki came out of retirement to direct this Studio Ghibli production, based on a fantasy novel by British author Diana Wynne Jones. A smashing success in Japan, it was brought to the United States by the team of Pixar and Disney, who dubbed it into English and gave it a limited theatrical release. It was nominated for the Oscar for Best Animated Feature.

Attack on Titan (2015) (Shingeki no Kyojin)

Shinji Higuchi is dead set on bringing *tokusatsu* cinema back to the forefront for Toho, and it seems like his two-part adaptation of Hajime Isayama's *manga* about gigantic humanoids attacking Earth may have been something of a dress rehearsal for Higuchi's resurrection of the Big G in *Shin Godzilla* (2016). But what a dress rehearsal it is!

17

The Humans

Actors Who Shared the Bill

Godzilla movies are about more than just monsters. Naturally, there are also human characters in every installment, whose stories parallel those of the big guy and his cohorts. Often overlooked by casual fans, the actors who played those crucial parts also deserve their due. For younger viewers (or those older ones with short attention spans), it's sometimes a challenge waiting for the human drama to pause and for the *kaiju* to appear on screen and do their thing. Granted, over the years, the human-oriented plotlines of Godzilla films—all the stuff that goes on while the monsters aren't destroying cities or each other—vary wildly in terms of "engagement factor."

Sometimes, we just want to see monsters kick butt, and that's OK. However, the actors speaking dialogue and *not* wearing rubber suits were quite a talented bunch, made up in many cases of some of the finest performers from the glory days of Toho's studio system. Overshadowed though they may be (both literally and figuratively), they are nonetheless greatly respected by connoisseurs of *tokusatsu* cinema, and the work they do on screen makes it easy to understand why. Here are just a few of the most important and lauded actors who helped wrap up all that *kaiju* chaos in rhyme and reason, and made us care about more than just the monster action.

Akihiko Hirata

Best known as the brooding yet good-hearted Dr. Daisuke Serizawa in the original *Gojira* (1954), Hirata was one of the biggest breakout stars to emerge from Toho's ambitious "New Faces" program of the 1950s, designed to groom the next generation of studio talent. He is also one of the actors most closely associated with Godzilla, having appeared in seven films in the *Showa* series, bringing his trademark intensity to every part.

Born Akihiko Onoda in Seoul, Korea, on December 26, 1927, he had the benefit of a wealthy family, initially studying interior design at Tokyo University. This interest led him to a passion for still photography, which eventually led him to the motion picture business. His older brother Yoshiki landed him a job as an assistant director at Shintoho, the company that had broken away from Toho just a few years prior. From there, he was recruited by Toho in 1953, but for a role in front of the camera, rather than behind it.

His first appearance was as a supporting player in the Toshiro Mifune vehicle *The Last Embrace* (*Hoyo*) (1953), and the following year he made the first of three appearances in Hiroshi Inagaki's *Samurai* trilogy alongside Mifune, as well. But it was his other 1954 assignment, in Ishiro Honda's top-secret new science-fiction project *Gojira*, that would change the course of Hirata's career.

Originally considered for the part of Ogata, the romantic lead, Hirata's maturity and serious demeanor made him a better fit for the part of Dr. Serizawa, the tortured and jilted scientist haunted by the knowledge of the only way to halt the monster's path of destruction. Hirata imbued the role with great pathos, nuance, and gravitas, setting a bar for dramatic performance that was rarely equaled in later installments in the Godzilla series.

But his work in *Gojira* was a blessing and a curse, as he was subsequently typecast by Toho brass, and spent most of the remainder of his career in *tokusatsu*. In a sense, this was good for the genre, as an actor of his caliber lent great merit to the proceedings in future films like *Rodan* (1956), *The Mysterians* (1957), *The H-Man* (1958), *Giant Monster Varan* (1959), *Mothra* (1961), and *Gorath* (1962). He returned to the Godzilla franchise in 1962 with a memorable role in the epic extravaganza *King Kong vs. Godzilla*. During the 1960s, he also appeared in classic *Showa* entries like *Ghidorah, the Three-Headed Monster* (1964) and *Godzilla vs. the Sea Monster* (1966), in which he played against type as the sinister leader of the criminal Red Bamboo organization.

As the series entered shakier ground both creatively and financially, Hirata was nonetheless there to take on the parts Toho gave him, appearing in typical scientist and professorial roles in *Son of Godzilla* (1967) and later in *Godzilla vs. Mechagodzilla* (1974). For his last turn with Godzilla, 1975's *Terror of Mechagodzilla*, Hirata came full circle, playing the cartoonishly insane Dr. Mafune, a broad mad scientist role that was the total opposite of his understated turn as Dr. Serizawa some two decades earlier.

Hirata went into semi-retirement after the *Star Wars* knockoff *The War in Space* (1977), but returned for one last role in the science-fiction picture

Bye, Bye Jupiter (1984). It was at that time that Toho was gearing up to reboot Godzilla with the first film in the series in nine years, and tapped Hirata to once again join the Big G on screen like in the old days. Hirata took part in a press conference to announce the new film, but unfortunately he was suffering from lung cancer at the time and was unable to appear in the film. He succumbed to the disease on July 25, 1984, at the age of fifty-six.

Yuriko Hoshi

A spunky ingénue with irresistible charm, Hoshi was a mainstay for Toho in the 1960s, and has enjoyed a career that began in her teens and continues to this day, into her seventies. In addition to a pair of roles with Godzilla during the *Showa* era (as well as one comeback role during the Millennium era), Hoshi also made a name for herself in a string of youth-oriented pictures that capitalized on her energy and charisma.

Born Yuriko Shimizu on December 6, 1943, she landed her first role at the tender age of fourteen, with a small part in *The Path Under the Plane Trees* (*Suzukake no sanpomichi*) (1959). Her second film was also her first with director Ishiro Honda, the baseball comedy *Inao: Story of an Iron Arm* (*Tetsuwan toshu Inao monogatari*) (1959). The following year, she collaborated for the first time with her eventual Godzilla co-star Akira Takarada in *The Dangerous Kiss* (*Seppun dorobo*) (1960). By age seventeen, she had gotten her first lead role in the youth-oriented drama *Young Wolf* (*Wakai okami*) (1961).

But the turning point for Hoshi's career came when she was cast in a supporting role in *Sir Galahad in Campus* (*Daigaku no wakadaisho*) (1961), the first in Toho's lucrative "Young Guy (*Wakadaisho*)" series starring Yuzo Kayama. Hoshi had been getting a lot of work in films geared toward the high school and college crowd, and the Young Guy films soon became the most popular. After the first installment, she took on the lead female role in the series, playing Sumiko Kishi, love interest of the dashing Yuichi Tanuma, in five of the next six films in the series between 1961 and 1968.

It was while riding the crest of her Young Guy fame that Hoshi crossed over into another Toho franchise and joined Akira Takarada as the female lead in *Mothra vs. Godzilla* (1964), playing the plucky photographer Junko Nakanishi to Takarada's hard-nosed reporter Ichiro Sakai. Her role was a breath of fresh air in the male-dominated series, and brought an element of fun to one of the finest of the *Showa* films. Hoshi's on-screen charisma was so strong that she returned in the next Godzilla film that same year, *Ghidorah, the Three-Headed Monster*, playing a very similar yet different character, Naoko

Shindo. Her popularity among young people at the time added wider appeal to both pictures.

When Toho fell on hard times in the 1970s, Hoshi's roles came along a bit fewer and far between, but she continued to work steadily into her thirties and forties, long after shedding her youthful image. Since the late 1990s, her focus has been on television roles, but she made an exception in 2000 when asked back by Toho to appear in the second film in the Millennium series, *Godzilla vs. Megaguirus*. A far cry from Junko the mod photographer, at fifty-six she appeared as physicist Dr. Yoshino Yoshizawa. Recently turned seventy-three, Hoshi is working more than she has in years, and appeared in three different films in 2016.

Hiroshi Koizumi

The perennial straitlaced scientist/professor, Koizumi was a regular face throughout the *Showa* era of Toho's *tokusatsu* cinema, and even made returns in both the *Heisei* and Millennium series. He was an important part of both the Godzilla and Mothra franchises, and was in fact the only actor to reprise two different roles in *daikaiju eiga* spanning the 1960s to the 2000s, and is perhaps best known as Dr. Shinichi Chujo, the scientist who first discovers Mothra. Along with Hirata, he was among Toho's promising crop of "New Face" actors in the early 1950s, and parlayed his early success into a career lasting more than half a century.

He was born August 12, 1926, in Kamakura City, Japan. He attended Keio University in Tokyo, graduating in 1948. He began his career as a television announcer working for Japanese national public broadcasting organization NHK, before being recruited by Toho in 1951 as part of the "New Faces" program. He had his first role in *Seishun kaigi* (1952) at the age of twenty-five, and next worked with rising star director Kon Ichikawa in *Mr. Lucky* (*Rakki-san*) (1952). Later that busy year, he first began to get noticed in Ishiro Honda's *The Man Who Came to Port* (*Minato e kita otoko*) (1952), appearing in a loaded cast that included Toshiro Mifune and Takashi Shimura. Critical acclaim continued with a strong supporting role in *Late Chrysanthemums* (*Bangiku*) (1954), the poignant story of a retired geisha.

Koizumi already had twenty-five films under his belt in just three years in the business when he was cast in his very first lead role, which happened to be in *Godzilla Raids Again* (1955), the immediate sequel to the original *Gojira*, which Toho rushed into production to capitalize on its surprise hit. In contrast to the somber and stoic men of science he would later be known for playing, in *Godzilla Raids Again* Koizumi plays dashing young pilot Shoichi Tsukioka, who heroically faces down the giant lizard in his plane during the film's climactic scene. Little did he realize it was just the beginning of his involvement with *tokusatsu* pictures.

Now a lead player, Koizumi began enjoying bigger roles, and was one of the major successes of the "New Faces" program. In 1961, he was given what turned out to be his most well-known part, as Dr. Shinichi Chujo in the original *Mothra*. Although he would play many different characters in the ensuing *tokusatsu* films in which he took part, many were iterations in the spirit of Dr. Chujo, and they were almost all mature authority figures. He appeared as a ship's captain in *Matango* (1963), a detective in *Atragon* (1963), and a scientist in *Dogora* (1964). When Mothra reappeared in *Mothra vs. Godzilla* and *Ghidorah, the Three-Headed Monster*, Koizumi was right there with her, playing the very Chujo-like Professor Miura. In fact, Koizumi is the only actor to star in more than one *Showa* Godzilla picture as the same central character.

In 1969, he was directed by Jun Fukuda in *Freshman Young Guy* (1969), and when Fukuda returned to the Godzilla series five years later for *Godzilla vs. Mechagodzilla* (1974), he brought Koizumi back as well, as yet another professor. And when Godzilla was rebooted a decade later for *Godzilla 1985*, Koizumi was there again, appearing as a geologist alongside his *Ghidorah* and *Dogora* co-star Yosuke Natsuki.

By age sixty, Koizumi had more or less retired, but would occasionally come back for a special part. One such part was offered in 2003, when the seventy-six-year-old actor was invited back by Toho to reprise the role of Dr. Chujo some forty-two years later, and share the screen with Mothra and Godzilla once again, in *Godzilla: Tokyo S.O.S.* Koizumi is endearing in the role, playing grandfather to child actor Itsuki Omori in the role of little Syun Chujo. It was a suitable cap to a career spent specializing in soft-spoken, professorial parts, and made up for some regrets the actor had later in life about being a bit too understated in his performances. *Godzilla: Tokyo S.O.S.* would be his final feature film. He passed away of complications from pneumonia on May 31, 2015, at the age of eighty-eight.

Akira Kubo

Possessing boyish good looks that later matured into an aura of urbane sophistication, Kubo maintained a successful career in dependable support-ing roles, working with everyone in Toho's stable of directors from Akira

Kurosawa to Ishiro Honda, from highbrow cinema to populist entertainment. From his teenage years in the early 1950s, right up to his eighties in the present day, Kubo has enjoyed one of the lengthiest careers of any actor in Japanese movie history.

He was born in Tokyo on December 1, 1936. At fifteen, he got his first movie role, a supporting part in the romantic teenage drama *Adolescence* (*Shishunki*), and also appeared in the sequel the following year, which was his first time working with director Honda. He attracted attention for the first time when, at age seventeen, he made an impressive starring turn in Senkichi Taniguchi's *The Sound of the Waves* (*Shiosai*) (1954), a teen romance in which he plays alongside Kyoko Aoyama, playing a beautiful young pearl diver. The part got Kubo noticed, and more prominent assignments began to roll in.

During the late 1950s, and into the 1960s, Kubo specialized in playing serious-minded young men, but his resume included everything from

怪獣総進撃

富士山の火口に根拠をかまえたキラアク星人は、地球人に挑戦してきた。ムーンライト SY-3 号の根長山辺（久保）たちは、基地に乗り込んだが、高度な文明を誇る宇宙人に撃退されてしまった。

Kubo (center) appears as heroic Capt. Katsuo Yamabe in *Destroy All Monsters*.

Movie Stills Database

"salaryman" comedies to war dramas. He landed a role in *Throne of Blood* (1957), Akira Kurosawa's brilliant adaptation of Shakespeare's *Macbeth*. This would not be the last time Kubo would work with Kurosawa, as five years later he appeared alongside Toshiro Mifune, Yuzo Kayama, and Takashi Shimura in *Sanjuro* (1962).

His first *tokusatsu* role came in 1962 in Ishiro Honda's *Gorath*, and the following year he played the starring role of Prof. Kenji Murai opposite Kumi Mizuno in Honda's *Matango*. Honda must have taken a liking to the young actor, because he brought him back in 1965 for the sixth installment in his Godzilla series, *Invasion of Astro-Monster*. Appearing as the enthusiastic and earnest Tetsuo Teri, inventor of a children's toy that winds up being the key to defeating an alien race, Kubo made the supporting part a memorable one. He returned to the Godzilla series two years later in *Son of Godzilla*, in which he played another self-righteous and well-meaning young man, the reporter Goro Maki who stumbles on unscrupulous scientific experiments in the South Pacific. Finally, in *Destroy All Monsters*, Kubo starred as Capt. Katsuo Yamabe, maverick fighter pilot who leads a crucial mission to the moon. His final Toho *tokusatsu* role came in Honda's *Space Amoeba* (aka *Yog: Monster from Space*) (1970).

Once the movie industry cooled down in the 1970s, Kubo, like many others, began to branch out into television, where he has worked for most of the past forty years. Still, there have been a few cinematic parts worthy of note in that time, including his appearance in *Zatoichi* (1989), a revival of Shintaro Katsu's classic samurai series, as well as his cameo in Daiei Studios' *Gamera: Guardian of the Universe* (1995), the movie that revived Japan's most revered non-Toho *kaiju* franchise. He has also done *anime* voice work, such as in the action-adventure series *Escaflowne* (*Tenku no Esukafurone*). His good looks and warm presence have served him well, and have endured over the decades. Now in his eighties, Kubo continues to work steadily, focusing on TV movies and miniseries.

Kumi Mizuno

A stunning beauty who ranks alongside the likes of Brigitte Bardot, Claudia Cardinale, Catherine Deneuve, Julie Christie, Jane Fonda, and Ursula Andress as one of the most internationally desirable actresses of the 1960s, Mizuno was a favorite leading lady of Ishiro Honda, who used her to unforgettable effect as the alluring and mysterious Miss Namikawa in *Invasion of Astro-Monster*.

Born Maya Igarashi in Niigata, Japan, on New Year's Day 1937, she attended drama school as a teenager, graduated at age twenty, and promptly began her film career. Still using her birth name, she made her debut for Toho rival Shochiku in *The Unbalanced Wheel* (*Kichigai buraku*; also known as *Crazy Society*) in 1957. By her second picture, Toho's romantic drama *A Bridge for Us Alone* (*Futari dake no hashi*) (1958), in which she starred opposite Akira Kubo, she had changed her professional name to Kumi Mizuno.

Possessing rare beauty and poise to rival any of Hollywood's leading starlets of the era, Mizuno was a top-billed superstar right from the start. She first caught the attention of Ishiro Honda in 1959 when he directed her, with Kubo once again, in *Seniors, Juniors, Co-Workers* (*Uwayaku, shitayaku, godoyaku*). When the *tokusatsu* boom hit in earnest at the start of the 1960s, and Honda found himself the director of choice in the new genre, he turned to Mizuno more and more as his lead actress. She appeared in the science-fiction disaster film *Gorath*, followed shortly by a starring part in *Matango*, in which she also sang.

One of the most in-demand Japanese actresses of the 1960s, Mizuno popped up in all manner of pictures, including Senkichi Tanaguchi's adventure epic *The Lost World of Sinbad* (*Dai tozoku*) (1963) alongside Toshiro Mifune and fellow screen diva Mie Hama. In 1965, she made two *kaiju* films for Honda back-to-back, starring both times with American actor Nick Adams. In both *Frankenstein Conquers the World* and *Invasion of Astro-Monster*, her on-screen chemistry with Adams is evident despite the obvious language barrier; the chemistry was so strong, in fact, that the two (both married to other people at the time) were romantically linked in the press, although they denied any involvement off screen.

Playing the conflicted Miss Namikawa, unwitting pawn of the devious Xiliens, Mizuno delivered the most memorable performance of her career. The following year, she appeared in two more beloved *kaiju* pictures. The first was *War of the Gargantuas* (1966), in which she starred with another American import, Russ Tamblyn (Adams had been offered the part initially, but had other obligations). The next was *Godzilla vs. the Sea Monster*, in which she played Daiyo, the island girl who becomes an object of fascination for the giant dinosaur—the film had originally been envisioned as a vehicle for King Kong, which would have put Mizuno in the familiar Fay Wray-style role.

Once the studio system in Japan collapsed, Mizuno could no longer rely on being the go-to studio girl, but she continued to work steadily nonetheless into the 1970s and beyond. In the 2000s, nostalgia for the *Showa* era led to her being cast once again in the Godzilla franchise, as by this point many of those in charge at Toho had grown up watching her on screen playing Namikawa and others. At age sixty-five, she played the prime minister of Japan in Masaaki Tezuka's *Godzilla Against Mechagodzilla* (2002), and two years later she appeared in the ultimate *Showa*-tribute free-for-all and the last film in the Millennium series, *Godzilla: Final Wars*, as the commander of the Earth Defense Force (who happened to be named Akiko Namikawa). She continued to find work in television until 2013, when she retired once and for all at age seventy-seven.

Megumi Odaka

The only performer to play the same character in a string of entries in the Godzilla series, Odaka was the darling of millions as Miki Saegusa, Godzilla's psychic muse during six of the seven films in the *Heisei* era of the 1980s and 1990s. A multimedia star, she enjoyed teen idol status in Japan, and was a recording artist as well as a star of stage and screen. She disappeared from the scene following her work with Godzilla, but remains a strong favorite among longtime *kaiju* fans.

Born May 9, 1972, in Kanagawa, Japan, Odaka first gained notoriety at the age of twelve, when she starred as the voice of Sandy in the children's animated TV series *Noozles* (*Fushigi na koala Blinky*), acting with Godzilla series legend Kumi Mizuno. In 1987, she captured first prize in Toho's "Cinderella" beauty contest, yet another talent development program reminiscent of the "New Faces" initiative of the 1950s. As a result, the fifteen-year-old Odaka was offered her first film role, in Kon Ichikawa's fantasy film *Princess from the Moon* (*Taketori monogatari*) (1987), starring 1984 Cinderella contest-winner Yasuko Sawaguchi as the titular princess, as well as the legendary Toshiro Mifune. The role garnered her a Japanese Academy Award for Newcomer of the Year.

Odaka's popularity grew with the youth of Japan, and like many young screen idols, she even attempted a singing career, releasing two albums, *Milky Cotton* (1988) and *Powder Snow* (1989). She got the role of a lifetime in 1989, when at only seventeen years of age, Toho cast her as the sensitive and beautiful telepath Miki Saegusa in *Godzilla vs. Biollante*, the film that picked up where the 1984 *Godzilla* reboot left off and kicked off the *Heisei* series in earnest. As the girl with a psychic link to the Big G, she won over audiences to such a degree that Toho decided to make Miki Saegusa a recurring character—something that had never before been attempted with the Godzilla franchise. Ironically, she had never seen a Godzilla film before being cast in the role, and was initially intimidated by the monstrous Godzilla costume, until she befriended the man inside the suit, Kenpachiro Satsuma.

The remaining five films of the *Heisei* era maintained an ongoing continuity. As Miki, Odaka played a pivotal role in *Godzilla vs. King Ghidorah* (1991), *Godzilla & Mothra: Battle for Earth* (1992), *Godzilla vs. Mechagodzilla* (1993), *Godzilla vs. Space Godzilla* (1994), and finally, *Godzilla vs. Destoroyah* (1995). Odaka brought great pathos to the films, helping to make the monster become more sympathetic with each entry in the series. Additionally, Toho capitalized on her teen idol status to help bring in a young audience.

After the conclusion of the *Heisei* series, Odaka stopped working in motion pictures at a mere twenty-three years of age. For the remainder of the 1990s, she could be seen in a handful of TV appearances, as well as Japanese stage productions such as *Peter Pan* and *Fiddler on the Roof.* She formally retired from show business in her late twenties due to illness, but has since recovered her health and has reportedly started a family. Although her work in movies was short-lived, she made the most of it, leaving an indelible mark on the minds of fans. In fact, she has gone on record as saying she would love to come out of retirement to reprise her role as Miki Saegusa in future installments of the Godzilla franchise, if such an opportunity ever arose.

Kenji Sahara

No featured actor has ever appeared in more Godzilla films, or for that matter, more Toho *tokusatsu* films, than Kenji "Ken-bo" Sahara. From *Gojira* to *Godzilla: Final Wars*, he can be seen in thirteen of the twenty-nine movies in the Godzilla franchise, and can boast ten more non-Godzilla Toho science-fiction classics to his credit, as well, including the original *Rodan* and *Mothra*. Beyond that, he is one of Japan's most accomplished stars, with a resume stretching across seven different decades.

Born Masayoshi Kato on May 14, 1932, in Kawasaki City, Kanagawa Prefecture, he first got Toho's attention at age twenty-one by winning "Mr. Ordinary," a magazine-sponsored modeling contest. Initially using the stage name Tadashi Ishihara, he was signed up for acting lessons by the studio and put under contract. One of the many fresh, new stars that Toho introduced in the early 1950s, he made his screen debut as an extra in Ishiro Honda's *Farewell Rabaul* (1954). His very next appearance would come in Honda's next motion picture, the original *Gojira*, in which he took on two uncredited background roles: that of a reporter and a terrified ship passenger.

Still a minor player, he was destined for much greater visibility in the near future. The big break happened in 1956, when Honda cast the twenty-year-old in the lead role of his next major *kaiju* picture, *Rodan*. Changing his stage name to Kenji Sawara (it would become "Sahara" in subsequent films), the young actor made the most of the opportunity, turning in a performance that instantly placed him among Toho's preferred leading men going forward.

Toho was on the verge of an explosion of science-fiction cinema, and Kenji Sahara became the actor most associated with the budding genre. Honda used him in a string of his genre films over the next few years, including the space epic *The Mysterians* (1957), the noirish thriller *The H-Man* (1958), the giant insect fantasy *Mothra*, and the disaster picture *Gorath*. He worked in many other films for Toho during this period, including Honda's acclaimed *Song for a Bride* (*Hanayome sanjûsô*) (1958), but it was for the *tokusatsu* pictures that Sahara is still best remembered to this day.

That's with good reason: Sahara was proving himself to be one of the most dependable actors on the Toho lot, pulling off heroic and villainous parts with equal aplomb, and displaying ease in a variety of genres. Still, the *kaiju* continued to come calling. When the Godzilla series started back up with *King Kong vs. Godzilla*, Sahara was there. He continued to co-star with Godzilla throughout the *Showa* era, featuring prominently in *Mothra vs. Godzilla*, in which he played the unscrupulous and devious Jiro Torahata; *Ghidorah, the Three-Headed Monster*, in which he played a determined newspaper editor; Jun Fukuda's *Son of Godzilla*; *Destroy All Monsters*, Honda's return to the series; *All Monsters Attack* (1969), in which he played the hardworking father of little Ichiro; as well as military roles in the last two *Showa* pictures, *Godzilla vs. Mechagodzilla* and *Terror of Mechagodzilla*.

And that wasn't all he was doing during Toho's golden age. He also played in most of Honda's other *tokusatsu* offerings, including *Matango*, *Atragon*, *Frankenstein Conquers the World*, *War of the Gargantuas*, and *Space Amoeba*. He appeared in Hiroshi Inagaki's *47 Samurai* (*Chushingura*) (1962); worked with Frank Sinatra in the Toho/Warner Bros. co-produced *None but the Brave* (1965); turned up in *Young Guy at Sea* (1965), part of the popular "*Wakadaisho*" series; and starred with Toshiro Mifune in *Battle of the Japan Sea* (*Nihonkai daikaisen*) (1969).

TV was about to take over as Japan's number-one entertainment medium, and Sahara was ahead of the curve. He dominated *tokusatsu* not only on the big screen but on the small screen, as well. In 1966, he first appeared in Tsuburaya Productions' acclaimed *Ultra Q* anthology series, and this led to a stream of work in the ongoing "*Ultra*" family of series that spanned more than forty years, including *Ultra Seven* (1967–68), *Return of Ultra Man* (1971–72), *Ultraman 80* (1980–81), *Ultraman Nexus* (2004–05), *Ultraman Mebius* (2006–07), and even the 2008 motion picture, *Superior Ultraman 8 Brothers*, which he appeared in at age seventy-six.

When Godzilla returned for the *Heisei* series in the 1990s, Sahara was brought back as well, appearing as Japanese Defense Minister Takayuki Segawa in *Godzilla vs. King Ghidorah, Godzilla vs. Mechagodzilla II*, and

Sahara signs autographs for fans at Chicago's 2009 G-Fest convention. *Photo by author*

Godzilla vs. Space Godzilla. Completing the trifecta, he appeared during the Millennium series as well, with a memorable turn as a paleontologist in *Godzilla: Final Wars.* Proud of his long-running work and continued association with Japanese *tokusatsu*, he enjoys meeting fans at conventions, and with his English-speaking wife as translator, has traversed the Pacific many times to appear at genre events in the United States.

Takashi Shimura

The elder statesman of Japanese cinema, Shimura was a classically trained thespian and scholar of literature who was just as much at home performing for Akira Kurosawa, for whom he appeared in a total of twenty-one films, as he was in the *tokusatsu* pictures of Ishiro Honda. He is best known as the lead samurai Kambei in Kurosawa's *Seven Samurai* (1954), but is beloved by *daikaiju eiga* fans as Dr. Kyohei Yamane, the grave paleontologist in the original *Gojira.* His formidable performance in the film is typical of the heft he brought to all his roles, and the seriousness with which he took even his "lower" science-fiction work.

He was born Shoji Shimazaki on March 12, 1905, in the town of Ikuno in Hyogo Prefecture. Perhaps fitting considering many of his later roles, he was descended from real-life samurai stock; nevertheless, by the twentieth century his family was working class, and he attended public school in his hometown of Ikuno, and later in Nobeoka, Miyazaki, where his father, a miner, had been transferred for work. Although his early education was disrupted temporarily by a bout of tuberculosis, he later threw himself into his studies in earnest, taking a particular interest in English literature, which would eventually lead him to Shakespeare and the dramatic theater.

Taking up poetry during his early school years, he entered Kansai University in 1923 to continue his studies in English literature. When his father retired, he was forced to take a job in the Osaka municipal waterworks to support his schooling. Developing his love for drama, he joined the University's Theatre Studies Society, and helped to found an amateur theatrical group, the Shichigatsu-za. After losing his job due to his increased involvement in the troupe, he dropped out of school, and began to tour with the Shichigatsu-za full time. It was his first taste of professional acting.

In his late twenties, Shimura took on acting roles both on the radio and on the stage, where he excelled as part of a series of touring groups. His first interest in motion pictures came in the mid-1930s when sound finally began to infiltrate the Japanese movie industry, which he felt would lend him a

Shimura springs to action in Kurosawa's *Seven Samurai*.   *Movie Stills Database*

great advantage as a theatrically trained actor (as it did many in the United States in the early 1930s). Although his film debut came in 1934 in the silent *Ren'ai gai itchome* for early movie studio Shinko Kinema, by his third film, *Chuji uridasu*, he was able to demonstrate the full range of his dramatic ability, speaking included.

By his fifth film appearance, as a detective in *Osaka Elegy* (*Naniwa ereji*) (1936), Shimura began landing substantial roles and making a name for himself as an actor of tremendous skill. In 1937, he parlayed his success into a five-year contract with top Japanese studio Nikkatsu, which saw him appearing in approximately twenty pictures a year. While there, he distinguished himself with a recurring role in the popular samurai film series *Umon Torimonocho*. His film career hit a bump in the road during World War II, when the increasingly oppressive and ultra-conservative Japanese regime detained Shimura for several weeks due to his involvement in perceived left-leaning theater groups. It was after emerging from detention, with help from his wife and some of his acting colleagues, that Shimura signed on with Toho Company in 1943.

Shimura's very first film for Toho would be an indicator of the path his career would take with the studio. It also happened to be the first film of maverick director Akira Kurosawa, *Sanshiro Sugata* (1943). Over the next thirty-seven years, Shimura would appear in a total of twenty-one of Kurosawa's thirty films, more even than the actor most associated with Kurosawa, Toshiro Mifune. These roles included that of a doctor in *Drunken Angel* (*Yoidore Tenshi*) (1948), a hardened detective in *Stray Dog* (*Nora Inu*) (1949), the woodcutter in *Rashomon* (1950), and of course, the part in *Seven Samurai* that immortalized him.

During production of *Gojira*, producer Tomoyuki Tanaka and director Ishiro Honda wanted an actor of some gravitas and experience to play their world-weary scientist Dr. Yamane. Shimura was just finishing up *Seven Samurai*, and seemed like just what they were looking for. Far from looking down on appearing in a monster movie, Shimura took the part just as seriously as anything he had ever done, and it shows. His work is among the highlights of the film, which is saying quite a bit for a movie about a massive dinosaur destroying Tokyo. Shimura was so good, in fact, that Honda and Tanaka kept turning to him to punch up future *tokusatsu* productions. He briefly reprised the role of Yamane in *Godzilla Raids Again*, and played another scientist, Dr. Tanjiro Adachi, in *The Mysterians*. He had a small but memorable part as a newspaper editor in the original *Mothra*, and played a paleontologist once again in *Gorath*. Even his appearances in *Ghidorah, the Three-Headed Monster* and *Frankenstein Conquers the World*, though brief, are enjoyable thanks to the genuine effort he puts into making them as real they can be, under the circumstances.

Entering his sixties during the height of Toho's glory days, Shimura continued to work in a variety of projects, a steady hand from the past in the midst of a sea of new, young faces. He appeared as a head priest in Masaki Kobayashi's cult horror classic *Kwaidan* (1964), and even had a chance to co-star in the 1965 remake of *Sanshiro Sugata*, which had been his first movie for Toho some twenty years previously. He worked nonstop through the 1970s, at a time when steady work for film actors was hard to come by. His prestigious work earned him Japan's Purple Ribbon Medal of Honor, awarded to outstanding academics and artists, as well as Japan's oldest accolade, the Order of the Rising Sun. In 1980, his old friend Kurosawa cast him one more time in *Kagemusha*, his first collaboration with the director in fifteen years, and a fitting end to a legendary career. The following year, Shimura died of emphysema at age seventy-six, leaving behind a profound legacy in theater and film.

Akira Takarada

Sophisticated and handsome, Takarada was to Japanese cinema of the 1950s and '60s what actors like Burt Lancaster, James Garner, Sean Connery, and Tony Curtis were to Western cinema of the period. Inextricably linked to Godzilla ever since his featured debut, which happened to be a co-starring role in the original *Gojira*, he enjoyed a career as one of Japan's premier leading men, a face and voice instantly recognizable to millions.

Born April 29, 1934, in Japan-occupied Korea, Takarada moved to Harbin, China, with his family at a very young age, where his father worked as a railroad engineer. The family stayed in China during the war, and it wasn't until Takarada was fourteen that they returned to Japan full time. Days before his nineteenth birthday, the good-looking youth was recruited by Toho Company as part of its now-legendary "New Faces" program in 1953. Although he had appeared briefly in the 1949 biopic *When the Liberty Bell Rang* while still in high school, he was now signed to a full-time contract, and made movies his career going forward.

Toho's first assignment would reflect the work he would later be best known for to Western audiences. As the headstrong Hideto Ogata, love interest of Emiko Yamane (Momoko Kochi), Takarada made quite a splash with filmgoers, and was immediately linked to a brand-new genre of Japanese film. He instantly became one of Toho's most relied-upon stars, his charisma only improving as he matured. He appeared in "salaryman" comedies, romances, samurai epics, war pictures, and much more. Honda used him in prominent parts in *tokusatsu* movies like *Half Human* (1958) and *The Last War* (1961).

When the Godzilla series exploded during the 1960s, Takarada enjoyed several starring turns alongside the monster. As reporter Ichiro Sakai, he appeared in *Mothra vs. Godzilla* with the lovely Yuriko Hoshi, a much more seasoned pro some ten years removed from playing Ogata. As Astronaut Fuji in *Invasion of Astro-Monster*, he enjoyed terrific chemistry with American actor Nick Adams, despite the fact that the two were speaking their lines in different languages on-set. Under director Jun Fukuda, he played the cynical fugitive Yoshimura in *Godzilla vs. the Sea Monster*, and was back working for Honda again in *King Kong Escapes* (1967) and *Latitude Zero* (1969).

As a mainstream celebrity in Japan, Takarada could be seen in commercials, and on countless guest appearances on game shows and other types of TV programs. He even lent his voice to the Japanese dubs of several imported American films, such as the Matt Helm pictures *Murderers' Row* (1966) and *The Ambushers* (1967), in which he provided the voice for Dean

Takarada poses with co-star Momoki Kochi on an original 1954 poster for *Gojira*.

Public domain

Martin's character; the musical *Doctor Dolittle* (1967), in which he spoke and sang for Rex Harrison; and even the later Disney films *The Great Mouse Detective* (1986)—in which he filled in for Vincent Price as Prof. Ratigan—as well as providing the voice of the villainous Jafar in the Japanese dub of *Aladdin* (1992).

During the 1970s and '80s, Takarada worked on screen less, focusing more on stage roles in Japanese productions of musicals like *My Fair Lady*, *South Pacific*, and others. He returned to motion pictures in the 1990s, and was even featured in the 1992 *Heisei*-era film *Godzilla & Mothra: Battle for Earth*. Over the past twenty years, he's focused on TV work and voice-over work for video games. He starred as the UN Secretary General in *Godzilla: Final Wars*, the last film of the Millennium series, and a decade later, at age eighty, he was even invited to the set of Legendary Pictures' American reboot, *Godzilla* (2014), to film a cameo appearance that was unfortunately left on the cutting-room floor.

Jun Tazaki

Perennially playing the stoic authority figures who struggle futilely to turn back the assaults of Godzilla, Tazaki had a face that's very recognizable to fans of *daikaiju eiga* as that of a string of generals, politicians, and the like. He came to motion pictures late in his career, and is remembered for the capable supporting performances he gave, often with only rather dry dialogue to work with.

Born Minoru Tanaka on August 28, 1913, in the northern coastal Japanese city of Aomori, he didn't make his feature film debut until the age of thirty-five, with a small part in *Body at the Gate* (*Nikutai no mon*) (1948), a film distributed by Toho but produced by the now-defunct Oizumi Studios. For the first two years of his film career, he was signed to Shintoho Studios (the company that had branched off from Toho), working for director Kon Ichikawa among others, and even appearing in the 1951 B-war-picture *Tokyo File 212*, produced in part by American studio RKO Pictures during the period of American occupation.

Tazaki's first part for Toho was in Hiroshi Inagaki's *Pirates* (*Kaizoku-sen*) (1951), in which he co-starred with Toshiro Mifune. He appeared throughout the *Jirocho sangokushi* samurai film series during the early 1950s, and later began to specialize in military-themed films, often as a general, admiral, or other high-ranked officer. In 1962, he made his first *tokusatsu* appearance, as the brave spaceship commander Raizo Sonoda in Ishiro

Honda's *Gorath*. Later that year, he debuted in the Godzilla series as Gen. Masami Shinzo in *King Kong vs. Godzilla*. He followed those up with the memorable role of Capt. Hachiro Jinguji in *Atragon* and Murata, the editor boss of Akira Takarada and Yuriko Hoshi in *Mothra vs. Godzilla*.

The successful character actor continued to appear in a string of beloved *kaiju* classics for the duration of the 1960s, including *Dogora, Frankenstein Conquers the World, Invasion of Astro-Monster, War of the Gargantuas*, and *Destroy All Monsters*, alternately playing detectives, generals, and scientists. He bucked the trend in Jun Fukuda's *Godzilla vs. the Sea Monster*, in which he played the nefarious and inscrutable commander of the Red Bamboo, seen only via remote screen. Aside from his work in science fiction, he also worked occasionally during this period for Akira Kurosawa, such as in *High and Low* (*Tengoku to jigoku*) (1963), and alongside fellow Godzilla-series scientist Takashi Shimura in *Kwaidan*.

He transitioned into TV work during the 1970s and 1980s, but continued working in film whenever the opportunity presented itself, as it did in 1985, when he cameoed one last time for Kurosawa in *Ran*. Shortly after his work on that final film, Jun Tazaki died of lung cancer on October 18, 1985, at the age of seventy-two.

And Also Featuring . . .

Hideyo Amamoto

A celebrated character actor in Japan, the distinguished Amamoto is most known to Godzilla fans as the eccentric inventor Shinpei Anami in *All Monsters Attack*. He can also be seen in *Gorath, Matango* (in which he is hidden in costume), *Atragon, Dogora, Ghidorah, the Three-Headed Monster, Godzilla vs. the Sea Monster*, and *King Kong Escapes*, in which he memorably plays the reprehensibly evil mastermind Dr. Who. At age seventy-five, he made a cameo appearance in *Godzilla, Mothra and King Ghidorah: Giant Monsters All-Out Attack* (2001) as the prophet Hirotoshi Isayama.

Yu Fujiki

Often used as comic relief, Fujiki was a favorite of Kurosawa's, and is remembered by G-fans as Tadao Takashima's sidekick in *King Kong vs. Godzilla*, as well as the hard-boiled egg-eating reporter Jiro Nakamura in *Mothra vs. Godzilla*. His other *tokusatsu* roles include *War of the Gargantuas*, *Space Amoeba*, and the Tsuburaya TV series *Ultraman Leo* (1974).

Mie Hama

Once a bus fare collector who happened to be spotted by Toho producer Tomoyuki Tanaka, Hama enjoyed a stellar career that saw her become one of the most internationally recognized Japanese actresses of her time. She played Fumiko Sakurai, the Fay Wray substitute in *King Kong vs. Godzilla*, as well as the alluring Madame Piranha in *King Kong Escapes*. She is perhaps best known to Western audiences as "Bond girl" Kissy Suzuki, one of Sean Connery's love interests in *You Only Live Twice* (1967).

Hiroyuki Kawase

His early 1970s film career was rather short-lived, but Kawase is fondly remembered as the heroic Ken Yano in *Godzilla vs. Hedorah* (1971), as well as Rokuro Ibuki, brilliant and dashing co-creator of Jet Jaguar in *Godzilla vs. Megalon* (1973).

Momoko Kochi

Striking yet demure, Kochi was immortalized as the brave yet fragile Emiko Yamane, daughter of Takashi Shimura's Dr. Yamane, in the original *Gojira*. One of Toho's "New Faces" discoveries of 1953, she had a stellar run during the 1950s, appearing in a wide range of films that included *The Mysterians* and *Half Human*. She worked much more sporadically after 1961, but returned to reprise her role of Emiko in *Godzilla vs. Destoroyah*, some forty years after the original.

Takehiro Murata

One of the most recognizable of the actors during Godzilla's *Heisei* and Millennium eras, Murata enjoyed the lead role of *kaiju*-chaser Prof. Yuji Shinoda in *Godzilla 2000* (1999). He had previously played the Indiana Jones-like Kenji Andoh in *Godzilla & Mothra: Battle for Earth*, and a newspaper editor in *Godzilla vs. Destoroyah*. He made brief cameos on *Godzilla, Mothra and King Ghidorah: Giant Monsters All-Out Attack* and *Godzilla Against Mechagodzilla*.

Shiro Sano

An actor as well as a director, Sano distinguished himself in two memorable sup-
porting roles during the Millennium series: as the nervous Prof. Shiro Miyasaka in
Godzilla 2000, and as the fidgety editor Haruki Kadokura in *Godzilla, Mothra and
King Ghidorah: Giant Monsters All-Out Attack*.

Katsuhiko Sasaki

Along with Hiroyoki Kawasa, Sasaki played one of the co-inventors of Jet Jaguar in
Godzilla vs. Megalon, and went on to appear in a string of Godzilla films in both the
Showa and *Heisei* eras, playing biologist Akira Ichinose in *Terror of Mechagodzilla*, a
soldier in *Godzilla vs. Biollante* and Prof. Mazaki in *Godzilla vs. King Ghidorah*. Today
he works extensively in animation voice-over work, as well as Japanese dubs of
American films, specializing in parts played by Robert De Niro and Alec Baldwin.

Tadao Takashima

An accomplished jazz musician as well as a prolific actor, Takashima was a popular
romantic leading man who also made a series of affable appearances in *tokusatsu*
pictures. Along with Yu Fujiki, he starred as the intrepid Osamu Sakurai in *King
Kong vs. Godzilla*. He can also be seen in *Atragon, Frankenstein Conquers the World*,
and *Son of Godzilla*. More than a quarter-century later, he returned to the franchise as Chief Hosono in *Heisei* entry *Godzilla vs. Mechagodzilla II*.

Yoshifumi Tajima

Among the favorite characters of Godzilla aficionados is the smarmy and slimy
Kumayama, the opportunistic head of "Happy Enterprises" in *Mothra vs. Godzilla*
(1964), perhaps Tajima's most memorable part. But the actor also did yeoman's
duty in a lengthy string of pictures for Toho, starting in 1956 with *Rodan*. Displaying
impressive range, Tajima also turns up in a variety of supporting parts in *The H-Man,
Giant Monster Varan, The Human Vapor* (1960), *Mothra, King Kong vs. Godzilla,
Atragon, Dogora, Ghidorah, the Three-Headed Monster, Frankenstein Conquers
the World, Invasion of Astro-Monster, War of the Gargantuas, King Kong Escapes,
Destroy All Monsters, All Monsters Attack*, and *Godzilla 1985*, as well as a recurring
role of *Daily News* editor Seki in the groundbreaking TV series *Ultra Q* (1966).

Chotaro Togin

A dependable supporting player for Toho during the 1960s, Togin first turned up in the Godzilla series as Ichino, one of the young, frightened stowaways in *Godzilla vs. the Sea Monster*. He can also be seen as a surveyor in *Son of Godzilla*; as Okada, one of the astronauts under Akira Kubo's Capt. Yamabe in *Destroy All Monsters*; and as a detective in *All Monsters Attack*. One of his final roles was in Ishiro Honda's *Space Amoeba*.

Akiko Wakabayashi

Along with Kumi Mizuno and Mie Hama, the beautiful Wakabayashi was one of the premier Japanese starlets of the 1960s. Her *tokusatsu* appearances include *King Kong vs. Godzilla* and *Dogora*, but she is best known as the brainwashed Princess of Sergina in *Ghidorah, the Three-Headed Monster*. Along with Hama, she appeared as "Bond girl" Aki in *You Only Live Twice*. Her career came to an abrupt end around the time the Japanese film industry virtually collapsed at the conclusion of the 1960s.

18

Shadows of Hiroshima

Godzilla as Allegory

When you pull back all the layers of silliness, popcorn movie fun, and monster effects, Godzilla is a symbol that can tell us a lot about the Japanese culture from which he emerged. There is certainly a mindset, or a combination of mindsets, that sets the stage for Godzilla, going back to a nation torn apart by nuclear fire, crippled by the aftermath of war and ambivalent toward an American enemy that was trying to turn itself into an ally. Some have pointed to Godzilla as a symbol of the atom bomb itself, or as a stand-in for America. Also, over the years the creature has vacillated from villain to hero in a pattern that corresponds with the tenor of Japanese/American relations. Without question, there's a level to Godzilla that goes far deeper than a guy in a rubber suit stepping on model buildings.

Over the years, it's become clear to even many casual fans that Godzilla is rife with symbolism. Some have seen him as a warning against the proliferation of technology in an overly industrialized age, as a force to keep the human race in check when it gets too big for its own britches. His Japanese origins also contain allusions to mythology and folklore, as *kaiju* have been suggested to be ciphers for ancient gods and divine forces beyond human control. And even though his transformation into a more lighthearted figure of good has much to do with commercial concerns and trends, there was also a philosophical shift in place that allowed audiences to accept as benevolent a being that once represented the worst disaster in the history of Japan.

The Atom Bomb Personified

It's impossible to overstate the horror that Japan underwent on August 6 and August 9, 1945, and the trauma that the nation was forced to cope with in the years that immediately followed. A once powerful empire, which had succumbed late to the temptations of fascism and aggressive colonialism thanks to the power of industrialization, Japan had been forced to pay for its transgressions in the most severe way possible. The terrors of the atomic bomb left a permanent scar on the psyche of the Japanese people, and what happened at Hiroshima and Nagasaki would be felt for generations to come. To this day, Japan is the only nation to be attacked by nuclear weapons, and the figurative fallout of those attacks forever transformed that nation.

Following the Japanese surrender in World War II was an American occupation that brought a formerly mighty world power low; a humbling experience, to say the least. Given Japan's part in Axis aggression, devastating attacks against the Chinese, as well as an unprovoked strike on American soil at Pearl Harbor, not to mention collaboration with Nazi Germany, it's not hard to understand why the American response would be thus, and even many circumspect Japanese realized that their nation had taken a dark path and needed to choose a different one. And although the need for such a harsh response by the Americans has been debated ever since, what cannot be denied is the multifaceted impact that response had on the Japanese people.

In addition to the A-bombs and the occupation, Japan also had to contend with the proximity of American nuclear weapons testing in the Pacific Ocean, adding proverbial insult to injury. In particular, Bikini Atoll, a chain of islands less than twenty-four hundred miles from the Japanese mainland, was the site of twenty-three different test detonations between 1946 and 1958. On one particular occasion, the Japanese fishing vessel the *Lucky Dragon No. 5*, or *Daigo Fukuryu Maru*, became irradiated with fallout from a test site, injuring and eventually killing most of the crew and contaminating fish that were unwittingly sold to the Japanese public. If the bombs hadn't completely focused the Japanese consciousness on the dangers of atomic weapons, then the infamous *Lucky Dragon* incident finished the job for sure.

It was in this environment, with these events in immediate hindsight, that Godzilla was created. In fact, the original *Gojira* (1954) went into production almost immediately after the *Lucky Dragon* incident, and was directly influenced by the event, which had been dominating national news in Japan. As a result, Tomoyuki Tanaka, Ishiro Honda, and Takeo Murata made a monster movie that could not have been more different from the monster movies being churned out in America. And even beyond that first film, they created a monster that was uniquely Japanese, and that reflected the horrors of war, the fear of nuclear annihilation, and the manner in

Castle Bravo, the first U.S. hydrogen bomb test. Bikini Atoll, March 1, 1954.   *Public domain*

which the Japanese people viewed themselves in the aftermath of unthinkable tragedy.

Rather than comment directly on current events, like most great science fiction, the Godzilla franchise uses symbolism and speculative elements to make social statements, and to comment on the human condition. Godzilla is born of radiation, a result of the aforementioned nuclear testing in the Pacific. And although America is never specifically mentioned or directly blamed, the insinuation is clear, as it was common knowledge who was conducting the tests in real life. Godzilla, particularly in his earliest incarnations, wreaks unholy havoc upon Japan, indiscriminately killing untold numbers of people and destroying property on a massive scale. A living nuclear weapon of sorts, he envelops cities in flame and levels buildings, the destruction spreading ever outward, like a mushroom cloud in slow motion. Also as with nuclear weaponry, conventional military might is powerless to stop him.

Certainly, to almost any Japanese sitting in a movie theater watching the scenes of destruction and mayhem in those early Godzilla films, the memories of Hiroshima and Nagasaki would be instantly conjured up. Indeed, the aftermath often resembles footage of those cities after the blasts, and in fact some of that real footage was even used. This makes sense, as director Honda was himself haunted by such imagery, having witnessed the damage done to Hiroshima firsthand during the war. It was something that stuck with him always, and informed his later work. The connection with real events was often a bit too real for some, as there were some complaints by film critics and others at the time that it was in poor taste for a monster movie to delve into such sensitive, real-life horror.

"The most significant and long-lasting one is that first movie, with its anti-nuclear message," says Steve Biodrowski, editor of *Cinefantastique Online*. "Everyone assumes in America that it's about the bombing of Hiroshima and Nagasaki, and it kind of is, but that movie is really about the H-bomb testing that irradiated the Lucky Dragon. It even starts with an attack on a fishing boat. The people who do object to the bomb, a lot of them first came to realize this by watching Godzilla films. . . . Honda hoped the movie would bring about the end of nuclear testing. He admitted that was naïve, but it wasn't totally useless, what he did."

It must be understood that in the years immediately following the end of the war, it was not really known how the postwar landscape would shake out, and what nuclear weapons would mean for the future of international relations. In the trauma of the moment, there was a lingering fear that what had happened could happen again, and maybe soon. This paranoia was embodied in Godzilla, the worst nightmare of the Japanese brought to life, in literally monstrous form. He represented not only the danger posed by nuclear war, but by war in general. The Japanese had seen the terrible destruction caused by man's inhumanity to man—including much they themselves had perpetrated—and people like Honda wanted to make it clear what a threat such behavior posed to the future. By using Godzilla, they were able to do so relatively "safely," in a manner that was free from outright politics.

"I always go back to what the filmmakers said," offers August Ragone, *kaiju* expert and author of *Eiji Tsuburaya: Master of Monsters*. "Honda said Godzilla is the embodiment of war. Not atomic war, but war in general. Having been the only one of the filmmakers that worked on the original film that was actually taken as a POW returning from Manchuria to Japan, being taken through the wreckage at Hiroshima, he really understood.

Honda said Godzilla was war incarnate, and his atomic breath was the H-bomb tests."

The Sleeping Giant

The parallel of the monster and the bomb is admittedly a simple one, perhaps overly simple. There are many who have read quite a bit more into it, and there are several other layers to the comparison. For example, Godzilla is often seen as a symbol for the United States, and this is a comparison that has been maintained not just during the creatures' early years, but throughout the history of the franchise. Certainly, the allegory is easy to perceive in the beginning, with Godzilla presented as a creature born of nuclear technology and bent on causing destruction to major Japanese cities. And yet, at the time the film was made in 1954, the United States had been an ally of Japan for several years, and in fact helped build the country back up following a prolonged occupation. So the comparison is a complex one.

Not all Japanese were thrilled at the notion of a humbling occupation, and so there may have been an element of bitterness in the Japanese attitude toward America. After all, the Americans were also the ones conducting the experiments in the Pacific that had led to the *Lucky Dragon* disaster in 1954. Nevertheless, making a film directly criticizing the U.S. for its decision to drop two atomic bombs on major Japanese cities, killing hundreds of thousands of civilians, would have been an unwise move politically, diplomatically, and otherwise. As is often the case in art, the less direct approach can be the more practical, and even more effective one.

The relationship between Japan and America was a conflicted one in those days, and that's mirrored in the portrayal of Godzilla. It's also worth noting that the attitude toward Godzilla, even when the monster is at his worst, is both fearful and respectful. Emperor Hirohito himself, after the bombing of Pearl Harbor, warned that Japan had "awoken a sleeping giant." This metaphor implies that not only could Japan be in serious danger, but also that perhaps the response that Japan would suffer as a result would be somehow deserved because of the country's hubris and foolhardiness. So perhaps the metaphor of Godzilla as America is not necessarily an indictment of America, but an indictment of Japan for somehow bringing destruction upon itself. That kind of introspection and self-blame wouldn't be entirely uncharacteristic of the Japanese mindset, especially among avowed pacifists like Ishiro Honda.

"With some of the Godzilla movies, the fan community desperately wants to read easy analogies into the different monsters and characters," says Dr. William Tsutsui. "The big one was always, does Godzilla represent America, and I think it's not that simple, really. But I do think because of the longevity of the Godzilla series, and the different social and political contexts it had to operate in, the narratives aren't as easy as they seemed at the time."

The Enemy of Industry

Implicit in the character of Godzilla, then, is also a rebuke; a punishment of the Japanese people for their sins. Godzilla has never been portrayed as the simple, two-dimensional beasts we usually see in American monster movies—in Godzilla films, there is often the sense that somehow, as horrific as it is, the mayhem caused by the monster is somehow at least partially earned or deserved. Even more than the notion of past military aggression, often, these sins are connected to industrialization, to technology, to all the trappings that come with the modernization of Japanese culture that occurred swiftly in the twentieth century.

Godzilla always targets man-made objects, including buildings, factories, and methods of transportation. The monster usually seems intent on crushing symbols of human civilization, as if he disapproves of Japan moving away from its more rural origins. After all, the more agrarian people who seem to fear and respect the monster the most are also spared the brunt of his wrath. Godzilla typically targets large cities and industrial complexes. Even in later films, when the monster is portrayed in a positive light, he still stands in opposition to Japan's disregard for the environment and its reliance on industrial development. This attitude was even carried over into the 2014 American reboot *Godzilla*, in which direct allusions are made to the 2011 Fukushima nuclear power plant disaster.

"Godzilla is perhaps unique in all of moviedom in that he's a character constantly evolving (and de-evolving) with the times and perceived requirements of his audience," says Stuart Galbraith IV. "Having lived in Japan for many years now, a country beset by all manner of unstoppable natural disasters—volcanoes, earthquakes, typhoons, and tsunami—Godzilla is, specifically, a manmade creation equally devastating and horrifying, a symbol of not only the dangers of nuclear weapons but also manmade war and the terrible weapons that derive from it. If that were the only Godzilla, what you'd have is a uniquely Japanese monster, but not the durably endearing character embraced around the world. That Godzilla is the product of 1960s Japanese moviemaking, a character that changed subtly with each new film. Some of that appeal grew out of this gradual anthropomorphization of Godzilla, as well as the direction Eiji Tsuburaya and suit actor Haruo Nakajima brought to the character."

Putting the "God" in Godzilla

Much more than a living, breathing animal, Godzilla is a force of nature. The "sleeping giant" metaphor is most apt, conjuring up as it does images of ancient, mythological beings. The *daikaiju* in general have often been compared to ancient gods, and there is something in their presentation that links them to Japanese folklore in a way that we never see in American movie monsters. This is directly shown in the case of Mothra, who is explicitly represented as a godlike entity; but it is also true to varying degrees with all the Japanese *kaiju*, and most certainly with Godzilla. The ancient obsession with reptilian gods in the form of the dragons of the East continues in the *kaiju* tradition, and even though King Ghidorah is a more direct allusion to this tradition, Godzilla is also informed by the fascinating and often ambiguous presence of dragons in Eastern culture. Those dragons are usually shown to be benevolent, but they are also just as often quite inscrutable and unknowable. They are beyond our power and understanding, much as Godzilla is.

In his very first appearance, Godzilla is spoken of as a divinity, which the people of Odo Island seek to perpetually appease. When unhappy, he lashes out with indiscriminate destruction, as many pre-Christian mythological divinities were known to do. He is never portrayed as an out-and-out evil creature (although the closest he comes to pure evil is in the 2001 film *Godzilla, Mothra and King Ghidorah: Giant Monsters All-Out Attack*, which is also ironically when he's at his most godlike), but is rather like a living natural disaster, as horrible as he is inevitable. Like many mythological gods, he is often ambivalent in his attitude toward humanity. He also seems to be quite immortal, immune and almost impervious to virtually all conventional forms of weaponry. Unlike American movie monsters, he can't be killed by bullets and bombs (and in fact, by changing this quality in the ill-fated 1998 American film, much of Godzilla's divine nature was wiped away).

"There have been plenty of dinosaur films," says August Ragone. "But why aren't more people having conventions for *Valley of the Gwangi*, or *Dinosaurus*, or *The Beast from 20,000 Fathoms*? The Japanese monsters are imbued and informed with a deep and very long history of Japanese culture and mythology. The creators of those films grew up in that culture: 2,000 years of mythology. These monsters are larger than life and quite different from Western creations, and removed from Western sensibilities. They become more attractive because they just don't simply die, and they're not simply living, breathing creatures. They're not animals, like dinosaurs. These are creatures that are divine, that have strange powers, in different films they manifest different types of personalities."

From Bad Guy to Good Guy and Back

Adding to the complexity of Godzilla's symbolism is the fact that the monster's attitude and perception change dramatically over the course of the series. As his longtime fans know, Godzilla goes from being an enemy of mankind to an ally, from a foe to a friend, from a destructive force to the literal guardian of the planet Earth. He also transforms back later in the series, and sometimes it seems even the filmmakers themselves can't make up their minds whether they consider Godzilla a force for evil or for good. He's often somewhere in the middle.

Granted, some of the reasoning behind the transformation of the character is sheerly commercial in nature. With each installment, Godzilla was becoming more popular with the audience, perhaps owing to the fact that he was always portrayed with varying degrees of sympathy. Children were attracted to the creature, and by the late 1960s, there was an entire generation of youngsters who were not even born at the time of the Hiroshima and Nagasaki bombings. Many, in fact, were not even born at the time the original *Gojira* was released. And so the direct connotation of Godzilla as an allegory for the bomb, or for an aggressive enemy nation, was lost on them. They just enjoyed seeing the monster action, and wanted to root for the mighty Godzilla. As time went on, Toho was more than happy to capitalize on that.

"Part of the reason Godzilla endures is the creators have always known how to evolve with the audiences," says Miguel Rodriguez. "It started out being a thinly veiled reference to H-bomb testing, and as the years progressed when the audiences became younger, they became more for kids. And they were not embarrassed about it."

And so, the creature that once stood for nuclear annihilation and the nightmare of genocide now was a brave superhero, bordering on cute and cuddly. The transformation didn't happen overnight, but continued steadily over the course of the *Showa* era. In addition to the aforementioned commercial concerns, many have also linked Godzilla's transformation with the developing attitude of the Japanese toward their American allies. As the war faded into a distant memory and Japan began to thrive, America was seen in a more benign light, and so was Godzilla. America was perceived as more of a friendly ally, and so was Godzilla. Even when the economic fortunes of Japan hit a downturn in the 1970s, the attitude toward America had shifted to the point where its cipher, Godzilla, was more than just a friendly face, but the actual protector and defender of the Japanese identity.

"It has changed, and that's what's been so brilliant and why it's been so enduring," says Rodriguez. "Godzilla is not a static character. In the first film, he's basically the H-bomb with a personality. And by the time it gets to *Smog Monster*, he's Ultraman. He's a superhero. It was a completely different take. As you watch the movies, you can see moments where the character changes. My favorite is from *Ghidorah*, when Mothra actually has to convince Godzilla and Rodan to band together against Ghidorah, and they're a little bit indignant at first! He sits down and puts his nose up in the air, shakes his head back and forth. You get to see more of where he changes, even the movie after that, when *Ghidorah* becomes a such a huge success that they make a direct sequel to it, *Monster Zero* [aka *Invasion of Astro-Monster*], where Rodan and Godzilla go to Planet X and defeat King Ghidorah and Godzilla does his infamous little dance. As absurd as that is, that dance sums up the *Showa* period in two seconds. That dance makes you fall in love with Godzilla just a little bit."

This *Showa* attitude was not a permanent one. As Japan's fortunes took an upturn again in the 1980s, and the nation became known as an industrial and technological giant, frictions once again developed between Japan and the U.S. Even though the two countries were and remain allies, a rivalry arose, and ironically, it would be many in the U.S. who grew suspicious of Japan's powers and prowess, somehow paranoid that Japan would overtake America's place as a preeminent and dominant world power. From an economic standpoint, for a time this seemed feasible to many. While relations were strained in this way, Godzilla once again returned to his menacing roots, and in the *Heisei* series which started in 1985, the creature is back to being an enemy of Japan. And never is the negative portrayal of the U.S. more direct than in the third *Heisei* film, *Godzilla vs. King Ghidorah* (1991), in which America's forces in World War II are shown as brutish cowards.

Tokyo's Godzilla statue pays tribute to one of Japan's cultural icons.

Subcommandante59/Wikimedia

But the portrayal of the creature gains nuance over the course of the *Heisei* and later Millennium series; just as perceptions between Japan and the U.S. were a mixed bag, switching between positive and negative, so is Godzilla represented with shades of gray. He never returns to his outright heroic demeanor, but he is also shown as a being worthy of respect and awe. He may still step on a town or two here and there as it suits him, but he can also be counted on to save the day whenever a worse threat to Japan and the world appears.

"When you watch an actor you're very fond of playing a villain, he's not quite as villainous as he should be, because you like him," explains Peter H. Brothers. "Each sequel gets further away from the original concept. Who worries about nuclear war anymore? It was a different time. It's not relevant to people anymore. Now it's terrorism, now it's climate change, so if you can have Godzilla tied in with those kinds of things, you can make him a little more relevant."

There are many who might find it frivolous to read so much serious social symbolism into such a camp/pop cultural icon as Godzilla, and yet those who are fans of the franchise, and many who take an interest in Japanese cinema, as well as Japanese culture in general, have been making these connections for decades. Certainly as originally envisioned by Honda, Godzilla was quite a serious creation, intended to deliver an important message to viewers. And even though that creation changed dramatically over the years, it's a testament to the potency of that original vision that there has always been much more to it than what appears on the surface. Whether a warning against nuclear war, a commentary on industrialization, or an ongoing allegory for East/West relations, Godzilla has had much to tell us beyond his piercing roar and the thud of his massive feet.

Godzilla's Changing Moods: A Kaiju Chronology

- 1954: With the release of *Gojira*, Godzilla is introduced to the world as a terrifying behemoth intent on wreaking as much havoc upon the Japanese people as he possibly can.
- 1962: Although Godzilla is still the bad guy in *King Kong vs. Godzilla*, this is the first time that the monster and his world are presented in a humorous, tongue-in-cheek light.
- 1964: Responding to the monster's growing popularity, in *Ghidorah, the Three-Headed Monster*, Toho has Godzilla come to humanity's aid for the first time, although he has to be begrudgingly persuaded by Mothra. He's still not truly

the hero, as he really just wants to be left alone. He'll step up to fight an outside threat, but humans are still very much afraid of the Big G.

- 1967: By giving Godzilla offspring in *Son of Godzilla*, Toho makes the monster even more sympathetic and benign.
- 1969: In a film aimed directly at children, *All Monsters Attack*, Godzilla becomes the idol of a little boy, who dreams of traveling to Monster Island to hang out with him and the other *kaiju*. Godzilla is presented as a fantastical product of youthful imagination, and for the first time seems to be devoid of all malice.
- 1971: By *Godzilla vs. Hedorah*, the Big G has completely morphed into his new role as defender of the planet, willingly answering the call to fight off the threat of the evil Smog Monster and "save the Earth" from the dangers of pollution.
- 1984: With the *Heisei* reboot that begins with *Godzilla 1985*, Toho brings Godzilla back to his original roots. The monster is now once again a remorseless bringer of destruction to mankind.
- 1991: In the third *Heisei* film, Toho seems unable to make up its collective mind, as Godzilla is still presented as a dangerous threat, and yet is also enlisted to defend humanity against King Ghidorah at the same time. It's a strange balancing act that would continue for the rest of the *Heisei* series.
- 1995: Godzilla's death in *Godzilla vs. Destoroyah* is presented in a completely tragic and sympathetic light, complete with a heartbreaking musical score by Akira Ifukube. We are clearly meant not to cheer, but to weep.
- 2001: Although most of the Millennium series continued the schizophrenic approach to Godzilla initiated in the *Heisei* series, in *Godzilla, Mothra and King Ghidorah: Giant Monsters All-Out Attack*, we see Godzilla at the most evil he has ever been, before or since. The tone is dropped after this film.
- 2014: Taking a cue from the latter *Showa* pictures, Max Borenstein and Gareth Edwards, respective screenwriter and director of Legendary Pictures' American *Godzilla*, surprise many fans by delivering a monster that is once again a valiant defender of Earth, who isn't bent on humanity's destruction, and who simply wants to be left alone.
- 2016: With the latest reboot of the franchise in *Shin Godzilla*, Toho has reestablished Godzilla once again as a dangerous, destructive force of nature. This is clearly a monster that has trouble making up his mind.

19

Legendary Reboot

Godzilla Returns to America

Sixteen years after TriStar Pictures' ill-fated American remake, genre powerhouse Legendary Pictures took on the daunting assignment of once again attempting to reinvent Toho's great monster for American moviegoers. The result was 2014's *Godzilla*, a modern-day special-effects extravaganza that made up for many of the mistakes of the 1998 misfire and successfully blended much of the Toho ethos with contemporary methods of CGI blockbuster storytelling. In many ways, the film made Godzilla relevant again for today's American audience.

Unlike the previous American attempt, which disappointed at the box office and became one of the worst-reviewed summer blockbusters of all time, alienating the fan base in the process, the new *Godzilla* was a triumphant success, and although not without its detractors (what movie has none?), it helped to restore the franchise and the character in the public consciousness, even inspiring Toho to reprise its own original Godzilla series. It was a long and tortuous process to get the Legendary picture to the big screen, stretching over the course of a decade. But the time put into developing the project was worth it, as in the end, the finished product was a piece of work that respected its source material while taking it in interesting and creative directions, and most importantly, delivering a highly engaging piece of entertainment.

"The attitude this time was that it's not enough to just put something on the screen where a lot of stuff gets destroyed," says Steve Biodrowski of *Cinefantastique Online*. "Let's make a movie that tries to show you how this would really feel if it happened for the first time. So we'll always shoot Godzilla from the eye level of people, and people will be in the foreground. It looks like something you'd see if you were there on the sidewalk looking up. It was respectful but not reverential. Not bound by what came before. They tried to make a real movie, and it's good by the standards of an American blockbuster. You're not coming out happy just because you're a Godzilla fan."

The 2013 teaser poster for Legendary's *Godzilla* piqued fan interest in a big way.

Global Panorama/Flickr

Smoggy Origins

Ironically, the film can trace its beginnings back to Japan, almost immediately following the release of *Godzilla: Final Wars*, the last entry in Toho's Millennium series back in 2004. Toho had decided to put its Godzilla franchise on hold, announcing that it would not make another installment for the next ten years. To prove how serious the decision was, Toho even demolished the fabled "Big Pool"—the expansive water stage used in an untold number of *kaiju* and other films dating back to the 1960s. Sony/ Columbia's TriStar division, which had produced the 1998 American *Godzilla* and had rights to make further American sequels, had allowed their rights to lapse in 2003. All seemed quiet on the Godzilla front.

Into this unique opening stepped a producer/filmmaker who had had an interesting history with the franchise in the past. Yoshimitsu Banno was the former wunderkind director whom Toho hired back in 1971 to write and direct the first Godzilla film in two years, which turned out to be the bizarre *Godzilla vs. Hedorah*, in which the Big G fights for the sake of the environment against a monster made of sludge and pollution. The studio was less than thrilled with the quirky offering, and Banno's directorial career was cut short. However, somehow, thirty-three years later in August 2004, Banno managed to secure the rights from Toho to make his own independent short Godzilla film. Intended as a 3D IMAX remake of *Godzilla vs. Hedorah*, the picture was to be called *Godzilla 3D to the Max*.

Soon, Banno had secured the services of American cinematographer Peter Anderson, as well as American producer Brian Rogers and visual effects giant Kerner Optical, recently spun off from George Lucas's Industrial Light and Magic. By 2007, Banno and his new partners had gotten more ambitious, and negotiated with Toho to turn their proposed short film into a feature-length film. After getting the OK from Toho, Banno and company turned for funding to American production company Legendary Pictures. Since 2005, the new company had been swiftly becoming a powerhouse in the area of blockbuster spectacle filmmaking, and had particularly impressed many in the industry (and the public) with its reinvention of Batman in the films *Batman Begins* (2005) and *The Dark Knight* (2008), as well as other big-budget projects like *300* (2007). It was thought that perhaps Legendary could do for Godzilla what it had done for the Caped Crusader. Legendary liked the idea, and in 2010 obtained the rights from Toho through the intermediary Banno, who would remain on the project as an executive producer.

Godzilla Begins

What had started as Banno's independent short film had evolved into a full-blown American reboot of Godzilla, something that had been attempted once before, with sad results. But much had changed in the movie industry; in addition to improved special effects, franchise properties were being treated with more respect than they had been, due in part to the vocal online fan community that had become a force in the age of social media. The American audience also seemed more ready for the return of the giant monster movie, as would be evidenced one year prior to the eventual release of the new *Godzilla*, with the surprising grassroots success of Guillermo del Toro's *Pacific Rim* (2013), a heavily *tokusatsu*-influenced film pitting giant human-operated robots against a host of assorted *kaiju* (as they were directly labeled in the movie).

As it had done in the past, Legendary partnered with Warner Bros. to co-finance and distribute its new venture (it would be the first time Warner Bros. had been involved in distributing a Godzilla picture since they took *Godzilla Raids Again* (1955) and released it in the U.S. as *Gigantis, the Fire Monster* in 1959). Intent on learning from the mistakes of the past, Legendary set out to make sure that its *Godzilla* would be a movie that fans and new audiences would enjoy, that would take its subject seriously, and succeed at the box office. This time, Godzilla would have other monsters to fight, which had not been the case in 1998. And although the creature would once again be brought to life with CGI—a decision that had once been controversial—the design would be more in line with the spirit of Toho's Godzilla, an upright saurian beast of building-squashing dimensions, with a sweeping tail, ridges down his back, and most importantly, the ability to spit nuclear fire.

In the fall of 2010, Legendary kicked the preproduction into gear by hiring a director, Gareth Edwards—a relatively untested Englishman known only for helming the 2010 British creature feature *Monsters*. Screenwriter David Callaham—known for the 2005 video game adaptation *Doom* and the Sylvester Stallone ensemble action flick *The Expendables* (2010)—was brought on board to flesh out the first draft of a script. Later, as is the custom with Hollywood blockbusters, additional writers were brought in to polish and rework the material, including respected genre scribe David S. Goyer, who had worked on Legendary's Batman franchise, as well as the *Blade* trilogy, among many other projects. Then, virtually unknown commodity Max Borenstein, whom Legendary had previously contracted to work on a script about Jimi Hendrix, was hired to complete the *Godzilla* script and get it into shootable shape (he'd also get the sole, official screenwriting credit on the picture). Finally, Frank Darabont, writer of such cult favorites as the remake of *The Blob* (1988) and *Mary Shelley's Frankenstein* (1994), and writer-director

A runaway MUTO leaves a wrecked Vegas Strip in its terrible wake.   *Movie Stills Database*

of *The Shawshank Redemption* (1994), *The Green Mile* (1999), and *The Mist* (2007), was hired to add his special touch as "script doctor"—a role he had filled for such films as Steven Spielberg's *Saving Private Ryan* (1998) and *Minority Report* (2002).

The final script was turned in to Edwards at the start of 2013, just in time for principal photography to begin. An all-star cast was put together, including *Breaking Bad*'s Bryan Cranston; Japanese actor Ken Watanabe, best known to American audiences for *Batman Begins* and Clint Eastwood's *Letters from Iwo Jima* (2006); Aaron Taylor-Johnson, young star of the underground superhero favorite *Kick Ass* (2010); Elizabeth Olsen, the younger sister of *Full House*'s Olsen twins, who had also just been cast as the Scarlet Witch in Marvel's *Captain America: The Winter Soldier* (2014); as well as Oscar-winner Juliette Binoche and Oscar-nominee David Straithairn.

Meet the MUTOs

In this version of the story, Godzilla was once again a force of nature—a mysterious underwater creature being tracked by the U.S. government. In a twist on the original nuclear origin, this Godzilla was not created by 1950s

Godzilla star Bryan Cranston discusses his role at the 2013 San Diego Comic Con.
Gage Skidmore/Wikimedia

nuclear testing, but rather awakened by it (in fact, it's later revealed that most of those tests were actually top-secret attempts to kill the creature). Meanwhile, Godzilla's eventual foes, two massive, dormant, prehistoric reptilian/insectoid creatures known as MUTOs (Massive Unidentified Terrestrial Organisms) are unleashed in the 1990s during a mining accident, and one of them causes a catastrophic meltdown at a nuclear power plant in Japan, strikingly reminiscent of the real-life meltdown of Japan's Fukushima Daiichi nuclear plant in 2011.

In a role of extraordinary power for a giant monster movie, Cranston plays Joe Brody, an engineer who loses his wife (Binoche) in the disaster and makes it his life's work to track down the hidden cause of it. When he finally stumbles onto the truth about the MUTOs, one of which is being studied by Watanabe's Dr. Ishiro Serizawa (named for both original *Gojira* director Ishiro Honda and Dr. Daisuke Serizawa, the character that helps to defeat the monster in that film), he enlists the help of his soldier son Ford (Taylor-Johnson). When Joe is killed (a shocking early death that many felt harmed the narrative flow of an otherwise engaging film), Ford must do what he can to aid the military, with Godzilla and the MUTOs on a collision course that leads to the film's climactic *kaiju* confrontation.

Inspired by movies like *Jaws* (1975) and *Close Encounters of the Third Kind* (1977), Edwards made the bold choice to hold the big reveal of Godzilla back for a large portion of the picture. And while this annoyed some fans (despite the same strategy being used in many classic Toho Godzilla films), the payoff is quite satisfying, as Godzilla and the MUTOs tear up portions of Honolulu, Las Vegas, and San Francisco. Many longtime fans were also shocked that Godzilla is portrayed not as a malevolent destroyer, but rather as an unstoppable force helping to keep the natural order of the world in balance. In a tone reminiscent of mid-*Showa* era Godzilla, here the Big G sets his sights on neutralizing the threat posed by the MUTOs, despite being targeted by military forces that mistakenly view him as just as much of a threat. Despite the protestations of dyed-in-the-wool "man-in-suit" proponents, the CGI monster sequences (supervised by Jim Rygiel of *The Lord of the Rings* fame) are quite effective, and Godzilla is suitably awe-inspiring, including a theater-shaking modern update of his trademark roar.

"They studied Shusuke Kaneko's *Gamera* trilogy very carefully, in terms of approach, in terms of how to stage the film and how to present the narrative," says leading Godzilla aficionado and author August Ragone. "At the same time, they turned it around where Godzilla's character in this is like Gamera's, he isn't one hundred percent a hero or a villain. You have elements of '70s Godzilla, where he's not purposely trying to kill people at all, he's just protecting his turf. That's essentially what's happening in Gareth Edwards's film. They hit the nail on the head in terms of getting the core of Godzilla's character to be true, in terms of the Godzilla they picked, the mid '60s and '70s Godzilla. They went for that style, and they got the spirit true, because Godzilla is not a dinosaur, he's a monster that obviously isn't a natural being."

A Worldwide Triumph

The finished product was delivered to Toho for approval in March 2014, and the company was reported to be quite pleased, not only with the creature design, but also with the story that dealt not only with the nuclear themes common to many past Godzilla films, but also with the more modern-day concerns raised by disasters such as Fukushima and the Indian tsunami of 2004. After Toho gave its blessing, Legendary released the picture world-wide on May 16, 2014, in IMAX 3D, as well as standard 3D and 2D formats. Warner Bros. handled distribution domestically and internationally everywhere except Japan, where Toho itself acted as distributor.

While a much bigger financial success than the 1998 *Godzilla*, Legendary's *Godzilla* was outmatched during the summer of 2014 by such tremendous blockbusters as *Transformers: Age of Extinction*, *Guardians of the Galaxy*, *Maleficent*, *X-Men: Days of Future Past*, and *Dawn of the Planet of the Apes*. It was a highly competitive season, but *Godzilla* still managed to set the all-time record for the highest opening weekend for a monster movie, earning $200.6 million in North America and a grand total of $528 million worldwide, making it a highly profitable endeavor for Legendary and Warner Bros.

Among fans and critics alike, the film received a relatively warm welcome, also a stark contrast to Roland Emmerich's 1998 movie. Most were impressed with the quality of the acting—often a point of mockery in Godzilla films—and pointed out the level of gravity that seasoned thespians like Cranston, Binoche, and Watanabe brought to the material. Many even compared Edwards's film to some of the genre work of Steven Spielberg, only fitting since Edwards had cited Spielberg as one of his main inspirations. All in all, the picture restored most of the goodwill that had been dashed by the previous American reboot, and pleased Godzilla enthusiasts with its faithfulness to the spirit of their beloved *kaiju*.

"The success of the Legendary film is that the Godzilla they have is being driven by this deeper primal force, but it's a recognizably heroic force," explains Dr. William Tsutsui. "It looks like the original, but not exactly. The problem with the 1998 *Godzilla* was that film really tried to separate Godzilla from his Japanese origins, and that just doesn't work. In the world, no matter where you go, Godzilla and Japan are of a piece. And that's what the Legendary film got back to. I didn't like the way they portrayed Japan in the film, but I do think having that link to Japan was what people expected to see, and what felt right."

With a sequel in the works—as well as another future crossover with King Kong—Gareth Edwards's *Godzilla* has helped to kick off a bone fide American Godzilla franchise for the very first time. Along with *Pacific Rim* and its upcoming sequel, it's part of what many hopeful fans see as a giant-monster-movie renaissance in the United States. Godzilla is a part of the mainstream American popular consciousness once again to a degree that he hasn't been since at least the 1970s, or perhaps ever, with a whole new generation introduced to the character that may not have ever been aware of his existence. The initial 1998 experiment may have flopped, but in 2014, the inexorable Godzilla succeeded in finally crossing the Pacific and conquering Hollywood.

20

Go, Go Godzilla!

A Pop Culture Phenomenon

More than just a motion picture or a movie monster, Godzilla has come to be a part of our cultural consciousness, arguably even more in the West than in Japan. From the classic Blue Oyster Cult song and the infamous *Bambi Meets Godzilla* (1973), to *Bridezillas* and *Pee-Wee's Big Adventure* (1985), the Big G has transcended his origins to become a bona fide icon. The creature has unquestionably had an ongoing life beyond the film series, and ironically, perhaps nowhere is this more apparent than in the United States, the country that has adopted him as one of its favorite entertainment imports.

Godzilla's name and image are instantly recognizable, and his pop culture ubiquity is on a rarefied stratum of fictional characters occupied by the likes of Superman, Mickey Mouse, Darth Vader, Dracula, and Sherlock Holmes. Some would even say that in recent years, his visibility has surpassed even that of his fellow giant monster icon King Kong. Over the past sixty-plus years, the character has pervaded every corner of the public space, and his name is even recognized by many who have little to no familiarity with the actual films in which he's appeared. Something about Godzilla has given him that rare ability of a fictional character to become something more than a character, but rather a symbol, a Jungian-style archetype that can suggest things that are sometimes totally independent of its actual fictional existence or nature.

"There's a kind of magic about Godzilla," says Japanese culture expert Dr. William Tsutsui. "On some level, Godzilla appeals to this fundamental sense in all humanity that goes across cultures and continents and languages, something about this big heroic figure we all stand in awe of, yet at the same time there's something about Godzilla we all want to be. Something liberating and exhilarating about being gigantic and dragging your feet through cities and watching them explode. It can't help but make us happy. That sense of fear and wonder, and also of joy. It's all tied up with

Godzilla's ubiquitous presence in our culture extends even to baked goods. *Photo by author*

childhood, especially for young people who often feel so disempowered in an adult world. So Godzilla keeps catching young fans, and those young fans become nostalgic middle-aged fans like myself, who always want to go back and capture some of that special time. It's a brilliant franchise that Toho could never have imagined would take off like it did. Because Godzilla is not a person like James Bond; he doesn't age. There's no 'Fat Elvis' phase of Godzilla, where he's not the same guy you grew up with. Godzilla can be refreshed, he can still be the same character and yet reflect the particular moment when he's depicted."

To say that Godzilla has taken on a life of his own would be an understatement, as even if no further films were made in the Godzilla franchise, the character would still retain nearly all its cultural currency, and would continue to do so for quite some time to come. Although Godzilla may technically be the intellectual property of one particular company, he truly belongs to the world, regardless of how that might be a source of ongoing frustration for that particular company. Defying all legal and other attempts to keep him under control, Godzilla has risen beyond the mundanities of proprietary boundaries. Godzilla is universal.

The enormous popularity of Godzilla in the West is so overwhelming that it even exceeds how the monster is perceived in his home country of Japan. In fact, over the decades, the profile of Godzilla has actually lowered in the Land of the Rising Sun, as his cinematic heyday recedes further and further into the past. American fans, who have come to revere the creature, might even be surprised at how "old hat" Godzilla has become in his birthplace, where the younger generation has little to no exposure to the character.

"If you go to Japan today and you ask about Godzilla, you'll find he is not someone the Japanese think about a whole lot," says Dr. Tsutsui. "They know who Godzilla is, but he's sort of a historic movie figure rather than someone who's living. I'm not sure the Japanese view Godzilla as such a strong representation of their country, as people abroad do."

Celluloid Cameos

Godzilla's special "guest" appearances in various movies and television shows outside of his own official series are virtually legion. But perhaps no other "unofficial" Godzilla appearance is as famous (or infamous) as the 1969 animated short film *Bambi Meets Godzilla*, created by young Los Angeles animator Marv Newland. The simple hand-drawn, two-minute film, which depicts Godzilla stomping on Disney's beloved cartoon deer, became an instant cult classic in 1973, when it was distributed to theaters as part of a package of underground animated shorts. It gained popularity over the years through play in repertory theaters, as well as on late-night TV and early cable channels like HBO, which used it as entertaining filler. By 1985, it was so well known that it was even paired with Toho's *Godzilla 1985* in American theaters and on its VHS home video release.

Over the years, filmmakers have enjoyed referencing Godzilla, either directly as a character or indirectly as a meta-reference, using his image as an easy cultural shorthand. Generation Xers fondly recall his appearance in *Pee-Wee's Big Adventure*, during a scene in which Pee-Wee Herman bicycles through a movie studio in which a battle between Godzilla and King Ghidorah is being filmed by a Japanese crew. In one of the Big G's least dignified and most random moments, the rubber-suited actor finds himself sitting in a sleigh with Santa Claus and being pulled through a Twisted Sister music video shoot. Rumor has it that director Tim Burton didn't even think to obtain the rights to the character from Toho (pointing to Godzilla's deceptive ubiquity), thus incurring the wrath of the Japanese company.

The following year, the Godzilla suit appeared again in the wacky comedy *One Crazy Summer*, in which comedian Bobcat Goldthwait becomes stuck in the costume and inadvertently crushes an assemblage of miniature buildings, much to the delight of Japanese onlookers. Tim Burton enlisted the monster again for his 1996 film *Mars Attacks!*, in which scenes of wanton destruction being perpetrated by the invading Martian fleet suddenly cut to a brief shot from *Godzilla vs. Biollante* (1989), which we quickly learn is the movie the aliens are enjoying in their spaceship during the attack. In *Austin Powers in Goldmember* (2002), the titular secret agent encounters a Godzilla-like statue, which, we are informed in an intentionally ham-fisted piece of dialogue, is not the *actual* Godzilla (a direct reference to Toho's notorious litigiousness).

On the small screen, the monster has been featured numerous times in that pop culture catchall *The Simpsons*, including a 1999 episode in which an animated Godzilla, along with fellow *kaiju* Rodan, Mothra, and even box-office rival Gamera, are attacking Tokyo during Homer and company's flight home from Japan. Another long-running TV animation staple, the bizarre *Robot Chicken*, has also featured Godzilla in several typically self-aware parodies and skits. In 1991, Comedy Central's snarky celebration of B-movie kitsch, *Mystery Science Theater 3000*, spotlighted two different Godzilla films, *Godzilla vs. the Sea Monster* (1966) and *Godzilla vs. Megalon* (1973), giving Joel Robinson, Tom Servo, and Crow T. Robot plenty of fodder for jokes on the Satellite of Love. And longtime fans of the beloved 1980s/90s sitcom *Roseanne* may recall that a Godzilla action figure was prominently displayed in the Conner family home during the course of the show.

The Sincerest Form of Flattery?

Due to Godzilla's universal nature in popular culture, it's been very hard to "contain" him like your run-of-the-mill piece of intellectual property. This has not made things easy for Toho, which has watched often help-lessly as its creation has proliferated in the popular consciousness and throughout media. Very often, as was the case with Tim Burton, those who use Godzilla's likeness or approximation don't even realize or even consider that the character may not be in the public domain. This has led Toho to become ever watchful of such occurrences, and many are those who thought they were paying tribute to the monster, or may not have even intended to directly reference him, who have found themselves the target of a Toho lawsuit.

The image of a giant reptilian monster attacking a city has become so commonplace that sometimes it doesn't even immediately seem to be a reference to Godzilla, but is more of a general cultural touchstone. Godzilla-like creatures have been casually featured in countless commercials and advertisements; for example, the 2008 commercial for the Subway sandwich chain that featured a quasi-Godzilla seeming to endorse the restaurant's "Five-Dollar Foot-Long" promotion, which attracted legal action from Toho. The 1986 arcade game *Rampage*, in which users can play as a variety of generic city-stomping monsters, featured "Lizzie," a titanic reptile who bore a striking resemblance to a certain radioactive Japanese dinosaur.

Even Godzilla's roar is such an instantly recognizable sound that it has been exploited countless times for dramatic or comedic effect. It can be heard in everything from the original 1958 *Hercules* starring Steve Reeves, made four years after the original *Gojira*, to *Star Trek: The Animated Series*, to the Rankin-Bass animated favorite *The Last Unicorn* (1982), to the 1990s sitcom *Malcolm in the Middle*, to the indomitable *Pokemon* animated series, which even featured Tyranitar, a Godzilla-inspired Pokemon.

The "Zilla" Phenomenon

If definitive proof is needed of the extent to which Godzilla has infiltrated our culture, one need look no further than the way in which the latter portion of his name, "-zilla," has become a generic suffix that is universally understood. Used to denote something of great size and/or anger, two qualities which Godzilla possesses in abundance, the suffix can be seen everywhere, and just as with the image of Godzilla himself, it is sometimes even used by those who have no in-depth knowledge or appreciation of Godzilla as a cinematic character. People who may not even make the immediate connection with the monster will hear the suffix "-zilla" at the end of a word or phrase, and the meaning is immediately conveyed.

"My favorite way that Godzilla has invaded the culture is actually through the lexicon," says Miguel Rodriguez. "The fact that '-zilla' is now a suffix, and a suffix that any English-speaking person immediately knows.

The scourge of Catholic school kids everywhere, "NunZilla" stomps and emits sparks from her mouth when wound up.

Author's collection

What better way to show the cultural ubiquity than to have changed the language in such a way?"

In order to connote power and robustness, in 1998, Netscape Communications decided to name its new software development branch "Mozilla." Today, Mozilla is best known for its Firefox web browser, and even sports a very dinosaurian logo that had to be slightly toned down from its original resemblance to Godzilla to avoid legal entanglements. American cable channel WEtv aired a reality series between 2004 and 2013 called *Bridezillas*, featuring difficult, rampaging brides-to-be who might even have made the Big G run and hide. On the mid-2000s sketch comedy series *Chappelle's Show*, African American host Dave Chappelle once appeared as "Blackzilla," a giant version of himself that attacks a Japanese city and even fights the "real" Godzilla.

It seems you can attach "-zilla" to the end of almost any word to indicate how great or powerful it is. Sometimes, a person or thing is even judged worthy enough to use the entire name, such as major league baseball player Hideki Matsui, a Japanese athlete who made the transition from Nippon Professional Baseball to play seven seasons for the New York Yankees. The New York press lovingly bestowed the nickname "Godzilla" on Matsui, which stayed with him his whole career, and even resulted in a brief cameo for Matsui in *Godzilla Against Mechagodzilla* (2002). The Nissan Skyline GT-R, a sleek Japanese sportscar, was in 1989 given the nickname "Godzilla," which has stuck with it to this day.

Songs in the Key of G

Godzilla's omnipresence has caused him to be referred to in popular songs, and sometimes even to be the subject of those songs—and that's not even including the "official" songs that Toho commissioned for some of its films over the years. Undeniably, the most famous Godzilla musical recording would have to be the song titled simply "Godzilla," by the rock band Blue Oyster Cult. Featured on its 1977 album *Spectres*, the guitar-heavy hard-rock number is a campy tribute to classic *Showa*-era Godzilla, with lyrics that detail his penchant for city-destruction. The recording even includes brief snippets of Japanese dialogue from actual Godzilla films. Perhaps second only to "Don't Fear the Reaper" as Blue Oyster Cult's most well-known song, it was even commonly used by cable networks TNT and Sci-Fi Channel to promote their Godzilla movie marathons during the 1990s.

Musical acts have even taken their name from the monster and his friends, such as French rockers Gojira and the rapper MF DOOM, who briefly went by the alias "King Geedorah." Hip-hop artists have enjoyed sampling sound effects and even musical cues from Godzilla, most notably Pharoahe Monch, who used the opening tones of Akira Ifukube's original Godzilla theme in his 1999 recording of "Simon Says," appearing on his solo debut album, *Internal Affairs*. Toho was so incensed at this particularly bold, unapproved usage that the company had the album completely pulled from stores.

Godzilla in Four Colors

As with so many icons of popular culture, Godzilla has had more than his fair share of representations in comic book form. In fact, there are several American comic book companies that have owned the official license to produce Godzilla comics over the past forty years. The very first Godzilla comic book produced in the U.S. was a small, crude, four-page promotional comic book version of *Godzilla vs. Megalon* that came out in conjunction with that film's American release in 1976.

Marvel Comics

From 1977 to 1979, Marvel Comics, perhaps the most popular comic book publisher of them all, held the official license from Toho Company, and produced a comic book entitled *Godzilla: King of the Monsters* that ran for twenty-four issues. It was written by Doug Moench, who specialized in Marvel's line of horror-tinged comics at the time and would later go on to fame as the writer of *Batman* and *Detective Comics* for rival DC Comics. The artist was Herb Trimpe, best known for his 1970s work on *The Incredible Hulk*. The *Godzilla* comic book incorporated the monster completely into the Marvel Universe, and he would interact with such Marvel stalwarts as the Fantastic Four, the Avengers, and even Spider-Man. The series even sparked the creation of the giant robot character Red Ronin, initially used as an adversary for Godzilla, but which continues to appear in Marvel Comics long after the company lost its Godzilla license.

Dark Horse Comics

The Godzilla comic book license lay dormant until 1987, when it was picked up by the new, upstart publisher Dark Horse Comics. Dark Horse would retain the license for the next dozen years, publishing straight through the 1990s. During that time, Godzilla appeared in a wide range of comics and trade paperbacks beginning with the 1987 one-shot *Godzilla King of the Monsters Special*. These also included *Godzilla*, Dark Horse's 1988–89 reprint of the Japanese *manga* adaptation of *Godzilla 1985*, as well as the ongoing series *Godzilla: King of the Monsters*, which ran for sixteen issues from 1995 to 1996. The latter series even featured Godzilla traveling through time to cause all manner of historic disasters from the San Francisco earthquake of 1906 to the sinking of the *Titanic*.

Issue #3 of Marvel's *Godzilla: King of the Monsters*, with a cover by Herb Trimpe.

Author's collection

IDW Publishing

In 2010, the twenty-first century's hottest new comic book publisher, IDW, best known for its comics based on licensed film and TV properties, stepped into the breach and picked up the Godzilla license after an eleven-year dearth of Godzilla comics. Since that time, the company has produced a long line of books, starting with the 2011–12 twelve-issue series *Godzilla: Kingdom of Monsters*, which kicked off with a gorgeous painted cover by renowned artist Alex Ross. Since then, Godzilla has appeared in other ongoing IDW series like *Godzilla: History's Greatest Monster* (2012–13) and *Godzilla: Rulers of Earth* (2013–15), as well as the miniseries *Godzilla: Gangsters & Goliaths* (2011), *Godzilla: Legends* (2011–12), *Godzilla: The Half-Century War* (2012), *Godzilla: Cataclysm* (2014), *Godzilla in Hell* (2015), and *Godzilla: Oblivion* (2016). IDW's Godzilla license is unique in that it extends to other Toho monsters as well, which has allowed appearances by a host of the monster's familiar allies and foes.

Pixelated Mayhem

The excitement of Godzilla, and of monster action in general, meant that his appeal as a video game property would be only natural. Even just taking into account, for the sake of brevity, the games produced in the United States, it's an impressive list that stretches back all the way to 1983 and the strategy game *Godzilla* made for the old Commodore 64 personal computer. Three years later, software developer Epyx introduced *The Movie Monster Game* for both the Commodore 64 and Apple II. In this unique game, players could choose to be Godzilla as well as a series of more generic giant monsters based loosely on movie creatures like King Kong, the Blob, and the Stay-Puft Marshmallow Man, and either fight other monsters or pummel the city of their choosing.

The original Nintendo Entertainment System (NES) took home video gaming by storm in the late 1980s, and in 1988 Toho produced its official game *Godzilla: Monster of Monsters* for the platform. In this game, Godzilla and Mothra must defend Earth against an invasion of monsters sent by the aliens of Planet X. Two years later, the first Godzilla game for Nintendo's Gameboy portable mini-system appeared: Entitled *Godzilla* and featuring a 1970s-era Big G on the box cover, the game involved Godzilla rescuing his son Minya from the clutches of some of his worst enemies. It was followed by a 1991 sequel, *Godzilla 2: War of the Monsters*.

The Super Nintendo Entertainment System (SNES), which had been unveiled in 1991, introduced its own Godzilla game, suitably titled *Super Godzilla*, in 1993. This game featured many of the *Heisei*-era monsters such as Biollante, Battra, and Mecha-King Ghidorah, and even included Bagan, a *kaiju* that had been deleted from the script for *Godzilla 1985*. A third Gameboy product, *King of the Monsters: Godzilla*, was released the same year, as well as *Godzilla: Battle Legends* for the short-lived Turbo Duo game platform. In the latter game, Godzilla fights a series of enemies from over the years, and takes on the appearance he did in the actual films in which he fought each monster.

At the end of the *Heisei* era, the game *Godzilla: Archipelago Shock*, based on the final *Heisei* film, *Godzilla vs. Destoroyah*, was released for the Sega Saturn, another relatively short-lived console. The next Godzilla film, which turned out to be the 1998 American *Godzilla*, was adapted into a series of games, including the first Godzilla CD-ROM game, *Godzilla Online*, as well as the online game *G-Patrol VR Combat Simulator*, and even the first Godzilla pinball game. Even the animated TV show based on that movie, *Godzilla: The Series*, got its own game adaptation for Nintendo's Game Boy Color.

Godzilla games continued aplenty in the twenty-first century, beginning with *Godzilla: Destroy All Monsters* for the Nintendo GameCube and Microsoft's original Xbox platform. That game received a sequel, *Godzilla: Save the Earth* (2004), named for the memorable song from *Godzilla vs. Hedorah* (1971). *Save the Earth* was the first Godzilla game released for Sony's PlayStation 2 system. The third game in the series, *Godzilla: Unleashed*, was playable on both PlayStation 2 and the new Nintendo Wii, and was an ambitious game that included more than twenty different *kaiju* from all three eras of Godzilla movies, as well as different versions of Godzilla from the 1950s, '60s, '80s, and 2000s.

In recent years, Godzilla has even invaded the world of mobile gaming. With the rising popularity of gaming apps at the end of the last decade came *Godzilla: Monster Mayhem* (2009) for the iPhone, as well as mobile games like *Godzilla: Strike Zone* (2014) and *Godzilla: Kaiju Collection* (2015). Spawned by the success of the 2014 American reboot film, the most recent *Godzilla* game for PlayStation 3 and 4 incorporates the revamped Legendary Pictures version of Godzilla alongside early Toho versions and other Toho monsters.

Here, There, and Everywhere . . .

Godzilla and his friends have made so many appearances over the years that some of them are just too bizarre or unusual to categorize. He's certainly the only fictional character to ever play one-on-one basketball with a major sports superstar, as he did in 1992 when he was pitted against a giant-sized version of NBA legend Charles Barkley in the streets of Tokyo, in a famous Nike sneaker commercial created by Industrial Light and Magic. Originally intended for Japanese viewers only, "Godzilla vs. Charles Barkley" proved so popular that it was debuted in the U.S. at the 1992 MTV Movie Awards. The following year, Dark Horse Comics even produced a comic book adaptation of the ad.

Much more than just a direct Godzilla parody, the highly irreverent animated series *South Park* parodied the entire Japanese *daikaiju eiga* genre in its 1998 first-season episode "Mecha-Streisand." In the notorious episode, an animated Barbra Streisand uses a magical relic to transform herself into a giant mechanical dinosaur that is a direct reference to Mechagodzilla. Further, Mecha-Streisand is opposed by a bizarre series of *kaiju* that include Sidney Poitier as a giant Gamera-like turtle, film critic Leonard Maltin as an Ultraman-style giant robot, and Robert Smith, lead singer of the Cure, as a giant moth (Smith was the only celebrity who lent his own voice to the episode).

And for those looking for the completely immersive Godzilla experience, there is now a Godzilla-themed hotel in the heart of Tokyo's Shinjuku ward. Opening its doors in April 2015, the Hotel Gracery Shinjuku (operated by Marriott) features a giant Godzilla statue that hovers over the building and can be directly viewed from some of the rooms. It also features an observation deck overlooking the statue, as well as an elaborate memorabilia room dedicated to the King of the Monsters, containing movie props and more. While reportedly not cheap, hordes of Godzilla fans the world over have already been making the pilgrimage to the thirty-story hotel, which is officially sponsored by Toho and is even located above the Toho Cinema, one of the theaters owned by the company.

Godzilla's status is such that, like Superman, Mickey Mouse, and others mentioned, he is treated almost as if he were a real, living entity beyond the films in which the character has been featured. As testament to this, in 1996, Godzilla received a Lifetime Achievement Award at the MTV Movie Awards, one of three fictional characters to receive the award, along with

Chewbacca of *Star Wars* fame and Jason Voorhees, the masked murderer of the *Friday the 13th* films. In 2004, as part of the marketing buildup to the release of *Godzilla: Final Wars*, the Big G received his very own star on the Hollywood Walk of Fame on Hollywood Boulevard—an honor usually bestowed to real people, and only reserved for pop culture creations of the most iconic order, including Bugs Bunny, Big Bird, Kermit the Frog, the Simpsons, and Snoopy.

Like the Frankenstein Monster, Tarzan, Capt. Kirk, or James Bond, Godzilla has become one of those rare fictional creations that completely transcends its creators, and even the media in which it was introduced, to become a totally free-standing, self-perpetuating figure in pop culture. Godzilla is more than a movie monster—his is an image and name burned into the minds of millions. Ironically, his notoriety has been sustained more strongly in the Western world, and the United States in particular, than even in his native Japan, making him the most pervasive foreign pop cultural export to impact the American consciousness.

Godzilla's star on the Hollywood Walk of Fame, dedicated in 2004 to commemorate his fiftieth anniversary, and the release of *Godzilla: Final Wars*.   *Ayustety/Wikimedia*

The *Kaiju* 'n' Wrestling Connection

The link between *daikaiju eiga* and another pop culture juggernaut, professional wrestling (or *puroresu* as it is colloquially known in Japan), has been a well-documented one, and makes perfect sense given the elements that make both genres so entertaining. In fact, the height of the *Showa* era coincided with a period in which *puroresu*'s popularity in Japan was also at an all-time high, thanks to the enormous popularity of Korean transplant Rikidozan, who became nothing short of a national hero, and later icons like Antonio Inoki, Giant Baba, and many others. The effect of wrestling on the Godzilla films of the 1960s and '70s is readily apparent, and often even manifested itself in the choreography of the *kaiju* fighting, which sometimes resembled pro-wrestling matches and even included identifiable pro-wrestling maneuvers like suplexes, dropkicks, and clotheslines.

Many years later in the United States, a performance entertainment troupe calling itself Studio Kaiju, originally composed of students of Boston's School of the Museum of Fine Arts, used this obvious *kaiju/puroresu* connection to create perhaps the most unusual and unorthodox pop culture riff on the *daikaiju eiga*, known as Kaiju Big Battel. Originally envisioned by founders Rand and David Borden as a video project, Kaiju Big Battel became something much more. Starting on Halloween night 1996 at the Revolving Museum in Boston, the Bordens and their colleagues have been presenting live, pro-wrestling-style spectacles, in which performers, dressed up as made-up *kaiju*, do battle inside a wrestling ring, which also contains miniature cityscapes—giving the impression of a fight scene from a *kaiju* movie taking place as a wrestling match.

Over the years, the "roster" of Kaiju Big Battel performers has grown tremendously, beginning with the first costumed performer Midori no Kaiju and expanding to include several factions, including the Heroes, the Rogues, Team Space Bug (made up of otherworldly *kaiju*), and the villainous posse of Dr. Cube. Each performer is given a colorful and outrageous background, typical of pro-wrestling characters but taken to a far more ludicrous extreme. Kaiju Big Battel has become a full-scale touring operation that continues to put on shows and even release DVDs of its performances to this day. The shows have even featured occasional appearances by actual pro wrestlers from outside the Kaiju Big Battel "universe," including Chris Hero and Kota Ibushi. Dr. Cube has even been known to make appearances for other wrestling companies such as CHIKARA Pro and Dragon Gate USA, proving that Kaiju Big Battel has been fully embraced by the pro-wrestling fan base and community at large as a "legit" independent operation.

21

Friends and Foes

The Kaiju Cast of Characters

When Godzilla first stomped onto the scene in 1954, he was the first *kaiju* of them all. But even a creature as mighty as Godzilla couldn't carry the entire load all the time, and before long Toho was introducing additional monsters for Godzilla to fight, or sometimes even to team up with. Toho's stable of bizarre behemoths grew over the years to become a pantheon of beings revered by fans the world over. As quirky as they are fascinating, they shared the screen with the Big G (and sometimes even got movies of their own) and helped provide diversity, color, and action to the *daikaiju eiga*. Mostly the work of the brilliant and visionary Eiji Tsuburaya and his creative team, they are now among cinema's most beloved nonhuman characters. Here's an in-depth look at the beasts that have stepped up to try to take out Godzilla, and occasionally lent him a helping claw.

Anguirus

Japanese Name: Angirasu
Appearances: *Godzilla Raids Again* (1955); *Destroy All Monsters* (1968); *Godzilla vs. Gigan* (1972); *Godzilla vs. Megalon* (1973); *Godzilla vs. Mechagodzilla* (1974); *Godzilla: Final Wars* (2004)
Size: 196 feet; 30,000 metric tons
Abilities: Spiky carapace, rolling into a ball (only in *Godzilla: Final Wars*)

Godzilla's most consistent ally, Anguirus (sometimes referred to as "Angilas") actually made his first appearance as a foe, in Motoyoshi Oda's *Godzilla Raids Again*. A massive irradiated dinosaur resembling the ankylosaurus, the remains of Anguirus were brought to new life by the same atomic bomb testing that unleashed Godzilla upon the world. He was the first *kaiju* that Godzilla ever fought, and although he was killed in his initial appearance in the first Godzilla sequel, a new Anguirus appeared in later *Showa* films to team up with Godzilla against common enemies like King Ghidorah, Gigan, Megalon, and Mechagodzilla.

Possessing three brains in his head, abdomen, and chest, Anguirus makes his home on Monster Island, along with Godzilla, and is often seen as the Robin to Godzilla's Batman. In *Godzilla vs. Gigan*, the monster is shown to converse with Godzilla in "monster language" (translated into English in the American dub of the film). Anguirus was gravely injured by Mechagodzilla in *Godzilla vs. Mechagodzilla*, his last *Showa* appearance. He made one last comeback thirty years later in the Millennium era film *Godzilla: Final Wars*, in which he returned to being an enemy of Godzilla, and also gained the unique ability to roll into a ball and propel himself at top speeds.

Designed by Tsuburaya, the original Anguirus suit appeared only in *Godzilla Raids Again*, in which it was worn by Katsumi Tezuka. The suit was shipped the following year to Hollywood, where the American film company AB-PT was making their own creature feature, *The Volcano Monsters*, and wished to include footage of Godzilla and Anguirus in the film. When AB-PT went under, the film was never completed, and the Anguirus suit was lost. A new and modified suit was constructed twelve years later for Anguirus's return in *Destroy All Monsters*, in which it was worn by Hiroshi Sekita. The same suit was used for his future appearances in *Godzilla vs. Gigan* (Koetsu Omiya), *Godzilla vs. Megalon* (Tadaaki Watanabe), and *Godzilla vs. Mechagodzilla* (Kinichi Kusumi). The final, modernized Anguirus suit was worn by Toshihiro Ogura in *Final Wars*. Just as he had done for Godzilla, composer Akira Ifukube created Anguirus's unmistakable honking cry, this time combining the sounds of a saxophone, harmonica, oboe, and tuba.

Baragon

Appearances: *Frankenstein Conquers the World* (1965); *Destroy All Monsters*;
    Godzilla, Mothra and King Ghidorah: Giant Monsters All-Out Attack (2001)
Size: 82 feet; 250 metric tons
Abilities: Heat ray, leaping, burrowing

With a name meaning "Rose Dragon" (due to the red, petal-like ridges along its back), Baragon was a prehistoric reptile that escaped the extinction of the dinosaurs by tunneling deep underground, but was awakened from his eons-long hibernation by noises from a nearby factory in *Frankenstein*

Conquers the World. After being trounced by the giant-sized Frankenstein Monster in that film, he returned three years later as one of the *kaiju* mind-controlled by the invading alien Kilaaks and compelled to attack major Earth cities (Paris, in the case of Baragon). After regaining his senses, Baragon joined forces with Godzilla and a host of other monsters to take down King Ghidorah.

Possessing a large, glowing horn in the middle of his head, Baragon is one of the most odd-looking *kaiju*. The only time he ever fought against Godzilla was in his big Millennium series return, in *GMK*. Portrayed as one of the three "guardian monsters" of Earth (along with Mothra and King Ghidorah), Baragon is the first to fight the reawakened and seriously ticked-off Godzilla, who kills the horned creature in the first battle of the film.

A Tsuburaya design, the Baragon suit was originally worn during the *Showa* series by Haruo Nakajima, who also portrayed Godzilla himself. The suit was borrowed by Tsuburaya to be modified into several monsters that appeared in his *UltraQ* and *Ultraman* series, including Pagos, Neronga, Gabora, and Magular. Because of this borrowing, the Baragon suit was unavailable for certain shots in *Destroy All Monsters*, and thus was replaced by Gorosaurus (even though the monster is still referred to as Baragon, a source of confusion for fans). Parts of the suit were later used by Teruyoshi Nakano in the construction of the Hedorah suit in 1971. The new suit designed for *GMK* was worn by Rie Ota.

Biollante

Japanese Name: Biorante
Appearances: *Godzilla vs. Biollante* (1989)
Size: 394 feet; 200,000 metric tons
Abilities: Grasping vines, radioactive spray

A living caution against the perils of genetic engineering, Biollante has one of the most unusual origins of any *kaiju*, having been created by splicing the DNA of Godzilla, a human (the deceased daughter of scientist Dr. Genshiro Shiragami), and a rose plant. The result is a creature that first manifests itself in Lake Ashino as a giant, mutant flower. After Godzilla incinerates the flower, its spores later manifest as a much more dangerous animal/plant hybrid that towers over Godzilla and nearly chokes him to death with its numerous vines. Although Biollante is defeated, its spores float into space and are believed to have possibly contributed to the creation of the mutated Space Godzilla of *Godzilla vs. Space Godzilla* (1994).

Although originally striving to use Godzilla's cells to create weather-resistant crops, Dr. Shiragami went down a dark path when his daughter Erika was killed in a bomb attack. Seeking to resurrect her, he meddled with the forces of nature to produce the menacing Biollante. The appearance of the final form of the creature was greatly influenced by that of Audrey II in the American horror comedy *Little Shop of Horrors* (1986), possessing a fanged, flytrap-like beak and an array of gripping vine tentacles.

Designed by *Heisei*-era special-effects maven Koichi Kawakita and costume designer Shinji Nishikawa after a concept by contest-winner Shinichiro Kobayashi, Biollante was one of the most complex and challenging monsters ever created by Toho. Performed by Masao Takegami inside the elaborate suit, the realization of Biollante was also aided by the use of a vast array of overhead wires used to manipulate the creature's head and vines. The fact that Biollante lives in water made the construction even more difficult to operate, stationed as it was in Toho's "Big Pool" aquatic set.

Destoroyah

Appearance: *Godzilla vs. Destoroyah* (1995)
Size: 393 feet; 80,000 metric tons
Abilities: Flight, oxygen destroyer beam, laser horn, tail energy beams

Godzilla has occasionally lost a fight here and there, but only once has he actually died while fighting another *kaiju*. And that *kaiju* was the fearsome Destoroyah, a hideous mutation caused by the fallout from Dr. Serizawa's oxygen destroyer contaminating the fossilized remains of prehistoric trilobites in Tokyo Bay. Even though Destoroyah does not actually deal the killing blow (Godzilla was overloaded with radiation from his previous battle with Space Godzilla and ready to blow anyway), it is unquestionably one of the most fearsome and memorable Godzilla foes, despite making only one appearance in the final *Heisei* film.

Taking several different forms, Destoroyah started out as a group of separate human-sized, clawed monstrosities with acid for blood, direct mutations of the underwater crustaceans exposed to the oxygen destroyer. When the separate creatures merged, they formed one horrific entity that continued to grow in size the more energy it absorbed, eventually taking its final, most terrifying form. At its largest and most dangerous, Destoroyah even managed to kill Godzilla's son before being killed itself by the combined might of the Japanese military and a dying Godzilla, in his final breaths.

Screenwriter Kazuki Omori wanted a truly unforgettable adversary for what was thought to be Godzilla's final Toho film, and worked closely with effects director Koichi Kawakita and suit designer Minoru Yoshida to pull it off. The monster was portrayed in its different forms by two suit actors, Ryo Hariya and Eiichi Yanagida.

Ebirah

Appearances: *Godzilla vs. the Sea Monster* (1966); *All Monsters Attack* (1969) (stock footage); *Godzilla: Final Wars*
Size: 164 feet; 23,000 metric tons
Ability: Gigantic claws

A mammoth shrimp mutated to unthinkable size by radiation generated by the terrorist organization known as the Red Bamboo, Ebirah had only one major film appearance, but he made it count, going one on one with Godzilla in a series of memorable encounters. Sometimes known only by his name in the film's title, "the Sea Monster," Ebirah possessed two claws of varying size, and like an actual shrimp or other crustaceans such as crabs and lobsters, he used both as deadly weapons—one as a giant, crushing pincer and the other as a stabbing, harpoon-like tool. Of course, none of that mattered after Godzilla ripped off one of those claws and sent the creature fleeing back into the ocean.

Pressed into service by the Red Bamboo that created it, Ebirah guarded the island on which they were conducting their terrorist activities and plans. Coincidentally, Godzilla also happened to be hibernating on the same island, and once he was awakened, he set about driving Ebirah away and taking out most of the Red Bamboo's operation before returning to the ocean himself. He wasn't seen again until nearly forty years later in *Final Wars*, in which he faced off with a squadron of mutant soldiers, before being taken out once and for all by the Big G.

Designed by effects director Teruyoshi Nakano, art director Akira Watanabe, and sculptor Teizo Toshimitsu, under the supervision of Eiji Tsuburaya, Ebirah is often mislabeled a giant lobster, which is understandable given his claws and red color. Inside the suit for its original appearance was Hiroshi "Yu" Sekita, while much later in *Final Wars* it was Toshihiro Ogura. Ebirah was originally scripted to appear in *Destroy All Monsters*, but was edited from the final cut.

Gigan

Japanese Name: Gaigan
Appearances: *Godzilla vs. Gigan*; *Godzilla vs. Megalon*; *Godzilla: Final Wars*
Size: 213 feet; 25,000 metric tons
Abilities: Buzzsaw abdomen, giant hooks for hands, optical beams and projectiles (*Final Wars* only)

Perhaps the most memorable of Godzilla's 1970s foes, the interstellar cyborg Gigan, scourge of Space Hunter Galaxy M, is also one of the most violent, drawing Godzilla's blood for the first time ever seen on film. Seemingly designed to be a machine of destruction, he sports an immense circular saw built right into his torso, and his hooked hands are designed only to tear and shred. He first appeared in the aptly named *Godzilla vs. Gigan*, in which he joined forces with Godzilla's archrival King Ghidorah to take on Godzilla and Anguirus, but was also recruited by the Seatopians to help Megalon against the combined team of Godzilla and the robot Jet Jaguar in *Godzilla vs. Megalon*.

Summoned by the nefarious Space Hunter alien race of Galaxy M in a bid to conquer Earth, Gigan twice abandoned his monster allies and fled into space. He even faced Godzilla in the monster's appearance on the Toho TV series *Zone Fighter*, in which it's revealed that he was captured by the Garogan army after his battle with Godzilla and Jet Jaguar, and returned to Earth to do more damage. For his big comeback in *Final Wars*, Gigan mutated into a sleeker, more muscular form, boasting a variety of new weapons built into his cybernetic body.

Sometimes criticized for lacking the creative spark often seen in early *Showa kaiju* designed by Eiji Tsuburaya, Gigan nevertheless has his fervent supporters. Designed by Teruyoshi Nakano's team, the costume was worn by Kenpachiro Satsuma, who would go on to portray Godzilla himself during the *Heisei* series. His Millennium-era refitting was overseen by effects director Eiichi Asada and creature designer Yasushi Nirasawa; the revamped costume was worn by Kazuhiro Yoshida.

Hedorah

Appearances: *Godzilla vs. Hedorah* (1971); *Godzilla: Final Wars*
Size: 197 feet; 48,000 metric tons
Abilities: Flight (in flying form), energy beams from eyes, corrosive skin, sludge projectiles

The physical embodiment of Japan's pollution problems of the 1960s and '70s, Hedorah was an alien life form that originated in the Orion constellation's Dark Gas Nebula, initially coming to Earth in tiny tadpole form, before growing dramatically in size by feeding on various pollutants and toxic waste. The creature was unique in that it mutated through several forms, first as an aquatic life form, then flying through the air, and eventually taking to land in its hugest and most sadistic form. Unlike with most other *kaiju*, Hedorah's human toll is directly shown, as the monster uses its powers of corrosion and acidity to disintegrate thousands of unfortunate Japanese before its weakness, dehydration, is discovered and exploited by Godzilla and the Japanese military.

Literally a walking pile of sludge, Hedorah is completely different in appearance from all of Toho's other *kaiju*. Sometimes known as "the Smog Monster" due to the American title of the movie, his piercing red eyes demonstrated genuine malice, and he was also shown to be totally impervious to Godzilla's atomic breath. Although he only made one major appearance, Hedorah did briefly return thirty-three years later for a cameo in *Godzilla: Final Wars*, in which he was unceremoniously thrashed by Godzilla in record time, along with fellow *Showa*-era one-off Ebirah the Sea Monster.

Writer-director Yoshimitsu Banno was looking to create a more serious type of monster that represented a real plight being faced by the Japanese, and decided that the threat to the environment had superseded the nuclear threat in the minds of most. Teroyushi Nakano and his team designed Hedorah for Banno, although Nakano would later have a major falling-out with him over creative differences regarding how the finished film came out. The name of the creature was derived from the Japanese word for chemical waste, and the extraordinarily heavy suit was created using elaborate foam rubber appliances. Tasked with wearing the costume was future Godzilla suit-actor Ken Satsuma, who endeavored to give the creature an otherworldly air via his unorthodox movements.

To his American audience, Hedorah was known as "the Smog Monster."

Toho Scope/Flickr

King Ghidorah

Japanese Name: Kingu Gidora

Appearances: *Ghidorah, the Three-Headed Monster* (1964); *Invasion of Astro-Monster* (1965); *Destroy All Monsters; Godzilla vs. Gigan; Godzilla vs. King Ghidorah* (1991); *Godzilla vs. Mechagodzilla II* (1993); *Rebirth of Mothra III* (1998); *Godzilla, Mothra and King Ghidorah: Giant Monsters All-Out Attack; Godzilla: Final Wars* (as Keizer Ghidorah); *Godzilla: King of Monsters* (Legendary's planned 2019 sequel)

Size: 328 feet; 30,000 metric tons

Abilities: Mach 3 flight, hurricane winds from wings, lightning bolts from all three heads

Generally considered Godzilla's greatest enemy hands down, King Ghidorah has menaced Godzilla (and Earth in the process) in multiple films during the *Showa*, *Heisei*, and Millennium series, and is even expected to be returning soon in Legendary Pictures' own American Godzilla franchise. A golden-scaled space dragon with enormous, demonic wings and three wildly flailing heads that fire rays of electricity sometimes called "gravity beams," he made his first appearance in the self-titled *Ghidorah, the Three-Headed Monster*, in which Godzilla is forced to join with Rodan and Mothra and help humanity for the first time, driving off a much worse threat to the planet.

Godzilla and Rodan once again met up with Ghidorah in the next film, *Invasion of Astro-Monster*, this time on the mysterious Planet X. He returned again to threaten Earth in *Destroy All Monsters*, in which it took a veritable army of *kaiju* to take him out. He was also the tag-team partner of Gigan in *Godzilla vs. Gigan*. King Ghidorah was such a popular enemy for Godzilla that he made a full-blown comeback in the 1990s with *Godzilla vs. King Ghidorah*, in which we learned more about his origins, and also witnessed his transformation into the robotic Mecha-King Ghidorah. His one appearance on the side of good occurred in 2001's *GMK*, and in *Final Wars* he morphed into the even more dangerous, quadripedal Keizer Ghidorah.

Inspired by both Greek and Japanese mythology, Ghidorah began as a suggestion of producer Tokoyuki Tanaka and turned into one of Eiji Tsuburaya and Teizo Toshimitsu's finest creations. The original suit was constructed by art director Akira Watanabe and originally worn by Shoichi Hirose, who had previously portrayed King Kong. A notoriously difficult suit to maneuver, it required extensive wirework to manipulate the heads and wings, especially during flight, and the actor in the suit had to hold onto an internal bar, as the costume had no arms. Hirose portrayed the monster in *Invasion of Astro-Monster*, while Susumu Utsumi did so in *Destroy All Monsters*, and Kanta Ina in *Godzilla vs. Gigan*. Illustrator and martial artist Hurricane Ryu donned the suit for the *Heisei* Godzilla films, while Akira Ohashi did so for his *Final Wars* turn. Ghidorah's trademark high-pitched warble was designed by Akira Ifukube using an electronic organ.

Mechagodzilla

Japanese Name: Mekagojira
Appearances: *Godzilla vs. Mechagodzilla*; *Terror of Mechagodzilla* (1975); *Godzilla vs. Mechagodzilla II*; *Godzilla Against Mechagodzilla* (2002); *Godzilla: Tokyo S.O.S.* (2003)
Size: 164 feet; 40,000 metric tons
Abilities: Mach 5 flight, eye beams, force field, electric discharge, assorted rockets and missiles

The proof of Mechagodzilla's persistence is in the fact that it has gotten top billing in Godzilla films in all three major eras (a source of confusion to many fans). Helping to popularize the concept of mechanized monsters in Japanese pop culture, Mechagodzilla has transformed drastically over the decades, with four distinct versions being seen. Each one possesses varying abilities and equipment, and the Millennium version even got a new name (Kiryu). Originally the product of evil extraterrestrial technology in his *Showa* incarnation, during both the *Heisei* and Millennium eras Mechagodzilla was a force for good, designed by the military to defend Japan against Godzilla.

In its first appearance in *Godzilla vs. Mechagodzilla*, Mecha-G resembles Godzilla in every way, until its outer skin is burned away by the real Big G to reveal his gleaming, metallic exoskeleton underneath. After besting Godzilla's pal Anguirus, the robot was wrecked by Godzilla, only to be rebuilt by the Black Hole Planet 3 aliens in *Terror of Mechagodzilla*, in which he teams with the massive aquatic reptile known as Titanosaurus. It was during the *Heisei* era that Mechagodzilla was first operated by human pilots. Finally, during his back-to-back Millennium appearances, Kiryu was built from the skeletal remains of the original 1954 Godzilla, making it some kind of cyborg/zombie hybrid.

Mechanized monstrosities were all the rage in the 1970s thanks to Japanese *anime*, and Toho had previously dabbled in the concept with Mechani-Kong from *King Kong Escapes* (1967). A break from the mutated animals faced by Godzilla in the past, Teruyoshi Nakano also found it easier to construct a creature that didn't have to appear organic or "alive." With its darker tone, the creation proved so popular that it appeared in an immediate sequel. Two complete redesigns were used, first by Koichi Kawakita in 1993 and then by Shinichi Wakasa in 2002. The robotic suit was worn in the 1970s by Ise Mori, in the 1990s by Wataru Fukuda, and in the 2000s by Hirofumi Ishigaki (*Godzilla Against Mechagodzilla*) and Motokuni Nakagawa (*Godzilla: Tokyo S.O.S.*).

Megalon

Japanese Name: Megaro
Appearance: *Godzilla vs. Megalon*
Size: 180 feet; 40,000 metric tons
Abilities: Mach 3 flight, napalm bombs from mouth, drill hands, electric bolts from horn, underground burrowing

Although not one of the most popular of Toho's *kaiju*, this gigantic beetle from deep beneath the Earth's surface did get one memorable/notorious run against the Big G in one of the kitschier entries in the series, *Godzilla vs. Megalon*. The avenger of the ancient subterranean civilization of Seatopia, Megalon was summoned to wreak havoc upon the Japanese people as payback for the manner in which they have abused and usurped the surface world from its original inhabitants. Possessing enormous burrowing powers, the massive insect rose to the surface on a mission of destruction.

Once Megalon was thwarted by the robot Jet Jaguar, the Seatopians summoned Gigan to help, which finally elicited the participation of Godzilla to drive both evil menaces from the scene once and for all. After being abandoned by Gigan, Megalon fled in defeat, burrowing back beneath the surface, never to be seen again. He remains the only top-billed *Showa* monster not to be given a comeback in later eras of the franchise.

The design of Megalon is often criticized for lacking creativity, and for being particularly unconvincing, even by *kaiju* standards. It is usually cited as an example of the decline of Toho's creature effects department after the death of Eiji Tsuburaya. The baggy and bulky Megalon suit was worn on screen by Hideto Odachi. It is assumed that it was due to the film's creative and financial failure that Megalon was never pressed into service again.

Minya

Japanese Name: Minira
Appearances: *Son of Godzilla* (1967); *Destroy All Monsters*; *All Monsters Attack*; *Godzilla: Final Wars*
Size: 50 feet; 2,400 metric tons
Ability: Radioactive smoke rings

Not to be confused with Godzilla Junior of the *Heisei* series, or for that matter with Godzilla's nephew Godzooky of the 1970s animated series *Godzilla*, Minya (sometimes called Minilla) was the original adopted son of the Big G, who hatched from an egg found on Sogell Island (later known as Monster Island). A timid, awkward creature who wanted badly to please his foster father, Minya displayed all the qualities of a petulant and exuberant human child, and tried to mimic Godzilla in all ways. Taking him under his proverbial wing, Godzilla attempted to teach Minya to spit atomic fire, and was marginally successful, although Minya's specialty remained the emission of comical smoke rings.

In his first appearance in *Son of Godzilla*, Minya was threatened by the dangerous denizens of Sogell Island, including the giant spider Kumonga and a pack of giant Kamacuras praying mantises. Godzilla repelled the attack and later sheltered Minya from the destruction caused by scientists on the island. Perhaps Minya's most memorable appearance was as a figment of childhood imagination in *All Monsters Attack*, in which he shrinks down to human size and befriends a little boy, even managing to speak to him. Although he was sometimes derided for his silliness, Minya fans were pleased to see the little guy turn up one last time by his foster father's side in *Godzilla: Final Wars*.

In order to accentuate the size difference between Minya and Godzilla, the Minya costume was worn by midget wrestler Little Man Machan, aka Masao Fukazawa. A pudgy, comical version of Godzilla with a cartoonishly humanoid face, Minya was a design of Tsuburaya's assistant Sadamasa Arikawa and art director Akira Watanabe. His appearance was typical of the more whimsical approach taken in Toho's late-*Showa kaiju* films. Although replaced with the more "realistic" Godzilla Junior during the *Heisei* era, Minya returned in *Final Wars*, this time portrayed by suit actress Naoko Kamio, who also played the Pink Ranger in many of Toei Company's *Super Sentai* (*Power Rangers*) series.

Mothra

Japanese Name: Mosura

Appearances: *Mothra* (1961); *Mothra vs. Godzilla* (1964); *Ghidorah, the Three-Headed Monster*; *Godzilla vs. the Sea Monster*; *Destroy All Monsters*; *Godzilla & Mothra: Battle for Earth* (1992); *Godzilla vs. Space Godzilla* (1994); *Rebirth of Mothra* (1996); *Rebirth of Mothra II* (1997); *Rebirth of Mothra III*; *Godzilla, Mothra and King Ghidorah: Giant Monsters All-Out Attack*; *Godzilla: Tokyo S.O.S.*; *Godzilla: Final Wars*; *Godzilla: King of Monsters* (Legendary's planned 2019 sequel)

Size: 262 feet; 15,000 metric tons

Abilities: Mach 3 flight, hurricane winds from wings, energy beams (*Heisei* and Millennium era only), silk shooters (larval form only)

Second only to Godzilla in popularity and notoriety, Mothra is also on par with the most legendary of movie monsters, and is the only other Toho *kaiju* that merited a series of starring appearances. Although she attacked Tokyo

Mothra is worshipped by the natives of Infant Island.   *Everett Collection*

in her first appearance in the original *Mothra*, the creature has usually been presented as an ally of mankind and a divine being with powers that extend into the magical. Accompanied by her twin *shobijin* fairies in almost every one of her appearances, Mothra has frequently been at odds with Godzilla, but has also teamed up with him on more than one occasion. A creature of fantasy and great beauty, Mothra is far from your average *kaiju*.

Worshipped by the natives of Infant Island, Mothra has taken several forms and had several incarnations over the years. After her first appearance, she returned to protect her giant egg, from which hatched two Mothra larvae. After her death, one of the larvae matured into the next incarnation of Mothra. Mothra has also been seen in both moth and larval form over the course of the *Heisei* and Millennium series, always answering the plaintive call of the *shobijin*.

Even Mothra's origins are unique, stemming as they do from a Toho-commissioned literary serial entitled *The Luminous Fairies and Mothra* by Shinichiro Nakamura, Takehiko Fukunaga, and Yoshie Hotta. The character was further developed for the screen by Shinichi Sekizawa, and designed by Eiji Tsuburaya as a giant, wire-controlled puppet. The Mothra larva was originally designed as a suit to be worn and controlled by six different performers, although in later appearances the larvae were radio-controlled puppets. The popularity of Mothra with the female audience is often cited for the creature's endurance over the years.

Rodan

Japanese Name: Radon
Appearances: *Rodan* (1956); *Ghidorah, the Three-Headed Monster*; *Invasion of Astro-Monster*; *Destroy All Monsters*; *Godzilla vs. Mechagodzilla II*; *Godzilla: Final Wars*; *Godzilla: King of Monsters* (Legendary's planned 2019 sequel)
Size: 164 feet; 15,000 metric tons
Abilities: Mach 1.5 flight, hurricane winds from wings, chest spikes, super breath

Rounding out Toho's "Big Four" is the mutant pteranadon whose history dates back almost as far as Godzilla's himself. Known in Japan as "Radon," there were originally two different giant irradiated pteranadons, born of nuclear testing just like the Big G was. Emerging from a coal mine, the two Rodans ravaged the countryside before turning their attentions to Japan's urban centers. Although one of the two died at the conclusion of the

Varan the Unbelievable leaps into frame for this 1958 publicity shot.   *Author's collection*

original *Rodan*, the other one continued to appear throughout the *Showa* series, one of the most persistent of Toho's creations.

Rodan faced off with Godzilla for the first time in *Ghidorah, the Three-Headed Monster*, before mending fences and teaming with him to defeat King Ghidorah. Along with Godzilla, he was abducted by the Planet X aliens in *Invasion of Astro-Monster* and compelled to attack the Earth once again. For his *Heisei* return in *Godzilla vs. Mechagodzilla II*, the creature mutated into Fire Rodan, eventually sacrificing his life to help Godzilla defeat his mechanized foe. In his last Toho appearance in *Final Wars*, Rodan turned his attentions West, attacking New York City.

As envisioned by *Rodan* screenwriter Ken Kuronuma, Rodan was meant as a nuclear warning, although not against the Americans as Godzilla was, but rather against the Soviets, who were also responsible for Pacific bomb tests at the time. As designed by Tsuburaya, Rodan was originally brought to life using a combination of a costume (worn by Godzilla actor Haruo Nakajima) and a giant marionette for flying sequences. For his later appearances, the costume was redesigned to appear less fearsome and more comical; this version of Rodan was portrayed by Koji Uruki (*Ghidorah, the Three-Headed Monster*), Masaki Shinohara (*Invasion of Astro-Monster*), and Teruo Aragaki (*Destroy All Monsters*). Rodan's iconic cry was created by sound technician Ichiro Minawa, who used the contrabass technique employed by Akira Ifukube for Godzilla, only speeding it up and adding human vocal sounds.

When Koichi Kawakita redesigned Rodan for the *Heisei* era, no costume was made; rather, the monster was created strictly with marionettes and puppetry. For his *Final Wars* appearance, creature designer Shinji Nishikawa incorporated a brand-new suit, this time worn by Naoko Kamio.

The Expanded Menagerie

Battra

Godzilla & Mothra: Battle for Earth

Gabara

All Monsters Attack

Gorosaurus

King Kong Escapes
Destroy All Monsters

Jet Jaguar

Godzilla vs. Megalon

Kamacuras (aka Gimantis)

Son of Godzilla
All Monsters Attack (stock footage)
Godzilla: Final Wars

King Caesar

Godzilla vs. Mechagodzilla
Godzilla: Final Wars

King Kong (Toho Version)

King Kong vs. Godzilla (1962)
King Kong Escapes

Kumonga (aka Spiga)

Son of Godzilla
Destroy All Monsters
All Monsters Attack (stock footage)
Godzilla: Final Wars

Manda

Atragon (1963)
Destroy All Monsters
All Monsters Attack (stock footage)
Godzilla: Final Wars

Megaguirus

Godzilla vs. Megaguirus (2000)

Orga

Godzilla 2000 (1999)

Space Godzilla

Godzilla vs. Space Godzilla

Titanosaurus

Terror of Mechagodzilla

Varan

Giant Monster Varan (Varan the Unbelievable) (1958)
Destroy All Monsters

22

Godzilla's Greatest Hits

The Top 10 Kaiju Smackdowns

There are so many things to love about Japanese giant monster movies. But if we're honest with ourselves, the most fun thing about Japanese giant monster movies is getting to watch unthinkably huge and exotic creatures pummel each other mercilessly, while taking out vast swaths of our environment in the process. Like a car wreck you just can't look away from, or a scrap in the schoolyard taken to the one-hundredth power, there's something about *daikaiju* action that fills Godzilla fans with ecstasy. We wait for those battles to happen, and when they do, we grab some popcorn, pick a side, and watch in gleeful rapture. And nobody does monster action like Godzilla does monster action. Over the years, the King of the Monsters has engaged in countless memorable confrontations. He's won some and lost some (spoiler: he's mostly won), but every time, he's given us our money's worth. And although it's a challenge to narrow it down to a mere ten, here's a look back at some of the Big G's finest squabbles, listed in chronological order (to attempt any other ranking system would be a fool's errand).

Because you can never have enough rubber-suited mayhem.

Opponent: King Kong

Film: *King Kong vs. Godzilla* (1962)
Winner: Kong

The two most famous giant monsters of all time cross paths more than once in Ishiro Honda's camp classic, but it's their final struggle that has etched itself into the annals of sci-fi cinema history. The whole thing is set up perfectly, with Kong being drugged and airlifted directly to the base of

Godzilla's trademark atomic breath, the tide-turner in many a hard-fought scrap.

Everett Collection

Mt. Fuji, to do battle with Godzilla there in the hopes that maybe the monsters will just destroy each other and spare humanity once and for all. Once there, the creatures use their respective strengths to their advantage, with Kong proving he is the more intelligent of the two, using plans and strategies to undo the massive lizard. Meanwhile, Godzilla has fierce atomic breath as his advantage, and is more than willing to fill the Fuji valley with the sickening scent of singed ape fur. Because Toho's version of Kong is able to absorb energy from electricity (like the Frankenstein Monster), a nearby storm cloud provides the big gorilla with just the extra boost he needs to take it to Godzilla in a big way. In the end, both beasts tumble off a steep cliff into the Pacific, and only the Eighth Wonder of the World emerges from the waters to swim safely home.

Opponents: Mothra larvae

Film: *Mothra vs. Godzilla* (1964)
Winner: Mothra larvae

Godzilla's track record isn't the best in the earlier films when he's still evil, because after all, you can't end a monster movie with the bad guy winning, can you? Even though Godzilla manages to fry the benevolent Mothra herself earlier in the film, sweet revenge is eventually enjoyed by the two grotesque Mothra larvae that emerge from the tremendous multicolored egg that had previously been the cash cow of the unscrupulous opportunists of Happy Enterprises. If you think a battle between Godzilla and two writhing, faceless, web-spinning worms couldn't possibly be engaging, then you need to think again, because watching those (relatively) little scrappers take it to the King of the Monsters with everything they've got provides one of the more satisfying experiences a Godzilla fan is likely to enjoy. Whether it's latching onto his tail like a rabid puppy dog or relentlessly hurling endless yards of unbreakable silk fibers at the big guy until he can't move, these two young *kaiju* put their hearts (do they have hearts?) into the affair, and eventually triumph when the webbing-encased Godzilla finally plunges helplessly into the ocean.

Opponent: Rodan

Film: *Ghidorah, the Three-Headed Monster* (1964)
Winner: No-Contest

Ironically, in some ways the most fun and memorable battle in *Ghidorah, the Three-Headed Monster* is not the final battle with the titular baddie, but rather the earlier confrontation between Godzilla and the giant pteranadon Rodan. The first-ever meeting between Toho's two oldest *kaiju*, it's a historic moment that doesn't disappoint. Shortly after emerging at the same time (in fulfillment of a Venusian prophecy), the two creatures first engage in a little collective property damage, before deciding it would be much more fun to try and tear each other apart. The humans flee the city, giving the two of them plenty of space to go at it. Perhaps the only thing not to like about this fight is that we don't get a conclusive winner, as goody two-shoes Mothra arrives on the scene to persuade Godzilla and Rodan to put aside their petty differences and unite against the common threat of King Ghidorah. Although eager to continue rumbling, the two monsters finally relent just in time to rescue the valiant Mothra from the golden clutches of Ghidorah.

Opponent: King Ghidorah

Film: *Destroy All Monsters* (1968)
Winners: Godzilla and a host of monster allies

In the ultimate testament to the fact that King Ghidorah may be the most powerful threat of them all, in *Destroy All Monsters* it takes the combined might of nearly all the denizens of Monster Island (here called Monsterland) to defeat him. Initially brainwashed by the invading Kilaaks in a bid to wipe out human civilization, when Godzilla and his cohorts are finally freed from their bondage and able to think for themselves, they team up to wipe out Ghidorah once and for all. Joining the Big G are the likes of Mothra,

Rodan, Gorosaurus, Baragon, Anguirus, Kumonga, Manda, Varan, and even Godzilla's son, Minya. Amongst the ingenious strategies employed is the use of Anguirus's spiky carapace to impale the three-headed dragon, and Minya finding the gumption (with a helpful step on the tail from Dad) to blast his very own atomic fire breath. Even so, Ghidorah nearly emerges victorious, but in the end the accumulated might of the monsters is just too much to handle.

Opponents: Gigan and King Ghidorah

Film: *Godzilla vs. Gigan* (1972)
Winners: Godzilla and Anguirus

By the 1970s, the Godzilla films were known to occasionally take a dark turn, as occurs in this film in which Godzilla comes up against the ruthlessness of the space cyborg Gigan. In one of the more brutal and violent *kaiju* encounters put to celluloid, the Big G teams up with his BFF Anguirus to tussle with the combined evil of Gigan and his fellow space monster and old Godzilla nemesis, Ghidorah. Unlike most *kaiju* battles staged by Toho, this one has copious amounts of blood, as the monsters viciously tear into each other with abandon. There's a killer instinct on display here that we rarely see in most relatively lighthearted *kaiju* films of the *Showa* era, and there's a genuine feeling of the stakes being significantly raised as the tag-team bout unfolds in the midst of the Godzilla theme park constructed by Gigan's masters, the Space Hunter Nebula-M aliens. The imposing Godzilla Tower, a weaponized structure built to look like Godzilla himself, even gets involved in the action, firing laser blasts at Godzilla and Anguirus as they struggle to repel their extraterrestrial adversaries.

Opponent: Biollante

Film: *Godzilla vs. Biollante* (1989)
Winner: Godzilla

Biollante is a strange and unusual monster that metamorphoses into several progressively more threatening forms, with Godzilla tangling with her (quite literally) at every stage of her transformation. Once she finally takes her largest and most fearsome form, the plant-animal-human hybrid monstrosity takes on Godzilla one last time. Dispatching all the abilities at her disposal, she gives Godzilla his toughest battle in years, and lives up to being the first monster opponent the Big G has faced since the *Showa* era. With deadly grasping vines and poisonous mist, as well as the ability to thrive both on land and in water, Biollante gives Godzilla more than he bargained for, even towering over him in size. It takes a potent blast of atomic breath fired directly into Biollante's mouth (foreshadowing Godzilla's 2014 battle with the MUTOs) to ultimately put down the creature and render it into a cloud of space-borne spores. As proof of the struggle required to defeat Biollante, Godzilla collapses in exhaustion after the fight is over, and needs time to recuperate before returning to the sea in triumph.

Opponent: Mechagodzilla

Film: *Godzilla vs. Mechagodzilla II* (1993)
Winner: Godzilla

Of all the many times that Godzilla has collided with his mechanized counterpart over the decades, perhaps the most epic clash of them all occurred in their *Heisei* film. Remembered by fans for its intensity and for its impressive action, the climactic contest between Godzilla and the military-operated Mechagodzilla that concludes *Godzilla vs. Mechagodzilla II* has many ups and downs that keep viewers on the edges of their seats. Linking up with Garuda, a second craft introduced by the military, to form the even-more-imposing Super Mechagodzilla, Mecha-G almost seems to finally have Godzilla's number, utilizing "G-crusher" technology to penetrate the monster's hide in an attempt to neutralize its nervous system. But when all hope seems lost, it's Rodan—nearly dead from a recent encounter with Mechagodzilla and Garuda—who comes to Godzilla's aid, lending his remaining life force to energize Godzilla to previously unheard-of levels. With a crimson blast of supercharged atomic breath, the Big G puts his robotic enemy out of commission.

Opponent: Destoroyah

Film: *Godzilla vs. Destoroyah* (1995)
Winner: Draw

After morphing from a collection of man-sized creatures into one gigantic nightmare of a super-*kaiju*, Destoroyah, Godzilla's bane, faces off with a

King of the Monsters who is on the verge of melting down due to absorbing an overabundance of cosmic radiation. But the stakes are higher than ever this time, as Destoroyah has also targeted Godzilla Junior. Enraged at the apparent murder of his offspring, Godzilla unleashes holy hell upon Destoroyah, and with some rare assistance from the Japanese military, manages to kill the creature. Unlike every other *kaiju* battle Godzilla has ever engaged in, this one concludes with his on-screen death, as he finally succumbs to the excessive radiation that has been disintegrating his body. Weakened by the battle with Destoroyah, and overcome with grief over the loss of Junior, Godzilla dissolves away to nothing in a scene sure to tug at the heartstrings of even the most hardened monster movie veteran. By the end of the film, both Godzilla and his foe are no more—although a recovered Godzilla Junior emerges to presumably take on the mantle of King.

Opponents: Mothra/Kiryu

Film: *Godzilla: Tokyo S.O.S.* (2003)
Winner: Kiryu

This monster pile-up is one of the most riveting and well-choreographed mash-ups of the Millennium era, in which Godzilla takes on not just Mothra, but also Mothra's newest larvae, as well as the Millennium incarnation of Mechagodzilla, also known as Kiryu. After Mothra flies in the path of Godzilla's breath in order to save her young ones, the noble creature is destroyed. But before Godzilla can follow through on toasting the larvae, the new and improved Kiryu springs into action, taking it to Godzilla with a powerful drill that it stabs directly into the monster's chest. The larvae do their part by trapping the Big G in an elaborate web of silk (shades of *Mothra vs. Godzilla*), putting the monster at Kiryu's mercy. It's at that moment that the soul of the original 1954 Godzilla, trapped inside the body of the mechanized Kiryu, causes the robot to latch onto the modern-day Godzilla and leap into the bay, taking the King of the Monsters past and present to the bottom of the sea.

Opponent: Keizer Ghidorah

Film: *Godzilla: Final Wars* (2014)
Winner: Godzilla

Godzilla: Final Wars is filled with one magnificent battle after another, as Godzilla goes through a round-robin tournament of sorts against many of his old foes. In the end, he faces his toughest challenge against the creature initially unleashed by the Xiliens as "Monster X," and later revealed to be "Keizer Ghidorah," a larger and more powerful version of King Ghidorah that stands on four legs and is rippling with muscles. A weakened and exhausted Godzilla faces off with the 'roided-out Ghidorah, with the fate of Planet Earth and the human race hanging in the balance. While mutant Ozaki and the crew of the Gotengo foil the plans of the insidious Controller of the Xiliens, Godzilla neutralizes the threat of Keizer Ghidorah, besting this new version of his greatest foe and driving the invading aliens from Earth forever.

23

Up from the Depths

The Animated Godzilla

O f all the many pop culture manifestations of Godzilla outside of his actual film franchise, there is perhaps no other that has endured, deservedly or not, in the memories of Godzilla fans quite like the late 1970s animated series *Godzilla*, produced by the venerable Hanna-Barbera Productions. Particularly amongst those who belong to Generation X, the Godzilla cartoon holds a special place in the heart, evoking polyester memories of Saturday mornings spent on shag carpets and bean-bag chairs with bowls of Captain Crunch, Froot Loops, and Golden Grahams, rejoicing in the freedom from school and homework. The cartoon came along during a time when production of Godzilla films had ceased in Japan, and so for some kids in the West, it was a first introduction to the character, which to this day remains the most indelible.

To the so-called Godzilla purist, there was certainly much to fault in the show, with its extremely loose attitude toward faithfulness to source material, and the Saturday-morning cartoon limitations definitely worked against it from the start. The animation is limited, the character design is uninspired, and the plots were repetitive and predictable. All in all, it was perfectly in line with what TV animation houses and more importantly, TV networks, believed was suitable kiddie fare to fill a half-hour slot. And yet there was also undeniable fun to be had in the silliness of the whole affair, and for a young child who loved dinosaurs and monsters, there were far worse ways to kill thirty minutes. The show stuck to Hanna-Barbera's tried-and-true formula, and many of the time-tested tropes known to viewers of its many beloved shows. It wouldn't be considered one of Hanna-Barbera's big hits, and it didn't last long, but it gave young Godzilla fans a fix when their local syndicated channel was between *kaiju* movie marathons.

The influence of the show on the memories of fans of a certain age is so strong that Gareth Edwards, director of the 2014 *Godzilla*, recalls that when he told his friends he'd be making the film, they immediately teased him with questions about whether there'd be an appearance from Godzooky, the comical little monster sidekick from the animated show (often confused

Hanna-Barbera's Godzilla and Godzooky.   *Everett Collection*

with Minya, the son of Godzilla seen in Toho's films, who was partly the inspiration for the character). For a show that featured a mere twenty-six episodes over two seasons, it lives on to a surprising degree, and forty-somethings still get a kick out of reciting the theme song. It has become part of the fabric of Godzilla's cultural history.

The Kings of TV Animation

Hanna-Barbera Productions was constantly on the lookout for new characters and properties on which to base its animated series. Founded by animation legends William Hanna and Joseph Barbera, creators of Tom & Jerry for M-G-M in the 1940s, the company had taken shape in 1957 when the two men decided to strike out on their own for the purpose of providing new animated programming specifically for television, a relatively novel concept at the time. Following its first two hits, *The Huckleberry Hound Show* (1958) and *Quick Draw McGraw* (1959), the studio really struck gold in 1960 with *The Flintstones*, the stone-age *Honeymooners* send-up that ran in prime time for years and changed the face of TV cartoons.

Other hot shows followed, including *The Yogi Bear Show, Top Cat, The Jetsons*, and *The Magilla Gorilla Show*. Starting in 1964, Hanna-Barbera began expanding beyond just goofy animals and comedic fare with *Jonny Quest*, its first adventure series, kicking off a trend that later included such action programs as *Space Ghost, Birdman*, and *The Herculoids*. In 1967, the studio started seeking out properties to adapt from other media, starting with Marvel's *Fantastic Four*. And two years later, kids across America fell in love with Scooby-Doo, perhaps Hanna-Barbera's most enduring character of all.

By the 1970s, Hanna-Barbera ruled the Saturday morning landscape, with new hits like *Hong Kong Phooey, Jabberjaw, Captain Caveman*, and its highly successful *Superfriends* franchise, featuring the adventures of DC Comics' Justice League. Truth be told, the company was not known for the quality of its animation, or for brilliant, satirical writing. Unlike the work Hanna and Barbera had done on Tom & Jerry in the '40s, most of their company's output was cheaply made, comparatively crudely drawn and animated, and written with no one over the age of twelve in mind. But it fulfilled its goal of providing a constant flow of content for Saturday morning television, much of which was beloved by more than one generation of American children.

Godzilla's First American Adaptation

Having had success with action-oriented cartoons, and with adaptations of proven properties, Joseph Barbera, the half of the duo in charge of developing new programming, looked in 1978 to Toho Company's Godzilla, a character that had gained enormous popularity with children in America thanks to a slew of Japanese monster movies played in endless rotation on syndicated TV. Seeing potential for a new Hanna-Barbera animated series, Barbera reached out to his good friend Henry G. Saperstein, the producer who had long been Toho's business partner and owner of the license to create Godzilla adaptations in the States. Saperstein brokered the deal with Toho, and before long Hanna-Barbera had permission to adapt the King of the Monsters as an animated cartoon, with Saperstein enjoying co-producer status on the project.

Hanna-Barbera attracted the interest of NBC, a network that had aired many of its programs in the past and wanted *Godzilla* for its fall Saturday morning lineup. The company quickly set to work on the new show, assigning its development to the team of Duane Pool and Dick Robbins, who had written the 1977 season of *The All-New Super Friends Hour* and worked on other Hanna-Barbera projects like *A Flintstone Christmas* (1977) and *Scooby's Laff-A Lympics* (1977) (Robbins's writing credits also included the initial 1973 season of *Super Friends*, and stretched all the way back to the cult favorite 1960s *Spider-Man* animated series). The directors assigned to manage the animation would be two revered cartoon luminaries: Carl Urbano, a key animator for the Harman-Ising Studio that produced shorts for M-G-M in the 1930s and '40s, and later a director of industrial shorts of the 1950s, who had come to work for Hanna-Barbera in the '70s; as well as the accomplished Ray Patterson, whose resume included work for Charles Mintz's Screen Gems outfit with Columbia Pictures, for Walt Disney on films like *Fantasia* (1940) and *Dumbo* (1941), and who had worked for Hanna and Barbera on Tom & Jerry shorts through the 1940s and '50s before following them to their new company in the '60s.

Although their schedule was limited as always, the team at Hanna-Barbera was initially very intrigued and energized by the potential of transforming Godzilla into animated form. Inspired by *Jonny Quest*, the idea was to incorporate Godzilla into the action cartoon format, while staying as true to the original material as possible. The company had only licensed Godzilla, meaning that new foes and friends would have to be created, as no other Toho characters could be used. The animators wanted to take the material as seriously as they could get away with.

Saturday Morning Makeover

Unfortunately, the problems began to arise when NBC network executives began to involve themselves in the creative process, and the limitations of what could actually be done became abundantly clear. Ludicrous restrictions began to be imposed by NBC's Standards & Practices division, limiting the level of violence or aggression that could be portrayed. Similar to how TV execs had hamstrung Hanna-Barbera's *Super Friends* by insisting that superheroes and supervillains couldn't physically fight, and that supervillains could never actually cause any serious harm to anyone, NBC declared that Godzilla could not be shown to cause any serious collateral damage, or take human life, in the interest of protecting the delicate sensibilities of young viewers (and avoid ticking off precious sponsors, no doubt). This forced the writers into making Godzilla friendly, as opposed to the destructive beast they had wanted to portray. Also, NBC wanted some humor and silliness to lighten up the proceedings, and so Hanna-Barbera wound up doing what had worked for them in many action series—introducing a comic-relief sidekick, in the form of Godzilla's awkward, cowardly little nephew, Godzooky.

The *Godzilla* show Hanna-Barbera developed revolved around the adventures of the *Calico*, a scientific research vessel manned by a crew of four: Capt. Carl Majors, first mate Brock Borden, the lovely Dr. Quinn Darien, and her brother Pete. Godzooky, designed as a whimsical ten-foot-tall flying dinosaur with webbed wings, is rescued from a coral reef by the crew of the *Calico*, and as a result, a grateful Uncle Godzilla agrees to offer his protection to the ship and her crew whenever serious threats arise—which would, of course, happen on a weekly basis. Godzilla could be summoned by the crew using a beacon device located on the ship, or using Godzooky's apparent telepathic link.

Sadly, the design of Godzilla as settled upon by Pool and Robbins looked almost nothing like Toho's Godzilla, other than being a giant bipedal dinosaur that swims in the ocean and has spiny ridges on his back. This Godzilla looked more like a traditional tyrannosaurus rex, and was colored green, unlike the charcoal gray of the movies. He was given the ability to shoot laser beams from his eyes, à la Superman, and his atomic breath was reduced to the more conventional fire spit by your run-of-the-mill fairytale dragon. His size also varied wildly over the course of each episode, as the plot required. Also, for whatever reason, Hanna-Barbera could not or would not use the patented roar created by Akira Ifukube, but instead used the deep bass voice of Ted Cassidy, a Hanna-Barbera voice-over stalwart best known as Lurch on the 1960s *Addams Family* TV show, giving Godzilla a distinctively human sound (rumors that Toho replaced Cassidy's voice with Godzilla's movie roar when the show aired in Japan are untrue). Meanwhile, providing the goofy voice of Godzooky was Hanna-Barbera legend Don Messick, the voice of Scooby-Doo. Hoyt Curtin, Hanna-Barbera's musical maven who had composed the catchy themes to shows like *The Flintstones, The Jetsons, Top Cat*, and *Josie and the Pussycats*, contributed the opening tune.

Must-See Monster TV

Godzilla premiered on NBC on September 8, 1978, packaged as one half of *The Godzilla Power Hour* along with another new Hanna-Barbera show, *Jana of the Jungle*. After two months, the hour was expanded to ninety minutes with the addition of *Jonny Quest*, making it *The Godzilla Super 90*. Thirteen episodes were produced, and then the show was renewed for a second season of thirteen. In the fall of 1979, *Godzilla* returned as a stand-alone half-hour show. Once the second season concluded in December 1979, the program was cancelled by NBC, having failed to attract a significant enough audience to warrant its continuation. Instead, the repeats were paired up with other Hanna-Barbera shows, including *The Super Globetrotters* (a show about the Harlem Globetrotters as superheroes), *Dynomutt Dog Wonder*, and *Hong Kong Phooey*. The repeats continued to be broadcast on NBC until the fall 1981 season, when they were replaced in the time slot by Hanna-Barbera's next Saturday morning juggernaut, *The Smurfs*.

Despite its short run and creative limitations, *Godzilla* is well remembered by many who enjoyed watching Saturday morning cartoons during the late '70s and early '80s. As they got older, its nostalgic fans clamored for the reruns to be shown again, which finally happened in 1993 when they were picked up by cable channel Turner Network Television (TNT). In later years, they would be carried on Turner's Cartoon Network as well, and even today can still occasionally be found on Turner's old-school animation channel, Boomerang. The first season of the show was finally released on DVD in three separate volumes in 2006 and 2007 entitled *Godzilla: The Original Animated Series*, but the second season remains unreleased to date.

Divorced from his movie origins and thoroughly watered down by the network, the animated *Godzilla* may not be the "real" Godzilla, but no survey of the monster's influence and reach would be complete without a nod to this animated series, a cultural artifact that was very much of its time. Godzooky may not be coming back any time soon, but a whole generation of kids will never forget him. Whether for good reasons or notorious ones, the *Godzilla* cartoon has a place in the *kaiju* canon, and in the hearts of middle-aged kids everywhere.

Godzilla: The Series

The 1970s *Godzilla* wasn't the only animated version of the monster produced in America. Some twenty years later, the Big G returned to Saturday morning television, in an entirely different form and from an entirely different source. This time, it was not Toho's franchise that inspired the cartoon; rather, *Godzilla: The Series* was intended as an animated continuation of TriStar's infamous 1998 American movie *Godzilla*, directed by Roland Emmerich. Far better than it had any right to be, the animated series is considered by most fans to be superior to the major motion picture on which it was based.

Before Sony Pictures (parent company of TriStar) had any inkling that its *Godzilla* was going to be the colossal flop it was, the company had already commissioned all kinds of tie-ins, including an animated series for kids and a line of toys and action figures based on that animated series. With the film still not even out in theaters, Sony Pictures Television set to work, passing the assignment to its animation division Adelaide Productions, which had previously been responsible for other movie-to-cartoon adaptations of Sony properties like *Jumanji: The Series*, *Extreme Ghostbusters*, and *Men in Black: The Series*. The new Godzilla series was developed for Adelaide by Jeff Kline and his partner Richard Raynis, whose earlier production credits included work on such animated TV hits as *The Simpsons*, *King of the Hill*, *The Critic*, and *The Real Ghostbusters*, and who had broken in as an animator on Ralph Bakshi's cult classic *The Lord of the Rings* (1978).

Even though the series was based on the American version of Godzilla, the central plot and themes were ironically somewhat similar to the 1970s cartoon, revolving around a group of scientific researchers called the Humanitarian Environmental Analysis Team (HEAT), who investigate and combat the ongoing threat of giant monsters. The team is led by Dr. Nick Tatopoulos, played in the movie by Matthew Broderick but voiced in the cartoon by Ian Ziering of *Beverly Hills 90210* and *Sharknado* fame. The show introduced several new characters not seen in the movie, but many characters including Audrey Timonds,

The title card for Sony's 1998 animated series.

Everett Collection

Victor "Animal" Pilotti, Philippe Roache, Mayor Ebert, and Major Anthony Hicks returned, some with new actors providing their voices, and some with the original actors from the film.

Even though the Godzilla of the TriStar movie was a destructive menace, the Adelaide version—much like the Hanna-Barbera version—was portrayed as heroic and helpful. Although Godzilla had died at the end of the movie, one of his surviving hatchlings grew up to be the Godzilla of the animated series, and forms a bond from birth with Dr. Tatopoulos, thereby explaining his benevolent behavior (although the real reason may very well be once again linked to the meddling of network Standards & Practices). Just like in the '70s, this Godzilla is called upon by the scientists to face up to the mounting threats of other giant monsters.

Godzilla: The Series premiered on the Fox Network on Saturday morning, September 12, 1998, as part of the popular Fox Kids cartoon block. Its first season ran for twenty-one episodes, broadcast sporadically along with repeats into the summer of 1999. Despite the infamy of the movie to which it was a sequel of sorts, the show proved popular, and was renewed for a second season in the fall. There it ran aground, as Fox Kids suddenly found itself in a Saturday morning war with the WB Network and its Kids WB package. At the time, Fox's *Digimon* and WB's *Pokemon* were two of the hottest cartoons on American TV and in direct competition; Fox began programming marathon blocks of *Digimon* on Saturday mornings, shuffling around *Godzilla*'s time slot and even postponing episodes. The show gradually lost its audience into 2000, until Fox cancelled it, never even bothering to air the last two episodes.

In April 2014, almost fourteen years exactly from when the show was cancelled, Mill Creek Entertainment put out the complete series on DVD for the first time—an honor that has yet to be afforded the 1970s series. *Godzilla: The Series* is also widely available on several streaming platforms as well, proving that unlike the film on which it's based, people still actually want to watch it.

24

Godzilla's Evolution

The Monster Through the Years

Over the past sixty-plus years, Godzilla has been a constant in Japanese and world cinema. But what hasn't been a constant is Godzilla's appearance. The monster has changed quite a bit between 1954 and today. Although it may not seem so to the eye of the layperson, Godzilla fanatics are well aware that numerous costume designs have been used over the years, and the overall design has gone through many changes, some of them quite major. The creature has transformed drastically over time, for a variety of reasons, ranging from the need to portray him in a different light, to simple, practical reasons of money and the requirements of effects technology.

Although recent incarnations of Godzilla in America, and even his most recent Japanese incarnation in *Shin Godzilla* (2016), have utilized CGI to bring the monster to life, the original conception was a fully sculpted and manufactured suit that was worn by an actor, and that was how the effect was traditionally pulled off by Toho over the course of fifty years. The "suitmation" technique perfected by Eiji Tsuburaya is beloved by devoted fans of *daikaiju eiga*, and was adhered to in Japanese cinema long after American genre filmmakers had made the complete switchover from practical to digital effects. There is something about the reality of the man-in-suit, and the whole phenomenon can be traced directly to Godzilla, and his legendary debut in *Gojira* (1954).

Serious Godzilla aficionados can determine which movie they are watching simply by analyzing the particular version of the costume being used. Unofficial nicknames for each costume, originally used by model kit companies to distinguish one version from another, were later adopted by Godzilla fandom at large, and expanded to include names for each iteration. For our purposes, these nicknames will be employed in this chapter to differentiate and spotlight the different costumes seen over the years, starting with the very first, known as *Shodai*-Godzilla.

Megaro-Godzilla poses with his 1973 co-stars (left to right) Jet Jaguar, Gigan, and Megalon.
Movie Stills Database

Shodai-Godzilla (1954)

When Tsuburaya was informed by producer Tomoyuki Tanaka that his grand ambitions for creating a stop-motion monster for *Gojira* were too impractical and expensive, he knew the only other way to go was to construct a suit that could be worn by an actor. The initial design for the costume came from comic book illustrator Wasuke Abe, who had previously worked with Shigeru Kayama, the novelist who had contributed the initial treatment for the film. Although some of Abe's elements were adopted, the final design came from the minds of Tanaka, Tsuburaya, and writer-director Ishiro Honda, who wanted to base it on the look of real dinosaurs. Production designer Akira Watanabe combined features of the tyrannosaurus rex, iguanadon, and stegosaurus, resulting in a bizarre yet familiar hybrid.

From there, the design was handed over to the artist Teizo Toshimitsu, who used it to build a clay sculpture that was used as the basis for the eventual construction of the suit itself. Under Tsuburaya and Watanabe's supervision, Toshimitsu and his crew constructed a cloth and wire frame, and applied layers of molten rubber over it, producing the desired rough, alligator-like skin. Following an initial model that proved too heavy and stiff to use, the team produced a final suit that could be utilized effectively by suit actor Haruo Nakajima. This finished version was notable for its large, rounded head, short arms, and creepy, almost doll-like eyes. It also boasted a profusion of jagged fangs and staggered dorsal-plate rows, producing a significantly monstrous appearance.

Gyakushu-Godzilla (1955)

Although rather similar in appearance to the original *Shodai* costume, the *Gyakushu* suit used in the immediate sequel *Godzilla Raids Again* (1955) was actually a completely new construction. Learning from experience, Tsuburaya's team designed the new suit to be narrower and more streamlined, and reduced the number of toes on each foot from four to three, thus making it easier for Nakajima to perform in. The size of the head was reduced and made less round, and more in keeping with what would be seen in later installments. Adding to the creature's expressiveness were eyes that were movable for the first time. This suit would be the one duplicated for American International Pictures (AIP) to shoot its proposed film, *The Volcano Monsters*. The film was never made, and the suit was lost.

KingGoji (1962)

The third Godzilla film, *King Kong vs. Godzilla*, was the first made in seven years, and also the first to be shot in color; a drastically redesigned costume was made for the occasion. The most reptilian-looking costume to date, *KingGoji* was distinguished by its wide, stocky build and a very small head with high-placed and narrowly spaced eyes. Owing to the much lighter tone of the film compared to what had come before, Godzilla was designed to be a lot less frightening—his fangs were gone, his hands were more humanoid, his dorsal plates were reduced, and his ears were removed (he wouldn't have visible ears for the remainder of the *Showa* era).

MosuGoji (1964)

By far one of the most popular of all Godzilla costume models, and perhaps the ultimate favorite of the *Showa* era among fans, the *MosuGoji* suit was utilized for both *Godzilla vs. Mothra* (1964) and its immediate follow-up, *Ghidorah, the Three-Headed Monster* (1964). Another bold departure, *MosuGoji* was the most streamlined costume yet, featuring a strongly defined chest and legs. The head was the perfect size, not too large or too small, and what stood out the most about it were the facial features. A prominent brow and decidedly menacing eyes made it clear that although he may not be as serious as before, this Godzilla was still a bad guy—at least for the time being.

For its second appearance in *Ghidorah*, the face of the costume was slightly altered, with movable eyes added and the tongue lengthened. This revised iteration is sometimes referred to as *SanDaiKaiju*-Godzilla. Tsuburaya got a lot of mileage out of this one, later repurposing it for use on his TV series *UltraQ*, in which it was modified to create the villainous creature Gomes, and later in the first season of *Ultraman*, in which it was combined with elements of a later model and given a pronounced, lizard-like neck frill to become the monster known as Giras.

Daisenso-Godzilla (1965–66)

By the mid-1960s, Godzilla had morphed into a good guy, and a new suit was designed to make him look less menacing while still retaining an intimidatingly monstrous appearance. First used in *Invasion of Astro-Monster* (1965), the costume bore some resemblance to the *MosuGoji* suit, but the design appeared more slipshod, with a less-defined body shape and a larger, more rounded face. With Tsuburaya's attentions elsewhere thanks to the launch of his own production company, some have felt that the suit designs for the remainder of the *Showa* era were of inferior quality, beginning with this one.

In spite of this, the suit did have a carefully detailed tail and retained the movable eyes. Unlike previous versions that possessed articulated fingers, this model had hands in which all the fingers were fused together, a detail that would be retained for the rest of the *Showa* era. Pressed into service again for *Godzilla vs. the Sea Monster* (1966), the suit was given minor repairs and additions that included movable eyelids (this revision is sometimes known as *Nankai*-Godzilla). The *Daisenso* suit would turn up briefly in a few later films for water scenes (a common practice when the filmmakers didn't want to unnecessarily damage the primary suit).

Musuko-Godzilla (1967)

Whenever discussion turns to the topic of, "What was the worst Godzilla suit of all time?," typically the answer is the *Musuko* suit, mercifully seen only once, in *Son of Godzilla* (1966). The classic example of how Toho's special-effects department had slipped since Tsuburaya stepped away from full-time supervision, the suit was ugly, overly comical, and unconvincing even by the standards of 1960s *tokusatsu* cinema. With a wide neck that gave away all illusion as to where the actor's head was hidden, a wide, floppy mouth, and giant, lifeless eyes, it was certainly a far cry from the nightmarish spawn of the atom bomb first seen a dozen years prior. Looking shabbily designed and hastily put together, the retention of moving eyes and eyelids was just about the only positive worth mentioning.

Soshingeki-Godzilla (1968–72)

No other costume got as much mileage as the *Soshingeki*, which was the primary suit used in *Destroy All Monsters* (1968), *All Monsters Attack* (1969), *Godzilla vs. Hedorah* (1971) and *Godzilla vs. Gigan* (1972). Perhaps with the economy and the movie business in general hurting, Toho decided to maximize its investment by riding this costume into the ground; still, it's a popular design and definitely a big step up from the *Musuko*. The head-to-body ratio is much better proportioned, and the structure of the neck and face are much improved, with Godzilla back to having expressive eyes and a strong brow.

After its initial appearance in *Destroy All Monsters*, slight alterations were made to the brow for *All Monsters Attack* (this version is sometimes called All Monsters-*Goji*). With Godzilla's image made more heroic than ever before in *Godzilla vs. Hedorah*, the eyes of the suit were made less menacing and more rounded, and the mouth was remolded into a determined frown (*HedoGoji*). For *Godzilla vs. Gigan*, the eyes were once again changed, and movable eyelids were restored (Gigan-Godzilla). Also by this point, the wear and tear of four feature appearances in a row had taken their toll, and the suit was visibly degraded and damaged.

Megaro-Godzilla (1973–75)

Often maligned, the *Megaro* suit was certainly the most kid-friendly of all the Godzilla costumes, designed for a time when the Big G was firmly entrenched as an Earth-defending superhero and friend to children everywhere. First appearing in *Godzilla vs. Megalon* (1973), it remained in use through the remainder of the *Showa* period, being featured in *Godzilla vs. Mechagodzilla* (1974) and *Terror of Mechagodzilla* (1975). Strongly influenced by the character design of children's *anime*, this Godzilla resembled a cute caricature of his former self, with stylized body and features that included a stumpy trunk and a rounded, almost feline face. After the hopelessly silly *Godzilla vs. Megalon*, slight alterations were made to the costume for its next two appearances in order to make it a bit less comical (these versions are sometimes called *Mekagoji* and *Meka-Gyakushu*-Godzilla, respectively). The *Megaro* suit can also be seen in the Toho-produced TV series *Zone Fighter* (*Ryusei Ningen Zone*), in which Godzilla appeared in five episodes in 1973.

84Goji (1984)

For the triumphant return of Godzilla in what came to be the *Heisei* series, Toho and special-effects master Teruyoshi Nakano (Tsuburaya's former assistant) came up with an entirely new and somewhat unique version of the creature to match up with his once-again evil demeanor. The Godzilla that appears in *Godzilla 1985* (1984) is quite different from what had been seen in the *Showa* era, and certainly different from the evolution that was to come in later *Heisei* movies.

For one thing, this was the first suit constructed not from scratch, but from foam-rubber-injected molds. During the *Showa* era, costumes had been built up by hand from nothing using raw materials, much as makeup legend Jack Pierce had done in the 1930s and '40s for Universal Studios when creating such movie monsters as Frankenstein and the Wolf Man. However, just as later Universal makeup chief Bud Westmore had seen the advantage of using molded rubber for such 1950s monsters as the Creature from the Black Lagoon and the Metaluna Mutant, so too did Toho begin using molds instead of building each suit from scratch. Although the result is more generic and has less of a human touch, using molds saves time and money, and also results in a more uniform look every time.

84*Goji* takes some elements from the original 1954 *Shodai*-Godzilla, bringing back the ears, the fangs, the four-toed feet, and the multiple rows of dorsal plates. These elements would remain for the remainder of the suits seen in the Godzilla franchise. Also unique about this costume was its mechanization, which included the ability for the lips to move and snarl.

BioGoji (1989–91)

New special-effects chief Koichi Kawakita stepped in beginning with 1989's *Godzilla vs. Biollante*, and he made his mark by drastically and permanently altering the appearance of the King of the Monsters. Making a clean break from what had been done in the previous film (more of a *Showa* holdover), Kawakita created a Godzilla that was muscular and powerful looking, with a much fiercer and animalistic face that suggested intelligence as well as evil. The legs were thick and stocky, the mouth had rows of sharp fangs, and the eyes were big and brown with almost no whites for the first time. With the aid of molds, a duplicate suit was made especially for scenes to be shot in water.

For the next film, *Godzilla vs. King Ghidorah* (1991), the same suit was used with some minor alterations, including a wider head. This altered version is sometimes known as *GhidoGoji*, and might have even been used for the fourth *Heisei* film, *Godzilla & Mothra: Battle for Earth* (1992), but it was unfortunately stolen from the Toho lot. Nevertheless, the molds established by Kawakita for *Godzilla vs. Biollante* would continue to be the basis for the suits made for the remainder of the *Heisei* series through the 1990s, resulting in a Godzilla who appeared much more uniform from one movie to the next than he had during the 1950s–70s.

BatoGoji (1992)

Due to the theft of the previous suit, a brand-new suit was constructed by Kawakita and his team for *Godzilla & Mothra: Battle for Earth*. A bit svelter than before, this Godzilla still retained a very powerful appearance, with a wider, ribbed neck and even more menacing eyes, this time bright golden in color. The *BatoGoji* suit also possessed the ability to maneuver the head up and down independently of the body, a first for Godzilla. Although this costume would only be center stage in one film, it was used in later entries *Godzilla vs. Mechagodzilla* (1993) and *Godzilla vs. Space Godzilla* (1994) for water scenes.

RadoGoji (1993)

Another modification of Kawakita's original 1989 *BioGoji* design, this suit, used for the 1993 installment *Godzilla vs. Mechagodzilla*, represented Godzilla at his bulkiest to date. Much of the changes added to the *BatoGoji* were retained here, including the brightly colored eyes, maneuverable head, and ribbed neck. This suit was also distinguished by slimmer legs and shorter, more easily movable arms. After filming on the movie, the *RadoGoji* costume would be used for the "Monster Planet of Godzilla," a 3-D amusement park ride at Japan's Sanrio Puroland that opened in 1994, featuring specially shot sequences of Godzilla battling Mothra and Rodan.

MogeGoji (1994–95)

The last of the major suits constructed for the *Heisei* series, the *MogeGoji* costume represented Kawakita's final take on the iconic design he had first introduced in 1989, and which is to this day considered the ideal design by many fans. It first appeared in *Godzilla vs. Space Godzilla*, and one of its most recognizable new changes were the eyes, which were much larger than before and slightly less demonic, perhaps owing to Godzilla once again inching toward reluctant hero status as the *Heisei* series wore on. Also worth noting is that this suit allowed Godzilla's head to fully rotate for the first time.

The suit was used once more for the final *Heisei* installment, *Godzilla vs. Destoroyah* (1995), with some major renovations to adapt to the story line of the new movie. Since the script called for Godzilla to be glowing with an overload of nuclear energy, Kawakita's team removed sections of the costume's skin and inserted arrays of small orange light bulbs, which were then covered over with transparent vinyl plates to achieve the glowing effect. The suit was also given glowing red eyes, and fitted to spew thick steam. According to suit actor Kenpachiro Satsuma, the steam was carbon monoxide, which nearly caused him to pass out several times during filming. This somewhat dangerous version of the suit is sometimes referred to as *DesuGoji*.

MireGoji (1999–2000)

With the advent of the third major phase of the Godzilla franchise, the Millennium series, came a major departure from Kawakita's classic 1989–95 design. Toho turned to suit maker Shinichi Wakasa, who was responsible for most of the costumes constructed during this period. Wakasa went for a much more decidedly reptilian look, giving Godzilla an almost pointed face, with a long tongue, massive fangs, and detailed scales covering the body. Further adding to the reptilian look was the decision to paint the entire costume a deep shade of green—despite misconceptions to the contrary, the suit in previous films had traditionally been colored charcoal gray. The dorsal plates were larger and more jagged than ever, and were painted purple, making this perhaps the most colorful Godzilla to date. His eyes featured dark pupils surrounded by white, a throwback to the *Showa* days. This suit would be used for *Godzilla 2000* (1999), as well as for the second Millennium film, *Godzilla vs. Megaguirus* (2000), with just a few slight alterations made to the face and body, including a different, lighter shade of green and purple color (*GiraGoji*).

SokogekiGoji (2001)

The only one of the Millennium films to not feature a variation of Wakasa's 1999 reptilian design, *Godzilla, Mothra and King Ghidorah: Giant Monsters All-Out Attack* featured an entirely new Wakasa design, created specifically at the request of director Shusuke Kaneko, who wanted his Godzilla to stand out from all others, due to his radical reimagining of the monster as an evil incarnation of vengeful human souls. The result is a one-shot costume that is memorably haunting, suggesting Tsuburaya's 1954 design while incorporating some of the fierceness that made Kawakita's *Heisei* suits so effective. The *SokogekiGoji* suit was the tallest Godzilla ever filmed, standing over seven feet tall, and the all-white eyes were another drastically different element that helped this new look stand out.

KiryuGoji (2002–03)

Kaneko's vision for Godzilla was confined to only one film, and once the Millennium series continued with what turned out to be the two-part saga of *Godzilla Against Mechagodzilla* (2002) and *Godzilla: Tokyo S.O.S.* (2003), Toho opted to return to Wasaka's previous design, with some changes. For one, the green color was replaced with the more familiar gray, and the purple dorsal plates went from purple back to white, although they were just as huge and jagged as they had been in *Godzilla 2000* and *Godzilla vs. Megaguirus*. For the *KiryuGoji* suit's second appearance in *Tokyo S.O.S.*, it was given a dramatic scar across the chest, representing an injury sustained in Godzilla's previous battle with Kiryu.

FinalGoji (2004)

The last entry in the Millennium series—and the final Toho Godzilla movie for a dozen years—*Godzilla: Final Wars* (2004) brought a costume that took the basic Wakasa design and incorporated elements of *Showa* and *Heisei* Godzilla, in keeping with the film's homage to the entire franchise. The face was altered to appear more in keeping with the 1960s and '70s Godzilla, and the dorsal plates were reduced in size as well, while the ears were the largest they had ever been. By utilizing lighter materials besides the customary foam rubber, the Final*Goji* suit was lightweight, leaner, and more easily maneuverable by suit actor Tom Kitagawa, known for his very physical performance style. This Godzilla costume would be the last one ever created by Toho.

ShinGoji (2016)

For the latest reinvention of Godzilla as seen in Toho's *Shin Godzilla* (2016), the studio attempted its most radical reimagining of Godzilla to date, and in keeping with the evolution of movie special effects, they achieved this reimagining not with a man in a suit, but rather with a combination of puppetry, animatronics, and CGI. The new look of the creature is perhaps the most frightening and disturbing ever seen, relying in part on the crazed, scarred appearance of the original 1954 Godzilla.

When first revealed to the world, the new look of *ShinGoji* surprised and alarmed many fans, with its bony body structure, featuring exposed musculature and glowing bright red from open sores, meant to represent the wounds suffered via radiation exposure. Beady lidless eyes, rough and misshapen fangs, and wiry clawlike hands distinguished *ShinGoji* as the antithesis of both the fun Godzilla of the late *Showa* era and the muscular, powerful Godzilla of the *Heisei* and Millennium eras. Adding to the creature's more monstrous reimagining were five-clawed feet that resembled those of a velociraptor and a tail that was monumentally long even by Godzilla standards, held aloft behind him at all times.

This newest look for the King of the Monsters may have caught some people by surprise, but it's really just the latest stage in the ongoing evolution and development of Godzilla, one of moviedom's more malleable monsters. Each iteration has suited its time, and the storytelling needs of filmmakers, while still remaining true to the core essence of what makes Godzilla Godzilla. The visions of numerous creative and talented artists from Eiji Tsuburaya to Koichi Kawakita to Shinichi Wakasa and beyond have informed and molded his appearance over the years, each one leaving his distinct mark on the creature and adding to his allure and mystique in the process.

Unsuited: Godzilla in Graphics

Both American versions of Godzilla produced to date featured an almost completely computer-generated creature, with American filmmakers rejecting the traditional suitmation of *tokusatsu* outright. As a CGI creation, Godzilla has been hit and miss, with the first attempt by TriStar being met with widespread disapproval and the newer Legendary version hewing a bit more closely to the classic Toho parameters, and thus winning over more of the monster's longtime enthusiasts. Both approaches added yet more layers to the many forms Godzilla has taken over the years.

TriStar*Goji* (1998)

Roland Emmerich wanted his *Godzilla* (1998) to be a complete overhaul from what had been done before, and as part of that overhaul he wanted a total rethinking of what Godzilla actually was, resulting in an appearance that bore only the slightest resemblance to anything that might remotely be called Godzilla. Special-effects designer Patrick Tatopoulos created an interpretation that was intended to be an agile, sly, and fast-moving creature, drawing even more inspiration from lizards and dinosaurs than any of his predecessors had (in keeping with the new concept of the creature as essentially a giant, irradiated iguana).

TriStar*Goji* hunched forward like a tyrannosaurus rex, had a massive head with a protruding lower jaw, and was colored with a spectrum of blue, brown, green, and gray hues, giving it a chameleon-like quality. The arms and legs were longer and almost humanoid, allowing Godzilla to bound through the streets of New York. Although CGI was predominantly used to bring the creature to life, Emmerich did still employ some animatronics, designed by former Disney designer Bob Gurr, who had also created the giant animatronic King Kong for the Universal Studios theme park. There was even a rubber suit used very sparingly, worn by suit actor Kurt Carley and seen in only a handful of shots in the finished movie.

Although approved by Toho, executives at the studio were reportedly unhappy with what TriStar had done, and eventually purchased the rights to the redesigned monster, which they renamed "Zilla" to avoid any

Early conceptual designs for Legendary's Godzilla were pretty close to the final product.
Movie Stills Database

confusion (with producer Shogo Tomiyama explaining that TriStar's version "took the God out of Godzilla.")

Legendary*Goji* (2014–)

Learning from the mistakes of TriStar*Goji*, for Legendary Pictures' 2014 *Godzilla*, Jim Rygiel, the Oscar-winning director of visual effects for WETA Workshop (best known for Peter Jackson's *Lord of the Rings* trilogy), designed a Godzilla that drew directly from Toho's recognizable and classic design, despite being a 100 percent CGI creation. Rygiel's design became known for its bulky girth, even leading some fans to refer to it as "Fat Godzilla" due to its thick neck, wide, square head, and swollen body. The color was the darkest ever, utilizing a shade of gray so deep as to be almost black. The eyes were yellowish in color, and for the first time, Godzilla appeared to have gills along his throat, suggesting an amphibious nature. Despite the liberties taken, this design balanced just enough tradition with modern special effects to please most fans old and new.

25

G-Fans

The Godzilla Community

I f there's one thing that the modern era of popular culture has taught us, it's that fans can be extremely passionate and creative about the things they love. Whether it's *Star Wars, The Lord of the Rings, Harry Potter, The Walking Dead, Dr. Who*, or any of the other countless entertainment properties that have each captured its own devoted following, fandom is a living, breathing, functional (and sometimes dysfunctional) entity unto itself. And in this respect, fans of Godzilla, or even more broadly of Japanese *tokusatsu* in general, are no different. Whether it's dressing up like their favorite *kaiju*, gathering together at annual conventions, or swarming to repertory screenings of old monster flicks, the Godzilla fan base is just as fervent and multifaceted as any genre community. There are devoted legions on both sides of the Pacific who have supported the Big G loyally and lovingly over the years.

Tokusatsu fans cover a wide range of material, including, of course, the monolithic Godzilla franchise itself, but also the many other films produced by Toho over the decades like *Rodan* (1956), *Mothra* (1961), *War of the Gargantuas* (1966), and countless others, as well as other *daikaiju eiga* from other Japanese studios, such as Daiei's enduring Gamera and Daimajin franchises, and Shochiku's Guilala. The fandom also covers enormously popular *tokusatsu* TV properties like Tsuburaya Productions' immortal *Ultraman*, the longest-running franchise in TV history, as well as Toei's *Super Sentai*, known in the West as *Power Rangers*, beloved by kids and adults worldwide.

But standing head and shoulders above all else, both literally and figuratively, especially amongst American fans, is the mighty Godzilla himself, the Godfather of *kaiju*. Godzilla fandom in the West also comes with a certain fascination with Japanese cinema and culture in general, often arising due to its "otherness," or its existence as an alternative to American entertainment and culture. Often its existence outside the American entertainment mainstream adds to its "hip" factor amongst American fans. *Tokusatsu* can

Godzilla cosplayers are common sights at genre conventions, such as this one at San Francisco's 2009 WonderCon.   © *BrokenSphere/ Wikimedia Commons*

be exotic and alien to those who grew up in a Western culture, reflecting values, priorities, and sensibilities often very different from our own, and therefore of great interest.

"Godzilla fandom is an odd animal, quite different from, say, the following the *Star Trek* franchise enjoys," explains author and critic Stuart Galbraith IV. "Whereas in that fan base people dress up, build model kits, collect toys, etc., at its core I think all *Star Trek* fans are rooted in the shows and movies—the stories and the characters that inhabit them. In the case of Godzilla, and of *kaiju eiga* generally, it's more splintered. Everyone watches the movies, to be sure, but their interests are more specialized and particular. Some love the films primarily for the special effects. Others like them because of their musical scores. Still others are into collecting toys or movie posters or building kits. My interest has always been primarily a fascination with the movies as movies, and how contextually they fit into the bigger picture of Japanese cinema. That's neither better nor worse than those who, say, are primarily fascinated with how the special effects are achieved, but it points to our wide-ranging interests in the same thing."

G-Fest

Godzilla fans of all stripes tend to enjoy gathering together to share their passion, exchange information, acquire new goodies, or just generally have fun; and long before the Internet made it much easier to do exactly that, fan conventions were traditionally the best method. To a large extent, they still are a major part of fandom. And when it comes to Godzilla and *tokusatsu*, the primary get-together each and every year since 1994 has been G-Fest, the annual mega-convention held in and around Chicago. The brainchild of Godzilla superfans J. D. Lees and the late John Rocco Roberto, G-Fest embraces all aspects of *kaiju eiga*, featuring something for virtually anyone, including movie screenings, costume contests, celebrity panel Q&As, and much more.

The G-Fest convention grew out of Lees's already existing (and ongoing) project, the *G-Fan* magazine. *G-Fan* was definitely not the first Godzilla-themed publication; there have been many others such as *Markalite*, edited and published by *tokusatsu* expert August Ragone in the early 1990s; as well as one of the oldest, *Japanese Giants*, founded by Mark Rainey and later edited by *tokusatsu* scholar Ed Godziszewski, which published sporadically between 1974 and 2004. These and others have satisfied American Godzilla fans starved for information on their favorite form of entertainment

Fans can find all manner of rare and coveted Godzilla toys at conventions like G-Fest.

Photo by author

(particularly during the pre-Internet days). However, *G-Fan* has proven to be the most enduring and popular of them all, beginning publication in 1993 and still going strong on a quarterly basis. A self-professed "fanzine," or fan-produced magazine, *G-Fan* has come to be the Bible of Godzilla, especially for Western fans—so much so that lovers of *kaiju eiga* often refer to themselves as "G-fans."

G-Fest initially began in 1994 as "Friends of *G-Fan*," a gathering of contributors to *G-Fan* magazine. The following year, it expanded into more of an organized convention, at first called G-Con. Although initially closed to the public, by 1996 it was a fully public and functioning Godzilla-themed convention, even bringing in suit actors Haruo Nakajima and Kenpachiro Satsuma as special guests. In 1998, the name was officially changed to

G-Fest, and the following year the convention began exhibiting films and giving out its now-prestigious Mangled Skyscraper Award. Since 1999, the award has been presented to such luminaries as Forrest J. Ackerman, publisher of the influential genre magazine *Famous Monsters of Filmland*; special-effects masters Koichi Kawakita, Teruyoshi Nakano, Shinji Higuchi, and Shinichi Wakasa; beloved actors Kenji Sahara and Akira Takarada; monster artist Bob Eggleton; author Don Glut; *tokusatsu* scholar August Ragone, and many others.

Other special guests have included Galbraith and other respected writer-critics like Steve Ryfle and Dr. William Tsutsui; directors like Shusuke Kaneko, Yoshimitsu Banno, Kazuki Omori, and Masaaki Tezuka; effects designer Sadamasa Arikawa; performers Megumi Odaka, Hurricane Ryu, Rhodes Reason, Don Frye, Tsutomu Kitagawa, and many others. G-Fest is truly a world-renowned gathering, and *the* place to be for fans of Godzilla

Even kids get into the act, such as this young girl who posed as Mothra at G-Fest 2009.

Photo by author

and friends, and those fans travel from all over the world to Chicago every year to be a part of it.

Getting fans together at G-Fest has also led to other fan-related endeavors, most notably the special international event known as G-Tour. Since 2004, Daikaiju Enterprises Ltd., Lees's company, which manages both G-Fest and *G-Fan*, has presented several guided tours of Japan, taking fans from America over to the Land of the Rising Sun. The tours have visited iconic landmarks featured (in miniature form) in Godzilla movies, such as the Diet Building, Tokyo Tower, and the Wako Building clock tower, and tours have even been taken through Toho Studios itself, where guests have rubbed elbows with actors and executives, and been given access to historic movie props and other memorabilia.

From Fans to Scholars

Amongst Godzilla fans, there are some who have taken their love of the Big G and gone on to become highly regarded and very well-informed scholars and writers on the subject, whom other fans look to for the latest news or in-depth analysis. These include previously mentioned critics and journalists like Galbraith, Ryfle, Ragone, and Godziszewski, who have become trusted names in Godzilla fandom, writing several important books on the subject and providing various commentaries for home video releases. Ragone's website *The Good, the Bad and Godzilla* is the ultimate source of breaking news, and the author and superfan also regularly hosts marathons of *kaiju* flicks and *Ultraman* episodes on the online streaming service Shout Factory TV. In recent years, fans have flocked to Godzilla-themed podcasts for more information and fan discussion; the most prominent and longest-running of these has been Kyle Yount's *KaijuCast*, which began in 2009 and has since provided in-depth commentaries, interviews, reviews, and news. The *KaijuCast* has proven so popular that it even enabled Yount to crowdfund his own lovingly made documentary *Hail to the King: 60 Years of Destruction*, completed in 2015.

Of course, there is also a negative side to all realms of fandom, and even Godzilla fandom isn't immune to the phenomena of fan entitlement, cynicism, petty bickering, and territorialism that seem bound to arise whenever passionate enthusiasts converge, especially in the age of social media. We've seen it recently in the ugly backlash against the female-led reboot of *Ghostbusters* (2016), as well as the outcry from fans of the maligned supervillain movie *Suicide Squad* (2016) to shut down the critics' aggregate site *Rotten Tomatoes* in outrage over negative reviews. The 2014 American *Godzilla* remake certainly divided fans of the Big G, and they continue to argue, sometimes to an unfriendly degree, over which version of Godzilla is superior, and other topics that seem of crucial importance to a certain segment of fandom and often leave more casual fans wondering what all the fuss is about.

"In that way, the fandom of Godzilla isn't that much different from any other kind of fandom," says Miguel Rodriguez. "There are lovely aspects and some very dark aspects. The dark aspects do come from feelings of entitlement. It's hard for fans to remember that people love various things for their own reasons, and bring their own baggage to it, and that's OK.

Fans show off their skills creating life-size props such as this Rodan costume on display at G-Fest 2009.   *Photo by author*

There are a lot of different ways to like something, and a lot of different reasons. Fans of every variety can get a bit too judgmental."

Some, including Stuart Galbraith IV, have occasionally been critical of the state of Godzilla fandom amongst both fans at large and even amongst professionals in the field, citing its lack of the cohesive unity that can often be found in other genres of fandom or film studies:

"It's enormously unfortunate that at both the fan level and at the professional/scholarly level—that is, people researching and writing about the films, selling merchandise, running fanzines, and operating conventions—there's been such a ludicrous amount of disunity. That's something I've tried to stay out of as much as possible—living on another continent helps—but I think we should all be supportive of one another's efforts to spread the word, share information, and our affection for this genre."

Nevertheless, despite any differences of opinion they may have, Godzilla fans are a joyous bunch, and enjoy celebrating a mutual love for something that they very often first discovered in their youth and remained fascinated with throughout their lives. As with many kinds of fandom, the love and celebration of *kaiju eiga* and *tokusatsu* in general comes from a place of innocence and wonder, and represents a way to remain close to something that has brought great happiness for many years. Godzilla fans of all opinions and types are united in their adoration and even reverence for a fictional character that has come to occupy a very real place in their hearts. Like an old pal from childhood, he is genuinely cherished. He may be a city-crushing monstrosity the size of a skyscraper, but to his fans, he will always be a friend.

26

Godzilla Marches On

The Future of the Franchise

Most would agree that it's a great time to be a Godzilla fan right now, with the monster's future looking about as bright as a blast of radioactive fire. For a franchise that is well over sixty years of age, not only does it show no sign of slowing down, but things have actually been ramping up more in the past few years than perhaps ever before. For the first time, there are Godzilla projects happening on both sides of the Pacific, with both Legendary Pictures in Hollywood and Godzilla's original home at Tokyo's Toho Company simultaneously continuing their respective series. Motivated in part by the success of Gareth Edwards's blockbuster *Godzilla* (2014), Legendary is moving ahead with plans to expand its own cinematic universe, while that same American success is finally convincing Toho to once again take Godzilla out of deep freeze for the first time in a dozen years.

The summer of 2019 is expected to bring the direct sequel to Legendary's *Godzilla*, but much more than that, the sequel will be part of a whole new monster-heavy franchise that will include much more than just the King of the Monsters. For the first time in an American film, Legendary plans to introduce other Toho creations Mothra, Rodan, and King Ghidorah in its next Godzilla installment. And beyond that, Godzilla will once again do battle with none other than King Kong in *Godzilla vs. Kong*, set to be released in the summer of 2020—Kong was reintroduced by Legendary in the recently released *Kong: Skull Island* (2017).

Meanwhile, Toho made history in July 2016 by kicking off what may well be its fourth official Godzilla series with the release of *Shin Godzilla*. Although inspired by Legendary's success, Toho's relaunch has nothing to do with the American franchise from a continuity standpoint, presenting an entirely new Godzilla, as envisioned by acclaimed genre filmmakers Hideaki Anno and Shinji Higuchi. One of the biggest Japanese releases in recent memory, the film thrilled legions of Godzilla fans worldwide that had been clamoring for the return of the "Toho" Godzilla. As of yet, it is unknown if *Shin Godzilla* will lead to a new full-blown series from Toho, but certainly if the reception to the film is any indication, it would be unwise to bet against it.

The Godzilla-Kong Universe

Toho has been making Godzilla movies for decades, but the concept of a continuing American Godzilla series is something very new. After TriStar's original attempt in the 1990s failed miserably, Legendary Pictures has finally pulled it off, with plans to use 2014's *Godzilla* as a launching point for an intriguing franchise, or more appropriately a "shared cinematic universe" à la Marvel Studios' superhero dynasty, which is the talk of genre fans of all stripes. Almost immediately after *Godzilla* became a runaway hit in its opening weekend, Legendary officially gave the green light to the continuation of the Big G's adventures, and the expansion of his world.

The Eighth Wonder Returns

This expansion would begin not with a new Godzilla movie, but ironically with a brand-new King Kong movie, something not seen since Peter Jackson's big-budget blockbuster of 2005. But this new picture would have no connection to Jackson's film, which was a remake of the 1933 original. Rather, the new film, first announced by Legendary at the 2014 San Diego Comic-Con and entitled *Kong: Skull Island*, would be a King Kong origin story. The new project was made possible by Legendary's 2014 partnership switch from Warner Bros., its original distributor and production partner, to Universal Studios, owners of the King Kong copyright. However, Legendary turned heads when it revealed that *Kong: Skull Island* would not be a Universal co-production, but a co-production of Warner Bros., the company with which Legendary had made *Godzilla*.

The announcement led to fervent speculation that Legendary was seeking to somehow link up Kong and Godzilla in the same movie universe, and that indeed turned out to be the case. Legendary soon revealed that *Kong: Skull Island* would be the beginning of a broader monster world only hinted at in *Godzilla*, and that the film would represent the first step on the road to Godzilla and Kong eventually crossing paths on screen, something that hadn't happened since 1962's *King Kong vs. Godzilla*. *Godzilla* scripter Max

Borenstein was brought in to write the first draft of the screenplay, to help establish continuity between the two movies.

Young director Jordan Vogt-Roberts, who had gained attention with the 2013 independent critical darling *The Kings of Summer*, was brought on board to helm the project, neutralizing rumors that *Pacific Rim*'s Guillermo del Toro had been offered the spot. The film tells the story of a team of explorers that stumbles upon the domain of the giant gorilla on an uncharted island deep in the Pacific in the 1970s, and includes direct references to Monarch, the top secret government organization first featured in *Godzilla*, that tracks the movements of giant monsters and other cryptids all over the world. In order to properly set up the eventual confrontation with Godzilla in a later film, this new incarnation of Kong would be vastly larger than his mere fifty-foot height as seen in the past (Toho's 1962 film had similarly skirted the issue).

The film features an all-star cast that includes Tom Hiddleston (*The Avengers*' Loki) in the lead role as the captain of the exploration team, Samuel L. Jackson as the team's helicopter pilot, and John Goodman as the government official in charge, as well as distinguished character actors John C. Reilly and Tom Wilkinson (Michael Keaton and J. K. Simmons had originally been attached, but dropped out before filming began in October 2015). Kong would be portrayed via CGI, using a motion-capture technique similar to what was done on Jackson's 2005 *King Kong*, this time with veteran stunt actor Terry Notary. It was released on March 10, 2017.

Big G Meets Some Old Friends

With *Kong: Skull Island* completed and released, the next phase in what is being called the "Godzilla-Kong film series" is the development of Legendary's direct sequel to *Godzilla*, entitled *Godzilla: King of Monsters*. Legendary first began to stir up interest in the possibility at the 2014 Comic-Con, the very same event at which *Skull Island* had been announced. With *Godzilla* a recent hit, the studio was proud to declare that it had secured the rights from Toho to use King Ghidorah, Mothra, and Rodan, three of Godzilla's most famous rivals, all of which had never appeared outside of Toho's own productions. Utilizing Ken Watanabe's memorable line from the first film, "Conflict: Inevitable. Let them fight," Legendary teased the concept to a most appreciative live crowd. A sequel would indeed be in the works, although it was not known for certain as of this writing if all three of the aforementioned *kaiju* would be appearing together in the film.

Legendary's mighty Godzilla will return to movie screens in 2019.   *Movie Stills Database*

While a script has not yet been completed, the film will be written by Max Borenstein as well, who has promised that Godzilla will have much more screen time in this go-round—a response to criticism from some fans of the monster's less-than-11-minutes on screen in the previous film. Gareth Edwards had been set to return as the director, but the timing of other projects (including the 2016 *Star Wars* franchise picture *Rogue One*) as well as a reported desire to step away from big-budget sci-fi blockbusters for a while, caused Edwards to withdraw from the project. This in turn led to a postponement of the film's release date, from June 8, 2018, to March 22, 2019. A new director had not yet been named as of this writing.

The Main Event

The plot of *Godzilla: King of Monsters* is not yet known, nor is it known how much the events of *Kong: Skull Island* will tie into it. What is known is that the movie will be the final step leading into the ultimate end-game of Legendary's franchise plans: *Godzilla vs. Kong*, set to be unleashed on the world in the summer of 2020. For decades, since the original *King Kong vs. Godzilla* (1962), the movie powers-that-be have been trying to bring the two greatest giant movie monsters together again for an all-out spectacular, and the stars finally aligned when Legendary Pictures switched production partners from Warner Bros. to Universal. Since Universal owns the rights to Kong, Legendary was able to secure rights to make Kong films. All it took after that was utilizing their old contacts at Warners, for whom they were continuing to make Godzilla movies anyway, and the deal bringing the two creatures together was finally able to be made.

After months of speculation following the news that Legendary would be working with both Warners and Universal on separate King Kong and Godzilla projects, fans finally got the official announcement they were waiting for in October 2015, when Legendary let it be known that what was once thought impossible, the reunion of Kong and Godzilla, would indeed be happening. What is known so far about the project is that the Monarch organization will continue to be involved, presumably monitoring the whereabouts of both monsters. That the two behemoths will do battle is a certainty; whether they will later team up against a common foe has yet to be clarified. Since the film will take place nearly fifty years after *Kong: Skull Island*, anything is possible, and whether the time shift has anything to do with Kong's change in size is also unknown.

A Japanese Resurgence

Meanwhile on the other side of the world, Toho Company brass decided they weren't going to let the Americans have all the fun, and made the decision to take advantage of the new worldwide wave of Godzilla mania by rebooting their own time-honored Godzilla franchise. After finishing *Godzilla: Final Wars* in 2004, Toho had declared that Godzilla would be given a ten-year break. True to their word, Toho executives announced their new project in December 2014. The announcement instantly caused a major buzz—this would not be America's Godzilla, but the "real deal," the Japanese version of Godzilla, given a whole new lease on life and relaunched for the third time in his sixty-year career.

The film was slated for a 2016 release, and was promised to be a total reboot, meaning not only would it have no connection to the American *Godzilla* films, but it would also be unconnected to any previous Toho *Godzilla* films; this one would depict Godzilla attacking Japan for the very first time. From the beginning, the initiative was to inject the Godzilla franchise with as much new blood as possible to produce something truly fresh and unique. Acting as chief producers on the film would be Akihiro

Yamauchi and Minami Ichikawa, both of whom had only risen in the Toho production ranks within the past dozen years (Ichikawa's first job at Toho had been as the publicist for *Godzilla vs. Biollante* in 1989).

Demonstrating its commitment to the future of its greatest franchise, Toho put into place what it called the "Godzilla Conference" ("*Goji-Con*") to act as a brain trust for the new picture and any forthcoming installments. Further illustrating this commitment and ratcheting up the excitement for the film was the revelation of who would be directing it: Hideaki Anno and Shinji Higuchi, the visionary filmmakers best known for the acclaimed *anime* series *Neon Genesis Evangelion*. While Anno had been more specifically involved in the direction of *Evangelion*, Higuchi had played a role in the writing and art design. Of the two, Higuchi was the one with the formidable *daikaiju* experience, having cut his teeth at Toho working on special effects for *Godzilla 1985* (1984) and *Godzilla, Mothra and King Ghidorah: Giant Monsters All-Out Attack* (2001), as well as on Daiei's *Heisei* Gamera trilogy of the late 1990s. In 2015, just prior to coming aboard with Godzilla, Higuchi had completed his two-part live-action adaptation of the popular *anime* *Attack on Titan*, about a race of giant humanoid creatures invading Earth.

Interestingly, the directorial partnership between Higuchi and Anno was to be quite similar to that established back in the '50s and '60s by the iconic team of Ishiro Honda and Eiji Tsuburaya, with Anno writing the script and directing the actors, while Higuchi handled the extensive special effects. The two men set to work creating something unlike anything Godzilla fans had seen before, combining the traditional nuclear element with influences including the 2011 Fukushima reactor disaster, and the earthquake/tsunami that ravaged Japan the same year. Seeking to bring true horror back to the Godzilla franchise, Higuchi strove to perfect a terrifying new design for the monster, which would emphasize its origins. It was also important that this be the hugest version of Godzilla ever imagined for the screen—at 389 feet, taller even than the one recently seen in the American *Godzilla*.

Higuchi brought in artist Mahiro Maeda, with whom he had worked on previous *Evangelion* projects, and who had recently provided concept art for the Oscar-winning *Mad Max: Fury Road* (2015). Maeda conceptualized a Godzilla partly in keeping with his 1954 origins, with large, jagged teeth; beady, staring eyes; clawlike hands; a sweeping tail; and a dark, rough hide covered in elaborate keloid scars. Breaking with time-honored tradition, Higuchi would not be employing "suitmation" to bring this Godzilla to life, but also would not be relying exclusively on digital effects. Instead, he would use a combination of practical techniques like puppets and animatronics, along with CGI (based on the motion-capture performance of actor Mansai Nomura).

Principal photography began in September 2015, and the official title for the new project was given as *Shin Gojira*, which can be approximated to mean "New Godzilla" in English, although the film's international title would be translated as *Godzilla Resurgence*; rejecting the international title as has happened before, American distributors instead would release the film in the U.S. as *Shin Godzilla*. After two months of filming, and another month of specials effects, the finished film was screened for the first time for international distributors in a highly successful bid to secure releases of the film in nearly one hundred countries all over the world.

Once again the product of nuclear radiation—although this time it is intimated that the radiation more likely stems from environmental pollution than from weapons testing—Godzilla emerges in the story after a series of mysterious attacks at sea, to wreak horrific damage and casualties upon mainland Japan, growing larger and more fearsome as he absorbs more energy, seeming to glow red from within due to the enormous amounts of radiation coursing through his body. Hiroki Hasegawa, star of Higuchi's *Attack on Titan*, appears as Rando Yaguchi, the Japanese Deputy Chief Cabinet Secretary with the daunting task of mounting a response and eliminating the creature. Fellow *Attack on Titan* veteran Satomi Ishihara plays Japanese American Kayoko Ann Paterson, special envoy to the President of the United States who helps the two nations coordinate a desperate attack against the creature. Once the military coalition determines that nuclear weapons alone can defeat the creature, Yaguchi and his team must race against time to prove that a safer, scientific method can be used to spare Japan from becoming the brunt of another nuclear assault.

After a marketing blitz designed to reacquaint the Japanese audience—many of whom may have been too young to recall Toho's Godzilla in his prime—with the original King of the Monsters, *Shin Godzilla* had its red carpet premiere in Tokyo on July 25, 2016, right down the street from the Godzilla-themed Hotel Gracery Shinjuku. Four days later, it was released wide to more than 350 theaters in Japan. International distribution followed, with the film making its way across Asia over the remainder of the summer, before reaching Western markets, including North America, in October 2016. Handling American distribution of the picture was Funimation, a company specializing in bringing many Japanese properties to the U.S., most notably Toei Animation's *Dragon Ball Z* (*Doragon Boru Zetto*).

While the specifics of the future of Toho's treasured Godzilla franchise are not fully known, the security and certainty of that future is more than clear. Over the course of seven different decades now, the monster has been making an imprint on audiences and the culture at large. *Shin Godzilla* proved that the creature is just as potent as ever, as has the resounding success of Legendary Pictures' own Godzilla franchise. A triumph on both sides of the planet, in two different simultaneous incarnations, Godzilla has been shown today to be an even stronger entertainment juggernaut than Tomoyuki Tanaka, Ishiro Honda, Eiji Tsuburaya, or any of his other creators and contributors could have possibly imagined back in those years not long after World War II.

Although Godzilla's fans are sometimes torn over their feelings about how their beloved monster is being represented on the big screen, both by the Americans and by the Japanese, there is no denying that this is a very thrilling time to be a Godzilla fan, perhaps the most thrilling time since the glory days of the early *Showa* era of the '50s and '60s. Godzilla is alive and well and a part of our lives, as a cinematic force and as a cultural one. With more American films on the horizon, and Toho just kicking off what may very well be the fourth great era in its megalithic franchise, we can be sure that Godzilla will be around for a very long time to come, just as much that inexorable, invincible force on the screen as off.

Selected Bibliography

Books

Barr, Jason. *The Kaiju Film: A Critical Study of Cinema's Biggest Monsters.* Jefferson, NC: McFarland Books, 2015.

Brothers, Peter H. *Atomic Dreams and the Nuclear Nightmare: The Making of Godzilla (1954).* Seattle: CreateSpace Books, 2015.

Brothers, Peter H. *Mushroom Clouds and Mushroom Men: The Fantastic Cinema of Ishiro Honda.* Seattle: CreateSpace Books, 2009.

Clutter, Bryan Matthew. *Titans of Toho: An Unauthorized Guide to the Godzilla Series and the Rest of Toho's Giant Monster Film Library.* Seattle: CreateSpace Books, 2014.

Debus, Allen A. *Dinosaurs Ever Evolving: The Changing Face of Prehistoric Animals in Popular Culture.* Jefferson, NC: McFarland Books, 2016.

Edwards, Matthew, ed. *The Atomic Bomb in Japanese Cinema: Critical Essays.* Jefferson, NC: McFarland Books, 2015.

Galbraith, Stuart, IV. *Japanese Science Fiction, Fantasy and Horror Films.* Jefferson, NC: McFarland Books, 2007.

Galbraith, Stuart, IV. *Monsters Are Attacking Tokyo! The Incredible World of Japanese Fantasy Films.* Venice, CA: Feral House, 1998.

Galbraith, Stuart, IV. *The Toho Studios Story: A History and Complete Filmography.* Lanham, MD: Scarecrow Press, 2008.

Galbraith, Stuart, IV and Paul Duncan, ed. *Japanese Cinema.* Los Angeles: Taschen America, 2009.

Kalat, David. *A Critical History and Filmography of Toho's Godzilla Series.* Jefferson, NC: McFarland Books, 2010.

Kirkland, Travis and Luca Saitta. *Memories from Monster Island: A Fun Stomp Through Toho's Godzilla Films.* Seattle: CreateSpace Books, 2015.

Lees, J. D. and Marc Cerasini. *The Official Godzilla Compendium: A 40-Year Retrospective.* New York: Random House, 1998.

Marrero, Robert. *Godzilla: King of the Movie Monsters.* Key West, FL: Fantasma Books, 1996.

Ragone, August. *Eiji Tsuburaya: Master of Monsters.* San Francisco: Chronicle Books, 2007.

Ryfle, Steve. *Japan's Favorite Mon-Star: The Unauthorized Biography of "The Big G."* Toronto: ECW Press, 1998.

Periodicals

Ackerman, Forrest J. *Famous Monsters of Filmland.* Encino, CA: Movieland Classics, LLC.

Lees, J. D. *G-Fan.* Steinbach, Manitoba: Daikaiju Enterprises Ltd.

Ragone, August, et al. *Markalite: The Magazine of Japanese Fantasy.* Oakland, CA: Pacific Rim Publishing Co.

Rainy, Mark, Brad Boyle and Ed Godziszewski. *Japanese Giants.* Japanese Giants, Ltd.

Web Sites

Becoming Godzilla. http://becominggodzilla.com/

"Being Godzilla: An Interview with Nakajima Haruo, The Man Inside the Suit." Nippon.com. http://www.nippon.com/en/views/b04002/

G-Fan Online. http://www.g-fan.com/

Godzilla and Other Monster Music. http://www.godzillamonstermusic.com/

"Interview with Yoshimitsu Banno, Executive Producer of *Godzilla* 2014." HJU. http://henshinjustice.com/2014/09/16/interview-yoshimitsu-banno -executive-producer-godzilla-2014/

"The Making of 'Godzilla,' Japan's Favorite 'Mon-Star.'" NPR. http:// www.npr.org/2014/05/02/308955584/the-making-of-godzilla-japans -favorite-mon-star

SciFi Japan. http://www.scifijapan.com/

SKREEONK! Home of the Kaiju Fan Network. https://skreeonk.com/

Toho Kingdom. http://www.tohokingdom.com

"The Tokusatsu Entertainment Genre That Godzilla Spawned." Nippon. com. http://www.nippon.com/en/views/b040/

"Voice of Gojira: Remembering Akira Ifukube." Music from the Movies. https://web.archive.org/web/20080418094016/http://www.musicfromthe movies.com/feature.asp?ID=52

"When Roses Attack: 25 Years of *Godzilla vs. Biollante* with Ed Godziszewski." Scified. http://www.scified.com/news/when-roses-attack -25-years-of-godzilla-vs-biollante-with-ed-godziszewski

Index

THE FAQ SERIES

AC/DC FAQ
by Susan Masino
Backbeat Books
9781480394506.................. $24.99

Armageddon Films FAQ
by Dale Sherman
Applause Books
9781617131196 .... $24.99

The Band FAQ
by Peter Aaron
Backbeat Books
9781617136139 .... $19.99

Baseball FAQ
by Tom DeMichael
Backbeat Books
9781617136061........................ $24.99

The Beach Boys FAQ
by Jon Stebbins
Backbeat Books
9780879309879................. $22.99

The Beat Generation FAQ
by Rich Weidman
Backbeat Books
9781617136016 .... $19.99

Beer FAQ
by Jeff Cioletti
Backbeat Books
9781617136115 .... $24.99

Black Sabbath FAQ
by Martin Popoff
Backbeat Books
9780879309572.................... $19.99

Bob Dylan FAQ
by Bruce Pollock
Backbeat Books
9781617136078 .... $19.99

Britcoms FAQ
by Dave Thompson
Applause Books
9781495018992 .... $19.99

Bruce Springsteen FAQ
by John D. Luerssen
Backbeat Books
9781617130939.................... $22.99

A Chorus Line FAQ
by Tom Rowan
Applause Books
9781480367548 .... $19.99

The Clash FAQ
by Gary J. Jucha
Backbeat Books
9781480364509 .... $19.99

Doctor Who FAQ
by Dave Thompson
Applause Books
9781557838544.................... $22.99

The Doors FAQ
by Rich Weidman
Backbeat Books
9781617130175 .... $24.99

Dracula FAQ
by Bruce Scivally
Backbeat Books
9781617136009 .... $19.99

The Eagles FAQ
by Andrew Vaughan
Backbeat Books
9781480385412.................... $24.99

Elvis Films FAQ
by Paul Simpson
Applause Books
9781557838582.................... $24.99

Elvis Music FAQ
by Mike Eder
Backbeat Books
9781617130496 .... $24.99

Eric Clapton FAQ
by David Bowling
Backbeat Books
9781617134548 .... $22.99

Fab Four FAQ
by Stuart Shea and
Robert Rodriguez
Hal Leonard Books
9781423421382........................ $19.99

Fab Four FAQ 2.0
by Robert Rodriguez
Backbeat Books
9780879309688................ $19.99

Film Noir FAQ
by David J. Hogan
Applause Books
9781557838551...................... $22.99

Football FAQ
by Dave Thompson
Backbeat Books
9781495007484 .... $24.99

Frank Zappa FAQ
by John Corcelli
Backbeat Books
9781617136030...................... $19.99

Godzilla FAQ
by Brian Solomon
Applause Books
9781495045684 .... $19.99

The Grateful Dead FAQ
by Tony Sclafani
Backbeat Books
9781617130861...................... $24.99

Guns N' Roses FAQ
by Rich Weidman
Backbeat Books
9781495025884 .... $19.99

Haunted America FAQ
by Dave Thompson
Backbeat Books
9781480392625.................... $19.99

Horror Films FAQ
by John Kenneth Muir
Applause Books
9781557839503 .... $22.99

James Bond FAQ
by Tom DeMichael
Applause Books
9781557838568.................... $22.99

Jimi Hendrix FAQ
by Gary J. Jucha
Backbeat Books
9781617130953....................... $22.99

Prices, contents, and availability
subject to change without notice.

Johnny Cash FAQ
by C. Eric Banister
Backbeat Books
9781480385405................. $24.99

KISS FAQ
by Dale Sherman
Backbeat Books
9781617130915...................$24.99

Led Zeppelin FAQ
by George Case
Backbeat Books
9781617130250...................$22.99

Lucille Ball FAQ
*by James Sheridan
and Barry Monush*
Applause Books
9781617740824.......................$19.99

M.A.S.H. FAQ
by Dale Sherman
Applause Books
9781480355897......................$19.99

Michael Jackson FAQ
by Kit O'Toole
Backbeat Books
9781480371064......................$19.99

Modern Sci-Fi Films FAQ
by Tom DeMichael
Applause Books
9781480350618 ....$24.99

Monty Python FAQ
*by Chris Barsanti, Brian Cogan,
and Jeff Massey*
Applause Books
9781495049439 ....$19.99

Morrissey FAQ
by D. McKinney
Backbeat Books
9781480394483..................$24.99

Neil Young FAQ
by Glen Boyd
Backbeat Books
9781617130373......................$19.99

Nirvana FAQ
by John D. Luerssen
Backbeat Books
9781617134500.....................$24.99

Pearl Jam FAQ
*by Bernard M. Corbett and
Thomas Edward Harkins*
Backbeat Books
9781617136122 ....$19.99

Pink Floyd FAQ
by Stuart Shea
Backbeat Books
9780879309503...................$19.99

Pro Wrestling FAQ
by Brian Solomon
Backbeat Books
9781617135996......................$29.99

Prog Rock FAQ
by Will Romano
Backbeat Books
9781617135873 ....$24.99

Quentin Tarantino FAQ
by Dale Sherman
Applause Books
9781480355880 ....$24.99

Robin Hood FAQ
by Dave Thompson
Applause Books
9781495048227 ....$19.99

**The Rocky Horror
Picture Show FAQ**
by Dave Thompson
Applause Books
9781495007477 ....$19.99

Rush FAQ
by Max Mobley
Backbeat Books
9781617134517 ....$19.99

Saturday Night Live FAQ
by Stephen Tropiano
Applause Books
9781557839510......................$24.99

Seinfeld FAQ
by Nicholas Nigro
Applause Books
9781557838575......................$24.99

Sherlock Holmes FAQ
by Dave Thompson
Applause Books
9781480331495 ....$24.99

The Smiths FAQ
by John D. Luerssen
Backbeat Books
9781480394490...................$24.99

Soccer FAQ
by Dave Thompson
Backbeat Books
9781617135989.......................$24.99

The Sound of Music FAQ
by Barry Monush
Applause Books
9781480360433...................$27.99

South Park FAQ
by Dave Thompson
Applause Books
9781480350649...................$24.99

Star Trek FAQ
(Unofficial and Unauthorized)
by Mark Clark
Applause Books
9781557837929......................$19.99

Star Trek FAQ 2.0
(Unofficial and Unauthorized)
by Mark Clark
Applause Books
9781557837936......................$22.99

Star Wars FAQ
by Mark Clark
Applause Books
9781480360181.................... $24.99

Steely Dan FAQ
by Anthony Robustelli
Backbeat Books
9781495025129 ....$19.99

Stephen King Films FAQ
by Scott Von Doviak
Applause Books
9781480355514 .... $24.99

Three Stooges FAQ
by David J. Hogan
Applause Books
9781557837882......................$22.99

TV Finales FAQ
*by Stephen Tropiano and
Holly Van Buren*
Applause Books
9781480391444 ....$19.99

The Twilight Zone FAQ
by Dave Thompson
Applause Books
9781480396180 ....$19.99

Twin Peaks FAQ
*by David Bushman and
Arthur Smith*
Applause Books
9781495015861.....................$19.99

UFO FAQ
by David J. Hogan
Backbeat Books
9781480393851 ....$19.99

Video Games FAQ
by Mark J.P. Wolf
Backbeat Books
9781617136306 ....$19.99

The Who FAQ
by Mike Segretto
Backbeat Books
9781480361034 ....$24.99

The Wizard of Oz FAQ
by David J. Hogan
Applause Books
9781480350625 ....$24.99

The X-Files FAQ
by John Kenneth Muir
Applause Books
9781480369740...................$24.99

HAL•LEONARD®
PERFORMING ARTS
PUBLISHING GROUP

Prices, contents, and availability subject to change without notice.

FAQ.halleonardbooks.com

0117